TO FORM A MORE PERFECT UNION

The Critical Ideas of the Constitution

UNITED STATES CAPITOL HISTORICAL SOCIETY
Fred Schwengel, President

PERSPECTIVES ON THE AMERICAN REVOLUTION
Ronald Hoffman and Peter J. Albert, Editors

Diplomacy and Revolution: The Franco-American Alliance of 1778

Sovereign States in an Age of Uncertainty

Slavery and Freedom in the Age of the American Revolution

Arms and Independence: The Military Character of the American Revolution

An Uncivil War: The Southern Backcountry during the American Revolution

Peace and the Peacemakers: The Treaty of 1783

The Economy of Early America: The Revolutionary Period, 1763–1790

Women in the Age of the American Revolution

To Form a More Perfect Union: The Critical Ideas of the Constitution

To Form a More Perfect Union

The Critical Ideas

of the Constitution

Edited by HERMAN BELZ

RONALD HOFFMAN

and PETER J. ALBERT

Published for the

UNITED STATES CAPITOL HISTORICAL SOCIETY

BY THE UNIVERSITY PRESS OF VIRGINIA

Charlottesville

THE UNIVERSITY PRESS OF VIRGINIA
Copyright © 1992 by the Rector and Visitors
of the University of Virginia

First Published 1992

Printed in the United States of America

Library of Congress Cataloging-in-Publication Data

To form a more perfect Union : the critical ideas of the Constitution / edited by
Herman Belz, Ronald Hoffman, and Peter J. Albert.
    p.   cm.—(Perspectives on the American Revolution)
Includes index.
ISBN 0–8139–1343–8
1. United States—Constitutional history.   2. United States—Politics and
government—1783–1789.   3. United States—Social conditions—To 1865.   I.
Belz, Herman.   II. Hoffman, Ronald, 1941–.   III. Albert, Peter J. IV. Series.
KF4541.T67 1992
342.73′029—dc20
[347.30229]   91–21152
                                                                              CIP

Contents

CONTENTS

Preface

IN 1832, four years before he died, James Madison, the man more responsible for the final structure of the Constitution than any of the other delegates who sat in Philadelphia during the summer of 1787, remarked to a visitor that the Constitution had two enemies—"one that would stretch it to death, and one that would squeeze it to death." While Madison proved an accurate commentator regarding the kinds of pressures that would continuously be brought to bear upon the Constitution as the founding document of the American political community and the final arbiter of the decisions that govern it, he would nonetheless be amazed, as would his Constitutional Convention colleagues, at the resilience, flexibility, and endurance of the instrument of governance they created. Within the constantly changing context of American society as it has evolved over the past two hundred years, a dazzling array of groups and individuals seeking to shape the character of this nation's history and to affirm their places within it have contended with the Constitution. Not surprisingly, the record of these struggles is a mixed one—a complex compendium of dignity and indignity, honor and dishonor, justice and injustice. Women, as well as native Americans, blacks, and other minority groups, have suffered discrimination and endured second-class citizenship by virtue of interpretations of the Constitution, while various special interest groups have managed to achieve wealth and preferential treatment through the manipulation of Constitutional doctrines. Although unable to prevent the Civil War, the Constitution survived it; although unable to prevent the assassinations of presidents, the Constitution allowed governance to continue in those times of severest crisis; and although it could not prevent betrayals like Watergate, the Constitution provided the mechanism through which the system of government continued to operate and preserve itself even as it corrected those abuses. Since 1787 the United States has changed from a rural to an urban society, from an agrarian to an industrial nation, and from a tenuous association of thirteen states strung from north to south along the Atlantic seaboard to a world power composed of fifty states. However stretched and squeezed by the incredible growth and transformation that have taken place in this country over the past two centuries, the Constitution has managed to accommodate and to endure. It is, therefore, altogether fitting and appropriate to commemorate the bicentennial of this remarkable document with the publication of these essays examining the political theories and the philosophies of governance that informed the minds of the men who created it.

The editors would like to acknowledge the valuable contributions made by the other participants at the U.S. Capitol Historical Society's symposium on the Constitution whose papers or commentaries are not published in this volume, namely, James MacGregor Burns, James H. Hutson, Edmund S. Morgan, and Jack N. Rakove.

RONALD HOFFMAN

Introduction

THE DEBATE over original intent jurisprudence that moved from the academy into the political arena in the 1980s expressed a basic fact about American political life, which in a less polemical and adversarial way is reflected in scholarly controversy over the nature and purpose of the Constitution of 1787. The basic fact is that government in the United States takes its direction and derives its purposes and values from the Founding. Although seeking to discredit their opponents by casting doubt on the possibility of ascertaining the original understanding of constitutional provisions, critics of original intent in their approach to constitutional interpretation were ultimately unwilling to ignore or reject the authority of the Framers.[1] Even if reference to the Founding as a source of legitimacy is seen as a political convention grounded in expediency rather than principled conviction, it is evidence of the shaping effect that constitutional forms, procedures, and ideas have on political life. Recognition of what at the least can be called the configurative, and possibly also the motivating philosophical or ideological, power of the Constitution, has always invested scholarship on the Founding with practical political importance.

In the early decades of the twentieth century, proponents

[1] This unwillingness was evident, for example, in the widely acclaimed argument, advanced by Powell, that recourse to original intent in the form of consulting contemporaneous historical documents to ascertain the purpose of the authors of the Constitution, should not be employed because the Framers did not intend that their speeches and writings, including what they said at the Constitutional Convention should be used in interpreting constitutional provisions. See H. Jefferson Powell, "The Original Understanding of Original Intent," *Harvard Law Review* 98 (1984–85):885–948. On the difficulty, if not impossibility, of ascertaining original intent, in the view of critics of original intent jurisprudence, see Leonard W. Levy, *Original Intent and the Framers' Constitution* (New York, 1988), pp. 1–29.

of reform sought to advance progressive causes by reeducating the public about the political ideas of the nation's founders. The Beardian, or progressive, interpretation of the making of the Constitution attributed to the Framers motives and purposes defined by personal and class economic interests, in contrast to the idealist and idealistic national and democratic motives that had figured in earlier historical accounts. After World War II, the progressive class-conflict, economic determinist view of the Constitution was superseded by explanations that recognized to a far greater extent the role of ideas as a causative force in the events of the Founding. In the counterprogressive interpretation advanced by consensus historians such as Louis Hartz and Edmund S. Morgan, the formative ideas of American nationality were understood to be those of John Locke, the great philosopher of early modern liberalism. The Revolution and the Constitution, expressing an emerging American nationality, embodied the theory of society and government based on the social contract and directed toward the end of protecting the natural rights of individuals to life, liberty, and property.

In the 1960s the reaction against the economic interpretation of progressive historiography continued in the writings of Bernard Bailyn, Gordon S. Wood, and J. G. A. Pocock. Instead of Lockean liberalism, however, these scholars identified classical republicanism or civic humanism, grounded in if not directly descended from ancient political philosophy, as the principal intellectual source of Revolutionary constitutionalism. Superficially the republican ideological interpretation, which rapidly gained ascendancy in accounts of the Founding, rejected the reductionist, economic determinist explanation of political events that characterized progressive history. In reality the ideological interpretation, no less than progressive historical theory, denied the autonomy of reason and deliberative reflection. Employing the concepts of semiotics, literary theory, or cultural anthropology, historians of republicanism made languages of discourse the ideologically decisive factors in human action that expressed social strains and anxieties and hence was ultimately grounded in perceptions of sociological and economic reality. Nevertheless, under the positivistic assumptions of modern historiography, the evidence relied on in the republican interpretation, dealing with constitutional and political arguments and principles, was judged to concern "ideas" more than "interests." The republican ideological account was therefore accepted in the historical profession as fundamentally different from the Beardian or progressive interpretation. This perception prevailed even though the most influential account of republicanism in the Founding, Gordon S. Wood's *The Creation of the American Republic, 1776–1787* (1969), told the story of a conservative constitutional reaction in 1787 which was based on the ideology of liberal self-interest and commercial expansion and which repudiated the community-oriented, egalitarian, and participatory democratic republicanism of the Revolution.

Although historians subsequently noted a variety of intellectual influences on American constitution making, including the Scottish Enlightenment, the French Enlightenment, the Protestant Reformation, and the English common law, controversy concerning the original intent of the Framers focused on whether republicanism or liberalism was the defining philosophy of the Constitution. Were virtue, political participation, and the common good the watchwords of the United States Constitution and the American political tradition, or self-interest, individualism, and economic acquisitiveness?

This formulation of the problem established a polarity as fundamental as the class and occupational division of the progressive interpretation. On the one hand, the Revolution was seen to spring from and express the communitarian spirit of classical republicanism, which regarded man preeminently as a political animal and imposed on citizens requirements of moral virtue that guarded against corruption and elevated the good of the commonwealth above the interests of individuals. On the other hand, the Federalist Framers of the Constitution were viewed as proponents of the ideology of modern liberalism, which regarded man as an economic animal and encouraged possessive individualism by conceiving the purpose of government to be that of protecting citizens' natural rights to life, liberty, and the pursuit of happiness.

Satisfying though the dichotomy between the moral community of Revolutionary republicanism and the possessive individualism of the Constitution of 1787 might be to many scholars, the distinction between classical republicanism and modern liberalism on which it rests is false. In fact the republicanism of the eighteenth-century English commonwealthmen on which Americans drew in their Revolutionary constitution making, and the republicanism found in Antifederalist writings that criticized the Constitution in the ratification controversy, was not ancient or classical but modern. Its modernity is signified in its acceptance of self-preservation and self-interest as fundamental to human nature and as providing the basic motivation of individual action. Furthermore, modern republicanism accepts the proposition that the protection of liberty, natural rights, and the acquisition of property by individuals is the proper end of government. In other words, notwithstanding continued references to virtue and corruption in the writings of commonwealthmen, American Revolutionaries, and Antifederalist critics of the Constitution, the republicanism of the Founding was modern and liberal.[2]

This is not to say that all aspects of classical republicanism were abandoned and eliminated from American constitutionalism. "Virtue," "morality," and "good government" were not expunged from political discourse or from the practical concerns of citizens and statesmen. These matters were understood, however, in light of the fundamental concern for individual liberty and self-interest that marked the emergence of modern political philosophy. Good government continued to be a goal of politics, but this goal was to be achieved not by government imposing a rule of virtue on citizens but by designing forms, procedures, and institutions that channel, direct, and encourage a constructive tension

[2] Thomas L. Pangle, *The Spirit of Modern Republicanism: The Moral Vision of the American Founders and the Philosophy of Locke* (Chicago, 1988), pp. 28–39; Barmak Nassirian, "Republicanism, Liberalism, and Conservatism" (unpublished manuscript), pp. 5–8.

between the interests, passions, and ambitions of citizens and officeholders alike. Self-interest was made to serve the common good in a constitutional order that, out of respect for the liberty, independence, and capacity for self-government of individual citizens, made virtue a matter of voluntary choice, rather than something to be guaranteed or coerced by government decree.[3]

At the national level the delegates to the Federal Convention created a liberal republican government of limited ends that would promote national unity mainly by protecting and regulating commerce among the states and with foreign nations, in addition to fulfilling the functions of national defense and diplomacy. At the state level the Framers accepted with approval constitutions and governing establishments that promoted the more traditional republican goal of training citizens in public virtue through religion, education, and the discipline of laws upholding community standards of civility and morality. A full understanding of the American regime requires recognition of the complementary emphases of modern republicanism as they were expressed in the divided sovereignty of American federalism.

The essays that follow elucidate the liberal character of modern republicanism in the critical ideas of the Constitution. Jennifer Nedelsky, for example, describes Madison's concern for property rights and liberty as essential to the stability and permanence of republican government. Madison's emphasis on property, she observes, makes him a liberal republican who successfully reconciled standards of justice and limitations on the will of the majority with popular representation and self-government in the extended republic. Similarly, John M. Murrin, while noting the several value systems that influenced American government in the eighteenth century, sees the Constitution as a device for establishing a republican government over a population of liberals. In the Framers' liberal republican regime, ordinary people would pursue their interests, while looking to the government and statesmen to prevent corruption and promote the public good.

---

[3] Harvey C. Mansfield, Jr., "Constitutional Government: The Soul of Modern Democracy," *The Public Interest*, no. 86 (Winter 1987):53–64.

INTRODUCTION

In J. R. Pole's interpretation the Framers, relying on philosophers concerned with the good of the community, paradoxically created a Constitution resting on liberal individualist foundations. A principal tenet of constitutional liberalism was the belief, expressed by Madison in *Federalist* No. 10, that protection of the diverse faculties and abilities of men that led to differences in propertyholding was the first object of government. Pole argues that the purpose of the Constitution was to assume fundamental responsibility for safeguarding the rights of individuals. Propounding an original intent argument, he discounts the significance of federalism in concluding that the "new Constitution cuts clean through the lines surrounding the states to operate directly on every individual . . . within the boundaries of the Union."

Edward J. Erler's account underscores the modern character of republicanism by interpreting the Constitution as an expression of the natural rights philosophy of the Declaration of Independence. In its emphasis on the principles of equality and consent, the Declaration defined a liberal philosophy that in essential respects contradicted the classical republican idea that the end of government is the inculcation of virtue and ultimately the attainment of philosophic knowledge. Erler points out further that the debate between the Federalists and Antifederalists over the proper scope of republican government was a disagreement over the means of achieving the liberal end of securing the natural rights of individuals.

In his analysis of the liberal republicanism of John Adams, John P. Diggins calls attention to the influence of Scottish commercialism and Calvinism. Adams, refuting the philosophical claims of the French enlightenment, rejected Montesquieu's definition of a republic as a regime in which virtue prevails over all self-regarding motives. Moreover, Adams believed, contrary to the French teaching, that commerce and virtue are not incompatible. Similarly, Isaac Kramnick's account of the interweaving of the political "idioms" of civic humanism, Lockean liberalism, radical Protestantism, and state-centered theories of power and sovereignty is a description of modern republicanism. In this new polity civic virtue coexisted with the nonpolitical private virtue of Calvinism and the individualism of market society. Philosophically pluralistic, modern republicanism reflected the redefinition of virtue that occurred with the spread of commercial enterprise.

The essays by Jean Yarbrough and Ralph Lerner examine the conjunction in modern republicanism of the commercial values embodied in the federal Constitution and the concern for religion, education, and civic virtue evinced at the level of state and local government. Yarbrough observes that commerce produced a new kind of liberal democratic virtue, superseding the self-denying aristocratic virtues of classical republicanism. Arguing that commercial bourgeois virtues are not sufficient for the preservation of republican government, she shows how the Framers looked to the states for the development and inculcation of character and virtue through family, church, school, and local political associations. Yarbrough points out that the Framers' silence on morality, religion, and virtue in the Constitution did not reflect indifference to these matters as a proper concern of republican government.

Lerner also demonstrates the fusing of commercial values and virtues with traditional public morality in the Founders' liberal republicanism. Noting that the modern republican regime calls forth a new kind of honor, Lerner states that the political challenge of self-government has a universal significance that elevates the prosaic nature of commercial republican life to a higher and more spirited level. Lerner explores the way in which John Quincy Adams and Abraham Lincoln responded to the legacy of republican self-government that the Framers conferred on future generations of Americans. He underscores the fact that the commercial character of modern republicanism does not preclude, and may well require, education acquired through political participation and action.

Calvin C. Jillson presents an account of modern republican politics in the Constitutional Convention. Describing a political culture in the new nation that was pervasively though not uniformly republican, he states that in New England, the Middle Atlantic region, and the South distinctive subcultures

INTRODUCTION

existed that contained elements of liberal market society which encouraged self-interested economic and political action. Liberal activity blended with corporate decisions aimed at creating the best government to implement shared moral principles. The delegates to the Federal Convention illustrated the tendency of modern republicanism to balance liberal interest aggregation and disinterested reflection and choice of constitutional principles, in the light of human nature and American social conditions.

Finally, in the course of analyzing the competing demands of state sovereignty and central government authority, Peter S. Onuf identifies modern republicanism as the political ideology of American constitutionalism. His main point is that the preservation of state sovereignty depended on strengthening the Union. In the ratification debate a convergence of goals occurred as both Federalists and Antifederalists claimed that their respective courses of action would preserve republican liberty. According to Onuf, the logic of American republicanism insisted on limited government and denied the despotic power to command submission from citizens. Modern republicanism, primarily concerned with the protection of individual liberty and natural rights, bore little relation to the classical republican regime of virtue that was fundamentally opposed to individual liberty.

The critical ideas of the Constitution were thus liberal republican in nature. The Framers believed in the need for public virtue in citizens and elected officials. They adhered to principles of honor and recognized the need for public support of morality through religion and education. They understood these traditional governmental purposes in the light of the central importance attached to individual liberty and natural rights in modern republicanism. In a manner that would have been inconceivable in the classical world, they intended to reconcile virtue and liberty. The Founders thus adopted a Constitution of limited government that divided sovereignty between the national government, designed as a commercial republic, and the states, where public morality and education in citizenship were proper concerns of republican government.

HERMAN BELZ

TO FORM A MORE PERFECT UNION

The Critical Ideas of the Constitution

JOHN M. MURRIN

Fundamental Values, the Founding Fathers, and the Constitution

"WE FORMED OUR Constitution without any acknowledgement of God," President Timothy Dwight told his Yale audience as the War of 1812 loomed threateningly over the community. "The Convention, by which it was formed, never asked, even once, his direction, or his blessing upon their labours. Thus we commenced our national existence under the present system, without God." Dwight traveled a great deal and knew personally some of the delegates to the Philadelphia Convention. Very likely one of them told him about the day on which the Fathers of the Constitution refused to invoke God in any form.[1]

During one of the stormiest moments of the Constitutional Convention, Benjamin Franklin tried to break the impasse between large-state and small-state advocates that threatened to paralyze the proceedings. Why, he asked on June 28, 1787, had the members "not hitherto once thought of humbly applying to the Father of lights to illuminate our understandings?" During the prolonged crisis with Great Britain that had led to Independence, the First and Second Continental Congresses had routinely opened their proceedings with

[1] Timothy Dwight, *A Discourse, in Two Parts, Delivered July 23, 1812, on the Public Fast, in the Chapel of Yale College*, 2d. ed. (Boston, 1813), p. 24. My thanks to Harry S. Stout for bringing this sermon to my attention. Dwight may have learned about the prayer incident at the Philadelphia Convention from Connecticut delegates Oliver Ellsworth, a personal friend, or Roger Sherman, a participant in the debate and a New Haven resident when Dwight attended Yale as a student. For Dwight's eulogies of the two men, see his *Travels in New England and New York*, ed. Barbara Solomon, 4 vols. (Cambridge, Mass., 1969), 1:219–21, 4:210–11.

1

public prayers, he noted. He did not point out that the Rev. Jacob Duché, the principal chaplain to Congress in those years, had somewhat spoiled the overall effect by becoming a loyalist. Instead, Franklin insisted that the United States had already benefited from "frequent instances of a Superintending providence in our favor." "*God governs in the affairs of men,*" he proclaimed emphatically. He therefore moved "that henceforth prayers imploring the assistance of Heaven, and its blessings on our deliberations, be held in this Assembly every morning before we proceed to business, and that one or more of the Clergy of this City be requested to officiate in that service."[2]

The motion drew a second from Roger Sherman of Connecticut, one of two born-again Christians at the Convention, although his modern biographer, Christopher Collier, considers him a "political" New Light—someone, that is, who knew that joining the New Light coalition could be a prerequisite to a successful public career and who probably persuaded his neighbors (this point remains unclear) that he had experienced the conversion required of a full church member.[3]

What happened after Franklin and Sherman urged the Founding Fathers to invoke God? Alexander Hamilton, we know, opposed the motion. However proper such a gesture might have been at the outset of the Convention, he argued, it was imprudent "at this late day" because it might indicate to the broader public "that the embarrassments and dissentions within the convention, had suggested this measure." So

[2] Max Farrand, ed., *The Records of the Federal Convention of 1787*, rev. ed., 4 vols. (New Haven, 1937), 1:450–52. On Jacob Duché, see Edmund Cody Burnett, *The Continental Congress* (New York, 1941), pp. 38–40, 252–53.

[3] Christopher Collier, *Roger Sherman's Connecticut: Yankee Politics and the American Revolution* (Middletown, Conn., 1971), pp. 36–37, 325. The other evangelical at the Convention was Richard Bassett of Delaware, a good friend and supporter of Francis Asbury, the first Methodist bishop in the United States. Bassett voted frequently at the Convention, but he served on no committees, and there is no record that he ever spoke. He later became a fairly prominent Federalist politician. See the *Dictionary of American Biography* and, for a hagiographic sketch, Robert E. Pattison, "The Life and Character of Richard Bassett," *Papers of the Historical Society of Delaware* 29 (1900).

James Madison recorded at the time.[4] According to the much later and highly problematic recollections of the youngest delegate at the gathering, Jonathan Dayton of New Jersey, Hamilton accompanied his objections with a highly irreverent speech. We shall probably never know whether Hamilton said anything of the kind at that particular moment, but the sentiments attributed to him by Dayton are quite compatible with the convictions of an admirer of David Hume, the skeptical Scottish philosopher whose writings Hamilton had devoured early in his military career.[5]

According to Dayton, Hamilton "commenced a high-strained eulogium on the assemblage of *wisdom, talent,* and *experience,* which the Convention embraced" and expressed his confidence in the delegates and their abilities. They, he declared, "*were competent* to transact the business which had been entrusted to their care." They "were equal to every exigence which might occur; and . . . therefore he did not see the necessity of calling in *foreign aid!*"[6] After considerable discussion, opponents of the proposal avoided voting explicitly on prayer or God by carrying a motion to adjourn instead.

This controversy is far more revealing than most brief political exchanges. Not only is God never mentioned in the text of the United States Constitution (an omission that has distressed believers ever since), but the delegates deliberately avoided invoking him throughout the four long months of the Convention. As Franklin's notes tersely summarized, "The Convention, except three or four persons, thought Prayers unnecessary."[7] Other than himself, Sherman, probably Dayton, and Edmund Randolph of Virginia, prayer attracted no backers.

This lack of support does not explain why the delegates opposed it. Their motives varied. The "true cause of the

[4] Farrand, ed., *Records of the Convention,* 1:452.

[5] John C. Miller, *Alexander Hamilton: Portrait in Paradox* (New York, 1959), pp. 46–47. Miller questions the authenticity of Dayton's version of what Hamilton said mostly because it suggests an uncharacteristic disrespect for Franklin (see p. 175n).

[6] Farrand, ed., *Records of the Convention,* 3:471–72.

[7] Ibid., 1:452n.

omission could not be mistaken," observed North Carolina's Hugh Williamson. "The Convention had no funds."[8] This obstacle may have seemed insuperable to him in 1787, but it had not deterred the First Continental Congress, an earlier body of delegates with no formal budget, from engaging Duché in 1774. George Washington and other members were wealthy enough to donate small stipends had they so desired. According to Madison, "several others" shared Hamilton's practical objection that to bring in a chaplain a month into the convention's proceedings would generate "alarm out of doors" about "the state of things within." Randolph offered an ingenious compromise. Because the Fourth of July was approaching, nobody could object if the Convention asked a clergyman to preach a sermon appropriate to the occasion. After the Fourth, the delegates could begin all daily proceedings with prayers, and no one would notice that a transition had occurred. Franklin seconded this substitute motion, but it failed to get any more support than his original proposal.[9]

Beyond any doubt, the Founding Fathers emphatically refused to pray together while they were drafting the fundamental charter of the new nation. We cannot tell how many of the fifty-five delegates were present for this debate, but the probable minimum is nineteen, and there is no inherent reason to assume that June 28 attracted fewer than the normal average of about thirty delegates present on a given day, unless Luther Martin's interminable oratory of June 27–28 drove from the room even those who showed up on the morning of the twenty-eighth. Prayer lost by at least four to one, and the margin may have been seven to one or even greater. The Constitution's failure to invoke God was no mere oversight. In that respect the document faithfully mirrored the attitudes of the delegates who wrote it.[10]

[8] Ibid., p. 452.

[9] Ibid.

[10] Fifteen delegates presided, spoke, or took notes on the proceedings of Thursday, June 28, which were abbreviated because of the early adjournment. These fifteen men represented nine states, but eleven states were present for a vote the next day. Few delegates would have timed an arrival at or return to the Convention for a Friday. Thus probably at least four other delegates were around for Thursday's debates. But I cannot

Today we like to think of the Revolutionary generation as a quiet repository for fundamental values, for our most cherished principles. When we get into trouble, we can turn to the Founders for guidance and certainty. Somehow we have grown more confused than they ever were. But as the prayer incident reveals, the Founders had no one set of principles that everyone could share. At a time when even Congress retained a chaplain and shared public prayers, the delegates refused to pray at all. Theirs was a world in upheaval, not a safe haven for basic truths. Even the fundamentals were changing. As the eighteenth century roared to its conclusion in the maelstrom of the French Revolution, Americans— much like Europeans—divided ferociously over *which* fundamental values they embraced.

Before turning to the broader question of the clash of value systems, perhaps we should look closely at a specific example of what this kind of conflict could involve. What, for instance, did "original intent" mean to the generation that drafted and implemented the Constitution? The question has obvious relevance to our time. During the administration of Ronald Reagan, Attorney General Edwin Meese, Judge Robert H. Bork, and other conservative spokesmen frequently asserted that the courts have gone astray by overinterpreting the Constitution. As a corrective, they insisted, we ought to rein ourselves in by returning to the original intent of the Founders. Disciplined by their restraint, modern judges will not make law. They will administer existing law according to the narrow intent of the Constitution itself.

The demand for original intent has obvious validity—at some levels, anyway. In interpreting the First Amendment,

---

account for one discrepancy. Early in Thursday's proceedings, Dayton asked that a vote be postponed because Gov. William Livingston would be absent until the next day. Until he returned, New Jersey would be unrepresented. This claim indicates that Dayton alone represented New Jersey at that moment. But William Paterson's notes cover June 28 in detail, even if they are in the handwriting of another New Jersey delegate, David Brearley. See ibid., pp. 444–79, for the two days. For Dayton's request, see p. 445. For Luther Martin's endless oratory on June 27–28, see 3:271–72.

for instance, any court would have to agree that the phrase "Congress shall make no law respecting an establishment of religion" means something fundamentally different from "Congress shall make laws respecting an establishment of religion." The prohibition was real then and still is now.

Problems arise only in cases of disputed meaning. When we disagree about what the Constitution mandates, permits, or prohibits, how do we determine what the Founders intended? The common sense of the matter today is that we should turn to the records of the Federal Convention to learn what individual delegates said about particular clauses. But even if we can agree on the validity of this method, it will not always address our concerns. The records of the Convention are corrupt, incomplete, or vague on many issues, making them an extremely perilous arbiter.[11] And uncertainties sometimes remain in cases where the record itself may be perfectly clear.

One example should illustrate the point. Article I, Section 8 empowers Congress "to raise and support Armies," "to provide and maintain a Navy," and "to make Rules for the Government and Regulation of the land and naval Forces." Article II, Section 9 names the president as "Commander in Chief of the Army and Navy of the United States." The Constitution never uses more general terms, such as the modern phrase, the "armed forces" of the United States. It speaks explicitly of the army, the navy, and also the state militias. Any serious application of the doctrine of original intent ought therefore to conclude that the National Defense Act of 1947 is unconstitutional because it created an armed force unknown to the Constitution and unintended by the Founders, namely, the United States Air Force. The obvious response—that the Founders never dreamed of the existence of an air force—has served us well for over forty years, even though the first successful balloon flight across the English Channel, a highly publicized event, occurred in 1783, and French Revolutionary armies were about to convert hot air

[11] See James H. Hutson, "The Creation of the Constitution: The Integrity of the Documentary Record," *Texas Law Review* 65 (1986–87):1–39.

balloons to military purposes.[12] While still a member of Congress in 1784, Thomas Jefferson described the early experiments in considerable detail. "The uses of this discovery," he explained, would probably include "traversing . . . countries possessed by an enemy" and "conveying intelligence into a beseiged place, or perhaps enterprizing on it, reconnoitring an army, &c."[13] Jefferson has been accused of many things, but creative military imagination is not one of them. If the military uses of balloons occurred instantly to him, no doubt the idea crossed the minds of informed delegates with considerable military experience, such as Washington and Hamilton. In their idle moments they may well have fantasized about an air force coming into being someday, but if so they did not write about these musings, and they experienced no need to empower the new government to create such an arm.

To take a very different issue, the delegates lived in a world in which nearly all blacks were still slaves except for a growing minority that had acquired freedom. The process of emancipation had gained real momentum in the North and still had power in the upper South in the 1780s, but a great majority of blacks would remain slaves until 1865. The Revolutionary generation's sense of civil rights for a mostly enslaved African-American population could hardly be adequate for our age in which all blacks are legally free and equal, a possibility that then must have seemed about as remote as the creation of an air force. Several governments in the South, for example, required the reenslavement of emancipated blacks who failed to leave their state by a certain deadline. Free blacks were free, but hardly as free as whites.

Yet those who demand a return to original intent have

[12] For the 1783 flight, see Charles C. Gillispie, *The Montgolfier Brothers and the Invention of Aviation, 1783–1784* (Princeton, 1983) and Mary Beth Norton, *The British-Americans: The Loyalist Exiles in England, 1774–1789* (Boston, 1972), pp. 91–92. Bernard and Fawn M. Brodie, *From Crossbow to H-Bomb,* rev. ed. (Bloomington, Ind., 1973), pp. 109–10, briefly describe early wartime uses of this invention.

[13] Thomas Jefferson to Philip Turpin, Apr. 28, 1784, in Julian P. Boyd et al., eds., *The Papers of Thomas Jefferson,* 24 vols. to date (Princeton, 1950-), 7:134–37.

problems only with the courts' extension of civil rights, not with their tolerance of the Air Force. This selectivity should tell us that a specific social agenda, far more than a passion for constitutional objectivity, energizes the call for original intent. Civil rights advocates can point to their very powerful bulwarks in the Thirteenth, Fourteenth, and Fifteenth amendments. No comparable constitutional guarantee yet sustains the Air Force.

So far this discussion has said nothing about what the Founders themselves meant by original intent. Interestingly, although they disagreed sharply among themselves, they all rejected the Meese-Bork doctrine. To them original intent could *not* mean referral to the records of the Philadelphia Convention to clarify their understanding of disputed clauses. For half a century under the new Constitution, there was no full text to refer to because Madison refused to publish his notes during his lifetime. He died in 1836, and his notes first appeared in print in 1840. He insisted on this delay precisely so that no one could cite his records in the way that modern conservatives now propose to use them. As he explained to one inquirer in 1821 (the year that Robert Yates's very incomplete notes appeared, silently altered in many particulars by their anonymous editor, Edmond Genet), he withheld publication "till the Constitution should be well settled by practice, and till a knowledge of the controversial part of the proceedings of its framers could be turned to no improper account." His reasoning was explicit. "As a guide in expounding and applying the provisions of the Constitution, the debates and incidental decisions of the Convention can have no authoritative character."[14]

On its face, Madison's logic seems strange, even perverse to us, but it made sense in the eighteenth century and well into the nineteenth. Legislatures and conventions kept journals of proceedings (all formal motions, amendments, votes, and committee assignments) and preserved the precise texts

[14]James Madison to Thomas Ritchie, Sept. 15, 1821, *Letters and Other Writings of James Madison, Fourth President of the United States,* 4 vols. (Philadelphia, 1865), 3:228. On Yates's notes, see Hutson, "Creation of the Constitution," pp. 9–12.

of the measures that they passed, but they did not even attempt to record debates. Those that survive are all unofficial. They reflect the initiative of some particular individual, who may have misunderstood what someone else said, deliberately misrepresented him, or simply omitted a good part of the argument. Some early reporters for the state ratifying conventions and the first federal Congress were alcoholic or doodled aimlessly in the margin while the debates droned on. Madison's own notes, detailed as they are, still compress speeches of several hours' duration into a few paragraphs.[15] Even if we decide to accept the accuracy of these accounts, they only tell us what one man thought, not why the majority voted as it did or what that majority assumed it was doing.

If original intent did not signify to the Founders what our common sense suggests it should have, what did they mean by the phrase? As H. Jefferson Powell has demonstrated, they split into two broad camps, each captained by an author of *The Federalist Papers,* Hamilton and Madison. Underlying their arguments was an ingrained sense of textual criticism derived ultimately from Protestant readings of the Bible. The central injunction remained to stick close to the text. Commentaries or glosses on the text are no substitute for the original and can be dangerous.

But what if the text itself is unclear? Did the Constitution empower Congress to incorporate the Bank of the United States, or did it not? Hamilton said yes. Madison and Jefferson said no. Arguing as a lawyer steeped in English common law, Hamilton insisted that one construed a constitution the way a court interpreted a statute. The preamble identified whatever evil the measure was trying to correct and indicated in what way doubtful phrases should be understood. In the case of the United States Constitution, the "general welfare" clause would thus give Congress broad discretionary powers, particularly when coupled with the "necessary and proper"

[15] For example, on June 27 Luther Martin of Maryland spoke, according to Robert Yates, "upwards of three hours." Yates's account of this effort runs just over three pages. Madison summarized Martin in a page and a half (Farrand, ed., *Records of the Convention,* 1:436–41. The quotation is on p. 438).

clause in Article I, Section 8.[16] This meaning of original intent was soon taken up by Chief Justice John Marshall, but it attracted much dissent.

Jefferson called for a strict-constructionist reading of the Constitution when he urged Washington to veto the bank bill, but only later in the decade would Madison provide a formidable justification for a narrow interpretation of all grants of power to the federal government.[17] A constitution, he insisted, differs from a statute. The majority that drafts a statute also gives it life, but those who draft a constitution have no power to implement it. Only the people can do that through the process of ratification. The real question is not what the drafters thought they were writing, but what the people believed they were implementing. Only the texts of the ratification resolutions—but not accounts of debates in the ratification conventions, which are even more imperfect and inadequate than those for the Philadelphia Convention—can tell us what the Constitution means. Those who ratified the Constitution intended to create a more limited government than either Hamilton or Madison (in their *Federalist Papers*, for instance) fought for in 1787–88, and their will must prevail.

By the 1820s most politicians accepted Madison's argument, even though the Marshall Court remained broadly Hamiltonian. From the Nullification Crisis of 1830–33 until the Civil War, the two views continued in sharp conflict, but Hamilton and Marshall gained strength in the North and finally emerged victorious at Appomattox. The Thirteenth, Fourteenth, and Fifteenth amendments restricted the latitude of the states still further and helped to guarantee that the Hamiltonian understanding of original intent would become the mainstream of American law, making possible even the judicial activism of the Warren Court. A return to the

[16] Alexander Hamilton's opinion on the constitutionality of the bank, dated Feb. 23, 1791, is in Harold C. Syrett et al., eds., *The Papers of Alexander Hamilton*, 27 vols. (New York, 1961–87), 8:63–134.

[17] See Jefferson's opinion on the constitutionality of the bank, Feb. 15, 1791, in Boyd et al., eds., *Papers of Jefferson*, 19:275–82; Irving Brant, *James Madison*, vol. 3, *James Madison: Father of the Constitution, 1787–1800* (Indianapolis, 1950), pp. 436–37.

Madison doctrine would now require a repudiation of the Civil War and its constitutional achievements. Even Madison would concede that the opinion of the people, expressed in its most solemn form as a constitutional amendment, must override earlier opinions by the public on the same subject. As matters now stand, the Meese-Bork position requires the repudiation of the only opinion of the Founders themselves on original intent that has had any validity for more than a century without even returning to the only alternative that they ever recognized as viable.[18]

Eighteenth-century differences over original intent suggest a larger problem about fundamental values. Although all the Founders probably believed that such values exist, they did not agree on what they are or how to find them. Instead, contemporaries had to choose among several competing value systems, each with brilliant articulation in the high thought of the day. Humans being what they are, few chose one set of values to the complete exclusion of all others. Most people absorbed strands from more than one source and did their best to reconcile the tensions that their efforts created. In that respect they were not much different from ourselves, except perhaps in their conviction that fundamental values could somehow be identified and affirmed. That question itself now divides, rather than unites us. Situational ethics and moral relativism had not yet found formidable defenders, although the eighteenth century did produce a generous share of religious skeptics who often embodied an incipient form of moral relativism.

The tensions among these systems were real, even if most contemporaries—in America, at least—struggled to reduce rather than magnify them. In general those who lived in the last half of the eighteenth century had to choose among six rival sets of fundamental values: Calvinist orthodoxy, Anglican moralism, civic humanism, early classical liberalism, Scot-

---

[18] My discussion of this issue rests heavily on H. Jefferson Powell's outstanding essay "The Original Understanding of Original Intent," *Harvard Law Review* 98 (1984–85):885–948.

tish moral sense and commonsense philosophy, and the artisanal radicalism best exposited by Thomas Paine.[19]

In North America, strict Christian orthodoxy meant some variant of Calvinism with its commitment to predestination, justification by faith alone, and the primacy of revelation over reason. Calvinists insisted that all men deserve damnation and can do absolutely nothing on their own to avert that terrible sentence. Only God can save them, and they have no chance at all until they realize beyond all equivocation that they have no chance at all, that their best deeds stink in the nostrils of the Lord. All Protestants (and most Catholics, for that matter) were confident that there can be no ultimate conflict between reason and revelation. What God tells us through creation or nature cannot contradict what he has specifically revealed. What separated the orthodox from others on this issue is what they did when they encountered apparent discrepancies. The orthodox began with Scripture and rethought their rationalistic arguments until the two were again harmonious. Their position was anything but obsolete between 1750 and 1800 when Jonathan Edwards and his followers produced the most consistent and persuasive body of Calvinist theology ever generated in North America. To many contemporaries, Edwardsian theology was the most exciting and compelling thought of the age. The unorthodox, by contrast, began to challenge Scripture in the light of reason, an enterprise that Voltaire in particular pursued with zeal, malice, and devastating wit.[20]

[19] For a somewhat different taxonomy of value systems, see Isaac Kramnick's important essay "The 'Great National Discussion': The Discourse of Politics in 1787," *William and Mary Quarterly*, 3d ser. 45 (1988):3–32. Kramnick is analyzing ideas about government and politics. My concern is more with the structured ethical systems available to the Revolutionary generation.

Other highly developed systems of values also existed in the early republic but had too few adherents to exert much impact beyond their own members, although civic humanism, classical liberalism, and the Scottish Enlightenment undoubtedly affected them in various ways. Examples include Roman Catholicism, Judaism, the Shaker religion, and various strands of German pietism. None of them will be discussed in this essay.

[20] Of an enormous literature, see Perry Miller, *Jonathan Edwards* (New York, 1949), and Voltaire, *Philosophical Dictionary*, trans. and ed. Peter Gay

Anglican moralism, or latitudinarian theology, took shape in England as an explicit critique of Calvinist orthodoxy. Its most popular manifestation was, beyond any doubt, Richard Allestree's *The Whole Duty of Man*, first published in London in 1658 and often reprinted, a work of practical piety that appeared in nearly every major private library in the colonial South and quite often in small ones as well. Only the Bible, *The Book of Common Prayer*, and various catechisms were more widely owned in colonies that had an Anglican establishment. The elegant writings of Archbishop John Tillotson ably developed the main points of latitudinarianism. Tillotson almost equaled *The Whole Duty of Man* in popularity in the southern colonies and also won many admirers in New England, particularly at Harvard College, after 1700. These Anglicans rejected Calvinist predestination, stressed the careful performance of religious and ethical duties, and assured believers that God would indeed forgive them for any remaining transgressions provided they repented and sincerely begged his pardon. Although Anglicanism was America's most rapidly declining religion by the 1780s, more delegates at the Philadelphia Convention shared that background than any other faith. Most southern planters and lawyers and such northerners as Benjamin Franklin, Gouverneur Morris, and William Samuel Johnson had been strongly affected by latitudinarianism.[21]

Civic humanism (or country ideology, or republicanism), to

(New York, 1962), esp. pp. 58–72, 230–32, 237–44, 248–53, 328–32, 400–405.

[21] John Spurr, "'Latitudinarianism' and the Restoration Church," *Historical Journal* 31 (1988):61–82; Norman Fiering, "The First American Enlightenment: Tillotson, Leverett, and Philosophical Anglicanism," *New England Quarterly* 54 (1981):307–44; Richard Beale Davis, *Intellectual Life in the Colonial South, 1585–1763*, 3 vols. (Knoxville, Tenn., 1978), 2:580–81, 715, and chap. 4. I have used the 1763 Edinburgh edition of *The Whole Duty of Man*. No doubt some estate inventories did not distinguish between that work and *The New Whole Duty of Man* (London 1747 and subsequent editions). *The New Whole Duty* differed from the original primarily in identifying deists rather than Puritans as the principal danger to the Church of England. It thus insisted strongly on certain points of doctrine that the former volume had generally avoided.

the degree that it can be traced to Polybius and Cicero, was older even than Christianity, but it had no significant impact on Great Britain until the last half of the seventeenth century or on North America until the second quarter of the eighteenth. To civic humanists the primary concern of man was not salvation but serving the public in a political capacity. There his preoccupation ought to be the preservation of liberty, which those who wield power are forever trying to destroy. In the modern world this attack was usually indirect—through corruption—not head-on through a military coup or other explicit application of force. In the entire history of the world, liberty had seldom held out long against power. In the eighteenth century, only the English and their American colonists could make it thrive. They identified a "mixed and balanced" constitution as essential to Britain's success, and the key to that balance was the "virtue" or "patriotism" of the individual citizen, particularly as embodied in the lower house of the legislature.

This ideology was intensely masculine. Virtue meant the voluntary subordination of one's self-interest to the public good. The supreme act of patriotism was, of course, the sacrifice of one's life for his country. Only autonomous adult males—those not subject to the will of another—could be virtuous. Anyone who was subordinate to someone else's will—women, slaves, children, economic dependents—could not be entrusted with the liberties of a free society. In its most cautious formulation, civic humanism confined liberty to the independent country gentry and the institutions they could control.[22]

[22] Within an extensive literature, the most important study of the Anglo-American origins and development of this tradition is J. G. A. Pocock, *The Machiavellian Moment: Florentine Political Thought and the Atlantic Republican Tradition* (Princeton, 1975). For American developments specifically, see Bernard Bailyn, *The Ideological Origins of the American Revolution* (Cambridge, Mass., 1967); Gordon S. Wood, *The Creation of the American Republic, 1776–1787* (Chapel Hill, 1969); Lance G. Banning, *The Jeffersonian Persuasion: Evolution of a Party Ideology* (Ithaca, N.Y., 1978); and John M. Murrin, "The Great Inversion, or Court versus Country: A Comparison of the Revolution Settlements in England (1688–1721) and America (1776–1816)," in J. G. A. Pocock, ed., *Three British Revolutions: 1641, 1688, 1776* (Princeton, 1980), pp. 368–453.

England's first civic humanists were self-conscious anti-Calvinists, and the implicit tensions between Protestant orthodoxy, whether Calvinist or Anglican, and civic humanism remained conspicuous. At the psychological level they could be overwhelming. The true Christian, a model of humility, must recognize his (or her) utter worthlessness. The patriot glories in the pride of his (there can be no her) virtue. A committed Christian could become a patriot and make the supreme sacrifice, but men who began as patriots first could not easily accept the full demands—emotional and intellectual—of Calvinist orthodoxy. When John Randolph of Roanoke experienced a severe religious crisis during the War of 1812, he could think of no way to love his neighbors and return good for evil except by retiring from public life for several years and living almost as a hermit. His was but an extreme example of a tension that could afflict any politicized man who had not already committed himself to a Christian denomination.[23]

The fourth option, early classical liberalism, derived from John Locke, particularly his *Second Treatise of Government*, published just after the Glorious Revolution, and was much amplified by Adam Smith's monumental *An Inquiry into the Nature and Causes of the Wealth of Nations*, which appeared in 1776. According to Locke, all humans have rights that antedate history and are even anterior to organized society. The acquisition and protection of property became to him a fundamental reason for creating societies and governments, and a government that refused to protect this right lost all legitimacy. As reworked by Smith and other Scots, the emphasis on natural rights receded but the justification of acquisitiveness increased in importance. Early liberalism worried many

[23] For the anti-Calvinist origins of civic humanism in England, see Blair Worden, "Classical Republicanism and the Puritan Revolution," in Hugh Lloyd-Jones et al., eds., *History and Imagination: Essays in Honor of H. R. Trevor-Roper* (New York, 1981), pp. 182–200. For a fuller discussion of Randolph in this context, see J. Jefferson Looney and Ruth L. Woodward, *Princetonians, 1791–1794: A Biographical Dictionary*, ed. John M. Murrin (Princeton, 1991), pp. 88–102. More generally, see Mark Valeri, "The New Divinity and the American Revolution," *William and Mary Quarterly*, 3d ser. 46 (1989): 741–69; and Ruth H. Bloch, "The Gendered Meanings of Virtue in Revolutionary America," *Signs* 13 (1987): 37–58.

contemporaries because it seemed to provide a license for greed and threatened to reduce the common good to a mere sum of individual interests prudently pursued. "That *Man* is designed for *Society*," warned evangelical Calvinist Gilbert Tennent, "appears from the original *Constitution* of the human *Nature*." He feared that men "will be tempted, against the *Law* of *Nature*, to seek a *single* and independent State, in order to secure their *Ease* and *Safety*," an urge that to him violated the "mutual *Love*" that is "the *Band* and *Cement*" of society. To Tennent obligation preceded right, and the very notion of a state of nature seemed morally repugnant.[24]

[24] For the argument that America was far more liberal than civic humanist, see Joyce Appleby, *Capitalism and a New Social Order: The Republican Vision of the 1790s* (New York, 1984), and, for the colonial period, Jack P. Greene, *Pursuits of Happiness: The Social Development of Early Modern British Colonies and the Formation of American Culture* (Chapel Hill, 1988). For discussions of this theme, see John Ashworth, "The Jeffersonians: Classical Republicans or Liberal Capitalists?" *Journal of American Studies* 18 (1984):425–35; Lance G. Banning, "Jeffersonian Ideology Revisited: Liberal and Classical Ideas in the New American Republic," *William and Mary Quarterly*, 3d ser. 43 (1986):3–19; Joyce Appleby, "Republicanism in Old and New Contexts," *William and Mary Quarterly*, 3d ser. 43 (1986):20–34; John M. Murrin, "Can Liberals Be Patriots? Natural Right, Virtue, and Moral Sense in the America of George Mason and Thomas Jefferson," in Robert P. Davidow, ed., *Natural Rights and Natural Law: The Legacy of George Mason* (Fairfax, Va., 1986), pp. 35–65; and James T. Kloppenberg, "The Virtues of Liberalism: Christianity, Republicanism, and Ethics in Early American Discourse," *Journal of American History* 74 (1987–88):9–33. For the civic consciousness of the Scottish Enlightenment in general and Adam Smith in particular, see the exceptionally strong set of essays in Istvan Hont and Michael Ignatieff, eds., *Wealth and Virtue: The Shaping of Political Economy in the Scottish Enlightenment* (Cambridge, 1983). See also John Robertson, *The Scottish Enlightenment and the Militia Issue* (Edinburgh, 1985). For the quotation, see Gilbert Tennent, *Brotherly Love Recommended, by the Argument of the Love of Christ: A Sermon Preached at Philadelphia, January 1747–8* . . . (Philadelphia, 1748), p. 3. (My thanks to Wilson Carey McWilliams for bringing this passage to my attention.) For Jonathan Edwards's similar anxieties about acquisitiveness, see the covenant that he persuaded his Northampton congregation to adopt in March 1741/42, in Perry Miller et al., eds., *The Works of Jonathan Edwards*, 9 vols. to date (New Haven, 1957–), 4: 550–54; and for a discussion, see Mark Valeri, "The Economic Thought of Jonathan Edwards," *Church History* 60 (1991): 37–54.

Smith's arguments were always much more sophisticated than such a criticism implied, and he was far more concerned to liberate the economic energies of ordinary people than to reward the rich with still greater wealth. But many orthodox Christians saw liberalism as a defense of the sin of greed, and civic humanists had to take alarm at the threat of corruption that any legitimation of acquisitiveness entailed. This question appeared far more urgent in the United States (where voters outnumbered college graduates by many hundreds to one and a high percentage of voters could hold office) than in Scotland (which had several times more college graduates than voters). In Smith's homeland, increasing the wealth and power of the kingdom through the private enrichment of thousands of individual families seemed just about the only civic act open to ordinary men.

The fifth set of fundamental values came out of the Scottish Enlightenment and tried hard to synthesize the other options into one compelling whole. Francis Hutcheson, who shared Locke's passion for natural rights, worried that Locke, by grounding these rights in the ability of ordinary men in a state of nature to deduce their mutual obligations by unaided reason, had hopelessly overintellectualized the process. On Locke's terms only a small elite would ever discover that they had natural rights to protect. Hutcheson's answer to this difficulty was moral sense philosophy. All humans, he insisted, possess an inherent moral sense that tells them without any need to reflect on the subject that certain acts are abominable and others benevolent. Orthodox critics worried that Hutcheson, a Presbyterian minister from Ireland who became professor of moral philosophy at the University of Glasgow, made the moral sense so powerful that it left little room for Original Sin. Hutcheson had to survive a heresy trial to win respectability. His arguments found a broad audience in Scotland, where he became the first academic to lecture in English and thus attracted great numbers of hearers from the community at large. His influence spread to America through excited disciples, such as Francis Allison, and reluctant converts, such as John Witherspoon, a critic of Hutcheson in Scotland who nonetheless appropriated nearly all of his moral philosophy into his own lectures when he became president of the College of New Jersey.[25]

The Scottish Enlightenment reached its most skeptical and daring phase in the writings of David Hume, a political moderate who denied that reason can prove the existence of God, challenged Locke's whole notion of a state of nature and natural rights, and strongly questioned the civic humanist reading of history. Where country ideologues saw only decline in the movement from the "Gothic constitutions" of the Middle Ages to the absolute states of Europe in the eighteenth century, Hume detected improvement in civility and wealth and refused to take alarm at the acquisitive habits of ordinary people. His successors, the moderate literati of Edinburgh and other university cities in Scotland, invented common-sense philosophy to give Protestantism a firm base in human reason, took over Hutcheson's moral sense, but extended Hume's attack on Locke's state of nature. At its peak, the Scottish Enlightenment became intensely historical, seeking answers to human problems in the recorded experiences of human societies.

To a remarkable extent, the Scots invented the social sciences. Hume and William Robertson became outstanding critical historians. Smith's *Wealth of Nations* inspired the modern discipline of economics. Adam Ferguson asked the kind of questions that have become central to sociology. Hume's essay "That Politics May Be Reduced to a Science" launched an endeavor that modern political science continues. These

[25] See Peter Jones, "The Scottish Professoriate and the Polite Academy," in Hont and Ignatieff, eds., *Wealth and Virtue*, pp. 89–117; David F. Norton, "Francis Hutcheson in America," *Studies in Voltaire and the Eighteenth Century* 154 (1976):1547–68; John Witherspoon, *Lectures on Moral Philosophy*, ed. Jack Scott (Newark, Del., 1982), esp. Scott's Introduction; Ned C. Landsman, "Witherspoon and the Problem of Provincial Identity in Scottish Evangelical Culture," in Richard B. Sher and Jeffrey R. Smitten, eds., *Scotland and America in the Age of the Enlightenment* (Princeton, 1990), pp. 29–45; Garry Wills, *Inventing America: Jefferson's Declaration of Independence* (New York, 1978), esp. pp. 167–319; Ronald Hamowy, "Jefferson and the Scottish Enlightenment: A Critique of Garry Wills's *Inventing America: Jefferson's Declaration of Independence*," *William and Mary Quarterly*, 3d ser. 36 (1979):503–23. Hamowy powerfully challenges Wills's specific claim for Hutcheson's impact on Jefferson and the Declaration, but the man's widespread influence on educated Americans is undeniable.

efforts and the more philosophical inquiries of Thomas Reid and Dugald Stewart all found admirers in America, where Scottish moral sense and commonsense philosophy banished all rivals in the colleges through most of the nineteenth century.[26]

For all of its synthesizing instincts, the Scottish Enlightenment could not escape dilemmas of choice. Hume's skepticism always lurked in the background, capable of ensnaring curious students under the most conscientious Protestant teachers. The Scots' emphasis on historical process weakened without repudiating the doctrine of Original Sin. To the gentlemen of Edinburgh, Adam's Fall no longer seemed to explain much about their world. This tendency provoked chronic quarrels between the moderate literati, who by mid-century dominated the patronage structure of the kirk, and evangelicals, who also looked to America for allies and found them in the Edwardsians. Witherspoon became distinctive because, not only did he appropriate most of the arguments of the moderates including their demand for complete religious toleration, but he also remained an evangelical who insisted on the need for religious conversion. Despite his efforts, his students at Princeton increasingly absorbed the secular side of the Scottish Enlightenment at the expense of the theological. The college, a major training ground for ministers before Independence, produced few of them after the war.[27]

A sixth set of values, artisanal radicalism, was much less fully developed as a coherent system through the 1780s. But in the next decade Paine became its most eloquent spokesman, and it found numerous adherents among artisans and

[26] The best introduction to this subject is Richard B. Sher's fine book *Church and University in the Scottish Enlightenment* (Princeton, 1985). See also Mark A. Noll, "Common Sense Traditions and American Evangelical Thought," *American Quarterly* 37 (1985):215–38; and Douglas Sloan, *The Scottish Enlightenment and the American College Ideal* (New York, 1971).

[27] See Mark A. Noll, *Princeton and the Republic, 1768–1822: The Search for a Christian Enlightenment* (Princeton, 1989), and John M. Murrin, "Christianity, Enlightenment, and Revolution: Hard Choices at the College of New Jersey after Independence," *Princeton University Library Chronicle* 50 (1989):221–61. This essay is superseded by Murrin, Introduction to Looney and Woodward, *Princetonians*, pp. xvii–lviii.

backcountry farmers. Until it built explicitly upon the labor theory of value (also traceable to John Locke) in the 1790s, its power to delegitimate the pretensions of others greatly exceeded its ability to legitimate its own claims. Paine's *Common Sense* (1776) demolished forever in America the foundations of hereditary monarchy and aristocracy without eliminating the civic humanist commitment to the common good and to checks and balances. New York City artisans, Philadelphia's radical militia, and such spokesmen for the Pennsylvania interior as William Findley scored brilliant successes in deflating the claims of specific opponents to disinterested benevolence, but by 1790 their own model of a simple unicameral constitution dependent entirely on the people had lost decisively to more complex forms that derived from civic humanism as modified for American society. By equating their artisanal skills with landed wealth as a basis for personal independence and political virtue in American society, radicals appropriated civic humanist values to their own purposes rather than repudiate them entirely. They also enjoyed using angry Protestant rhetoric to bring the elite down a notch or two, although most American churches remained close to conventional orthodox attitudes toward the social order. But with the widespread dissemination of Paine's more systematic writings in the 1790s, the labor theory of value achieved an astonishing impact in Britain and a still greater influence in America. In the 1760s, political spokesmen had often portrayed themselves as disinterested men of leisure. By 1820 any American who hoped to retain an audience had to earn his own living.[28]

[28] Important studies include E. P. Thompson, *The Making of the English Working Class* (London, 1963); Margaret and James Jacob, eds., *The Origins of Anglo-American Radicalism* (London, 1984); Gary B. Nash, *The Urban Crucible: Social Change, Political Consciousness, and the Origins of the American Revolution* (Cambridge, Mass., 1979); Bernard Friedman, "The Shaping of the Radical Consciousness in Provincial New York," *Journal of American History* 56 (1969–70):781–801; Steven Rosswurm, "The Philadelphia Militia, 1775–1783," in Ronald Hoffman and Peter J. Albert, eds., *Arms and Independence: The Military Character of the American Revolution* (Charlottesville, 1984), pp. 75–118; Gordon S. Wood, "Interests and Disinterestedness in the Making of the Constitution," in Richard Beeman, Stephan Botein, and Edward C. Carter II, eds., *Beyond Confederation: Origins of the Constitution*

In a word, the tensions among these systems could be muted, but they refused to disappear. On some occasions and for some purposes, individuals could overcome the inherent obstacles and draw upon several different systems to create a powerfully persuasive argument. On other occasions people had to make painful choices between them. Jefferson provides marvelous examples of both kinds. The Declaration of Independence put together into a compelling whole central aspects of three of these competing systems. But his effort to grapple with the morality of slavery forced him to choose which value was more fundamental and for whom.

The Declaration of Independence is Lockean in its appeal to natural rights, equality, and the right to revolution. Although Jefferson changed Locke's trinity of life, liberty, and property into life, liberty, and "the pursuit of happiness," he may even have derived that intriguing phrase from Locke's *Essay concerning Human Understanding*. Sufficiently exposed to Scottish historicity to feel uncomfortable with the state of nature, he usually subordinated the right to property to the more fundamental right of each person to migrate from the society in which he was born. If a man moved to a place with vacant and unclaimed land, he could occupy it himself and thereby establish good title. In effect the migration argument provided him with a functional substitute for the state of nature. It gave him something which really existed in historical time and which acquired impressive explanatory power for North America. Jefferson probably also shared Jean-Jacques Burlamaqui's reservations about making property a natural right. Historically, as eighteenth-century jurists well understood, governments have defined what property is, and the law of property has varied considerably from one society to another. Like many of his contemporaries, Jefferson could accept property as a very basic civil right, defined by govern-

---

and American National Identity (Chapel Hill, 1987), pp. 69–109; Isaac Kramnick, "Republican Revisionism Revisited," *American Historical Review* 87 (1982):629–64; Gary B. Nash, "The American Clergy and the French Revolution," *William and Mary Quarterly*, 3d ser. 22 (1965):392–412; and Sean Wilentz, *Chants Democratic: New York City and the Rise of the American Working Class, 1788–1850* (New York, 1984), pp. 23–103.

ment but not anterior to it, provided government adopted uniform rules and enforced them impartially. After 1776 he did not often resort to natural rights arguments.[29]

The civic humanist portion of the Declaration—the indictment of George III—is the longest section of the text. The complaints against swarms of officeholders, the corruption of the colonial judiciary by undermining its independence, and the use of a standing army without colonial consent are vintage items from this tradition. Many of the others could come from both a Lockean or a civic humanist perspective, although the Declaration never explicitly mentions a social contract that the king has violated. Instead it insists that George III "has abdicated Government here, by declaring us out of his Protection and waging War against us"—a rather more legalistic position and perhaps a deliberate echo of Parliament's own position in the Glorious Revolution of 1688 and 1689 when it declared that James II had abdicated his throne by fleeing to France.

Scottish common sense appears in the appeal to "self-evident" truths, and Scottish moral sense emerges in Jefferson's discussion of the relationship between the British and American peoples. In a passage that Jefferson wrote and Congress deleted, he declared that the insensitivity of the British people to American appeals has "given the last stab to

[29] An important recent study is Richard K. Matthews, *The Radical Politics of Thomas Jefferson: A Revisionist View* (Lawrence, Kans., 1984), esp. pp. 19–29. For the migration argument, see Jefferson's *A Summary View of the Rights of British America* (1774), in Boyd et al., eds., *Papers of Jefferson*, 1:121–23. For Locke's use of the idea of the pursuit of happiness, see John Locke, *An Essay concerning Human Understanding*, ed. Alexander Campbell Fraser, 2 vols. (Oxford, 1894), 1:341. (My thanks to Thomas L. Pangle for alerting me to this possibility.) The connection between Locke, Burlamaqui, and Jefferson is explored in Morton White, *The Philosophy of the American Revolution* (New York, 1978). For a revealing discussion of the actual restraints upon property in eighteenth-century America, see Forrest McDonald, *Novus Ordo Seclorum: The Intellectual Origins of the Constitution* (Lawrence, Kans., 1985), pp. 9–55. See also Boyd et al., eds., *Papers of Jefferson*, 21:452, index entry under "Rights, natural," an exercise suggested to me by my colleague Daniel Rodgers. For the larger context of the Founders' attempts to tame the radical potential in natural rights theory, see Daniel T. Rodgers, *Contested Truths: Keywords in American Politics since Independence* (New York, 1987), chap. 2.

agonizing affection." Americans must reject these "unfeeling brethren" who, like their king, had flunked the moral test of empire. "We must endeavor to forget our former love for them, and to hold them as we hold the rest of mankind [—]enemies in war, in peace friends," he added. "We might have been a free and a great people together; but a communication of grandeur & of freedom it seems is below their dignity. Be it so, since they will have it. The road to happiness & to glory is open to us too."[30]

Although the Declaration does invoke "nature's God," it is in no sense an orthodox Calvinist document. Jefferson made no appeal to that tradition in preparing his argument for Independence. Nor did he in any explicit way draw upon Anglican moralism. But American culture soon supplied what he withheld. In all probability, cosmopolitan gentlemen of latitudinarian tastes favored it in disproportionate numbers. Clergymen from a Calvinist tradition rapidly appropriated the full Puritan heritage to explain Independence as a providential act by a people in special covenant with God. This emphasis often acquired a millennial dimension as well.[31]

The Declaration's continuing success as a justification for American nationhood stems largely from Jefferson's ability to combine arguments drawn from widely diverse systems. What did not persuade one person might convince someone else. Orthodox Americans quickly sanctified it in a way that Jefferson had not imagined doing. But he had far less success coping with slavery.

Jefferson considered slavery a violation of natural rights. The king's protection of the slave trade against colonial attempts to abolish it, the Virginian claimed in 1774, placed the interests of "a few British corsairs" above "the rights of human nature deeply wounded by this infamous practice." One

[30] Boyd et al., eds., *Papers of Jefferson*, 1:315–19, 413–33, esp. pp. 319 and 431, for the various drafts of the Declaration, the quotation omitted from the final version, and the abdication passage.

[31] See generally John F. Berens, *Providence & Patriotism in Early America, 1640–1815* (Charlottesville, 1978). On the tendency of cosmopolitan gentlemen to support the Constitution, see Jackson Turner Main, *Political Parties before the Constitution* (Chapel Hill, 1973).

of his rejected passages in the Declaration of Independence made a similar argument. Scottish moral sense theory only strengthened this conviction, for it gave Jefferson a way of affirming the moral equality of people whom he could never acknowledge as his intellectual peers. Yet unlike George Washington, Patrick Henry, Robert Carter of Nomini Hall, Richard Randolph, and other Virginia patriots, he never emancipated his own slaves. Until his death in 1826, he kept several hundred people in bondage.[32]

Jefferson justified his slaveholding in civic humanist terms. Throughout his life he felt a horror of debt that makes sense only in the language of country ideology. Debt could destroy his or any Virginia planter's capacity to function as an autonomous and virtuous citizen. The connection between debt and slavery became explicit in an agonized letter that he wrote in 1787:

> The torment of mind I endure till the moment shall arrive when I shall not owe a shilling on earth is such really as to render life of little value. I cannot decide to sell my lands. I have sold too much of them already, and they are the only sure provision for my children. Nor would I willingly sell the slaves as long as there remains any prospect of paying my debts with their labour. In this I am governed solely by views to their happiness which will render it worth their while to use extraordinary cautions for some time to enable me to put them on an easier footing, which I will do the moment they have paid the debts from the estate, two thirds of which have been contracted by purchasing them.[33]

To protect his personal independence, Jefferson came close

[32] See Jefferson, *A Summary View* and "Notes on Proceedings in the Continental Congress," June 1–Aug. 7, 1775, in Boyd et al., eds., *Papers of Jefferson*, 1:130, 317–18; Wills, *Inventing America*, pp. 218–28.

[33] Jefferson to Nicholas Lewis, July 29, 1787, in Boyd et al., eds., *Papers of Jefferson*, 11:640. In quoting this passage, William Cohen renders "cautions" as "exertions." See his "Thomas Jefferson and the Problem of Slavery," *Journal of American History* 56 (1969–70):516. The original manuscript is blurred and a case can be made for either reading, but Boyd's is more plausible, according to Eugene R. Sheridan, associate editor, the Papers of Thomas Jefferson, Princeton University.

to blaming his slaves for their condition. It was their fault that he ran into debt buying them. They should be grateful for the opportunity to work harder to pay off that obligation and not be sold. Yet in the 1790s Jefferson had to sell about fifty slaves to satisfy his creditors. He struggled conscientiously not to break up families in the process, but his definition of family did not always coincide with theirs. The subsequent resentment and grumbling from the quarters seemed offensive to his refined sensibilities. Slaves refused to understand why a future president of the United States sometimes felt the need to protect his civic humanist identity at the expense of their Lockean rights.[34]

The conflict of values in the eighteenth century was starkly real, and it affected the Constitution. In different ways civic humanism, classical liberalism, and the Scottish Enlightenment all challenged Calvinist orthodoxy and, to a lesser degree, Anglican moralism. Religious leaders responded by appropriating parts of each. But as the prayer incident reveals, Christian orthodoxy in any form was in short supply at the Philadelphia Convention.

The Founding Fathers did their best to minimize these antagonisms. Franklin, John Adams, and Jefferson all claimed to be Christians. They all thought of themselves as religious men. Franklin routinely said family prayers in his household and in the decade before Independence worked with Sir Francis Dashwood to revise *The Book of Common Prayer* in a rationalist direction. Young John Adams graduated from Harvard College expecting to become a clergyman, but then he veered into law because of particular religious scruples. Jefferson put enormous amounts of time and energy into compiling two religious works that he called "The Philosophy of Jesus" and "The Life and Morals of Jesus." First he selected the passages of the New Testament that he considered morally edifying, mostly from Matthew and Luke. Then he took the best Greek, Latin, French, and English versions of the Bible and put them together as parallel texts for each pas-

[34] Cohen, "Jefferson and Slavery," pp. 503–26.

sage. He, of course, decided which passages to include and which to omit.[35]

All three—as well as Madison, Washington, and other patriot leaders—claimed to be Christians. And yet the truly orthodox quite rightly wondered about the nature of their Christian commitment, except in the case of Washington, whose lack of fervor, distaste for dogma, inability to invoke the word "Christ," and refusal to receive the sacraments seems never to have attracted adverse comment. When Franklin died in 1790, rumors flew throughout Philadelphia. Had he expired with calm resignation? Had he made any formal profession of Christian beliefs? In his case the discrepancies among contemporary witnesses are minor. Franklin affirmed no set of doctrines, but he remained a Christian moralist who believed, or felt that he ought to believe, in an afterlife. Yet popular reports of his skepticism would not vanish. The Constitution, proclaimed *The American Annual Register . . . for the Year 1796*, "betrays as much indifference about religion, as if it had been exclusively penned by Benjamin Franklin himself. It is well known that the doctor believed *nothing*. He was by far the greatest philosopher of whom America can boast. Yet all the world knew that this great man disbelieved Christianity."[36]

Jefferson's "infidelity" finally became a major issue during the presidential campaign of 1800, but he refused to go public with his religious convictions. His decision was prudent, for in some parts of the country he could still have been arrested for blasphemy. Unable to accept the virgin birth, he believed that Jesus was not only the world's greatest moral teacher but also its most important bastard. In advising young Peter Carr about his education in 1787, Jefferson gave

[35] See Alfred Owen Aldridge, *Benjamin Franklin and Nature's God* (Durham, N.C., 1967), chap. 13; Lyman H. Butterfield, ed., *Diary and Autobiography of John Adams*, 4 vols. (Cambridge, Mass., 1961), esp. 1:42–43, 73; Eugene R. Sheridan, Introduction to Dickinson W. Adams and Ruth W. Lester, eds., *Jefferson's Extracts from the Gospels: "The Philosophy of Jesus" and "The Life and Morals of Jesus"* (Princeton, 1983), pp. 3–42.

[36] Aldridge, *Franklin and Nature's God*, pp. 264–69, esp. p. 268 (quotation).

him two options about Jesus. Carr could agree with those "who say he was begotten by god, born of a virgin, suspended and reversed the laws of nature at will, and ascended bodily into heaven." Or Carr could decide that Jesus "was a man, of illegitimate birth, of a benevolent heart, enthusiastic mind, who set out without pretensions to divinity, ended in believing them, and was punished capitally for sedition according to the Roman law." But Jefferson did not give Carr much real choice in deciding between these alternatives. Everyone, Jefferson insisted, ought to "read the bible . . . as you would read Livy or Tacitus." Reason alone must "call to her tribunal every fact, every opinion." "Do not be frightened from this enquiry by any fear of it's [*sic*] consequences," Jefferson added, even if "it ends in a belief that there is no god," because "you are answerable not for the rightness but the uprightness of the decision."[37]

Jefferson may not have been an ethical relativist in quite the twentieth-century sense, but on religious and even social questions he came rather close. Like most other Founders, he optimistically favored broad toleration because he hoped that human reason could improve on the confusion and bigotry that competing orthodoxies had brought to mankind. Reason, not revelation, was primary. Humans still had much to learn about social ethics, and he was convinced that what was morally proper in one society could even be utterly wrong in another. The criterion, he explained, is utility. "Men living in different countries, under different circumstances, different habits and regimens, may have different utilities; the same act, therefore, may be useful, and consequently vir-

[37] Constance B. Schulz, " 'Of Bigotry in Politics and Religion': Jefferson's Religion, the Federalist Press, and the Syllabus," *Virginia Magazine of History and Biography* 91 (1983):73–91; Jefferson to Peter Carr, Aug. 10, 1787, Boyd et al., eds., *Papers of Jefferson*, 12:15–17. Jefferson never changed his mind about the illegitimacy of Jesus. "And the day will come when the mystical generation of Jesus, by the supreme being as his father in the womb of a virgin," Jefferson wrote John Adams on Apr. 11, 1823, "will be classed with the fable of the generation of Minerva in the brain of Jupiter" (in Lester J. Cappon, ed., *The Adams-Jefferson Letters: The Complete Correspondence between Thomas Jefferson and Abigail and John Adams*, 2 vols. [Chapel Hill, 1959], 2:594).

tuous in one country which is injurious and vicious in another differently circumstanced."[38]

John Adams aroused less controversy among the orthodox, but his religious convictions were not that different from Jefferson's. "Twenty times, in the course of my late Reading, have I been on the point of breaking out, 'This would be the best of all possible Worlds, if there were no Religion in it!!!'" he wrote Jefferson in 1817. "But in this exclamati[on] I should have been as fanatical as Bryant or Cleverly. Without Religion this World would be Something not fit to be mentioned in polite Company, I mean Hell." These remarks seem to be a preface to an affirmation of Original Sin, but Adams took his argument in quite a different direction. "So far from believing in the total and universal depravity of human Nature; I believe there is no Individual totally depraved. The most abandoned Scoundrel that ever existed, never Yet Wholly extinguished his Conscience, and while Conscience remains there is some Religion."[39] In other words, Adams could affirm Christianity only if Scottish moral sense triumphed over orthodoxy. He refused to subordinate his judgment to anyone else's doctrine or theology, and insisted that he must decide for himself what was or was not orthodox. Like Jefferson, he could not bring himself to accept the divinity of Jesus.

How did this conflict of values connect with the drafting of the Constitution? Of course Jefferson and Adams were both abroad in 1787 and not even at the Convention, but the two men had an important indirect impact on the drafting and acceptance of the Constitution. Through four long months of deliberations, the delegates moved from a prototype that resembled the Virginia constitution of 1776, to which Jefferson had made important contributions, toward one that looked much more like the Massachusetts constitution of

[38] Jefferson to Thomas Law, June 13, 1814, Thomas Jefferson, *Writings*, ed. Merrill D. Peterson (New York, 1984), p. 1338.

[39] Adams to Jefferson, Apr. 19, 1817, Cappon, ed., *Adams-Jefferson Letters*, 2:509.

1780, of which Adams was the principal author.[40] When it became clear that the federal Constitution could not be ratified unless the Federalists agreed to add a bill of rights, Jefferson employed all his powers of persuasion in urging Madison to respond positively and creatively to this demand.[41] The views of both Jefferson and Adams are quite relevant to the achievements of 1787–88.

The Framers were not atheists. They all affirmed some degree of Christian commitment. But they were not orthodox, either—not many of them, anyway. Forced to choose between orthodoxy and enlightenment, nearly all of them evaluated the word of God by the reason of man, not human reason by the word of God.

The two chief architects of the Constitution, James Madison and James Wilson, had both been heavily influenced by the Scottish Enlightenment, including Hume. Madison as a young man studied Hebrew for a year with John Witherspoon at Princeton, which probably indicates that he seriously considered a ministerial career. As late as 1778 he still defended Calvinist predestination, but as an adult he never joined a church and was much more successful than Jefferson in keeping his religious opinions private. Other than an acceptance of a divinely sanctioned higher law, it is hard to know what he still believed by the 1780s, but he was no longer an orthodox Calvinist.[42] Wilson, like young John Adams, had rejected the clerical career for which his family had sent him

---

[40] For a fuller discussion of this point, see John M. Murrin, "1787: The Invention of American Federalism," in David E. Narrett and Joyce S. Goldenberg, eds., *Essays on Liberty and Federalism: The Shaping of the U.S. Constitution* (College Station, Tex., 1988), pp. 20–47.

[41] The relevant portions of this correspondence have been collected in Alpheus Thomas Mason, ed., *The States' Rights Debate: Antifederalism and the Constitution,* 2d ed. (New York, 1972), pp. 170–88.

[42] Madison's explicit defense of Calvinism is no longer extant, but much of its contents can be inferred from the recipient's reply. See Samuel Stanhope Smith to Madison, Nov. 1777–Aug. 1778, William T. Hutchinson et al., eds., *The Papers of James Madison,* 19 vols. to date (Chicago and Charlottesville, 1962-), 1:194–212. See also Ralph L. Ketcham, "James Madison and Religion—A New Hypothesis," *Journal of the Presbyterian Historical So-*

to college. He, too, chose the bar instead. His law lectures place him close to the moderate literati of Edinburgh, fully committed to moral sense philosophy and unwilling to concede any real conflict between it and revelation. The Scriptures, he told his students, "are addressed to rational and moral agents, capable of previously knowing the rights of men, and the tendencies of actions; of approving what is good, and of disapproving what is evil." In other words, the Scriptures "support, confirm, and corroborate, but do not supercede the operations of reason and the moral sense."[43]

Madison, Wilson, and the other delegates at Philadelphia set themselves a daunting task, the creation of a government that—through checks and balances, the separation of powers, and a viable division of legitimate authority between state and national levels—would contain within itself a potential for indefinite endurance. Madison no longer believed, as had many of his countrymen in 1776, that the American people were more virtuous than others. Americans could be as greedy and repulsive as anyone else. Although he too hoped for elementary decency and integrity from average citizens, Madison thought the Framers must devise a government that would behave more virtuously than the people at large. By pitting faction against faction in an enlarged republic run by gentlemen, no majority faction was likely to emerge, and minority factions could fairly easily be controlled through the majority principle. The Constitution thus became a device for establishing a republican government over a population

---

ciety 38 (1960):65–90; idem, "James Madison and the Nature of Man," *Journal of the History of Ideas* 19 (1958):62–76. Ketcham reads more positive religious affirmations into his sources than I can find. Madison would not have remained so secretive about his convictions, or lack of them, unless he feared exposure.

[43] Charles Page Smith, *James Wilson, Founding Father, 1742–1798* (Chapel Hill, 1956), p. 17; Robert Green McCloskey, ed., *The Works of James Wilson*, 2 vols. (Cambridge, Mass., 1967), 1:144. Compare Stephen A. Conrad, "Polite Foundation: Citizenship and Common Sense in James Wilson's Republican Theory," *Supreme Court Review, 1984,* ed. Philip B. Kurland et al. (Chicago, 1984), pp. 359–88. See also Daniel Walker Howe, "Why the Scottish Enlightenment Was Useful to the Framers of the American Constitution," *Comparative Studies in Society and History* 31 (1989): 572–87

of liberals. Ordinary people would still pursue their self-interest every day, but government would try to accomplish something grander, the common good. Although every national politician was potentially factional on questions that concerned his own or his constituents' interests, no harm would follow unless this minority somehow became a majority. "In the extended republic of the United States, and among the great variety of interests, parties and sects which it embraces," Madison affirmed, "a coalition of a majority of the whole society could seldom take place on any other principles than those of justice and the general good."[44] He hoped that he had created what a later commentator called "a machine that would go of itself."[45]

In the language of today's television evangelists, the Founders drafted a secular humanist text. The Constitution meets all the essential criteria of today's angry preachers, even though "secular humanism" was not a phrase used by the Founders.[46] The Constitution is not Christian in any doctrinal sense. Throughout their deliberations, the Founders consciously rejected any appeal for divine aid and neglected even to mention God in their completed text. This omission was all the more striking because Congress had invoked "the Great Governor of the world" in the Articles of Confederation, and most state constitutions or bills of rights had used at least a similar metaphor for God somewhere in the document.[47]

[44]*Federalist* No. 51 in Jacob E. Cooke, ed., *The Federalist* (Middletown, Conn., 1961), pp. 352–53. Too often *Federalist* No. 10 is taken as Madison's celebration of liberal America. This passage from No. 51 indicates the republican context in which his acceptance of liberal behavior belongs.

[45]See generally Michael Kammen, *A Machine That Would Go of Itself: The Constitution in American Culture* (New York, 1987), p. 18. The phrase comes from James Russell Lowell's 1888 celebration of the Founders' achievement, but the metaphor of a machine began much earlier (pp. 17–19).

[46]However, men of the Enlightenment often called themselves "the party of humanity." See Peter Gay, *The Party of Humanity: Essays in the French Enlightenment* (Princeton, 1959).

[47]For a fuller discussion, see John M. Murrin, "Religion and Politics in America from the First Settlements to the Civil War," in Mark A. Noll, ed., *Religion and American Politics from the Colonial Period to the 1980s* (New York,

31

Nor does the Constitution rest on any broad consensus about Original Sin, a favorite method of Christianizing the document today. Few Founders held orthodox views on that question. Humans, they assumed, are easily corruptible, not irremediably corrupt from conception. I exaggerate just a little in suggesting that, to the Founders, Original Sin, if it existed at all, was a disability that afflicted other people. The men of the Revolution were forever affirming their own disinterestedness and the purity of their motives while denouncing the corruption of their political opponents. As the machine metaphor powerfully suggests, the Constitution is a purely human answer to human problems within history.

These attributes, and the ethical relativism that the Founders shared in an incipient form, are the criteria for secular humanism as defined by the Evangelical Right today.[48] The consequences may be serious. A few years ago William B. Hand, chief justice of the United States District Court for the Southern District of Alabama, declared secular humanism a religion and banned from the public schools all books that, in his opinion, embraced such convictions, including several dangerous home economics textbooks which point out that divorce occurs often these days. He was quickly overturned by a higher court, but if his judgment should ever prevail, and if my analysis is correct, the obvious conclusion is a trifle unsettling. It ought to be unconstitutional to teach the Constitution in American public schools.

Perhaps I should stop there, but the American people did not, and neither shall I. The Constitution did not long remain a distillation of secular humanism, eighteenth-century style. Although the Revolutionary era probably marked the low point in church attendance throughout American his-

---

1990), pp. 19–43, esp. pp. 29–30. For the Articles of Confederation, see Samuel Eliot Morison, ed., *Sources and Documents Illustrating the American Revolution, 1764–1788, and the Formation of the Federal Constitution*, 2d ed. (Oxford, 1929), p. 186, Art. 13.

[48] So a number of TV evangelists have declared in numerous television sermons, although I have not taken notes while watching them and cannot cite any particular one.

tory, average citizens were more likely to be orthodox than the Founders, and they soon invested the document with their own religious values and aspirations. What had happened earlier to the Declaration now occurred with the Constitution. The culture Christianized it. Because nothing in the Constitution is inherently anti-Christian, that process began early and achieved considerable but always incomplete success.

No incident better displays this process than what the public learned about Franklin's motion for public prayers at the Convention. The notes of Robert Yates were published in 1821. They give a brief account of what happened. Franklin first acknowledged the difficulties the delegates faced. "As a sparrow does not fall without Divine permission," he asked, "can we suppose that governments can be erected without his will? We shall, I am afraid, be disgraced through little party views. I move *that we have prayers every morning.*" Without explaining why, Yates added in a separate one-line paragraph: "Adjourned till to-morrow morning." He did not specifically record that Franklin's motion never carried.[49]

The Yates entry was ambiguous enough to encourage the public to believe what it wished, especially once the ghost of Jonathan Dayton provided encouragement. Around 1815 he had recounted his version of the event to William Steele, who reported it to his son Jonathan D. Steele in 1825, a year after Dayton's death. Steele's version badly garbled what happened. How much of the blame was his and how much was Dayton's we shall never know.

When Franklin finished his speech on behalf of prayer, "never," asserted Dayton, "did I behold a countenance at once so *dignified* and *delighted* as was that of Washington . . . ! Nor were the members of the Convention, generally less affected." While Hamilton attacked the invocation of foreign aid, "Washington fixed his eye upon the speaker, with a mixture of *surprise* and *indignation.*" The delegates shared Washington's scorn, for "no one deigned to *reply,* or take the smallest notice of the speaker, but the motion for appointing a chaplain was instantly seconded and carried; whether under the

[49] Farrand, ed., *Records of the Convention,* 1:457–58.

silent disapprobation of Mr. H———, or his *solitary negative,* I do not recollect." The Convention then adjourned for the weekend, which Dayton made a part of Franklin's motion. It met on Monday with tempers calmed and a chaplain present, and after prayers it quickly passed the Connecticut Compromise.[50]

Steele's account of Dayton's version of what happened reached the public on August 26, 1826, about seven weeks after the deaths of Jefferson and Adams on the fiftieth anniversary of the Declaration had quite dramatically confirmed to nearly all contemporaries God's overt approval of the American republic. (Former president James Monroe confirmed this tradition by dying on July 4, 1831, but Madison had to pay for his misdeeds. As the last Founder to die, he did not quite make it to July 4 when his time came in 1836. Instead, he expired on June 28, the anniversary of the occasion when he and fellow delegates had defeated prayer at the Philadelphia Convention.) Although Madison denied the accuracy of the Dayton version in private letters, no adequate account became available before Madison's notes were published in 1840.[51] Until then the American people had every reason to believe that the delegates used prayer to solve their most ferocious dispute.

The process of sanctifying the Constitution began with its adoption and has continued ever since. The most common method has been the creation and invocation of a "civil religion," a language representing the lowest common denominator of religious values that most of the public can accept. It permits government officials to invoke God's aid and guidance in a way that comforts and sometimes inspires an audience. At moments of strife or danger, the old Puritan rhetoric of a chosen people can also emerge, and so can the jeremiad when a manifest need to repent and reform seems at hand. At first Federalists, Whigs, and Republicans were rather more comfortable with these devices than were Jeffersonian and Jacksonian Democrats. As the nineteenth century pro-

[50] Ibid., 3:467–73, esp. pp. 471–72.

[51] Madison to Jared Sparks, Apr. 8, 1831; Madison to Thomas S. Grimke, Jan. 6, 1834, ibid., pp. 499–500, 531.

gressed, Whigs and Republicans also tried to give America's civil religion a much more explicit Protestant evangelical content. By the age of William Jennings Bryan and Woodrow Wilson, even many Democrats had joined in, but overt evangelicalism was much more likely to divide than to unite the polity.[52]

What then became of the conflict of values that had helped to generate the Constitution? The competing systems were by no means unique to the United States, but the way that the republic resolved its disagreements about fundamental values probably was. In Britain, for example, early classical liberals knew that they were not orthodox Christians. Although Locke managed to combine much of Anglican doctrine with his own Unitarian convictions, Hume was a skeptic, and the mature Adam Smith may have been an atheist, as were such prominent utilitarians and liberals as Jeremy Bentham and John Stuart Mill. Civic humanism, still a powerful force in Britain during the American Revolution, weakened rapidly thereafter, while Scottish philosophy continued to find adherents even as it lost its base in Edinburgh and became more widely diffused throughout the kingdom.[53]

The United States displays no such pattern. Probably because of the close association between classical liberalism and religious infidelity, almost no American thinkers proclaimed themselves committed liberals. Americans were so proud of their progressive Revolution that virtually no one accepted the label of conservative. The liberal-conservative dichotomy did not become a prominent part of the language of politics,

[52] Catherine L. Albanese, *Sons of the Fathers: The Civil Religion of the American Revolution* (Philadelphia, 1976); John F. Wilson, *Public Religion in American Culture* (Philadelphia, 1979).

[53] Locke's religiosity, once widely doubted, has been generally accepted since the publication of D. G. James, *The Life of Reason: Hobbes, Locke, Bolingbroke* (London, 1949). On Smith, see John Dunn, "From Applied Theology to Social Analysis: The Break between John Locke and the Scottish Enlightenment," in Hont and Ignatieff, eds., *Wealth and Virtue*, p. 120. For later utilitarians and liberals, see Elie Halévy, *The Growth of Philosophic Radicalism,* trans. Mary Morris (Boston, 1955). For a fine study of the indirect ways in which civic humanism continued to affect nineteenth-century British thinkers, see J. W. Burrow, *Whigs and Liberals: Continuity and Change in English Political Thought* (Oxford, 1988).

I suspect, until the middle decades of the twentieth century. Wealthy Mahlon Dickerson provides an amusing example of this absence and what it meant. A lifelong Jeffersonian and Jacksonian officeholder who served as senator and secretary of the navy for extended periods, he heard a rumor in 1838 that some people were calling him a "conservative." Though nearly seventy, he spent an exhausting day prowling the state to track down and quash this horrid slander. To him both liberals and conservatives were British, and he rejected nearly everything about the British political system.[54]

Yet as Madison knew as early as *Federalist* No. 10, liberal behavior was quite conspicuous in the United States. In the nineteenth century it became more characteristic of America than of any other society in the world. In its most overt entrepreneurial forms it won enthusiastic support among evangelicals. Liberal values and behavior, if not the philosophical system of liberalism, made converts of the orthodox in America.

To an unusual degree, Americans resolved these tensions through role-playing. The typical liberal was the head of a household trying to feed his family and if possible get rich through intense involvement in the market. Yet he expected his political leaders to be statesmen who, while looking after his local interests, would fight corruption and stand for the public good. Civic humanism continued to provide the conscience of American public life, as the nation's obsession with corruption reveals. The truest Christian was, of course, the American mother in an age that saw the churches drastically feminized. Whether republicans or liberals, nearly all men in the nineteenth century still insisted that women must remain humble and serve others—their parents first and later their husbands and children. Most women probably agreed or at least learned to be resigned to their role, but increasing numbers of them either resisted or used this public acknowledgment of their selfless virtue to demand improved legal and political rights. Scottish commonsense and moral sense philosophy also survived in the United States for most of the

[54]Mahlon Dickerson, entry for Aug. 20, 1838, Diary, July 16, 1832–Aug. 26, 1845, typescript copy, p. 104, Mahlon Dickerson Papers, New Jersey Historical Society, Newark.

nineteenth century, at least in the colleges where the faculty continued to assure generations of students that Scottish thought retained the power to reconcile reason and revelation.

Much of American uniqueness lies in the nation's refusal to admit that the differences in these systems are as fundamental as the values each affirms. The pluralism of the republic has extended, not just to ethnic and religious diversity, but to its basic value systems as well. The main line of political development has pitted a largely nonevangelical Jeffersonian-Jacksonian coalition against a disproportionately evangelical Whig-Republican alignment that has usually derived some kind of reform agenda from its commitment to liberal entrepreneurial values and born-again piety. This compound remains highly unstable but has also been extremely persistent. It can rarely control the country for long, but it never goes away. Two hundred years later it is still battling to reduce the republic and its secular humanist Constitution to a Christianized homogeneity.[55]

The purpose of the Founders was startlingly different from what the Evangelical Right hopes to impose on America. Without the contributions of eighteenth-century secular humanists, the American republic would never have become what it is today. If the original intent of the Founding Fathers survives into the coming century, secular humanism will continue to interact with other value systems in constantly reshaping the nation.

[55] For these purposes, perhaps the best single introduction to nineteenth-century American political culture is Paul A. Johnson, *A Shopkeeper's Millennium: Society and Revivals in Rochester, New York, 1815–1837* (New York, 1978). On the transformation of American Protestantism, see Nathan O. Hatch, *The Democratization of American Christianity* (New Haven, 1989).

JENNIFER NEDELSKY

The Protection of Property in the Origins and Development of the American Constitution

THE UNITED STATES Constitution has a coherent institutional design that shapes the structure of power in America. Its design reflects the constellation of ideas about the importance of property and the objects and limits of government that prevailed at the Constitutional Convention of 1787. This conception was essentially Madisonian, as was the structure of power it generated. Both are still with us today.

These statements imply relationships between the origins of the Constitution and its current form, between the institutional structure of our government and its underlying conceptual framework, and between all of these and the distribution of power in the United States. A better understanding of the thought of influential Framers such as James Madison helps us to understand the purpose of the Constitution's design, and, conversely, the structure of the Constitution and its subsequent development shows the extent to which our system incorporated a Madisonian, property-centered conception of government.[1] This two-way approach indicates the relationships between institutions, power, and ideas encompassed in the Constitution.

[1] For an example of the argument that the Constitution must be understood and interpreted as a coherent structure, see Charles Black, *Structure and Relationship in Constitutional Law* (Baton Rouge, 1969).

The Constitution may properly be seen both as a concrete system of institutions and as a document that exists in the realm of ideas, concepts, and values.[2] The institutions and the ideas shape and reinforce each other. When I first began this project, I saw it as a case study of the translation of political theory into practice. There are important ways in which the writing of the Constitution was such an endeavor, but this characterization is also misleading. I found it impossible to sort my note cards into neat piles of "theory" and "institutional embodiment." The Framers were practical statesmen whose concerns with designing institutions shaped their theoretical inquiry as much as their commitments to theory shaped the institutions they proposed for the new Constitution. Property is a characteristic and central instance of the way in which theoretical conceptions such as justice and representation mixed with pragmatic concerns such as stability, and of the way in which institutional designs distributed power.

To examine the conceptual framework of the Constitution and the system of institutions it established, I turn to the political thought of James Madison, for the Constitution is essentially Madisonian. I argue that there are important weaknesses in his political theory that can be traced to the central importance he accorded to property. Their significance is clearest when Madison is compared with two of his most influential allies at the Convention: James Wilson and Gouverneur Morris. Such a comparison illustrates the ways in which the Constitution of 1787 embodied both the strengths and weaknesses of the Madisonian approach. I conclude with a brief discussion of how the rise of judicial review entailed both a culmination and a subtle transformation of the Madisonian Constitution. In the subsequent development of the Constitution, its basic strengths and weaknesses have remained despite a dramatic shift in the formal constitutional status of property—once the core of Madisonian constitutionalism.

[2] For a discussion of this dual nature see William F. Harris II, "Bonding Word and Polity: The Logic of American Constitutionalism," *American Political Science Review* 76 (1982):34–45.

A concern with property is the foundation of Madison's major contribution to republican theory: his perception that majority rule alone is an inadequate basis for republican government. The catalyst for this conclusion was the instability and injustice of state laws under the Articles of Confederation. Madison saw the paper money and debtor relief laws of this period as attacks on property, which raised fundamental questions about republican government as the solution to the age-old problem of tyranny. These laws were not confiscations of property without representation; they were infringements on property rights by duly elected representatives of the people and, as such, were formally legitimate. Consequently, they brought "into question the fundamental principle of republican government, that the majority who rule in such governments are the safest Guardians both of the Public Good and private rights."[3]

Madison saw in the legislative attacks on property proof that the process of popular representation would not of itself achieve the ends of government. The problem was not that the system did not adequately reflect the people's views or that it thwarted the will of the majority. The problem was that government gave effect to their will, and their will was often unjust. This required a qualification of the basic principle of republican government: the consent of the people was the basis for the legitimacy of government, but not everything the people consented to was legitimate. The end of government was justice, and Madison believed that there were "rules of justice"[4] that set a limit to what even popular government could legitimately do. The question was how to design a republican government that would respect those limits; the protection of property was central to this.

Madison's concern with property dominated his writings at the time of the Convention, and in his single most important statement of republican theory he asserted that "the first object of government" was "the protection of the different and

---

[3] James Madison, "Vices of the Political System of the United States" (April 1787), in Marvin Meyers, ed., *The Mind of the Founder: Sources of the Political Thought of James Madison* (Indianapolis, 1973), pp. 83–92.

[4] *Federalist* No. 10.

unequal faculties of acquiring property."[5] But Madison also claimed that there were not one but two "cardinal objects of Government: the rights of persons, and the rights of property"[6] and that, consequently, "the most either can claim, is such a structure [of government] as will leave reasonable security for the other."[7] How to design such a structure was the problem he wrestled with throughout his life. In his view, "the most difficult of all political arrangements is that of so adjusting the claims of the two Classes as to give security to each, and to promote the welfare of all."[8] The priority he claimed for property in *The Federalist* was thus not a settled principle but the core of a fundamental problem that involved practical politics, not theory. There was no inherent tension between the two sets of rights. Madison did not think that the full security of property rights would of itself infringe on or threaten the rights of persons—or vice versa. The problem arose out of the inevitable division of the population into two classes: those with and those without property. It was the conflict between these two classes that required the statesman to treat the two sets of rights as separate and in tension with one another.

Both classes would, if given the power, be likely to violate the rights of the other: "Give all power to property, and the indigent will be oppressed. Give it to the latter and the effect may be transposed."[9] But the rights of property were more

[5] Ibid.

[6] James Madison, "Remarks on Mr. Jefferson's Draught of a Constitution" (Oct. [12], 1788), Meyers, ed., *Mind of the Founder*, p. 58. For Madison the "rights of persons" or "personal rights" do not include all individual rights. Thus he says, "Government is instituted no less for the protection of the property than of the persons of individuals" (*Federalist* No. 54). The rights of persons do not include nonbodily rights such as freedom of conscience. These are truly inalienable: the individual need never surrender any control over them to government. Consequently, they are not, properly speaking, objects of government.

[7] Max Farrand, ed., *The Records of the Federal Convention of 1787*, rev. ed., 4 vols. (1937; reprint ed., New Haven, 1966), 2:204. All references are to Madison's notes unless otherwise indicated.

[8] Ibid.

[9] Madison, "Remarks on Jefferson's Draught," Meyers, ed., *Mind of the Founder*, p. 58. A later statement makes explicit that the rights that would

vulnerable in a republic than the rights of persons. In the first place, the propertied class would inevitably be the minority: "It is now observed that in all populous countries, the smaller part only can be interested in the rights of property."[10] The majority, having no property, would have no interest in protecting the rights of property and, indeed, were likely to think they had an interest in violating those rights. The propertyless majority could only be relied on to protect the rights of persons.[11] The interests of the propertied, on the other hand, were such that those with property were less likely to violate the rights of others: "As the holders of property have at stake all the other rights common to those without property, they may be the more restrained from infringing, as well as the less tempted to infringe the rights of the latter."[12] It would nevertheless not be safe to entrust them with exclusive power.

The problem of how to balance these two classes in order to protect the rights of both—to weigh their power, their threat, and the importance of each set of rights—was compounded by republican principles. Madison recognized a "fundamental principle that men cannot be justly bound by laws in making of which they have no part,"[13] that is, men have a fundamental right to suffrage. But if this right were extended equally to all, the controlling power in the government would be a majority "not interested in the rights of property."[14] If property rights are to be secured, therefore,

---

be violated are, respectively, those of persons and property: "Allow the right [of suffrage] exclusively to property, and the rights of persons may be oppressed. . . . Extend it equally to all, and the rights of property or the claims of justice may be overruled by a majority without property" (Note on Madison speech of Aug. 7, 1787 [1821], ibid., p. 503).

[10] Madison, "Remarks on Jefferson's Draught," ibid., p. 58.

[11] Ibid.; Madison, Note on Aug. 7, 1787, speech, ibid., p. 501.

[12] Madison, Note on Aug. 7, 1787, speech, ibid., p. 501.

[13] Madison, Note on Aug. 7, 1787, speech, Farrand, ed., *Records of the Convention*, 2:204.

[14] Madison, Note on Aug. 7, 1787, speech, Meyers, ed., *Mind of the Founder*, p. 503.

some restriction of this fundamental right is required. In principle, there was no conflict between the rights of persons and the rights of property; in principle, suffrage was the right of all. But in practice, if political rights were given equally to all, the rights of persons and the rights of property would not be equally protected. Madison was thus faced with the problem of balancing not only the rights of property and the rights of persons, but political rights as well. There were several interrelated reasons why property weighed so heavily in this balance, why it was Madison's primary concern even though he could not accord it priority in principle. The first of these has to do with the requirements of republican government, the second with the nature of property itself.

Madison emphasized property in part because it was inherently vulnerable in a republic. In America the problem began with the neglect of property rights in the political thought of the Revolution:

> The necessity of thus guarding the rights of property was for obvious reasons unattended to in the commencement of the Revolution. In all Governments which were considered as beacons to republican patriots and lawgivers the rights of persons were subjected to those of property. The poor were sacrificed to the rich. In the existing state of American population and American property the two classes of rights were so little discriminated that a provision for the rights of persons was supposed to include of itself those of property, and it was natural to infer from the tendency of republican laws, that these different interests would be more and more identified. Experience and investigation have however produced more correct ideas on the subject.[15]

---

[15] Gaillard Hunt, ed., *The Writings of James Madison*, 9 vols. (New York, 1900–1910), 5:287. In 1787 Madison assumed the importance of personal rights and emphasized "property as well as personal rights." During the 1790s, however, there was a brief reversal of his emphasis. The political developments between 1787 and 1792 apparently made him think that a concern with property rights had become predominant in America and that the rights of persons might need special emphasis after all: "In a word, as a man is said to have a right to his property, he may equally be said to have a property in his rights. . . . Government is instituted to protect property of every sort; as well that which lies in the various rights of individuals, as that which the term particularly expresses" ("Property," *National Gazette*, Mar. 29, 1792, Meyers, ed., *Mind of the Founder*, p. 244). In

Madison thought that the Revolutionary principles of government assured the respect for the rights of persons but left the right of property vulnerable to the excesses of popular government.

Property was vulnerable, not simply because of the tradition of American thought, but also because of the age-old division between the many and the few, a division to which America would not be immune. The few were the rich, and even though the many in America in 1787 were not yet poor, they had already advocated violations of property rights. Matters would only get worse: ultimately America would have a propertyless majority who would "labor under all the hardships of life, and secretly sigh for a more equal share of the blessings of life." [16] Thus popular government clearly posed a special problem for the protection of property.

The intrinsic dangers of threats to property were, as we shall see, serious enough. But the issue took on a wider significance as well: it pointed to the fundamental problem of the vulnerability of any minority rights to majority faction. Faction, Madison argued, was an inevitable part of any free society, and factions could be composed of the majority as well as the minority. It was the former that posed enduring problems for republican government; the threat to property was the chief example of this larger problem: "the most common and durable source of faction has been the various and unequal distribution of property." [17] For Madison the protection of property was always of both great intrinsic and symbolic importance. A government that could not protect property demonstrated its inability to ensure justice and security either generally or with respect to a crucial particular.

This dual quality is apparent in the dominant theme of

---

fact, here Madison was urging concern not simply for the rights of persons, but for all individual rights.

This broad use of property was an isolated example. He used it only for rhetorical purposes to make a particular point. In all other instances Madison's use of "property" did not incorporate other individual rights.

[16] Farrand, ed., *Records of the Convention*, 2:422.

[17] *Federalist* No. 10.

Madison's discussions of property: stability. The core of his argument is that the protection of property rights is essential to the stability of society and government, and stability in turn is necessary if republican government is to endure. He argued from both the historical particular and the general. The current attacks on property were producing such instability that Americans' confidence in republican government was being undermined: "The state of affairs under the Articles of Confederation was marked by symptoms which are truly alarming, which have *tainted the faith of the most orthodox republicans,* and which challenge from the votaries of liberty every concession in favor of stable Government not infringing fundamental principles, as the only security against an *opposite extreme of our present situation.*"[18] Madison was convinced that the precarious experiment with republican government could not survive if it could not prevent the abuses to which it was prone. The people would finally not tolerate the insecurity and instability and would look to nonrepublican forms of government for a remedy. Should this happen, the American republic would succumb to the fate of all other popular governments: "The instability, injustice and confusion introduced into the public councils have, in truth, been the mortal disease under which popular governments have everywhere perished."[19]

The threat of instability and injustice was a constant refrain in Madison's discussions of republican government, and it was always clear that the "vicissitudes" of state policy he referred to were those involving property rights.[20] "One legislative interference is but the first link of a long chain of repetitions, every subsequent interference being naturally produced by the effects of the preceding."[21] Further, such laws undermine confidence in both public engagements and

[18] James Madison to Thomas Jefferson, Mar. 19, 1787, in Julian P. Boyd et al., eds., *The Papers of Thomas Jefferson,* 24 vols. to date (Princeton, 1950-), 2:219.

[19] *Federalist* No. 10.

[20] See, for example, Mar. 19 and Apr. 8, 1787, in Hunt, ed., *Writings of Madison,* 2:326 and 339.

[21] *Federalist* No. 44.

private contracts and hence undermine the possibility of regular, ordered, long-term enterprise.[22] In short, from Madison's perspective, the laws of property are a central part of the order of society; if these fluctuate, the entire society will be unstable.

A system of government that could not secure property rights invited not only social and economic disorder but political instability. The source of this instability was not only the immediately precarious situation of the young republic but Madison's vision of the future propertyless majority. According to Madison, those who have neither property nor the prospect of acquiring any would have no "interest in the security of property rights."[23] Indeed, they were likely to mistakenly think it in their interest to violate those rights. Without the proper structure of government, the propertyless would pose a serious threat to republican liberty:

> Liberty not less than justice pleads for the policy here recommended [providing protection for property rights by annexing a property qualification to the right to vote for senator]. If *all* power be suffered to slide into hands not interested in the rights of property, which must be whenever a majority fall under that description, one of two things cannot fail to happen; either they will unite against the other description and become the dupes and instruments of ambition, or their poverty and dependence will render them the mercenary instruments of wealth. In either case liberty will be subverted; in the first by a despotism growing out of anarchy, in the second, by an oligarchy founded on corruption.[24]

One can see here the supreme political importance of protecting property from the majority: Madison could not imagine either a coherent strategy based on opposition to the vested rights of the minority or an ordered political society

[22] *Federalist* No. 62.

[23] See "Remarks on Jefferson's Draught," Meyers, ed., *Mind of the Founder,* p. 59: "In all populous countries, the smaller part only can be interested in preserving the rights of property."

[24] Ibid.

based on a denial of the property rights of a well-off minority. If the propertyless should unite against the propertied, Madison saw them becoming "the dupes and instruments of ambition"—being used by demagogues and tyrants to satisfy such men's ambitions. He could see nothing solid or useful around which the poor could unite in a positive movement to further their interests; if this group were to gain power, the political result would be anarchy leading to despotism. (Madison was perhaps assuming more generally that there could be no liberty based on the denial of any individual rights.) He considered it equally likely that the majority would sell out to the rich, further underscoring his belief in the political incapacity and unreliability of the propertyless. These dangers could only be averted if the structure of government secured property against the designs of both demagogues and the masses.

Most of Madison's discussions of property were directed to the political consequences of a failure to secure this essential right. He had comparatively little to say about the intrinsic value or importance of property, or about exactly what he thought this right entailed. Nevertheless, it is possible to make reasonable assumptions and deductions about these issues, and it is important to do so because they bear on two important elements in the Madisonian conception of government: justice and equality.

The first thing to note is that the value of property was apparently so widely accepted in 1787 (at least in circles of men such as the Framers), that there seemed little need to defend or articulate it. More specifically, it is quite clear that the traditions of political thought the Framers drew on, in their various ways, all saw property as essential for autonomy, independence, and political capacity.[25] There was a strong American version of this in the Jeffersonian ideal of the republic of yeoman farmers. Madison sympathized with this ideal (although he thought it could not be maintained), and

[25] See generally Gordon S. Wood, *The Creation of the American Republic, 1776–1787* (Chapel Hill, 1969), and J. G. A. Pocock, *The Machiavellian Moment: Florentine Political Thought and the Atlantic Republican Tradition* (Princeton, 1975).

47

he almost certainly believed that one of the essential political values of property was autonomy and independence.[26]

The relation Madison saw between property and unequal political capacity is clearest in his view of the dangers from the propertyless (noted above) and in the kinds of attributes he associated with property. He spoke, for example, of "men of intelligence, patriotism, property, and independent circumstances"[27] and of "men of abilities, of property, of influence."[28] The men suited to govern were the men who had these attributes and the other advantages property brought: education and "superior information."[29] A properly designed system would select men of respectability and sympathy with the rights of property (and only the propertied fell into this last category).

In Madison's view, the object of government was protection of the rights to exercise one's faculties for acquiring property. This and the free exercise of man's reason were the basic aspects of liberty that made faction inevitable in a free society. "The most common and durable source of faction" could perhaps be mitigated or eliminated if the exercise of faculties for acquiring property were limited. But this would be to limit a basic aspect of man's liberty, which Madison clearly stated would be a remedy worse than the disease.[30]

There was a kind of egalitarianism about Madison's focus on faculties for acquiring property. The exercise of these faculties was the only right of property that everyone could actually enjoy. (Both use and possession are of course restricted to those who actually acquire property.) And the focus on faculties carried with it a view of a society with economic mobility. It was not the protection of vested rights as such that Madison emphasized, but the opportunity for all to ex-

[26] See Drew R. McCoy, *The Elusive Republic: Political Economy in Jeffersonian America* (Chapel Hill, 1980).

[27] Madison to Jefferson, Dec. 9, 1787, Meyers, ed., *Mind of the Founder,* p. 209.

[28] Madison to Jefferson, Feb. 19, 1788, ibid., p. 101.

[29] Madison, Note on Aug. 7, 1787, speech, ibid., p. 508.

[30] *Federalist* No. 10.

ercise whatever faculties they have for acquiring property. But while this allows a kind of equal opportunity,[31] it is explicitly opportunity for *unequal* faculties. An unequal distribution of property must follow and is thus built into Madison's view of liberty and government's responsibility to protect it.[32]

Madison was explicit that "the personal right to acquire property, which is a natural right, gives to property, when acquired, a right to protection, as a social right."[33] The point here was not that the right to protection was a "mere" social right but that this social right had its origins in a natural right and was an essential aspect of man's liberty. Madison certainly made clear that any attempt to redistribute property was unjust and iniquitous: in *Federalist* No. 10 he referred to "a rage for paper money, for an abolition of debts, for an equal division of property, or for any other improper and wicked project." For Madison, the protection of unequal faculties for acquiring property (the first object of government) must involve protection of unequal possessions that resulted. The redistribution of property, therefore, involved not simply a rearrangement of material goods of society or a redefinition of a merely social right; from Madison's perspective, the redistribution of property had serious implications for the protection of man's liberty.

The place of property in Madison's political thought should be increasingly clear: property is the central instance of the basic problem of minority rights; the protection of property is essential to the stability and endurance of republican government; property is tied to liberty. These are all

[31] Madison gave no indication that he saw that when the majority are poor and the minority rich, the equal protection of faculties will not of itself guarantee equality of opportunity. He never suggested that the government might have to take positive steps to ensure that all have equal opportunity to exercise their unequal faculties.

[32] An unelaborated comment in *Federalist* No. 10 shows in yet another way that inequality is not a contingent, but an essential, aspect of property rights: the rights of property originate in the diversity of the faculties of men.

[33] James Madison, speech in the Virginia Constitutional Convention, Dec. 2, 1829, Meyers, ed., *Mind of the Founder*, p. 512.

49

compelling reasons for conceiving of property as the primary object of government. But as I noted at the outset, the most important aspect of Madison's views on property was their relation to the issue of majority rule, to the basic principle and structure of republican government. Madison's chief concern was to prevent the majority from violating the property rights of the few, and thus to place an important limit on the majority's ability to implement its will. He viewed property as an end in itself and rejected both the notion that it was simply a means to an end and the idea that the property rights of the few should be conditional on the need of the many.

Given the prevailing views on property, it would be no surprise if Madison had ignored these ideas although both were suggested to him. His close and respected friend, Thomas Jefferson, wrote from France about his dismay over the plight of the poor and his conclusions about the necessary modifications of property rights. Madison responded with his own thought about the problem of the poor. This correspondence deserves extensive quotation because it is important to see exactly what suggestions Madison had to consider and how he chose to respond to them.

Jefferson wrote:

> I am conscious that an equal division of property is impracticable, but the consequences of this enormous inequality producing so much misery to the bulk of mankind, [is that] legislators cannot invent too many devices for subdividing property, only taking care to let their subdivisions go hand in hand with the natural affections of the human mind, the descent of property of every kind therefore to all the children, or to all the brothers and sisters, or other relations in equal degree is a politic measure, and a practicable one. Another means of silently lessening the unequality of property is to exempt all from taxation below a certain point, and to tax the higher portions of property in geometrical progression as they rise. Whenever there is in any country, uncultivated lands and unemployed poor, it is clear that the laws of property have been so far extended as to violate natural right. The earth is given as a common stock for man to labour and live on. If, for the encouragement of industry we allow it to be appropriated, we must take care that other employment be permitted to those excluded from the appropria-

tion. If we do not the fundamental right to labour the earth returns to the unemployed.[34]

Jefferson suggested here that property originated as a means to an end; men allowed the earth to be appropriated in order to encourage industry, which, presumably, would be to the advantage of all. But this appropriation necessarily excluded some, and Jefferson argued that the use of this means carried a responsibility to provide employment for those excluded. The rights of property were contingent on the fulfillment of this responsibility. He also suggested that since the rights of property were only a means, they must be judged by their results; they must be measured against other rights.

Madison did not comment directly on any of these suggestions.[35] But he respectfully implied that Jefferson's perception of both the problem and the solution was too simplistic. It failed to go to the root of the problem, which was that "a certain degree of misery seems inseparable from a high degree of populousness." Even if the unemployed did reclaim their right to employment, the problem would not be solved: "If the lands in Europe which are now dedicated to the amusements of the idle rich, were parcelled out among the idle poor, I readily conceive the happy revolution which would be experienced by a certain proportion of the latter. But still would there not remain a great proportion unrelieved?" Madison suggested that the problem must be seen not in terms of property laws but in terms of population:

> No problem in political economy has appeared to me more puzzling than that which relates to the most proper distribution of the inhabitants of a country fully peopled. Let the lands be shared among them ever so wisely, and let them be supplied with laborers ever so plentifully; as there must be a great surplus

[34] Jefferson to Madison, Oct. 28, 1785, William T. Hutchinson et al., eds., *The Papers of James Madison*, 19 vols. to date (Chicago and Charlottesville, 1962-), 8:386–87.

[35] This is itself an indication of disagreement. Madison usually made detailed responses to Jefferson's ideas. When he disagreed, however, he generally passed over the idea in silence or with a vague or general response.

of inhabitants, a greater by far than will be employed in clothing both themselves and those who feed them, and in administering to both, every other necessary and even comfort of life. What is to be done with this surplus?[36]

Many would be absorbed into undesirable occupations, such as domestics and soldiers, but even these occupations will not absorb them all. Once a certain level of population has been reached, even with the wisest distribution of the land and employment on the land, there will be unemployed poor left over. Population, not property law, was the basic cause of poverty.[37]

Because Madison did not accept the view that property laws were at the root of the problem, he missed or rejected Jefferson's most important point: that property laws must be seen as means and judged in terms of their consequences. Since property laws were not the cause of poverty, its existence did not suggest to Madison that they ought to be re-evaluated. The misery of some was inevitable; their needs were not rights against which the rights of property must be balanced. The suffering of the poor was not itself evidence of any injustice in the system of property.

As an analysis of the cause of poverty, Madison's view may be said to go beyond Jefferson's to a broader understanding of the problem. But Madison missed the ethical challenge of Jefferson's perspective. Like Jefferson he saw that in a system of private property some will be "excluded from the appropriation" and, indeed, from useful employment, but he did not address the question of what responsibility those who enjoy the benefits of the system have to those who do not. He did not suggest that the rights of property were in any way contingent upon the fulfillment of such a responsibility. For Madison, the only problem the vision of a propertyless ma-

[36] Madison to Jefferson, June 19, 1786, Hutchinson et al., eds., *Papers of Madison*, 9:76–77.

[37] There is, however, no suggestion in Madison's thought that all systems of property were just. It was widely accepted at the time that the feudal system was unwise and unjust. And Madison agreed with Jefferson that the French system should be changed.

jority raised was how to prevent them from violating the rights of property.

We must then ask whether there was a conflict in Madison's thinking between his commitment to free, popular government, the will of the majority, and the good of the whole body of people on the one hand, and his commitment of the property rights of the minority on the other. We must question how he could confidently discuss the necessity of measures to prevent the majority from claiming a more equal share of the property held by the minority, when he foresaw not only a majority without property but some without either property or employment. For Madison, this conflict was an unavoidable difficulty. A statement in 1785 shows the terms in which he saw the problem: "True it is that no other rule exists, by which any question which may divide a society, can be ultimately determined, but the will of the majority; but it is also true that the majority may trespass on the rights of the minority."[38] Majority rule was, then, a political necessity, but it was no solution to the problem of justice: "It is well understood that interest leads to injustice as well as where the opportunity is presented to . . . an interested majority in a Republic, as to the interested minority in any other form of Government." Madison suggested that the majority must be prevented not only from trespassing on the rights of individuals, but from subverting the government: "At first view, it might not seem to square with republican theory to suppose . . . that a majority have not the right . . . to subvert a government. . . . But theoretic reasoning in this as in most cases, must be qualified by the lessons of practice. Why may not illicit combinations, for purposes of violence, be formed as well as by a majority of a State, especially a small state, as by a majority of a country, or a district of some state."[39]

But on what principle could the majority be prevented from implementing its will, from taking steps to achieve its desire for a larger share of the benefits of society, or, indeed, from ordering the society however they chose? Madison's an-

[38] James Madison, Memorial and Remonstrance against Religious Assessments (1785), Meyers, ed., *Mind of the Founder*, pp. 9–10.

[39] *Federalist* No. 43.

swer was clear: there were "rules of justice" that stood above the will of the majority.[40] And it is clear that property rights—which are based on natural rights—are covered by these rules of justice. Majority rule, on the other hand, "does not result . . . from a law of nature, but from compact founded on utility."[41]

The rules of justice provided Madison with a political standard of right and wrong; he therefore had little hesitation about thwarting the will of the majority. Majorities had the power in republican government, but force and right were not necessarily on the same side. To decide that the best government was one in which the will of the majority was the final arbiter was not to declare that the interest of the majority determined what was right. Madison discussed this explicitly:

> There is no maxim in my opinion which is more liable to be misapplied, and which therefore more needs elucidation than the current one that the interest of the majority is the political standard of right and wrong. Taking the word "interest" as synonymous with "ultimate happiness," in which sense it is qualified with every necessary moral ingredient, the proposition is no doubt true. But taking it in the popular sense, as referring to immediate augmentation of property and wealth, nothing can be more false. In the latter sense it would be the interest of the majority in every community to despoil & enslave the minority of individuals; . . . In fact it is only re-establishing under another name and a more specious form, force as the measure of right.[42]

This standard rests on Madison's understanding of "ultimate happiness." He is not simply making the distinction between permanent and temporary interests; the majority will always want the property of the minority, and it is explicitly clear that he does not consider the attainment of this desire necessary for their "ultimate happiness." His conception of

[40] The phrase is from *Federalist* No. 10.

[41] Madison to Jefferson, Feb. 4, 1790, Hunt ed., *Writings of Madison*, 5:440.

[42] Madison to James Monroe, Oct. 5, 1786, ibid., 2:273.

what constituted ultimate happiness was such that anything that came into conflict with the rules of justice, as he understood them, could not contribute to it. Thus, it was impossible for him seriously to consider the idea that it might be in the true interest of the majority to appropriate a share of the property held by the minority. Justice as well as the interests of all required a structure of government that could prevent or minimize the likelihood of any such attempt.

We can now see the major components of Madison's approach to property in republican government: stability, liberty, inequality, and justice. Liberty produces conflict and inequality, which, in popular governments, threaten all minority rights and property in particular. Justice is the end of government, and stability is the prerequisite for enduring government. Liberty, justice, and stability all demand that minority rights, and particularly the rights to unequally distributed property, be protected from the will of the majority. This set of ideas resulted in a conception of republican government that today we would call constitutional democracy: a system based both on popular representation and on independent standards of justice against which the results of the political process can be measured; a system in which simple popular consent is not sufficient for legitimacy. The vulnerability of property was the catalyst for Madison's perception of the need for such a system, and property became the focal point for defining limits to what popular government could legitimately do.

The full implications of this conception of government can best be seen when Madison's thought is contrasted with that of Gouverneur Morris and James Wilson. If Madison's views were characterized by an ongoing attempt to balance conflicting rights and a continuing unease about the balance he struck, Morris's were characterized by a confident single-mindedness. Morris was unequivocal in his claim that government was instituted to protect property, and that all other claims should be measured against this defining purpose. Like Madison, he saw a tension and conflict between property and political liberty. But Morris was explicit that the Framers had to make a choice between the two. He saw two, distinct categories: first, civil liberties, among which was property and the right to use it freely, and, second, political liberty. The latter was merely the means to the former. The degree of political liberty that was appropriate was one that was consistent with the security of property. For Madison the choice was not simple, but agonizing, and he was less candid about the consequences of his decision. But as we shall see, he was willing greatly to limit the political rights of the poor, and thus put their personal rights at risk, in order to protect property.

Morris also saw an inevitable division between the rich and the poor, but the implications of this division were quite different from what they were for Madison. From Morris's position of complete certainty about the priority of property, he was able to recognize and acknowledge things that Madison could not. Morris, for instance, made no attempt to disguise the fact that his system was designed to protect the interests of the rich, and that as long as it was successful in doing so, the poor would not be able to satisfy their desires for a greater share of property, power, or privilege. Madison, by contrast, never acknowledged that his preferred system would also have had this effect. Both Madison and Morris believed that this was the best the poor could hope for. Both were certain that if the poor were given the power to pursue their desires, their misguided efforts would cost them their political liberty.

Morris also candidly recognized that the inequality of property had implications for other rights. He saw that without equality people would have rights they could not exercise.[43] But in keeping with the absolute priority of property in his system, his response was not to consider whether the

[43] Contemporary constitutional law has now directly confronted this issue. In *Maher* v. *Roe* (432 U.S. 464 [1977]) and *Harris* v. *McRae* (448 U.S. 297 [1980]) the Supreme Court was asked to decide whether a Medicare policy refusing medical payments for abortions, while covering all other pregnancy-related expenses, amounted to a denial of equal protection on the basis of wealth. The court did not deny that women who could afford abortions could exercise their constitutional right to decide whether to carry their pregnancies to term, while poor women could not. But it clearly said that the American Constitution has never required the government to provide the means for people actually to exercise their rights. The

rights of property should be modified to give effect to other rights. His conclusion was that proclaiming the equality of rights is dangerous; it must necessarily give rise to challenges to the inequality of property. He was the only one of the three to see or comment on the radical implications for private property of the equality of rights. This was typical of the perception that distinguishes Morris's thought. It is as though the unequivocal priority he accorded to property gave him the clarity of perception necessary to see the implications of his position. No unease or conflicting values clouded his vision.

Morris's most important perception, and his most distinctive contribution, is his recognition of the power of property. While virtually everyone else was talking about the danger of the people, Morris saw that the wealthy few, not the propertyless many, posed the major threat in a commercial republic. Property gave advantages of talent, influence, connections, and power that outweighed the numerical power of the poor. This perception of Morris's points to one of Madison's most serious and dangerous failings: in his preoccupation with protecting property, he failed to take adequate account of the danger and power of the wealthy minority. Madison acknowledged the influence of the propertied, but he saw it only as a salutary counterbalance to the power of the many.[44] He did not see the danger of all governmental offices being held by the few, a situation that, like Morris, he expected the system to produce. Madison believed that republican government solved the problem of minority faction: "If a faction consists of less than a majority, relief is supplied by the republican principle, which enables the majority to defeat its sinister views by regular vote."[45] From Madison's perspective, minor-

---

fact that rich people and poor people have different capacities to exercise and enjoy their basic rights is part of the American tradition.

Of course this whole constitutional argument is only possible because of the addition of the Fourteenth Amendment. The Constitution of 1787 did not guarantee equality.

[44] *Federalist* No. 54; Madison to Caleb Wallace, Aug. 23, 1785, Meyers, ed., *Mind of the Founder,* pp. 49–50.

[45] *Federalist* No. 10.

ity factions were must less dangerous than majority, because the former could not use the guise of legitimate authority to carry out their evil designs. But Morris saw that this was exactly what the wealthy could do. By monopolizing government offices and exerting their extragovernmental influence and power, the wealthy could establish an oligarchy while republican forms remained intact. Madison did not address this problem. He focused on what he saw as the characteristic republican problem, majority oppression, and the consequent need to control the people. Neither his theory nor his institutional design was directed toward preventing undue overlap between economic and political power.

James Wilson provides the basis for a critique from the other direction. Wilson was the only one of the Framers to say that property was not the object of government. He was concerned with things other than material welfare or even liberty. Property was only one element of liberty, and liberty was not sufficient for happiness. The proper objects of government were improvement of men's minds, development of men's characters, and relations between men. Wilson stressed that both the proper character and proper community were necessary for republican government to thrive. Active popular participation in public affairs was the way to achieve both. His emphasis on participation provided the answer to the problems of popular injustice. Madison and Morris were fearful of the power of the people because both thought the people incapable of intelligently pursuing either their own interests or those of society. Wilson believed that participation would develop political competence. When the people were given political responsibility they would take an active part and lively interest in public affairs. Their political life would not be restricted to voting in periodic elections. Politics would be a daily and ongoing interest; neighbors would meet at the end of the day to discuss the latest political issues. The result would be that the people would learn to exercise power responsibly and intelligently. What would prevent schemes detrimental to the public interest would be a widespread understanding of what constituted the public interest. A politically active and intelligent populace would also be capable of choosing and evaluating their leaders. Active participation would contribute to men's happiness and excellence and minimize the dangers of republican government.

Madison by contrast virtually ignored the importance and potential benefits of participation. His concern was to control popular excesses, not to facilitate citizens' active involvement in public affairs. He thought of political liberty as a means only, not as an important exercise of man's faculties. Popular participation essentially meant suffrage, and Madison thought even that should be limited. He had virtually nothing to say about what would foster citizens' political competence, their understanding of, or interest in, public affairs. Madison thought he had a realistic view of the people's capacities; they could not understand many important political issues, but they generally knew this and would recognize the superiority of the elite. The object was thus to design a system in which the people could select and follow good leaders. But in his inattention both to participation and community Madison had little to say about what would foster a population in which at least some would rise above the conflict of interests and which would select such men as their representatives.

We can now see the full dimensions of Madison's property-centered conception of government. First, his emphasis on the protection of property was the core of an essentially liberal rather than classically republican approach to government. Character, duty, virtue, and community may all have been moral values, but they were not the relevant objects of government. The problem of property itself reflects a libertarian split between civil rights and moral duty. Whatever moral obligations individuals or even communities may have had to the poor, the central problem economic inequality posed for government was how to protect the property of the few from the injustice of the many.

Madison's values of justice and stability also implied a distinction between civil and political liberty: "Justice is the end of government. It is the end of civil society. It ever has been and ever will be pursued until it be obtained, or until liberty be lost in the pursuit. In a society under the forms of which the stronger faction can readily unite and oppress the weaker, anarchy may as truly be said to reign as in a state of nature, where the weaker individual is not secured against

the violence of the stronger."[46] Political liberty must be subordinate, or at least contingent, for it could only be sustained
if instituted in a manner compatible with order, stability, and
justice.

Madison's preoccupation with property was not the origin
of his concern with individual rights, but it shaped his approach to the problem. It may have hardened the lines between morality and politics, and ordered the ranking of civil
over political liberty. The focus on property put inequality
and the control of the people's will at the center of Madison's
concerns. The result was the neglect of two crucial issues,
participation and the relation between economic and political
power. With this neglect Madison not only accepted that economic inequality could limit political equality, he ran the risk
that the pattern of economic inequality would be reproduced
in the political sphere. A Madisonian system designed to prevent injustice could easily serve to protect and consolidate the
wealth, power, and control of the elite.

Whether or not Madison saw these implications, he was left
with an unease about his own system. He never abandoned
his goal of protecting the rights of persons, the rights of
property, and political rights. The will of the people needed
to be bounded by the rules of justice, but he was never entirely certain how to achieve this boundary consistently with
his threefold goal. Madison's thought was dangerously
skewed by a preoccupation with property, but it was also characterized by an unresolved tension. Both these aspects were
reflected in the structure of the Constitution.

The protection of property was of course not the only concern of the Framers of the United States Constitution. There
were such major conflicts as those between large states and
small and between the North and the South that had little to
do with property, and such other basic issues as the respective
powers of the state and federal governments in which the
security of property was only one of many aspects. Such matters often determined the final design of institutions, such as
the Senate. I am not suggesting that all the issues at the Con-

---

[46] *Federalist* No. 51.

vention can be reduced or subordinated to the issue of property, but rather that the Madisonian constellation of ideas about the problems and possibilities, the objects and limits, of government provided the dominant framework of republican principles and their institutionalization. The resulting structure of institutions was not Madison's but it was Madisonian—with the strengths and weaknesses implicit in his ideology.

Madison had three basic approaches to the problem of preventing popular injustice without sacrificing republican principles: a mediated system of representation, specific prohibitions aimed at the most likely abuses, and a federal government whose extended sphere would minimize the effectiveness of factions. All three were incorporated, with modifications, into the Constitution.

There was a general consensus at the Convention that republican government had to have a popularly elected branch of the legislature. This would be the base of the government, the essential connection with the people. But there were disagreements about what the nature of this connection should be. The dominant Madisonian version was that the function even of this first branch was not to reflect but to refine the views of the people. From this perspective the people's sense of connection with or control over their government was of minimal interest. The requirements on this score were only that the people recognize the government as legitimate. The real issue was how to construct the institution so that the people would be likely to elect men capable of refining the popular views. Large election districts were most likely to return "enlightened" men, "superior to local prejudices," men of "probable attachment to the rights of property."[47] The plan agreed to by the Convention was attacked as aristocratic by Antifederalists on just this ground.[48] With the proper system Madison was confident that property would be a factor in the people's choice. Property qualifications for

[47] *Federalist* No. 10; Madison, Note on Aug. 7, 1787, Meyers, ed., *Mind of the Founder*, p. 508.

[48] See the discussion and examples in Jennifer Nedelsky, "Confining Democratic Politics: Anti-Federalists, Federalists, and the Constitution," *Harvard Law Review* 96 (1982–83):340–60.

the members of the legislature were unnecessary, because electors would discriminate between real and ostensible property "more effectively than stated qualifications could."[49] Madison wanted a relatively long term—three years—to make this branch "more capable of stemming popular currents taking a wrong turn."[50] But here those advocating a closer connection between the people and their representatives held sway.

The Convention also rejected property restrictions on suffrage for the first branch (restrictions that Madison considered desirable, but problematic for getting the Constitution adopted).[51] In Madison's view, the design for the first branch was such that, even with the advantages of large election districts, the popular branch would be liable to the errors, passion, fickleness, and lack of information of the people.

He wanted the Senate to be a small select body to counterbalance this potential for error and excess. Here, too, Madison was in the mainstream of thought at the Convention.[52] There was general agreement that the legislature should be divided to protect the people from both their rulers and themselves. Madison wanted a Senate that would guard against the dangers of the "leveling spirit" and all "interested coalitions to oppress the minority." The Senate should be "sufficiently respectable for its wisdom & virtue, to aid on such emergencies, the preponderance of justice by throwing its weight into that scale."[53] The design for the Senate was shaped in part by other concerns, but it emerged as small, with a long term, and was indirectly elected. Such a select body was suitable for the checking purposes Madison had in mind, although he would have liked to have the Senate represent property more directly.[54]

[49] Farrand, ed., *Records of the Convention*, 2:121.

[50] Madison, Note on Aug. 7, 1787, speech, Meyers, ed., *Mind of the Founder*, p. 508.

[51] See Farrand, ed., *Records of the Convention*, 2:203–4.

[52] Note that I am interested here in the extent to which the political thought of the Framers was Madisonian, not whether Madison himself was influential.

[53] Farrand, ed., *Records of the Convention*, 1:423.

[54] Ibid., pp. 158 and 562.

The executive branch was to serve the purpose of acting as still a further check on the legislature through a qualified veto. The object of the veto was both to protect the executive from encroachments on his power and to "control the National Legislature so far as it might be infected with a . . . propensity" like that of the state legislature, to "a variety of pernicious measures."[55] In particular, "a negative in the Ex[ecutive] is . . . necessary . . . for the safety of a minority in Danger of oppression from an unjust and interested majority."[56] Madison wanted to ensure that the means of election and the term of the executive would give him the strength and independence to exercise his veto in defiance of popular demands. (Madison was not particularly interested in the ties between the people and the executive, a concern of some who wanted direct election.) But he doubted that the president alone would have such strength in a popular government. He therefore wanted to add the "wisdom and weight" of the judiciary to form a council of revision that would be adequate to check the legislature. This mixing of judicial and political functions did not, however, prevail.

Madison did not rely only on this system of successive mediations and refinements of the people's will. In his view the most hopeful aspect of popular government in America was the extent and diversity of the country. His now famous position was that conflict in a large and free country would be so various and diffused that it would be difficult for any majority to combine to effect unjust schemes. The advantages of the extended and pluralistic republic, combined with the structure of checks, meant that only a national majority, sustained over many years, could control all the branches necessary to implement their schemes.

It was only with respect to the state governments that the Convention adopted specific prohibitions to limit the unjust exercise of the people's will.[57] The threats to property that had been most prevalent were outlawed in the provisions against bills of credit and impairments of the obligation of

[55] Ibid., 2:110.

[56] Ibid., 1:108, King's notes.

[57] There were some specified limits on the federal government in Article I, Section 9, such as protections from suspension of the writ of habeas

contract.[58] The state governments did not have the advantages of the federal government's structure of checks, and were thus particularly liable to laws infringing on property rights, which would undermine the stability of the whole system.[59] (Madison actually believed that nothing short of a blanket power of national veto over state legislation would solve the problem. Not foreseeing the ingenuity of the Supreme Court, he was sure that the state legislatures would find ways around the specific wording of the provisions.)

The system that emerged from the Convention of 1787 was shaped by perceptions of the tension between political liberty and private rights. This tension was in fact sustained rather than simply resolved in favor of civil rights. There is nothing in the structure that violated the principle of political equality (unlike the structure that Madison proposed). The system relied instead on a structure in which the links be-

---

corpus, from bills of attainder and ex post facto laws, and against misuse of public funds. But these limits were aimed at the more traditional problems of usurpation of power and abuse of office. The abuses are not those associated with the threat of the majority. The prohibitions are not a list of things they needed to be protected from. They are abuses likely to be generated by regional conflict (for example, no preference to the ports of one state over another) or by tyrannical officials acting in their own interest. In addition there is the special prohibition resulting from the slavery compromise and what may be described as a basic tax policy. The prohibition of granting titles of nobility may be seen as both a matter of republican policy and a protection against the abuse of power by legislators. These prohibitions reflect different concerns from that of majority tyranny.

[58] Article I, Section 10. The choice of limitation with respect to contract reflects not only the kinds of law that the states had passed but the extent to which the concern with the rights of property was a concern with economic liberty as well as vested rights.

[59] Questions of the distribution of power between the state and federal government may thus also be seen as related to the general issue of how to secure individual rights and sound policy under popular government. All power lodged in the federal government was safer than that in the hands of the states. Madison would for this reason have preferred a government more national than federal. This issue, too, may be one where the subsequent developments have seen an even greater shift toward one side of the Madisonian balance.

tween the people and the government were mediated both by indirect election and by size of election districts. Both the proponents and opponents of the Constitution expected that those who would actually hold positions of power would be a propertied elite. The system was designed not only to encourage the active participation of the people, but to rely on deference and a process that would make it difficult for the people immediately to effect their wishes should they in fact become actively involved in some issues—such involvement was the very popular passion and turbulence that the system was designed to mitigate. Seen from this perspective, the inattention to the overlap between economic and political power is consistent with the rest of the pattern. Some overlap was in fact anticipated in the expectation that the economic elite would also be the political elite. Both the removal of the people and the power of the wealthy were indirect effects of the system, but effects that served to sustain property rights. The system was designed not to limit, but to control popular will—and the control was to be in the hands of the propertied.

It is a question whether the indirect effects were so strong that the power of property upset the republican balance. Madison anticipated one aspect of this problem in his recognition that too much power for the propertied would put the rights of persons at risk—a risk he was prepared to take. Another aspect was whether public participation would atrophy into a purely formal exercise that gave the people no sense of control over or responsibility for their government. While the republican forms (especially when expanded to include more people in the formal exercise) might sustain the popular sense of the government's legitimacy, the result would be to further skew the structure of power away from its nominal base in the people. This was a problem outside the Madisonian realm of thought.[60]

The development of judicial review was a continuation, and in some ways a culmination, of the Madisonian conception of government. The core of this conception is the idea of civil

[60] But of course it is a current problem given the low rate of voter turnout.

rights as limits on what the majority may legitimately do. I have argued that Madison's elaboration of this idea was shaped by his concern with protecting the property rights of the few from popular injustice. But the Constitution of 1787 stopped short of setting up property as a general limit on popular will. The Constitution was designed to minimize the danger to property (and other minority rights) but not, at the federal level, to prevent it. The early development of judicial review placed property squarely as the boundary to legitimate state action. As the vulnerability and importance of property had focused Madison's attention on the need to control popular will, property continued to exert its influence in defining and justifying the powers of judicial review.

The importance of property in the early development of judicial review is clearly shown in Edward S. Corwin's article "The Basic Doctrine of American Constitutional Law."[61] He argues that the doctrine of vested rights gave legal reality to the notion of governmental power as limited power. He shows that natural rights doctrines were given constitutional force through the concept of separation of powers, and that property was the instance the courts used to define the limits to legislative power. A classic example of this natural rights approach to the limits of legislative power is *Fletcher* v. *Peck*.

It may well be doubted whether the nature of society and of government does not prescribe some limits to the legislative

---

[61] Edward S. Corwin, "The Basic Doctrine of American Constitutional Law," *Michigan Law Review* 12 (1914):247–76. In moving from the 1787 Convention to the early development of judicial review, I have, perhaps startlingly, skipped the first ten amendments. I do so in large part for reasons of space, but also because they reflect and raise quite different issues from those I am dealing with here. The Bill of Rights was to a large extent a concession to the Antifederalists, designed to address their fears of government tyranny and abuse which were quite different from Madison's preoccupation with majority tyranny. (The Antifederalists were afraid that the government would act against the wishes of the people; Madison was afraid it would implement them.) It is questionable whether the first ten amendments actually reshaped the Constitution by providing protections that would otherwise have been absent (Madison thought they did not). But the Bill of Rights certainly has been important for the development of judicial review. The aspect most directly related to my argument here is that the Fifth Amendment may be seen as placing the protection of property clearly in the judicial realm.

power; and if any be prescribed, where they are to be found, if the property of an individual, fairly and honestly acquired, may be seized without compensation.

To the legislature all legislative power is granted; but the question, whether the act of transferring the property of an individual to the public, be in the nature of the legislative power, is well worthy of serious doubt.[62]

In this case, as in others, the Court went beyond the specific provisions of the Constitution to argue that violations of essential property rights are inherently beyond the power of the legislature. The Court was also building upon the major instance in which the Constitution did set up property as a limit to popular will—the contract clause. This clause, combined with natural rights arguments, was central in the development of judicial review: in the late nineteenth century it was (excluding the commerce clause) the "constitutional justification for more cases involving the validity of state laws than all of the other clauses of the Constitution together." Through the doctrine of vested rights, the power of judicial review transformed the balance between majority rule and minority rights, between republican principles and the sanctity of property, into a balance between the proper sphere of the legislature and that of the courts—a balance which the courts would determine.

The fact that property was the basic issue in the development of judicial review is important for several reasons. First, issues of property strengthened the courts' claims to define rights and determine boundaries. Property was a clearly established common law concept. Who could better claim to know what constituted the basic, inviolable rights of property than the courts? And the courts in fact relied on common law definitions of property rights in determining whether the legislature had exceeded its bounds. Second, for the same reasons, the emphasis on property may have been responsible for the highly legalistic cast to the American conception of rights. Had the central issue been the freedom of conscience, a right not legal in its form, the courts could hardly have made the same claims for special competence to define and defend it. Finally, independent of its vulnerability, prop-

---

[62] 6 Cranch 87 (1810) at 135–36.

erty is a particularly good focus for the boundaries to legitimate governmental power. Property may quite literally provide a sphere of autonomy against both public and private interference. Its power as a symbol or focal point for the limits of government is enhanced by the correspondence between its real and symbolic functions. Similarly, governmental interference with property may have a tangible quality that makes it easy to recognize and useful as a reference point for less tangible inferences.[63] The focus on property and the identification of the courts as arbiters of legislative legitimacy provided a powerfully concrete if also legalistic realization of the abstract concepts of the "rules of justice."

The history of property as a judicially protected boundary to legislative action has been mixed, but the basic elements of the underlying conception of limited government continue. Between the 1830s and the 1870s the courts quietly ignored their much vaunted guarantees of protection. Vested rights were systematically undermined by radical redefinition of property rights and legislative encroachment sanctioned by the courts.[64] Yet despite judicial articulation of an "instrumental" approach, American legal and political thought offered no clear reassessment of the importance of private property or the judiciary's responsibility to define and protect it. The contingency of property rights on the public good did

[63] Despite this concrete quality, property could not actually provide a clear-cut boundary. It is one of the inherent complexities of the role of property in American political thought that while it was conceived of as a boundary to legitimate government activity, it could never in fact be independent of the state. Unlike freedom of conscience, property must be defined and protected by the state. It requires positive action in the form of legal rules, not merely negative protections, to exist. Even the most ardent advocates agreed that property was not an absolute right; it was subject both to taxation and eminent domain. Thus in some ways property rights served a theoretical function (defining the boundaries to legitimate government action) for which they could provide a focus, but no definitive solution.

[64] See Morton Horwitz, *The Transformation of American Law* (Cambridge, Mass., 1977), and Harry Scheiber, "The Road to Munn: Eminent Domain and the Concept of Public Purpose in the State Courts," *Perspectives in American History* 5 (1971):329.

not replace the sanctity of private property in the mainstream of American thought.

Between the 1870s and the 1930s there was a dramatic resurgence of emphasis on judicial protection of private property and its corresponding right of contract. Rejecting the role of government implicit in social welfare legislation, conservatives on the Supreme Court drew on all the old (and, at the level of theory, long revered) arguments about property as the boundary (both real and symbolic) between individual rights and legitimate governmental authority. The maintenance of that boundary and the freedom it ensured were, they argued, essential to free government and the stable endurance of the republic. The original ideology was in full force, serving as an active limit on the will of the majority.

After 1937 there was another reversal: the Supreme Court decided that the definition and protection of the rights of property and contract were political questions properly determined in the legislatures. Property was no longer the boundary to, but the subject of, legitimate governmental action. Since then the courts have virtually abandoned the use of any of the traditional means of protecting property from legislative infringement.[65] Clearly, this raises the question of what this departure has meant for the role of property in our conception of limited government. I have three kinds of answers. The first deals with the question of autonomy, one of the original elements of this conception.

Property no longer provides most people with the basis for independence and autonomy in the eighteenth-century sense (neither wages nor stock dividends provide this traditional political independence, although both may provide the insulation and security of wealth). Property has thus lost part of its original political significance. In addition, once property is itself subject to regulation, it can no longer serve sym-

[65] This does not mean that the Supreme Court has not protected property rights when in conflict with other values such as free speech. See Norman Dorsen and Joel Gora, "Free Speech, Property, and the Burger Court: Old Values, New Balances," *Supreme Court Review, 1982,* ed. Philip B. Kurland et al. (Chicago, 1983), pp. 195–241.

bolically or otherwise as the boundary between individual rights and the legitimate scope of governmental power. Once this traditional sphere of autonomy is permeated, we need new ways of thinking about the sources and protections of autonomy. It is arguable that the recent judicial protections for privacy and procedural rights in administrative law are the response to this challenge. The new legal developments recognize that autonomy in the modern age requires not only a sphere (now provided entirely by law, without any independent material base) into which government cannot intrude, but also one in which government may legitimately act. The old conception of a boundary beyond which government may not legitimately go is no longer of the same importance. From this perspective, the traditional liberal (once property based) concerns with individual liberty in the face of government power have transformed themselves into forms appropriate to a regulatory state.[66]

My second answer deals with why the judicial abandonment of property did not lead to the instability conservatives had feared for 150 years. My suggestion is that what accounts for the ultimate acceptance of wide regulatory powers infringing on traditional rights of property and contract was the perception on the part of powerful business leaders that such powers would further the goals of stability at a minimal economic cost. Regulation, not rigid insistence on judicial enforcement of antiquated notions of individual rights, would provide a stable climate for business and discourage the discontented poor from mobilizing around radical attacks on the system. Moreover, the new system may have provided an alternate means of insulating sensitive areas from democratic turbulence: independent regulatory agencies. This argument also suggests that "the propertied"—or a powerful segment of them—in the end accepted the abandonment of traditional judicial protections of property because they were so confident of their control of the political processes that they did not think the essential features of the capitalist system or its structure of power would be endangered. If this

[66] See Jennifer Nedelsky, "Reconceiving Autonomy," *Yale Journal of Law and Feminism* (1989).

account is correct, then the removal of property from its original privileged place does not suggest that the original failure to take account of the overlap between political and economic power has been overcome. On the contrary, it suggests that the original structure, including the emphasis on private property that prevailed between 1880 and 1937, permitted such a consolidation of economic and political power that the original fears of a democratic legislature could be abandoned.

Finally, it seems that despite the judicial abandonment of property, the sanctity of property, with all its original implications, remains an important part of popular ideology. A recent study suggests there is a deep division between American views about economic rights and political rights.[67] Both rich and poor believe in the principle of political equality, and they believe in the justice of economic inequality. The belief in the legitimacy of economic inequality and the sanctity of property rights sets limits on the use to which political rights may be put. Indeed, the more a measure looks like infringement on property, the more likely that it will be opposed even by those whom redistribution would benefit. The effect of economic inequality on effective political equality also seems to be accepted by contemporary Americans as it was by Madison. Such popular acceptance of his perspective was, of course, beyond his wildest dreams, and is surely one of the most impressive accomplishments of the regime.

My conclusion, then, is that despite the change in the role of property itself, both the best and the worst of the Madisonian scheme are still with us. Madison's genius was to transform a concern with private property into protections for minority rights. This transformation has continued and now includes a thoughtful judicial response to the problems of autonomy in a regulatory state. The judicial retreat from property did not mean that the system had overcome its original weaknesses, but rather that those weaknesses had become entrenched. We now have a system in which popular participation is so largely formal and the confluence of eco-

[67] Jennifer Hochschild, *What's Fair: American Beliefs about Distributive Justice* (Cambridge, Mass., 1981).

nomic and political power is so thorough, that the original concern with protecting private property is now irrelevant. Add to this the extraordinary popular acceptance of the sanctity of property and the paradoxical triumph of the Madisonian scheme is complete: the American system protects the values of the original property-based conception—autonomy, stability, and the security of the wealth and power of the elite—but traditional private property is no longer the vehicle for this protection.

J. R. POLE

The Individualist
Foundations of
American
Constitutionalism

ALL GOVERNMENT, David Hume said, rests on opinion. This observation came to be exemplified—to an extent that he could hardly have anticipated—in the Constitution of the United States, which was ratified by elected state conventions and was generally presumed to enjoy the consent of the people it governed. But Hume's dictum may be applied to the American republic in a more subtle sense. For the question as to what the Constitution actually *means* in any particular case can be answered only by giving an *opinion* as to what it means. The operative opinion is that of the Supreme Court, or a majority of it. These opinions are rendered at such remote distances of time and circumstance from the original text that they depend on inference, colored as a rule by social philosophy. Very occasionally, however, the Court has occasion to recur to first principles, as happened when the problem of legislative apportionment arose, beginning with *Baker* v. *Carr* in 1962.[1]

That case was returned for judgment to the state judiciary. But two years later, in *Reynolds* v. *Sims*, Chief Justice Earl Warren gained the opportunity for a definitive pronouncement of constitutional principle. "Legislators represent people, not trees or acres," he said; "legislators are elected by voters, not farms or cities or economic interests." It had been argued that certain interests deserved to be given special consideration in

[1] *Baker* v. *Carr* 369 U.S. 186 (1962).

73

the electoral system; the Chief Justice replied that it was "inconceivable that a State law to the effect that, in counting votes for legislators, the votes for citizens in one part of the State would be multiplied by two, or five, or ten, while votes for other persons in another area would be counted only at face value, could be constitutionally sustainable."[2] These decisions were fundamental in the literal sense because they restored the American system of government to its foundations; they put into effect a doctrine well understood by the generation of the Founders, that a republic must return periodically to its founding principles in order to survive—as was well known to the republics of the Italian Renaissance in the injunction *"redurre ai principii."*[3] Even in a case like this we are dealing with opinion, and in fact with differing opinions; all of them involve inference from the text, and even self-evident truths are more self-evident to some than to others.[4] Most judicial decisions reflect a process of inferential reasoning from the language of the Constitution; most if not all modern cases arise from situations which the Founders could not have envisaged. I think we can usefully distinguish here between two types of inferential reasoning that for simplicity's sake I will call explicit and implicit. On this basis we can state that the Warren Court's judgment in the apportionment cases so far mentioned was correct because it rested on the explicit meaning of the Constitution; we may say this because the Constitution's arrangements for representation could not have meant and could not now mean anything else. To mean something else we would have to use different words.

[2] *Reynolds* v. *Sims* 377 U.S. 533 (1964).

[3] Pennsylvania in 1776 provided a particularly clear example of the principle with its Council of Censors—whose ineffective record exposed the near impossibility of operating a system under which a specially delegated body was at odds with the elected legislators (J. G. A. Pocock, *The Machiavellian Moment: Florentine Political Thought and the Atlantic Republican Tradition* [Princeton, 1975], pp. 204–5). For discussions of case histories in relation to general questions of American policy, see J. R. Pole, *The Pursuit of Equality in American History* (Berkeley, 1978), chap. 9.

[4] For a philosophical discussion of this point, see Morton White, *The Philosophy of the American Revolution* (New York, 1978), pp. 9–96.

This brings us to a second line of argument, which is slightly more legalistic, but none the worse for that. If you take a certain theoretical position A, and you later find that in circumstances you did not, perhaps, originally envisage position B *necessarily* follows from A, then you logically *meant* B when you adopted A. Since these cases usually rest on inference, which in turn is usually affected by judicial preference, more than one reasonable inference is often possible. Different judges often draw diverse conclusions from the same set of premises.[5] I shall argue in this paper that the constitutional foundations of the United States are in certain respects explicitly individualistic, and that from this one can draw certain implicit inferences about the relationship of public policy to American first principles.

At this early point I should acknowledge that if this essay were a judicial opinion, it would not be satisfactory to rest it on historical evidence of the Founders' intentions. Even if legislative intent could be recovered with confidence from periods in the distant past (an enterprise fraught with epistemological difficulties) it could seldom be considered to have the last word in the altered circumstances of later times.[6] But historical and legal reasoning are in some ways dissimilar processes, and the historian's interest in reconstructing the thought of the past in its depths and complexities may give him or her a better understanding of the problem without in any way conflicting with the appropriate legal inference. Without intending to deprive myself of the resources of the historian, I hope to show why as well as how legal inferences may be drawn from the political thought underlying the Constitution. Nor do I wish to imply that one branch of these activities is intrinsically more valuable or important than the other. The historian of law and the lawyer both have pro-

[5] Edward Levi, *An Introduction to Legal Reasoning* (Chicago, 1948), esp. chap. 3; also John Hart Ely, *Democracy and Distrust* (Cambridge, Mass., 1980), esp. chap. 4; I take my own argument to be consistent in principle with Ely's.

[6] H. Jefferson Powell, "The Original Understanding of Original Intent," *Harvard Law Review* 98 (1984–85); Ronald Dworkin, *Law's Empire* (Cambridge, Mass., 1986), chaps. 9 and 10. For a subtle critique of Powell, see Philip Bobbitt, *Constitutional Interpretation* (Oxford, 1991), pp. 123–24.

foundly significant kinds of intellectual commitment, neither of which is fully intelligible without the other. The historian however, will find it more difficult to escape a gnawing sense of paradox, which has an unfortunate tendency to obscure the clearer lines of the lawyer's logic—for if life were logical, history, which is its chronicle, would be logical. The thesis of this paper is a thesis about political individualism, and I hope to establish that whatever else may be intended by the Constitution, and notwithstanding the reserved representation of the states, it is in essence a Constitution of individuals and for individuals. The Constitution was drawn up and approved at a moment in history when men were to an unusual extent dedicated to the idea of individual rights, and at a moment when Americans took these ideas more literally than practically anyone else had ever done. People are inclined to agree about this dedication to the concept of individual rights without pausing to appreciate that it was being carried to historically very unusual lengths.

Yet the paradox is that the political philosophers of the eighteenth century to whom Americans were heavily indebted were also occupied with the overriding purpose of serving the good of the community as a whole. If private vices were to be justified, it was because public good might come to them, as Bernard Mandeville had argued early in the century; and the most intensely individualistic and egalitarian of the philosophes, Jean-Jacques Rousseau, was also in a strong sense the most collectivist. For was not the individual will ultimately subordinate to the general will, of which it could only be a fraction?[7] The Scottish philosophers had views on individual psychology and on the origins of human sentiments, but it did not occur to them to doubt that the benevolence which actuated men (and presumably women) toward the good of their kind was a deeply collective sentiment and a collective aim. Adam Smith, the greatest of them, understood very well the self-seeking urge toward individual accumulation and aggrandizement; but the ultimate justification for releasing these impulses, as the very title of his best-

[7] Bernard Mandeville, *The Fable of the Bees, or, Private Vices, Publick Benefits*, 4th ed. (London, 1725); Jean-Jacques Rousseau, *Du Contrat Social* (1762) (Paris, 1960).

known book proclaimed, was *The Wealth of Nations,* not the wealth of mere individuals.

The significance of these doctrines was hardly likely to be lost on Americans, who had absorbed a wealth of the Scottish nation's moral philosophy from some of Smith's immediate predecessors. As for the clergy, they may have felt—they often preached as though they did—that they were fighting a losing battle against the sinful prevalence of self-gratification as the dominant motive in human life—more particularly in the male sex: it seems that these sermons were addressed to masculine traits.[8]

American life, economic, social, and religious, was lived in various forms of community. It may reasonably be argued that the more exposed facets of life in the colonies, particularly in the thinly settled and frontier areas, brought home most intensely the physical and, not less, the psychological necessity for mutual support and for collaborative effort and protection in everything from house-building to military defense. Much of this communal effort, whether rural or urban, was directed to needs that had very little bearing on politics— or to the self-image of political society; but when political spokesmen drew out the themes that knitted the communal experience of life into a political society they seldom failed to recognize that politics was essentially the prescriptive system of social order. The balance was nicely struck by Enos Hitchcock, a Fourth of July orator in 1788. "Society is composed of individuals . . . they are part of the whole," he said. And in America, Gordon S. Wood has added, "such individuals were the entire society: there could be nothing else—no orders, no lords, no monarch, no magistrates in the traditional sense."[9] He might have added that in terms of social psychology, these apparently separate individuals were in a very strong sense surrogates for *families*—the real basic element of society. But this social truth does not seem to have detracted from the force of the individualist image, and the fact

[8]See in this connection J. E. Crowley, *This Sheba, Self: The Conceptualization of Economic Life in Eighteenth-Century America* (Baltimore, 1974).

[9]Gordon S. Wood, *The Creation of the American Republic, 1776–1787* (Chapel Hill, 1969), p. 607.

that so sensitive a historian as Wood failed to make this distinction shows how forcefully it has survived in the American mind.

It fell to Thomas Jefferson, because he was deputed to draft the reasons for American independence, to claim for all his fellow countrymen the character of being "one people." We are not in the habit of analyzing this phraseology quite as closely as some other passages in the Declaration of Independence, but when we note that the time had come for "one people to sever the political bands which have united them with another," it is worth reflecting that this highly collective description of the scattered and heterogeneous colonies was by no means the only one that was available. Jefferson was endeavoring to form an image of this collectivity in anticipation of the facts.

New imperatives tended to concentrate people's minds on fundamentals. It is not surprising that we have a variety of reflective statements from which to study those ideas of political obligation under whose influence the colonists converted their institutions into those of self-governing republics. John Adams, in his influential little tract *Thoughts on Government,* took care to distinguish between government and society. Society, he explained, is from the nature of man, not from God.[10] This may seem a rather curious distinction when one considers that Adams would hardly have denied that the nature of man was itself from God; but it was important to distinguish between man before and after the Fall, and, no doubt, to exonerate God from responsibility for the natural propensities that had followed from that unhappy event. Government, on the other hand, was a result of deliberate choice, which meant of the aggregation of *individual* choices. Another influential voice was that of James Wilson, who gathered his thoughts in the Law Lectures he delivered, soon after the launching of the Constitution, in the College of Philadelphia. He is an instructive witness because he stood out at Philadelphia as a strong proponent of political individ-

[10]Charles Francis Adams, ed., *The Works of John Adams,* 10 vols. (Boston, 1850–56), 4:193–209.

ualism. But when lecturing on "Man, in the Great Common-wealth of Nations," Wilson adopted Rousseau's formula and described a nation as a "moral person," and went on from this to a more collective philosophy of property than we generally think of as fashionable for the time and place. "From the same principles," he argued, "the property of each of the members must, with regard to other states, be deemed the property of the whole nation." Not wholly comfortable with this position, he goes on, "In some degree, this is, in truth, the case; because the nation has power over the riches of the citizens; and because those riches form part of the national wealth." For this reason, when one nation had a grievance against another, it had a right to seek redress from the wealth of the offending nation's citizens.[11]

The problem of how society came into existence was not one with which American thinkers were much concerned. They felt no need to justify the existence of society, but they did have to justify and in a sense explain to themselves the existence of government. This need, which seems at times to have been of quite pressing psychological importance to them, went beyond formalities and beyond the practical problem of setting up particular governments, which tended to assume forms whose outlines were historically familiar. They often seem to have taken literally Thomas Paine's rhetorical dictum that all government was "a badge of lost innocence," and to have set about their work with a felt need to apologize for the defects of human nature that made it necessary.[12]

The hint of paradox with which these remarks began gives

[11] Robert Green McCloskey, ed., *The Works of James Wilson*, 2 vols. (Cambridge, Mass., 1967), 1:275; the statement that a state is a moral person is also to be found in, and may be a transcription from, a passage in the article on *l'Etat* in the *Encyclopédie*, in which the chevalier de Jaucourt writes, "On peut considérer l'*état* comme une personne morale, dont le souverain est la tête et les particuliers les membres" (The state may be considered as a moral person, of which the sovereign is the head and the individuals are the limbs) (Paris, 1756).

[12] Philip S. Foner, ed., *The Complete Writings of Thomas Paine* (New York, 1945), p. 4.

rise to a contrast that should now be a little clearer. No one felt that living in society was for ordinary people a matter of choice; men—by which was obviously meant men and women, not to mention their children—were by their natures social beings. But living under *political* society, under government, was strongly felt to be a matter of choice, or to have been a matter of choice at some period of apparently mature human experience. It was a society fully aware from experience as well as from religion and philosophy of the fundamentally collective nature of the human condition, a view that human experience in America confirmed, and yet it was at the same time a society whose thinkers repeatedly uttered the most precisely individualistic affirmations about the moral foundations of the political order.

It is not part of the purpose of this paper to pursue the problem which this contrast suggests. (There is, I think, room for such a pursuit.) I do think it necessary to take note of it, if only to safeguard ourselves against being trapped by contradictory evidence, often from the same sources. Some of these sources have already been introduced. John Adams, also in *Thoughts on Government,* lays down that "the happiness of society is the end of government" and that "the happiness of the individual is the end of man." A happy society must by inference be a society of happy men, but Adams does not explore the problem of reconciling these aims on occasions when they come into conflict. It is difficult to resist the implication that social happiness outweighs that of one or a very few individuals, however, and we seem to have here the beginnings of a utilitarianism that Adams could have acquired from English and French contemporaries, or might have arrived at from his own premises; he was not a systematic thinker and seems not to have taken the analysis any further. But by the same token it is the individual's sense of his own condition that gives value to the efforts of society; there is nothing here to give countenance to any idea that society might be the judge of whether its members were happy or not. The individual retains an unmistakable primacy of self-knowledge and self-interest.

A Philadelphia essayist argued on comparably individualist lines that property is prior to government and that govern-

ment came into existence to protect its rights and interests.[13]
William Livingston, editor of *The Independent Reflector* and
subsequently governor of New Jersey, in an attack on Adams's
*Defence of the Constitutions of Government of the United States of
America,* described man as "by nature a gregarious animal,"
distinguished as clearly as Adams had done between society
and government, and argued that while society was founded
on man's appreciation of his natural condition, government
was formed deliberately—a truth which, he thought, particularly applied to the governments of the United States.
Livingston illustrated the texture of the weave between individuals and society with a statement that was rapidly becoming an American commonplace—that "the governments in
these states are in fact nothing more than social compacts for
the mutual advantage of the individuals of whom they are
composed."[14] Thus, in the act of recognizing the fundamentally social nature of man, Livingston joined Adams in sub-
scribing to the doctrine that society was composed of
individuals, and that a principle of individual interest lay at
the basis of all American government. Addressing the principal question before him in writing the essay, Livingston had
no doubt that this individualist interest had been transferred
to the new federal government, which was to be its custodian:
"All this will signify nothing without an effective FEDERAL
GOVERNMENT."[15]

Examples of these principles could easily be multiplied
from pamphlets and newspapers. But some of the states sub-
scribed to them in very explicit language in the act of founding independent constitutions. Virginia's formulation,
written by George Mason and adopted by the General Convention in Williamsburg as early as May 6, 1776, declared that
all men were "by nature equally free and independent, and
have certain inherent rights, of which, when they enter into
a state of society, they cannot by any compact deprive or di-

---

[13] Adams, ed., *Works of Adams,* 4:193; [Anon.], *An Essay on Government
Adopted by the Americans* (Philadelphia, 1775), pp. 11, 20–21.

[14] William Livingston, *Observations on Government* (New York, 1787).

[15] Ibid., p. 53.

vest their posterity."[16] The rights have become familiar with repetition; the present point is that men entered voluntarily into society in order to protect them. But the doctrine was nowhere more explicit than in Massachusetts, where the preamble to the constitution adopted in 1780 explained exactly how political society came into being. "The body politic," it declared, "is formed by a voluntary association of individuals: it is a social compact, by which the whole people covenants with each citizen, and each citizen with the whole people, that all shall be governed by certain laws for the common good."[17] It may be of some significance that this formulation succeeded a rejected constitution that had been put together by the legislature and contained no reference to rights—or other theoretical framework.[18] The authors of the constitution of 1780 were making sure that the consent of the people was woven into the fabric of that document. But it is equally significant that the radicals who seized power in Pennsylvania in 1776 put "the protection and security of the community as such" ahead of the natural rights of "the individuals who compose it."[19] Even here, however, in a more collective formulation than the one that Massachusetts adopted four years later, we note the significant indication that the elements composing the community are *individuals*—and we are entitled to infer that they are thought to have given their consent to membership.

Even before constitution making became the custom of America, however, the future author of the Declaration of Independence had given an indication of the unusual force of the idea of the individual as the basic social and political unit. In his *Summary View of the Rights of British America*, Jefferson asked, "Can any reason be assigned why 160,000 elec-

[16] Samuel Eliot Morison, ed., *Sources and Documents Illustrating the American Revolution, 1764–1788, and the Formation of the Federal Constitution*, 2d ed. (Oxford, 1962), p. 149.

[17] J. R. Pole, ed., *The Revolution in America, 1754–1788: Documents on the Internal Development of America in the Revolutionary Era* (London, 1970), p. 479.

[18] Ibid., pp. 435–46.

[19] Ibid., p. 529.

tors in the island of Great Britain should give law to four millions in the states of America, every *individual* of whom is equal to every *individual* of them, in virtue, in understanding, and in bodily strength?"[20] Earlier in the same essay Jefferson asserted that the American continent had been settled and tamed by the efforts of *individuals.*

The historical writing of recent years has been unusually resourceful in drawing politically scientific inferences from historical sociology, a process that has concentrated a great deal of attention on signs of nascent individualism in colonial culture. It is fortunately not necessary to enter into these debates about the character or concept of individualism to recognize certain points of salient importance for the understanding of American constitutional theory. When men observed the life lived by themselves and their families, they observed a state of a naturally formed—we might now say, an organic—society; but when they *theorized* about government, they saw something different: a series of acts founded in the rational intent of independent individuals—in psychological terms, acts that combined the faculties of reason and will. For our present purpose of understanding the presuppositions of American constitutional theory, questions arising about the status of these individuals are less important than the one universally recognized truth about them: that as members of society under government, and indeed before the formation of government, they all had *rights.* When the town meeting of Concord, Massachusetts, voted its resolutions of October 21, 1776, it had something to say on this point: "We conceive that a Constitution in its proper idea intends a system of principles established to secure the subject in the possession and enjoyment of their rights and privileges, against any encroachment of the governing part."[21] True, the concept of "subject" was about to give way to that of "citizen"; but putting that aside, the good people of Con-

[20] Julian P. Boyd et al., eds., *The Papers of Thomas Jefferson,* 24 vols. to date (Princeton, 1950-), 1:423. I have added the emphasis in this quotation.

[21] Oscar and Mary Handlin, eds., *The Popular Sources of Political Authority: Documents on the Massachusetts Constitution of 1780* (Cambridge, Mass., 1966), pp. 152–53.

cord were comfortable in the knowledge that they were affirming a faith with which their fellow countrymen would
readily agree—and so was Jefferson when he framed the sentiments that open the Declaration of Independence.

Few people in the United States could be counted on to
reaffirm universal opinions with more conviction than
George Washington. In his circular letter to the state gover-
nors, written at the end of the War of Independence, Washington sounded a note of serious warning about the
responsibilities that went with independence: "The foundation of our empire was not laid in the gloomy age of ignorance and superstition," he told them, "but at an epocha
when the rights of mankind were better understood and
more clearly defined, than at any other period." And it followed that if the citizens of the United States were not "completely free and happy, the fault will be entirely their own."[22]
It was a heavy burden to lay upon the conscience of a people
so near to the beginning of their political life, and I am not
sure whether the people of the United States have ever fully
recovered from the responsibility of bearing it. Four years
later, when transmitting the draft Constitution to the Congress, Washington introduced the familiar analogy of the origin of political society to justify the new national departure:
"It is obviously impracticable in the federal government of
these states, to secure all the rights of independent sovereignty to each, and yet provide for the interest and safety of
all: individuals entering into society, must give up a share of
liberty to preserve the rest."[23]

Views such as these were not confined to those who held
the more nationalist vision of the American future. When
opinions were bitterly divided over the draft Constitution
during the ratification process, Antifederalist voices were as
firmly committed as the Federalists' to the conviction that

[22]Quoted by Edward S. Corwin, "The Progress of Constitutional
Theory between the Declaration of Independence and the Meeting of the
Philadelphia Convention," *American Historical Review* 30 (1924–25):511–
36.

[23]George Washington to the President of Congress, Sept. 17, 1787, in
Winton U. Solberg, ed., *The Federal Convention and the Formation of the Union*
(Indianapolis, 1958), pp. 363–64.

government, even society itself, existed to protect individual rights. It was this that gave force to the reiterated Antifederalist demand for a bill of rights. Agrippa—generally supposed to have been James Winthrop, a former librarian of Harvard College—warned Massachusetts of the necessity to defend the individual against the majority in a republic as much as against the king in a monarchy. He feared that the new Constitution would not prove as effective as the states under the old Confederation.[24] Where James Madison would rely for the protection of individual rights on the mutually blocking action of collectively represented interests, Agrippa preferred to rely on the entrenched protection of specified rights. (The two programs were certainly not incompatible: Madison soon afterwards sponsored precisely the sort advocated by Winthrop when he introduced the Bill of Rights into Congress.) Elbridge Gerry, another prominent opponent, agreed with "a justly celebrated writer [John Locke, presumably], that the principal aim of a society is to protect individuals in the absolute rights vested in them by the immediate laws of nature, but which could not be preserved in peace without the mutual intercourse which is gained by the institution of friendly and social communities." It was the individual who counted. "The rights of individuals," he added, "ought to be the primary object of all government." John Hampden and John Pym were called in support, and Niccolò Machiavelli was cited for the view that no republic ever stood on a stable foundation without satisfying the common people.[25] Gerry does not seem to have shared the habit of distinguishing between society and the more formalistic concept of government, but if rights existed before society, then government, which existed to protect society, manifestly protected these individual rights.

Rights were venerable entities in the history of political thought, and it would hardly be worth going to these lengths of illustration to argue that Americans had a high regard for them, or again that Americans belonged to a generation

[24] Cecelia M. Kenyon, ed., *The Antifederalists* (Indianapolis, 1966), p. 154.

[25] [Elbridge Gerry], "By a Columbian Patriot," in *Observations on the New Constitution* . . . (Boston, 1788), pp. 6, 10–11.

whose education and experience had taught them to regard government as the primary source of danger. Yet the truth was that the rights Americans had in mind were not quite as old, and in historical opinion not quite as universal, as they seemed. And their recent history was of some significance for an understanding of the uses to which they were being put.

In medieval England and in Renaissance Italy, both of which were source material for Americans, men were very well aware of the attributes of individual human nature, and they lived under laws that protected specific rights. But these were not general rights; they were the consequences of commitments, entered into voluntarily by oneself or by some lawful guardian. Political philosophers had no theory of a voluntarist origin for society or for government, nor was there any conception of property as antedating the formation of government; but they did regard as in a sense voluntary the relations following from contracts. Thus it has been possible to describe man in Renaissance Italy as "propertyless" because he was "rightless."[26]

At about the same time that English commercial interests were coming into collision with the Dutch and the English were emigrating to North America, Hugo Grotius developed the theory that rights of property derived from physical attachment: labor attaches the object to its maker. Grotius's *Introduction to the Jurisprudence of Holland* (1619–20) has recently been called "the ancestor of all codes based on rights." The law of nature did not decree protection for universal and inalienable human rights, which no one had yet heard of, but it did decree the obligation of contract, which entailed respect for the rights of another. And "sociability," the necessary condition of human life, similarly entailed respect for individual rights. This, Richard Tuck tells us, was the first major expression of a strong rights theory in Protestant Europe. Grotius, however, considered that obligation itself was constituted by the act of a superior will; by contrast, the Englishmen John Selden and Thomas Hobbes saw obligation as

[26] Richard Tuck, *Natural Rights Theories: Their Origin and Development* (Cambridge, 1979).

proceeding from rational principles based on egoistic motivation.[27]

From these sources the concept of rights gradually struggled free from the ground and rose into the empyrean of universal ethics. It does not fall to us to follow or explain the course of this development, which no one could have foreseen. What matters, and matters immensely for our understanding of the American Constitution, is that Americans caught the idea of rights at full flow; and the First Continental Congress was persuaded—against the judgment of some of its more conservative members—to adopt a reference to natural rights in its protest known as the Suffolk Resolves.[28] The precedent was exalted and dangerous; hitherto it had always been thought sufficient to rest on the rights of free-born Englishmen as known through the common law and such statutes as habeas corpus. But the process that was now taking formal shape was to have rapid and momentous implications, because the Americans were entering into their period of constitution making. The American concept of a constitution itself grew in large part from the formalization of the individual rights into fundamental law.[29]

Nothing I have so far said proves anything about the Constitution. The Articles of Confederation, which satisfied the demands of the people in their states, said nothing about individual rights, because rights were left entirely to the protection of the states, whose sovereignty was explicitly reserved under Article II.[30] The ground so far laid out, however, does strongly suggest that any national constitution, if it came into being, would be expected to protect individual rights either directly or indirectly, or at least not to impair them. The dis-

[27] Ibid., pp. 68, 90–94, 127.

[28] Quoted in J. R. Pole, *The Decision for American Independence* (London, 1977), pp. 60–64.

[29] Gerald Stourzh, "Fundamental Laws and Individual Rights in the Eighteenth-Century Constitution," *Bicentennial Essay Number Five*, Claremont Institute for the Study of Statesmanship and Political Philosophy (Claremont, Calif., 1984).

[30] Morison, ed., *Sources and Documents*, p. 178.

appointment of that expectation in a Constitution that greatly strengthened national power gave rise to the strongest of Antifederalist protests and to the demand for a bill of rights as part of the Constitution. But state constitutions could give no clear guidance as to the form this would take. Five states failed to adopt a bill of rights and some of the others were curiously episodic. Some fundamental rights seem to have been more fundamental than others; several omitted all reference to double jeopardy, acts of attainder, and even the writ of habeas corpus itself.[31] Alexander Hamilton was able to make great play with the fact that New York had no bill of rights and that its citizens were therefore less well protected than they would be under the Constitution, which was itself in certain respects a bill of rights. Legislative majorities had ridden rough-shod over existing state bills of rights, which caused Madison to feel a skepticism that he expressed to Jefferson.[32] The whole issue became entangled in the politics of ratification, and there is strong ground for suspecting that Antifederalist leaders used it as a stratagem for calling a second convention, at which they hoped to undo the work of the first.[33] These political tactics do nothing to detract from the force of the popular feeling for a bill of rights, however; the leaders would hardly have used the issue if it had not had popular appeal.

The failure of the Philadelphia Convention to appreciate this state of the public mind can be understood in part as a result of its self-imposed isolation; its reasons may have made good sense, but its political tactics were insensitive. When, however, Hamilton resorted in *Federalist* No. 84 to arguing that the case for a bill of rights was undermined by the fact that no such bill was included in the Articles of Confederation, his tactics were not only specious but potentially self-

[31] Leonard W. Levy, *Constitutional Opinions* (New York, 1986), pp. 111–12, 130–31; Jacob E. Cooke, ed., *The Federalist* (Middletown, Conn., 1961), pp. 575–81. Subsequent references to *The Federalist* are from Cooke.

[32] James Madison to Thomas Jefferson, Oct. 17, 1788, in Marvin Meyers, ed., *The Mind of the Founder: Sources of the Political Thought of James Madison* (Indianapolis, 1973), pp. 205–9.

[33] Levy, *Constitutional Opinions*, pp. 106, 124.

defeating; for the deeper purpose of a national Constitution would be to assume fundamental responsibility for protecting the rights of individual citizens, which, of course, the Articles left under the care of state sovereignty. The fact that the Articles did not make this provision was not an argument that it was not needed, and could have been turned against Publius.[34] But it is fair to say, in defense of the Framers against the repeated charges that they had endangered the people's liberties by neglecting this duty, that they had taken care to include some of the cherished rights of individuals in the list of prohibitions on Congress contained in Section 9 of Article I, as Hamilton pointed out in the penultimate *Federalist* essay.

In the end it was the Antifederalists who lost the battle of tactics; for when those of them who really wanted to defeat the Constitution insisted on a bill of rights and, against their own expectations, were taken at their word, they found perforce that the new Constitution had taken over some of the most distinctive obligations of the states. This, of course, was exactly what the Federalists had intended. Some—to judge by the decline of opposition—were honestly satisfied: the leaders no doubt saw that they had been outflanked.

Americans of this era were heirs to a political philosophy that owed much of its persuasive power to certain forms of individualistic psychology. Selden and Hobbes in their psychology of motivation and Locke in his epistemology identified the individual as the object of interest and knowledge, without any reference to the psychology of groups.[35] *The Federalist* is permeated with a powerful sense of the driving force

[34] *Federalist* No. 84.

[35] Tuck, *Natural Rights Theories,* pp. 82–100; Thomas Hobbes, *Leviathan* (1651), ed. Michael Oakshott (Oxford, 1960); John Locke, *An Essay concerning Human Understanding* (London, 1691), esp. book 2, chap. 2. The whole work is a study of individual psychology, but his rejection in chap. 2 of innate ideas seems to leave no room even for a theory of preexisting group, family, or collective psychological dispositions. John Selden, *Opera* (London, 1726), cols. 1197–98, etc., as cited by Tuck in *Natural Rights Theories;* idem, *Of the Dominion, or Ownership, of the Sea,* trans. Marchamont Nedham (London, 1652), pp. 23–25. Selden derives the right of property from "some such Compact or Covenant [as] was passed in the very first

of personal ambition and motivation—a force extending to public as much as to private life. Hamilton was far from being alone in holding that fame was "the ruling passion of the noblest minds."[36]

In *The Federalist* itself, the most interesting passage relating personal psychology to political science was written by Madison and occurs in No. 10, in the discussion of the nature and effects of faction in the body politic. As long, Madison says, as a connection exists between man's reason and his self-love, opinions and passions will have a reciprocal effect on each other, and man's self-esteem will attach itself to his opinions. Rights of property originate from the fact that diverse faculties—that is, abilities—exist among men; the point here being that "different and unequal faculties of acquiring property" lead immediately to the actual possession of different amounts of property; and these differences in turn influence the sentiments and views of different owners, causing interests and parties to spring up in society.

This analysis has often been quoted for its profound insight into political motivation, but it has seldom, perhaps never, been subjected to critical comment. It is in itself a singular example of a very specific type of motivated reasoning. Differences in amounts of property actually owed their origins to very much more complicated causes than the highly individualized differences of personal "faculty" to which Madison attributed them. Inheritance was hardly a trivial source of economic and social differentiation in his own state of Virginia, to say nothing of other aspects of social class, family background, and education. But it is the inborn individual faculties that absorb Madison's interest and motivate his political science. For in the midst of the language quoted he makes one salient remark that I have so far omitted: "The

---

beginnings of private Dominion or possession." The original is admittedly rather vague, but the individual character of the act is clear.

[36] *Federalist* Nos. 1, 6, 72. This phrase of Alexander Hamilton's (which scans) seems to be a vulgarization, in the less flattering sense of the word, of Milton's lines on Fame in *Lycidas:* "Fame is the spur that the clear spirit doth raise / (That last infirmity of noble minds)."

protection of these faculties is the first object of Government."[37]

These comments strike a different note from those usually associated by scholars with the meaning of *Federalist* No. 10, but it is no less significant for that. We have already seen men, as rational, independent animals, making up their minds after due deliberation to enter into political society, primarily with the object of protecting their property. We now see that differences arising from different faculties under government will be no less entitled to protection, itself hardly a matter for surprise; and we are also told that the primary reason for the existence of government is to protect these different faculties. It is not the property itself, but the individualized faculties of acquiring property, that government exists to protect. Many examples can be found of statements regarding the duty of governments to protect individual rights, but I doubt whether we could find a more specific assertion of the claim that this is the reason why they were brought into existence in the first place.

The view sometimes expressed, that this discussion of rights is out of place because the whole emphasis of *The Federalist* has shifted from the earlier preoccupation with rights to a new, Madisonian preoccupation with *interests,* has no effect on the force of this argument.[38] Rights are included in interests. An interest has no legal force from its mere existence, but derives its claim on juristic attention from the fact—or claim—that a right exists. That indeed is why it had been necessary for Madison to say that property arises from the exercise of different faculties.

The passage from these views, which are statements belonging to a historical political science, to the meaning of the Constitution to which they refer, is not a very troublesome one. It must be acknowledged at once that *The Federalist,* a work of high propaganda, does not have the same signifi-

[37] *Federalist* No. 10. Since this was written, the analysis has received cogent support in Jennifer Nedelsky, *Private Property and the Limits of American Constitutionalism: The Madisonian Framework and Its Legacy* (Chicago, 1990).

[38] Most recently by John P. Diggins, *The Lost Soul of American Politics: Virtue, Self-Interest, and the Foundations of Liberalism* (New York, 1984), p. 62.

cance for the Constitution as Revelation does for the Christian religion (though it has been rather too often treated in that light), but these views are in general consistent with contemporary opinion. They were agreed to on all sides. In the long debate in which Federalists and Antifederalists rebutted each others' arguments, no one denied that these expressions reflected the true meaning of the Constitution.

The new Constitution cuts clean through the lines surrounding the states to operate directly on every individual subject to its jurisdiction—which means every individual within the boundaries of the Union. It has this power because it confers on Congress and the president the power to make and sign laws that will affect individuals regardless of any form of protection or privilege conferred by state citizenship. The Constitution also brings into being a new class of citizens—those of the United States—which at a stroke makes every citizen of any state into a citizen of the United States. The Constitution also makes it the duty of Congress to establish "a uniform rule of naturalization."

These statements have a clarity of outline that was less apparent to contemporaries. Hamilton argued in *Federalist* No. 32 that the power conferred on Congress must be an exclusive power because "if each State had power to prescribe a DISTINCT RULE there could be no UNIFORM RULE," which seems plain enough; but debates on naturalization laws and judicial decisions nevertheless continued to show some tolerance for the notion that the main object was to establish uniform procedures, leaving leeway for the states to make their own variations on the actual conditions of naturalization.[39] Two types of citizenship, of the state and of the United States, continued to stand side by side. A state made laws for those residing within its jurisdiction and had the power to tax them. But any individual entering a state was subject to these laws whether he or she was legally defined as a "citizen" of that state or not, and anyone proposing to reside there would presumably at once become a citizen of it; nothing in the Constitution would countenance a situation in which a state claimed power to *deny* citizenship to a citizen of another state.

[39] *Federalist* No. 32. James H. Kettner, *The Development of American Citizenship, 1608–1870* (Chapel Hill, 1978), pp. 231–47.

If such action had been contemplated by a state it would—or ought—to have been overruled by the Comity Clause of the Constitution, which establishes the essential uniformity of the rights of citizens. With masterly if somewhat elliptical brevity, Section 2 of Article IV says simply that "the Citizens of each State shall be entitled to all the Privileges and Immunities of Citizens in the several States." A citizen of Massachusetts, traveling in South Carolina, might not be a citizen *of* South Carolina, but while *in* that state he was entitled to all the privileges and immunities of its citizens. There could be no other meaning, and laws passed by South Carolina to restrict the freedom of sailors from northern states whose ships were docked in its ports were plainly unconstitutional.[40] The sailors in question, of course, were blacks; and it is central to the argument of this paper that state laws restricting the privileges and immunities of citizens of the United States, *or of other states,* on grounds of racial designation were incompatible with the equality of rights protected by the Constitution, not only after the Fourteenth Amendment but before the Civil War.

In the light of the intense controversies over these questions in the nineteenth century—controversies that were to be resurrected as recently as the 1950s—it is instructive to observe that no such doubts seem to have been entertained when the draft Constitution was under debate. The federal government, said Hamilton, "must carry its agency to the persons of the citizens. It must stand in need of no intermediate legislations; but must itself be empowered to employ the arm of the ordinary magistrate to execute its own resolutions." And Hamilton discerned in sovereign power "an impatience of controul."[41]

Hamilton was a highly partial witness, but strong support for those views and for the Constitution for putting them into effect was to be found rather unexpectedly in South Carolina, where the motion to call a convention was debated at length in the House of Representatives. Charles Cotesworth

---

[40] Charles S. Sydnor, *The Development of Southern Sectionalism, 1819–1848* (Baton Rouge, 1948), p. 223.

[41] *Federalist* Nos. 15, 16.

Pinckney, after going over the failings of the states in their obligations under the Confederation, declared that it was "essential to have a government that operated on the people, not on the states," and added that this was seen by everyone, whatever differences they might have about questions of power.[42] Antifederalists, on this as on other questions, did not speak with one voice. Melancton Smith, attacking the Constitution in the New York convention, admitted that it was necessary "to some extent that the government should operate on individuals."[43] But William Findley, a prominent western Pennsylvania politician who emerged as a strong Antifederalist, attacked the Constitution precisely because it was not— as he thought it ought to be—"a CONFEDERATION of STATES, but a GOVERNMENT of INDIVIDUALS." The sovereignty of individual states, he charged, was destroyed, and he went on to the ritual charge that a bill of rights was omitted.[44] Antifederalists took this to mean that the Federalists intended to use the cover of the Constitution to undermine these rights.

These arguments are devastating to the claims of later generations of southern political leaders in favor of state sovereignty and the right of secession. That such thoughts were not in the minds of contemporary leaders is demonstrated by evidence from South Carolina itself. Charles Cotesworth Pinckney's cousin, Charles Pinckney, made a cogent contribution to the same debate. "This admirable manifesto," he declared, reading from the Declaration of Independence, "sufficiently confutes the honorable gentleman's doctrine of individual sovereignty and independence of the several states. In that declaration the several states are not even enumerated. . . . The separate independence and individual sovereignty of the several states were never thought of by the enlightened band of patriots who framed this declaration." Opponents took the same point. Rawlins Lowndes, as a leading Antifederalist, confirmed Pinckney's views with opposite

---

[42] *Debates in the House of Representatives of South Carolina on the Ratification of the Proposed Constitution of the United States* (Charleston, 1789), pp. 3–4.

[43] Kenyon, *The Antifederalists*, p. 379. This, he said, was "agreed."

[44] [William Findley], *Address from an Officer* (Philadelphia, 1787), pp. v, 3, 6.

intent; after giving a eulogy of the Confederation, he attacked the Constitution on the very grounds that it "wipes out state sovereignty."[45]

The extreme sensitivity on this issue suggested the need for considerable tactical flexibility during the composition of *The Federalist* essays. The tone adopted by Publius undergoes a distinct modification with the progress of the argument. Earlier essays argue trenchantly and even scornfully against the absurdities of trying to retain local sovereignties—on the same lines as Madison's arguments in the Convention; but by the beginning of the new year, Hamilton in No. 32 was trying to reassure the states that they would retain the authority to raise revenues to supply their own wants. Shedding the political burden of "consolidation," he now assures them that "the plan of the convention aims only at a partial Union or consolidation," under which "the State Governments would clearly retain all the rights of sovereignty which they had before and which were not by that act *exclusively* delegated to the United States." Considered analytically this might be little more than a truism; but as Hamilton did not believe in dual sovereignty, his choice of language represented a concession to the opposition.

This flexible trend culminated in *Federalist* No. 39 in which Madison moved further toward a notion of shared sovereignty, a doctrine which, like Hamilton, he held to be self-contradictory, an oxymoron in political science. Soon afterward he was writing of a "residual sovereignty" in the states.[46] None of this could wash away the powers actually conferred on the federal government by the Constitution, not least by the clause granting power to enact all measures "necessary and proper" to the purposes of the Constitution itself; Antifederalists who attacked this clause were certainly aiming at the right target.

For all that these modest concessions might have been worth, there remained one feature of the Constitution that decisively overturns the claim that the powers retained by the

[45] *Debates in South Carolina*, pp. 35, 25–26.

[46] *Federalist* Nos. 6, 9, 15, 16, 39, 62; Max Farrand, ed., *The Records of the Federal Convention of 1787*, rev. ed., 4 vols. (New Haven, 1937), 1:446–49.

states can be considered as "sovereign" powers in any conventional sense of that word as it had come down in the works of Jean Bodin, Hobbes, Samuel von Pufendorf and, more recently, William Blackstone. The Constitution provides for its own amendment, by either of two processes; and the federal Constitution, being superior to any state constitution, can overturn any provision of a state constitution. It thus follows that when the states gave their consent to the federal Constitution, they relinquished their control over their own fundamental law. This condition is compatible with a very considerable measure of self-government, as no one would have denied and as was genuinely intended; but it is not compatible with the concept of sovereignty. In 1860 honest secessionists admitted that secession was revolution.

There was no doubt in anyone's mind, Federalist or Antifederalist, that the Constitution reached every individual in the Union, and reached them all equally, with its powers of government; could there be any doubt that it reached them equally with its powers of protection? The principle of the political equality of individual voters, which emerged from Revolution politics, the well-established common law principle of equality before the law, and the obvious meaning of the Constitution, all pointed in the direction of this duty of equal protection. That was the teaching of all the political philosophy that we have discussed, and it was a teaching that no one on either side disputed. What was in doubt was not whether government had a duty to protect individual rights, but *which* government, state or federal, was to do it. If, as everyone who spoke on the subject seemed to agree, men had entered into political society to protect their rights, they could hardly be expected to have divested themselves of those rights when they endorsed the Constitution.[47]

The first American bill of rights was issued in 1215 and was called the Magna Carta. But a more recent and more

[47] On the theory of the Declaration, it is doubtful whether they would have had the power to divest themselves of rights that were by definition "unalienable." As Morton White has shown, what is inalienable *cannot* be transferred, either voluntarily or by the will of another (*Philosophy of American Revolution*, pp. 195–210).

relevant version dated from as late as 1787 and was contained in the Northwest Ordinance. Article II of that charter laid down that the peoples of territories administered by the Congress should have in essence all the rights and immunities that were soon afterward confirmed in the first batch of constitutional amendments. The language is in most cases strikingly similar.[48] The implications are interesting. The old Congress, so much derided for its debility, was actually exerting extensive powers over future states, and seemed to be assuring future Americans of guarantees that exceeded those assured in the original thirteen states. In view of the way I began this paper, we may note that the inhabitants of future territories were entitled to the benefits of "a proportionate representation in the legislature." This principle, though in fact of recent origin, had already entered into the precepts of fundamental republican law.[49]

When James Madison somewhat wearily decided to honor the implied promises made when Virginia ratified the Constitution and began to draft a federal bill of rights, he had ample precedent. But the language of the amendments had to deal with new circumstances. Although the general intention was to draft amendments that would implement the principle of equal protection throughout the Union, the sensibilities of the states had still to be respected.

The legislative history of the amendments can be traced in the *Annals of Congress,* so far as they can be considered a reliable record, but even so it cannot be recaptured in full because of the secrecy of the Senate. (It is also unfortunate for the historian that Sen. William Maclay's diary reveals nothing about the debate on the amendments.) But one inference we can draw with confidence is that the amendments were intensely scrutinized and that their ultimate language

[48] Pole, *Revolution in America,* p. 386.

[49] The way in which this process came about during the Revolution is explained in J. R. Pole, *Political Representation in England and the Origins of the American Republic* (1966; reprint ed., Berkeley, 1971), pp. 169–249, 372–73, 538. For the observation that the Ordinance of 1787 was "the first federal bill of rights," see Robert Allen Rutland, *The Birth of the Bill of Rights, 1776–1791* (Chapel Hill, 1955), pp. 103–5.

conveys meanings reflecting the maximum degree of obtainable agreement. We are not in the presence of inexperienced, vague, or unskillful draftsmanship.

When Madison introduced the amendments that would be transmuted into the Bill of Rights, most of them were directed against possible abuses of government power. And in view of the consensus that existed about rights, the most important question from the individual's point of view was not so much what rights they protected but to what form of government they are addressed. With this question in view we can observe that the amendments follow the essential forms of the Constitution by speaking in more than one voice. Some speak in what William Crosskey called "the single active voice," as when the First Amendment says: "Congress shall make no law respecting an establishment of religion." Clearly this is directed to Congress and not to the states. But where the Constitution intends to add specific prohibitions *on the states* to those imposed on Congress, the amendments instead adopt a "general passive voice" to achieve a general prohibition on both federal and state governments. Amendments Two to Eight are all in this style and all restrain the states as well as Congress. Thus in the Fourth Amendment, "no Warrants shall issue, but on probable cause," and in the Fifth Amendment, "no person shall be held to answer."

The intention can be illustrated from an episode in the legislative history. When Madison introduced the article that was eventually to become the Fifth Amendment, he planned it as part of a rather comprehensive First Amendment. But the general context of that amendment is national; it restrains Congress, not the states. To make this distinction between restraint on Congress and intended restraint on the states for the clause in question, Madison's draft began with the words, "No state shall." But when this clause took its place as a separate amendment, that distinction was no longer necessary, and the clause now adopted the general passive voice, "No person shall be held to answer," meaning that no one in the United States was to be deprived of any of the listed rights by federal, state, or for that matter, local government.[50]

[50] William W. Crosskey, *Politics and the Constitution in the History of the United States,* 2 vols. (Chicago, 1953), 2:1070. For the controversy over Crosskey's interpretation, see Charles Fairman, "The Supreme Court and

Madison had wanted to draft amendments to the actual text of the Constitution, which might have left less room for subsequent disagreements, but when the House insisted on amendments in the form of *additions* to the text, the single active voice—"No state shall"—was at first used to restrain the states. This proposal, which applied only to certain sections, was rejected by the Senate, but the record does not tell us why. Crosskey points out that in doing so the Senate "destroyed the sole surviving basis for regarding the *other* amendments as applying only to the nation"—adding that it was so perceived and intended.[51]

It was on the question of religious establishment that the defenders of state sovereignty put up their most determined and successful resistance. And precisely for this reason the First Amendment restraints on religious establishment begin by naming Congress without restraining the states—several of which had retained support for religion. It is now clear that the *other* amendments, Two to Eight, apply equal restraints to both types of government existing in the Union. But so sensitive was Madison to the danger of reaction from the states that in withdrawing his motion intended to prohibit a "national" religion, he went as far as to say that he had not intended to imply that the government was a national one; the author of the recent *Federalist* No. 39, whose identity could not long be expected to remain undisclosed, had by this time a reputation to preserve for masterly ambiguity.[52]

The tenor of these amendments was in no way disturbed by the Tenth, which states that the powers not delegated to the United States nor prohibited to the states "are reserved to the States respectively, or to the people." *Or* to the people? Why "or," if anyway to the states? The answer must be that the *people of the United States* do not constitute the same entity as the respective states; the people as a whole made the Constitution, acting through the agency of their respective states;

---

the Constitutional Limitation on State Authority," *University of Chicago Law Review* 21 (1953): 40–78; Crosskey's reply, 22 (1954): 19–43; and Fairman's rejoinder, 22: 144–51.

[51] Ibid.

[52] *Annals of Congress*, 1st Cong., 1st sess., 731.

and it is the people who have amended the Constitution, through their representatives in the appointed manner. "It is true," said Chief Justice John Marshall in *McCulloch* v. *Maryland,* "they assembled in their several states [for ratification]—and where else could they have assembled? No political dreamer was ever wild enough to think of breaking down the lines which separate the states, and then compounding the American people into one common mass." (Some distinguished political dreamers had come rather close to this in the Convention, whose proceedings remained unpublished.) "Of consequence, when they act, they act in their States. But the measures they adopt do not, on that account cease to be the measures of the people themselves, or become the measures of the State governments."[53] And it is the people, as individuals, who fall within the reach of federal power; and just as they fall within its authority, so are they objects of its protection. That is the meaning of the Bill of Rights.

It would be pleasant to be able to record that the Framers had succeeded in handing down their work intact to future generations. But one of the heaviest blows at the record of the Framers' intent—and not only their intent but, more important, the express meaning of their language—came from the hands of Chief Justice Marshall in his last important case before death took him from the bench. In *Barron* v. *Baltimore,* decided in 1833, a private citizen claimed the protection of the Fifth Amendment's due process clause against the government of his state. The Court held that the claim must fail because *none* of the first eight amendments reached into state jurisdictions. With regard to the First Amendment this judgment was clearly correct; the amendment contains an express prohibition on Congress. But if the remainder of the judgment conformed to the language of the Framers, then, as Crosskey observes, the draftsmanship of these amendments was "bungling in an extreme degree." We may feel persuaded

---

[53] Quoted by Gottfried Dietze, *The Federalist: A Classic on Federalism and Free Government* (Baltimore, 1960), pp. 261–62; 4 Wheaton's Reports 400. The judgment may also be consulted in Gerald Gunther, ed., *John Marshall's Defense of* McCulloch v. Maryland (Stanford, 1969).

to agree with Crosskey that *Barron* v. *Baltimore* was "without any warrant at all."[54]

Only a civil war could bring a reversal of this political reconstruction of the Constitution, and the outcome of the war presented the problem of equal protection on an unprecedented scale. It was resolved, first, by the Civil Rights Act of 1866, which established the citizenship of all persons born in the United States and confirmed the principle of national protection.[55] But a statute is a frail thing on which to rest a fundamental civil right, and the contentious politics of Reconstruction soon produced the Fourteenth Amendment. Some of the Amendment's provisions are hardly clear at first sight, but its basic aims are unmistakable. The moral and political purpose was to destroy the foundations of the *Dred Scott* decision and to affirm that Negroes enjoyed equal rights of citizenship with native or naturalized whites. It was to ensure that all Americans and all persons under American jurisdiction were equal under the law. No state could henceforth deprive a citizen of the United States of the privileges or immunities that he or she enjoyed in virtue of United States citizenship. There was nothing new about the category of citizenship of the United States, which was coeval with the Constitution itself; there was in truth nothing new about the doctrine that gave equal protection to American citizens. The Comity Clause, as we have seen, bridges the gap between

---

[54] Crosskey, *Politics and the Constitution*, 2:1058, 1056; *Barron* v. *Baltimore*, 7 Peters 243 (1833). The argument heard by the Court was confined to the question of jurisdiction. John Marshall also looked into the language, distinguishing between such expressions as "no bill of attainder shall" and "no State shall," which seems a false distinction since the first applies to the body of the Constitution, the second occurs in an amendment to it. He then fell back on the argument that "the Amendments contain no expression indicating an intention to apply them to the State government." No such expression was called for. But see the conventional, and opposite, view as expressed by Andrew C. McLaughlin in *A Constitutional History of the United States* (New York, 1935), p. 225. Charles Grove Haines, *The Role of the Supreme Court in American Government and Politics, 1789–1835* (Berkeley and Los Angeles, 1944), pp. 608–9, reports Marshall without critical comment.

[55] U.S. *Statutes at Large*, 14:27.

United States and state citizenship. It was the turbulent political situation rather than the language of the Constitution that made this new affirmation a necessary act on the part of the nation.

This condition of equal protection was already present in the Bill of Rights; its power to operate at the federal level had been removed, however, by *Barron* v. *Baltimore,* another reason why the amendment was now necessary. But I would go further than that; for if we reach a little further back, to the Constitution itself, we surely find an equality of individual standing that in turn brings an equality of protected rights. If that view is unsound, then the Constitution itself was doing less than was claimed for it and less than was intended by the men who created it.

It would be an exaggeration to claim that the Fourteenth Amendment did nothing more than confirm existing truths. The many persons whose protection was ambiguous in the past were now covered by the language extending protection to "all persons." But it would not be an exaggeration to claim that the amendment was *consistent* with the Bill of Rights and to claim that it gave explicit meaning to the value of the individual already present in the Constitution.

This benign state of affairs was not long allowed to remain undisturbed. It was disrupted in *The Slaughterhouse Cases,* decided in 1873 by a Court, most of whose members owed their appointments to Lincoln. The interests of Negroes were not involved in the suit, which arose from the corrupt grant of a monopoly to a New Orleans slaughtering corporation. But in an unusual adaptation of the common principles of legal reasoning, the majority held that it could therefore be decided on different grounds, a departure which implied that the constitutional protections afforded to blacks were somehow of a different order from those afforded to all other Americans. The point of the amendment, however, was that they were exactly the same. Blacks were no longer in some constitutional sense "blacks" but were individual Americans like all others, and by the same token all others were constitutionally like them.

The issue was the meaning of citizenship. "It is quite clear, then," declared Justice Samuel F. Miller for the Court, "that there is a citizenship of the United States and a citizenship of a State, which are distinct from each other and which depend on different characteristics or circumstances in the individual." This was in fact far from clear to Justice Stephen J. Field, as he indicated in his dissent. "A citizen of a State is now only a citizen of the United States residing in that State. The fundamental rights, privileges and immunities which belong to him as a free man and a free citizen, now belong to him as a citizen of the United States, and are not dependent on his citizenship of any State."

The argument I have advanced about the meaning of the Fourteenth Amendment appears to gain weight from the next step in Field's opinion. For he went on to say that the amendment did not attempt to confer any *new* privileges and immunities on citizens, but assumed that they already existed, and ordained that they should not be abridged by state legislation. Apparently, Field did think that a gap had existed between state and federal citizenship that states could fill with laws of their own; historically this was certainly true, and Field was wise to take it into account. It led the way to the devastating conclusion that if the majority of the Court was right, then the Fourteenth Amendment "was a vain and idle enactment, which accomplished nothing, and most unnecessarily excited Congress and the people in its passage."[56] Crosskey's comment on the Court's decision is that the minority was right in charging that the majority must have determined, if they dared,[57] to destroy the new provisions of the Constitution completely. Why they may have wished to do so, and indeed whether they took into consideration the deeper implications for the power of American citizenship to protect civil rights, are questions that lie beyond the scope of this paper.

The status of the individual as a protégé of the Constitution grew worse before the end of the century in the more notorious case of *Plessy* v. *Ferguson* in 1896. This judgment, which validated the doctrine of "separate but equal" under the aegis of the Fourteenth Amendment, has been frequently

[56] *Slaughterhouse Cases*, 16 Wallace 36 (1873).

[57] Crosskey, *Politics and the Constitution*, 2:1119–30.

attacked on the grounds that the conditions provided for the two races, black and white, on Louisiana's segregated railroad cars, were not physically equal and the Court was therefore dishonest about the facts behind the case. This is a spurious argument, which conceals a more subtle issue of greater moral and constitutional importance. For even if physical conditions on railroad cars, or anywhere else under state authority, had been identical, the legislation would still have been objectionable because it had the effect of denying the equal status of *individuals* and their right to make free, independent choices, by designating them not as individuals but as members of prescribed racial blocs. So long as the liberty of any one individual was restrained by this group designation, just so long was his liberty curtailed. The equality described here was only an equality of unfreedom; and as this unfreedom actually affected some individuals differently from others, equality of individual protection was not preserved.[58]

The charge against these decisions is that they departed from the basic precept that the Constitution requires all individuals to be treated alike. When laws are passed that single out specified groups, as must often be done in a changing society, their justification must not be that they treat individuals differentially, but that their *aim* is to bring about some condition that will, when accomplished, more closely resemble that of primal equality.

Nothing in this paper is intended to detract from the pluralistic character of the Constitution. To do so would be unhistorical and would be inconsistent with the features of the Constitution that leave all the powers associated with local government, together with criminal and civil law, in the hands of the states. The states could still do nearly everything they could do before. What they could not do, or ought not to have been able to do, was to deprive American citizens— before 1869—and any person under American jurisdiction after the Fourteenth Amendment, of the right to equal treatment under the law.

[58] *Plessy* v. *Ferguson,* 163 U.S. 537 (1896). For comment, see Noel T. Dowling and Gerald Gunther, *Cases and Materials on Constitutional Law* (Brooklyn, 1965), pp. 1160–62; Pole, *Pursuit of Equality,* pp. 195–98.

The primal activity in a democracy is voting. The principle that each politically participating individual's vote shall have equal weight is as basic as anything that can be attributed to the American Republic under its Constitution. The first section of Article I lays down that representation is to be according to population, and to ensure that this principle is maintained, it adds that distribution is to be revised in accordance with each decennial census of population. (It was for violation of this principle, laid down in the state constitution, that the case of *Baker* v. *Carr* was taken and returned for rehearing in Tennessee in 1962.) It is difficult to see how the principle of individuality could have been made more explicit, but the case is open to one perhaps minor objection that should be mentioned at this point. For the same article leaves to the states the power to determine suffrage qualifications and thus permits them to continue the existing practice of disqualifying certain individuals, who in other respects qualify as citizens, from participation in elections. Property qualifications were slight, but they were widespread and varied from state to state. How, then, can we speak of a fundamental political equality of individual citizens?

The Revolutionary generation had not acquired the comparatively modern idea that citizenship necessarily carried with it the right to take part in electing representatives: Americans had more room in their thinking for their own version of "virtual representation" than many would have cared to confess.[59] It was very generally accepted that the right to vote demanded a certain level of social responsibility reflected in property. But once people did have the right to vote, the right was based on individual equality; no state permitted some people to cast two, five, or ten votes and others only one, and no such practice was contemplated. The question of what to do if such a bizarre departure occurred simply did not come up for debate. A clash between the indubitable federal principle of equal protection for *all* American citizens and the power of individual states to make their own election laws thus did not occur and was never contemplated. If it had, one must recognize that the outcome would have been

[59] On which, see Pole, *Political Representation*, pp. 54, 155.

as likely to have depended on the local political climate as on the best reading of the Constitution; that was a burden the Constitution had to bear on many actual occasions.

The significant thing from the present point of view is not only that the Founders understood the matter in the individualist light I have described, but that the language they employed is clearest, most intelligible, and most internally consistent when read in this light. If the Warren Court had failed to affirm these principles and instead had followed the dissenting voices of justices Felix Frankfurter and John Marshall Harlan, it would indeed have been able to find ample precedents in American history, but the United States would have been deprived of its claim to be a republic based on equal representation. Once lost, that foundation could not have been recaptured. There was no base in the *political* system from which to reclaim it, and no constitutional means would have existed to check the growth of largely self-appointed and self-perpetuating legislative oligarchies. Jefferson observed in his *Notes on Virginia* that the Americans had not fought for an alternative form of tyranny.[60]

What exactly happens when the Supreme Court hands down bad constitutional law, as it did in *Barron* and as it did in *Plessy,* and people live under and adapt themselves to that law for generations, is a question for philosophers if not for theologians. Some would say that the bad law was never part of the Constitution; there is at least the saving grace of a text—not of a recoverable "original intent," but of a readable original text.

Earlier in this essay I observed that if life were logical, history would be logical. Oliver Wendell Holmes once wrote that the life of the law had not been logic but experience.[61] The half-truth of that much-quoted observation may have deflected attention from the fuller truth that it only half reveals: the life of the Constitution, which is the supreme law of the land, has been neither wholly logic nor wholly experience, but a constant and creative tension between them.

[60] Thomas Jefferson, *Notes on the State of Virginia,* ed. William Peden (Chapel Hill, 1954), pp. 120–29.

[61] Oliver Wendell Holmes, *The Common Law* (Boston, 1881), p. 1.

JOHN P. DIGGINS

John Adams and the French Critics of the Constitution

"THERE IS NO country in the world," wrote Alexis de Tocqueville, "in which the boldest theories of the eighteenth century are put so effectively into practice as in America." Tocqueville was not alone in seeing America as a "truly philosophical republic," one founded upon carefully considered political ideas rather than upon force, accident, or long enduring custom and tradition. French writers who hailed America—like the marquis de Lafayette, Auguste Comte, and Mme. de Staël—believed in the efficacy of reason in politics as well as science. In contrast to Edmund Burke, who insisted that the origins of all governments must remain veiled in secrecy, French thinkers were rationalists who wanted to strip away old customs in order to lay the basis for a new regime founded upon the liberal principles of reason and nature. Even as rationalists the French were tempted to romanticize America and see it as a place where "wisdom" had triumphed over "prejudice, dogma, and superstition" and had paved the way for "liberty, virtue and reason." Parisian intellectuals looked to America as evidence that the French Enlightenment had found fertile soil in the New World and that the American system of government proved the validity of its universal principles.[1]

The American thinker who assumed the burden of refuting that claim was John Adams. Before becoming America's second president, Adams was one of the great political phi-

[1] René Rémond, *Les Etats-Unis Devant L'Opinion Française, 1815–1832* (Paris, 1962), pp. 553–59; Alexis de Tocqueville, *The Old Regime and the French Revolution*, trans. Stuart Gilbert (Garden City, N.Y., 1955), p. 153.

losophers of the Counter-Enlightenment, the skeptical questioning of the rationalists' claims for human goodness and wisdom. In his two eccentric texts, *A Defence of the Constitutions of Government of the United States of America* and *Discourses on Davila,* Adams drew on the philosophers of the Scottish Enlightenment to challenge the claims of the French Enlightenment. In doing so, he also had to defend the constitutional systems that the American states had adopted under the Articles of Confederation, most of which had been based on the principle of "mixed" and "balanced" government that the new United States Constitution was about to incorporate.

French philosophers and statesmen had followed closely America's daring experiments in constitution making, particularly in the newly founded journal *Affaires de l'Angleterre et de l'Amérique.* The major figure who touched off the controversy over the New World constitutions was Anne-Robert-Jacques Turgot. Baron Turgot had been unsuccessful in his effort to reform France's government under Louis XVI; hence he had good reason to question any new political system that was reluctant to break completely with Old World models. Turgot and other French critics saw no need in America for such cumbersome devices as bicameral legislatures, checks and balances, strict separation of powers, and a strong executive branch of government. Adams, drawing on Scottish thinkers as well as his own Calvinist convictions, believed it essential not only to defend such mechanisms but also to call into question many of the French Enlightenment's assumptions about power, liberty, and human perfectibility. The following discussion, which examines ten of those assumptions, deals not so much with the Constitution as such but with the transatlantic debate that it generated in the late 1780s. After examining Adams's defense of the Constitution, the paper will conclude with a brief evaluation of some of his arguments on the basis of validity, relevance, and the issue of "American exceptionalism."

(1) *The role of reason.* In Enlightenment thought reason was seen as both a method of analysis—in which the nature of things is grasped by breaking them down into their component parts—and as the container or vessel of truth itself; it is

not simply a technique of thinking but its goal, or *telos*.[2] Both types of reason assumed that the universe was inherently reasonable and that there existed a sufficient measure of human rationality in man's thinking faculties. Adams was a rationalist to the extent that he thought critically and analytically and believed that the world could be understood in proportion to man's ability to understand the laws of nature. As an intellectual, he also believed that it was up to the "lawgivers and philosophers, to enlighten the people's understandings, and improve their morals, by good and general education." Yet Adams could not bring himself to believe that the authority of political institutions lies in the rational nature of the individuals who make up society. With David Hume and the Scottish skeptics, he doubted that political man's volitions had a rational character; as to the irrational nature of the "laws of passion and action," he doubted that their causes could be known or, even if known, controlled.[3]

Such somber conclusions forced Adams to take issue with the seemingly more optimistic convictions of the many ancient philosophers he had admired. In the *Defence* he quoted at length several passages from Cicero's *De Re Publica* in order to define republicanism. He also drew upon Plato's *Republic* to sketch the degeneration of various polities from the ideal republic to timocracy, oligarchy, democracy, and tyranny. But Adams could not rely upon reason in politics because he doubted that man's cognitive faculties were sufficient to overcome his sinful nature:

> If Socrates and Plato, Cicero and Seneca, Hutchinson and Butler, are to be credited, reason is rightfully supreme in man, and therefore it would be most suitable to the reason of mankind to have no civil or political government at all. The moral government of God, and his vicegerent Conscience, ought to be sufficient to restrain men to obedience to justice and benevolence, at all times and in all places; we must therefore descend from the

[2] Ernst Cassirer, *The Philosophy of the Enlightenment*, trans. Fritz C. Koelln and James P. Pettegrove (Boston, 1955).

[3] John Adams, *A Defence of the Constitutions of Government of the United States of America*, 3 vols. (1787–88; reprint ed., New York, 1971), 3:385–86.

dignity of our nature, when we think of civil government at all. But the nature of mankind is one thing, and the reason of mankind another; and the first has the same relation to the last as the whole to a part: the passions and appetites are parts of human nature as well as reason and the moral sense. In the institution of government, it must be remembered, that although reason ought to govern individuals, it certainly never did since the Fall, and never will till the Millennium; and human nature must be taken as it is, as it has been, and will be.[4]

(2) *The promise of virtue.* Closely related to the Enlightenment's claims for reason was the promise of virtue that had been inherited from classical antiquity. In the *Defence* Adams scrutinized all the meanings of virtue: the Roman ideals of courage and manliness, the ancient principles of prudence, justice, temperance, and fortitude, and even the Christian concept, "so much more sublime," observed Adams, of Jonathan Edwards's Calvinist ethic of "universal benevolence." Of all the concepts of virtue, the one that troubled Adams most was Montesquieu's notion of the individual sacrificing his private interests for the sake of the public good. The idea that man could go against his natural inclinations and engage in what Montesquieu called "a renouncement of self" seemed preposterous to Adams. Thus Adams rejected Montesquieu's definition of a republic as a regime in which virtue prevails over all the self-regarding motives. "If the absence of avarice is necessary to republican virtue, can you find any age or country in which republican virtue has existed?"[5]

The various ways Adams critically analyzed and then refuted the classical idea of civic virtue need not be elaborated here.[6] But the sources he drew upon do bear mentioning, for they were a curious combination of Calvinist faith and Humean doubt. First the Christian reminder: "To expect self-denial from men, when they have a majority in their favour, and consequently power to gratify themselves, is to disbelieve

[4] Ibid., p. 363.

[5] Ibid., pp. 488–89.

[6] On this point see John P. Diggins, *The Lost Soul of American Politics: Virtue, Self-Interest, and the Foundations of Liberalism* (New York, 1984).

all history and universal experience; it is to disbelieve Revelation and the Word of God, which informs us, [that] the
heart is deceitful above all things, and desperately wicked."
Then the Scottish connection: "I am not often satisfied with
the opinions of Hume, but in this he seems well founded,
that all projects of government founded in the supposition
or expectation of extraordinary degrees of virtue are evi-
dently chimerical."[7] Adams, as we shall see, disagreed with
Hume over the matter of political representation, but he did
share the philosopher's skepticism about the prospect of reason subduing the passions, and education and the Enlightenment leading to a future reign of virtue.[8]

(3) *Liberty as power.* Two decades after its publication, Adams's
Defence provoked John Taylor of Caroline into writing *An
Inquiry into the Principles and Policy of the Government of the
United States.* Taylor raised the awkward question of how it
was possible to insist, as did Adams, that the American Constitution as a system of mechanistic structures was "virtuous"
while the people it governed were regarded as "vicious." He
also wondered how a system of government so preoccupied
with controlling power could sustain liberty. Perhaps Taylor
was trying to recapture the older, Revolutionary distinction,
which had been pronounced in Montesquieu's writings, between liberty as defined as independence of another's will,
and power as something determined by forces external to
one's own will. The distinction appeared to be part of the
ideological origins of the Revolution. According to Bernard
Bailyn, in much of whig opposition thought liberty had been
regarded as the antithesis of power, the assumption being
that the former signified freedom from restraint and the latter the coercions of the state. However valid that distinction
may have been in the 1770s, in the post-Revolutionary situation the Federalists had to come to grips with power and to
demonstrate that its augmentation in the new central govern-

[7] Adams, *Defence,* 3:289; John Adams to Samuel Adams, Oct. 18, 1770,
in Adrienne Koch, ed., *The American Enlightenment* (New York, 1965),
p. 201.

[8] Adams, *Defence,* 1:158.

ment would be compatible with liberty. Thus, in his reply to Taylor, Adams felt it necessary to reconsider liberty as itself a form of power. Like Alexander Hamilton in the *Federalist,* Adams considered liberty as efficacy, the ability to do something whether right or wrong:

> Liberty, according to my metaphysics, is an intellectual quality, an attribute that belongs not to fate nor chance. Neither possesses it, neither is capable of it. There is nothing moral or immoral in the idea of it. The definition of it is a self-determining power in the intellectual agent. It implies thought and choice and power; it can elect between objects, indifferent in point of morality, neither morally good nor morally evil. If the substance in which the quality, attribute, adjective—call it what you will, exists, has a moral sense, a conscience, a moral faculty; if it can distinguish between moral good and moral evil, and has power to choose the former and refuse the latter, it can, if it will, choose the evil and reject the good, as we see in experience it often does.[9]

Whether or not Adams's idea of liberty as the power to choose and act had been influenced by Hume, his conviction that liberty must be subordinated to law would have been readily endorsed by the Scottish philosopher. Assuming with Hume that freedom can only be secured through order and established procedures, Adams rejected Turgot's claim that a citizenry dedicated to the "public good" is sufficient to insure the rights of both minorities and majorities. Nor could he agree with Turgot that the honored dictum that "liberty consists in being subject to the laws only" contradicts the republican principle stipulating the "general interest" must prevail in all cases. Adams found absurd the French claim that "human nature is so fond of liberty, that, if the whole society were consulted, a majority would never be found to put chains upon themselves, by their own act and voluntary consent." Adams could hardly believe that man's attachment to liberty was so deep a commitment as to be a natural right

[9] John Adams to John Taylor of Caroline, Apr. 15, 1814, in George A. Peek, ed., *The Political Writings of John Adams* (Indianapolis, 1954), p. 196; Bernard Bailyn, *The Ideological Origins of the American Revolution* (Cambridge, Mass., 1967).

which he would never forsake or alienate. Thus, "all men, as well as republican writers, must agree, that there can be no uninterrupted enjoyment of liberty, nor any good government, in society, without laws, or where standing laws do not govern."[10]

(4) *Liberty and property.* In the eighteenth century it was commonly assumed that liberty and property were synonymous, and that power followed property. No one, not even the most severe critic of the Constitution, not even Thomas Paine, who would become a hero to later generations of radicals, questioned the conventional assumption that property provided the foundation of liberty. Some French writers, however, did raise the issue of property on the eve of their own revolution. This was particularly true of Gabriel Bonnet de Mably, a writer Adams had earlier befriended when he proffered advice on undertaking a book on the American Revolution. In the *Defence* and elsewhere, Adams, though expressing great respect for Mably, felt compelled to challenge the Frenchman's notion that austerity and equality of wealth provided the healthiest basis for political society. Mably even went so far as to claim that the desire for wealth arises from the "envy" and "avarice" born only in situations of inequality. Thus Adams had to defend not only property but the psychology of motivation behind it.

It is curious that in the Constitution property received no conceptual definition and that even in the more theoretical *Federalist* Hamilton and James Madison did not pause to provide a philosophical rationale for the institution. In the *Defence* Adams also avoided relating property to a philosophical doctrine like natural right. In the liberal, Lockean tradition, for example, it was assumed that property arises from man's adding value to natural objects by means of his own labor. And because labor is the essential means of preserving life, man had a natural right to the products of his labor. Adams did not partake in this Lockean tradition that held up productive man as moral man. Indeed, he seems closer to the Scottish tradition that saw property as a social convention

[10] Adams, *Defence*, 1:128.

deriving from custom and habit. The desire to possess property, as opposed to actually creating wealth, may have more to do with leisure and pride than labor and productivity. Adams also assumed, as did some Scottish philosophers, the scarcity of goods in relation to the infinite nature of human needs and desires, and he, too, believed that man had no innate drive to be productive. "Indolence is the natural character of man to such a degree that nothing but the necessities of hunger, thirst, and other wants equally pressing can stimulate him to action, until education is introduced in civilized societies and the strongest motives of ambition to excel in arts, trades, and professions are established in the minds of all men. Until this emulation is introduced, the lazy savage holds property in too little estimation to give himself trouble for the preservation or acquisition of it." Assuming human nature to be basically lazy and indolent, and assuming as well that America could witness a country in which the majority are without property and the vital work habits, Adams came close to predicting the outbreak of class warfare unless the propertied minority were protected under the Constitution:

> Suppose a nation, rich and poor, high and low, ten millions in number, all assembled together; not more than one or two millions will have lands, houses, or any personal property; if we take into account the women and children, or even if we leave them out of the question, a great majority of every nation is wholly destitute of property, except a small quantity of clothes, and a few trifles of other movables. . . . Property is surely a right of mankind as really as liberty. Perhaps, at first, prejudice, habit, shame, or fear, principle or religion, would restrain the poor from attacking the rich, and the idle from usurping the industrious; but the time would not be long before courage and enterprize would come, and pretexts be invented by degrees, to countenance the majority in dividing all the property among them, or at least in sharing it equally with its present possessors. Debts would be abolished first; taxes laid heavy on the rich, and not at all on others; and at last a downright equal division of every thing be demanded, and voted. What would be the consequence of this? The idle, the vicious, the intemperate, would rush into the utmost extravagance of debauchery, sell and spend all their share, and then demand a new division of those who purchased from them. The moment the idea is admitted into

society, that property is not as sacred as the laws of God, and that there is not a force of law and public justice to protect it, anarchy and tyranny commence.[11]

This passage warrants quoting in full for two reasons. First, it indicates that Adams saw the threat of tyranny coming not from the executive branch, as in classical republicanism, but from the masses of people themselves. Second, and perhaps more important, when Tocqueville visited America a half century later he saw many of Adams's worst fears realized in the "tyranny of the majority," and yet property remained as safe as ever. Why the many became no threat to the few in America is a problem that we shall leave to Tocqueville to explain later in the paper.

(5) *Equality.* Perhaps nowhere was the distinction between the French and Scottish Enlightenments greater than on the issue of equality. Adams could accept with Thomas Jefferson the Lockean principle that all men are "created equal" in the sense that in the state of nature no one has the authority to dominate another, and everyone has the right to self-preservation. In this respect all people are entitled to equality of the law and the right to participate in the legislative branches of government. But Jean-Jacques Rousseau's *Discourse sur inégalité*, which depicted the modern world of private property and unequal social classes as a deviation from the primitive conditions of noble savagery, could hardly be endorsed by Adams, Hume, and Adam Smith, all of whom defended various degrees of ownership as an incentive to work and progress. Then in 1790, during the first stage of the French Revolution when the aristocracy lost its status and privileges and a general assault was waged against all forms of social distinctions, Adams responded with a series of newspaper articles later collected and published as *Discourses on Davila.* Here he drew upon Smith's analysis of ambition and the origins of distinction and ranks to explain why, in contrast to Rousseau's claim of natural equality, society conspires with man's human propensities to produce different class strata

[11] Ibid., 3:216–17.

because people are driven by a desire to outdo one another and achieve recognition. "We are told that our friends, the National Assembly of France," scoffs Adams, "have abolished all distinctions. But be not deceived, my dear countrymen. Impossibilities cannot be performed. Have they levelled all fortunes, and equally divided all property? Have they made all men and women equally elegant, wise, and beautiful. . . . Have they blotted out of all memories, the names, places of abode, and illustrious actions of all their ancestors?"[12]

As we shall see shortly, Adams's conviction about the desirability of social distinctions was not based on the assumption that a given class is superior to others but on a theory of human action that derived straight from Adam Smith. Indeed it was Jefferson, not Adams, who believed in the possibility of a "natural aristocracy" that would be superior because of its virtues and talents. Adams agreed with the Scots that all social phenomena are as "artificial" as distinctions are inevitable. Ironically, it was the Jefferson who believed in equality who condoned slavery whereas Adams could both uphold the necessity of class distinctions and condemn slavery.

(6) *The inevitability of classes.* To those historians and social scientists of the 1950s who told us that America is an "open-class society," one in which the whole notion of class relations was too European an idea to apply, it must surely seem strange that the major author who defended the Constitution against its European critics argued the case for class. Here one encounters another irony in American intellectual history. Many former Marxists came to believe in American "exceptionalism," the conviction that America's historical development was unique and therefore would not lend itself to an orthodox class analysis. This view had also been entertained, however passingly, by Karl Marx himself and by Friedrich Engels and Antonio Gramsci, and in the eighteenth century it was emphatically upheld by Turgot, Mably, and

[12] John Adams, *Discourses on Davila* (1805; reprint ed., New York, 1973), p. 78.

116

other French critics of the American Constitution.[13] The latter philosophers wondered why America's state constitutions, and later the federal, had to be so mired in a mosaic of checks and balances. America was not England; it did not possess the social constituencies of the Old World—monarchy, aristocracy, commons: the one, the few, and the many. Why disperse power among differentiated class strata when America remained an undifferentiated mass of people? Why have an upper and lower house when America had no aristocracy? Why have an executive branch when America had no king?

It was Adams's deep conviction that America would replicate Europe's social structure and produce "monarchical," "aristocratical," and "democratical" constituencies that preferred to be governed by either a single leader, an educated elite, or by the voice of the majority. It mattered little to Adams that America had no feudal heritage and established aristocracy, for he remained convinced that the "passion for distinction" was a universal trait of human nature whose manifestation did not necessarily depend upon historical circumstances. Even patriotism, a fundamental virtue in classical republicanism, evolved from the emotion of pride, and Adams agreed with Smith and Adam Ferguson that pride was instinctual and beyond the control of the rational faculties:

> Perhaps it may be said, that in America we have no distinctions of ranks, and therefore shall not be liable to those divisions and discords which spring from them; but have we not labourers, yeomen, gentlemen, esquires, honourable gentlemen, and excellent gentlemen? and are these distinctions established by law? have they not been established by our ancestors from the first plantation of the country? and are not those distinctions as earnestly desired and sought, as titles, garters, and ribbons are in any nation of Europe? We may look as wise, and moralize as gravely as we will; we may call this desire of distinction childish and silly; but we cannot alter the nature of men: human nature is thus childish and silly; and its Author has made it so, undoubtedly for wise purposes; and it is setting ourselves up to be wiser

[13] See John P. Diggins, "Comrades and Citizens: New Mythologies in American Historiography," *American Historical Review* 90 (1985):614–49.

than Nature, and more philosophical than Providence, to censure it. All that we can say in America is, that legal distinctions, titles, powers, and privileges, are not hereditary; but that the disposition to artificial distinctions, to titles, and ribbons, and to the hereditary descent of them, is ardent in America, we may see by the institution of the Cincinnati. There is not a more remarkable phenomenon in universal history, nor in universal human nature, than this order. The officers of the army, who had voluntarily engaged in a service under the authority of the people, whose creation and preservation was upon the principle that the body of the people were the only fountain of power and of honour; officers too as enlightened and as virtuous as ever served in any army; the moment they had answered the end of their creation, instituted titles and ribbons, and hereditary descents, by their own authority only, without the consent or knowledge of the people, or their representatives or legislatures.[14]

(7) *Class realities, classical politics, and the French Enlightenment.* Strictly speaking, there was nothing in Adams's observations of the behavior of the Cincinnati that would have disturbed the exponent of classical republicanism. Niccolò Machiavelli himself expected glory to be accorded to those who first conquered power and established a republic. And Adams, Hamilton, and other Federalists believed that "fame" and "honor" were among men's deepest motives. But Adams's larger point was to demonstrate that social "divisions" grew out of such emotions, whether they were the desire for military glory, wealth and its conspicuous display, or social status and its haughty mannerisms. What this meant was that political power was a phenomenon of social class, for without class divisions there would be no need for a "balanced" government to control them. And Adams made it clear that power was inexorable since it reflected the emotions from which it sprung. Power was not, as it was for Rousseau and later for Marx, some independent force that stood over and above man and stunted his full human development. Rather than being alien to man, it was inherent in his own nature. What, then, was to be done?

Machiavelli, the brilliant Florentine who understood poli-

[14] Adams, *Defence*, 3:207–8.

tics as the struggle for power among men, was wise enough to see that only out of the ceaseless clash of opposing groups can liberty survive. But somewhere along the way of Machiavellianism's historical evolution the principle of pluralism was lost from sight; and by the time of the French Enlightenment, Rousseau, whom the historian J. G. A. Pocock along with many other scholars regards as the heir of Machiavelli, sought to reformulate classical republicanism. Rousseau regarded the history of power as the history of man's alienation from forces beyond his control. Equality and virtue, Rousseau insisted, could only be realized by constructing a polity that would resist the divisiveness of commercial society and liberal politics. Here is another instance where Adams drew upon the Scottish Enlightenment to refute the French.

Smith, Hume, and Ferguson had argued, in contrast to Rousseau, that commerce could be virtuous and just, that liberty could be sustained in a state of conflict, and that society itself could survive and prosper without the rational designs of the philosopher. "The public interest is often secure," wrote Ferguson, "not because individuals are disposed to regard it as the end of their conduct, but because each, in his place, is determined to preserve his own. Liberty is maintained by the continued differences and oppositions of numbers, not by their concurring zeal in behalf of equitable government."[15] Adams adopted such reasoning in his reply to the French critics of the Constitution who wanted to see a unicameral legislature and no emphatic separation of powers. Whereas Rousseau and his followers had identified society with the unanimity of the "general will," Adams denied that all power could be invested in a single entity such as a national assembly that presumably would represent all the people. Whereas the classical tradition had insisted that the purpose of politics was to transcend the differences among interest groups, Adams and the *Federalist* authors recognized such differences ("factions") as permanent, natural, and unalterable. Thanks to the Scottish philosophers, Adams could equate liberty not with unity but diversity, and liberty would survive precisely because America was a class society that defied the heritage of classical politics.

[15] Adam Ferguson, *An Essay on the History of Civil Society* (New Brunswick, N.J., 1980), p. 128.

(8) *Commerce and corruption.* The French Enlightenment sought to demonstrate to the world that society could be rearranged according to the rational nature of man. For Rousseau, man's true nature could be realized to the extent that he rediscovered his natural condition and used it as the norm with which to criticize the creature comforts that accompany progress and modernity. Rousseau was a romantic as well as a rationalist, and he believed that man's passions, instead of needing to be controlled as outlined in the *Federalist,* could be made to serve the public good by means of citizen participation and the nurturing of civic culture and religion. Above all, Rousseau and other radical exponents of the Enlightenment regarded civic virtue as incompatible with commerce, and thus they saw as the mission of classical republicanism the unswerving resistance to the coming of bourgeois society—an idea put into practice in Robespierre's reign of terror in the name of virtue.

Thinkers of the Scottish Enlightenment had postulated a different set of propositions about the meaning and direction of history and, indeed, the meaning and value of life. They were less interested in showing how political virtue is to be sustained than in explaining how wealth is created and liberty preserved in the face of an emergent market economy. Thus Hume relied on self-interest as both a motive of explanation and the motor of economic progress. Society, Hume pointed out, is held together not by "passion for the public good" but by "a spirit of avarice and industry, art and luxury."[16] His friend Adam Smith, who addressed Rousseau in a series of articles in the *Edinburgh Review* in 1756, refused to see the moral degeneration of people as the precondition of progress and social and civil life. On the contrary, Smith held that the pursuit of self-interest emancipated man from natural scarcity and thereby enlarged the possibility of human freedom.[17]

[16] David Hume, "Of Commerce," in *David Hume: Political Essays,* ed. Charles W. Hendel (New York, 1953), pp. 130–41.

[17] Louis Schneider, *The Scottish Moralists on Human Nature and Society* (Chicago, 1967); on Adam Smith and Jean-Jacques Rousseau, see Michael Ignatieff, *The Needs of Strangers* (New York, 1984), pp. 105–32.

In the *Defence* Adams shared the Scottish thinkers' skepticism about the incompatibility of virtue and commerce. What led to the decline and fall of the Roman republic was not the economic pursuits of its citizens but the poorly conceived political system in which they had to live, particularly the absence, as we shall see, of any reliable technique of balancing power. The lesson of Rome "may lead us to doubt the universality of the doctrine, that commerce corrupts manners." [18] Adams believed with Hume that the austere Spartan state had distorted man's natural drives and thereby smothered the lifeblood of liberty instead of nurturing it. But he also believed that democracy fed the appetite for affluence. In the "late war," he noted, Americans delighted in the influx of huge amounts of money, and "without the least degree of prudence, foresight, consideration, or measure, rushed headlong into a greater degree of luxury than ought to have crept in in a hundred years." Yet the war was fought, the Revolution won, and the Constitution established. The lesson?

A free people are the most addicted to luxury of any: that equality which they enjoy, and in which they glory, inspires them with sentiments which hurry them into luxury. A citizen perceives his fellow-citizen, whom he holds his equal, [to] have a better coat or hat, a better house or horse, than himself, and sees his neighbours are struck with it, talk of it, and respect him for it: he cannot bear it; he must and will be upon a level with him. Such an emulation as this takes place in every neighbourhood, in every family; among artisans, husbandmen, labourers, as much as between dukes and marquisses, and more—these are all nearly equal in dress, and are now distinguished by other marks. Declamations, oratory, poetry, sermons, against luxury, riches, and commerce, will never have much effect: the most rigorous sumptuary laws will have little more. [19]

Sensitive to the gaudy spectacle of luxury, Adams nevertheless saw no way to turn back the clock as he questioned the classical assumption that a properly constructed political

[18] Adams, *Defence*, 1:212.

[19] Ibid., 3:336–37.

system could restrain such behavior. "But what has poverty or riches to do with the form of government? If mankind must be voluntarily poor in order to be free, it is too late in the age of the world to preach liberty."[20] How then should liberty be preached?

(9) *The primacy of the executive and the end of the republican doctrine of legislative supremacy.* Adams answered that question in one simple statement: "The Romans charged the ruin of their commonwealth to luxury: they might have charged it to the want of a balance in their constitution."[21]

In the entire three volumes of the *Defence,* a variation of this statement appears again and again. It goes to the heart of Adams's quarrel with both Machiavelli and the French Enlightenment, and it represents one instance where Adams departs from the Scottish Enlightenment. Many of the Scottish philosophers treated politics as a branch of sociology in that they tended to see law and political systems as reflecting society's conflicts rather than causing them. Adams, in contrast, saw political institutions as primary and determinative, so crucial that one weak conceptual joint in the architecture of government could bring down the entire edifice like a house of cards.

In the *Defence* Adams praised Machiavelli "to whom the world is so much indebted for the revival of reason in matters of government, and who appears to have been himself so much indebted to the writings of Plato and Aristotle."[22] But Adams questioned Machiavelli's "pious exhortations" about virtue and patriotism and asked readers to take a closer look at what was really going on in Roman and Florentine history. As did the Oxford historian Ronald Syme a century and a half later, Adams insisted that the high-sounding rhetoric of ancient politics merely concealed the deeper, uglier factional strife, and that the cry of *libertas* was really in the service of

[20] Ibid., p. 339.

[21] Ibid., p. 337.

[22] Ibid., 2:114.

power.[23] Although Adams was pleased to find that Machiavelli also looked to politics as a means through which man can gratify his ambitions, he concluded that the Florentine had a misleading view of human motivation. Thus he quoted from *The History of Florence*. "The commonwealth," wrote Machiavelli, "might have continued quiet and happy, if the nobility could have been content to confine themselves within the bounds of that moderation which is requisite in all republican governments." Why, asked Adams, would the nobility or any faction be content or moderate under any form of government? "When we know human nature to be utterly incapable of this content, why should we suppose it? Human nature is querulous and discontented wherever it appears, and almost all the happiness it is capable of arises from this discontented humour. It is action, not rest, that constitutes our pleasure."[24] Machiavelli had assumed that the man of virtue would be the citizen of few needs. Adams the Calvinist and Scottish skeptic believed that all men are creatures of insatiable desires. But the even more serious flaw in Machiavelli's reasoning was not so much motivational as institutional, and here Adams emerged as much a political architect as a social psychologist.

Adams appreciated Machiavelli's perception of social conflict, and he agreed that politics in Rome was basically a contest between the patricians and the plebians and in Florence between the Guelphs and the Ghibellines. But whether conflict derived from class tensions or filial rivalry, why could it not be controlled? Machiavelli erred, according to Adams, in attributing the collapse of ancient republics to either the exigencies of "fortune," the selfish ambitions of individual leaders or factions, or the lack of political imagination on the part of the prince. Adams replied that ancient republics collapsed because their leaders failed to balance class against class, the rich against the poor, and the many who were poor against the few who were rich. The only mechanism for achieving

[23] Ronald Syme, *The Roman Revolution* (New York, 1960), esp. chap. 11 on "Political Catchwords," pp. 148–61.

[24] Adams, *Defence*, 2:45–46.

such a balance was the executive branch of government, which Machiavelli failed to distinguish sufficiently from the legislative branch in his idea of a representative council system. Adams saw the executive branch as moderating factional strife and controlling class warfare. "A balance can never be established between two orders in society, without a third to aid the weakest."[25] Adams's concern for the weaker class led him to rebuke Hume for weighting representation in favor of the senate against the lower house. Hume failed to consider, Adams observed, that a senate behaves even worse after the expulsion of the king; now it can, as an unfettered nobility in a purely republican form of government, manipulate and dominate the representatives of the people.[26] Adams would isolate (or impose a "polite ostracism" upon) wealthy elites in the upper house so they would be unable to prey upon members of the lower, while at the same time government could both exploit their abilities and control their power in order to "have the benefit of their wisdom, without fear of their passions." But the key institution that Adams prized was the executive:

> The rich . . . ought to have an effectual barrier in the constitution against being robbed, plundered, and murdered, as well as the poor; and this can never be without an independent senate. The poor should have a bulwark against the same dangers and oppressions; and this can never be without a house of representatives of the people. But neither the rich nor the poor can be defended by their respective guardians in the constitution, without an executive power, vested with a negative, equal to either, to hold the balance even between them, and decide when they cannot agree. If it is asked, When will this negative be used? it may be answered, Perhaps never: the known existence of it will prevent all occasion to exercise it; but if it has not a being, the want of it will be felt every day.[27]

In the *Defence* Adams answered the European critics of the Constitution with much the same reasoning he used against

[25] Ibid., 1:108.

[26] Ibid., pp. 369–71.

[27] Ibid., p. 140, 3:294.

Hume and Machiavelli. Mably, Turgot, and Marchamont Nedham had argued that America had no need of bicameral legislatures and a strict separation of powers because the New World lacked the constituencies those divisions were designed to represent. They also maintained that external controls were unnecessary since the people were themselves the best guardians of their interests and liberties. Thus in the New World all power could be invested in "the centre," a single assembly representing all the people and requiring no mediating executive. In response Adams pointed out that there is no such thing as "the people," since the masses do not meet, think, discuss, and arrive at conclusions together. There are only discrete social divisions whose interests must be represented by the discrete branches of government.[28]

In addition to denying the motivational efficacy of the idea of virtue,[29] there are several other ways in which Adams's *Defence* departed from the conventions of classical republicanism. First of all, Adams saw the danger to republics as inherent in the people and their representatives who needed to be controlled, and not in the corrupt few who manipulate ministerial politics and compromise the principle of separation of powers. Moreover, Adams had a kind of Calvinist-Newtonian concept of politics as the inexorable movement of power whose path could only be halted by counterforce. Thus the only answer to power in one branch of government was equal power in another. Politics was never unitary but binary, and it required the mediation of an independent force. What this meant was that politics presupposed opposition, the factional interest group behavior that had been the scourge of classical ideals. Finally, there is Adams's deep conviction about the primacy of the third branch of government. In denying any role for the executive, the French critics of the American Constitution were rejecting the lessons of their own Montesquieu, perhaps because they saw monarchy as the only source of tyranny. But Adams saw the abuse of power as even more threatening in a national assembly claiming all sovereign authority. As a result, he made the separation of

[28] Ibid., 3:209–374.

[29] See Diggins, *American Politics*, pp. 69–99.

powers so paramount that his *Defence* signified the abandonment of the classical republican assumption that in all circumstances the legislature is the supreme branch of government.

(10) *The human condition.* Although it had antecedents in Polybius and Montesquieu, Adams's adamant conviction about the absolute necessity of the separation of powers was in many respects his own contribution to political thought. The reasons why he felt such institutional controls were so vital involved a theory of human nature that derived from Scottish philosophy as well as his own Calvinist ancestry. His view of man as restless, weak, and divided against himself at the core of his being is a portrait of the human condition that seems to echo more of twentieth-century existentialism than the eighteenth century age of reason. "You and I," he wrote in a letter to Dr. Richard Price in the *Defence,*

> admire the fable of Tristram Shandy more than the fable of the Bees, and agree with Butler rather than Hobbes. It is weakness rather than wickedness which renders men unfit to be trusted with unlimited power. The passions are all unlimited; nature has left them so: if they could be bounded, they would be extinct; and there is no doubt they are of indispensable importance in the present system. They certainly increase too, by exercise, like the body. The love of gold grows faster than the heap of acquisition; the love of praise increases by every gratification, till it stings like an adder, and bites like a serpent; till the man is miserable every moment when he does not snuff the incense: ambition strengthens at every advance, and at last takes possession of the whole soul so absolutely, that the man sees nothing in the world of importance to others, or himself, but in his object. The subtilty of these three passions, which have been selected from all the others because they are aristocratical passions, in subduing all others, and even the understanding itself, if not the conscience too, until they become absolute and imperious masters of the whole mind, is a curious speculation.[30]

Curious indeed. Adams is almost Freudian in his insight that the self plays hide and seek within the mind. But many

[30] Adams, *Defence,* 1:129–30.

of Adams's convictions—that liberty cannot be unified, equality realized, conflict eliminated, and the passions subdued—derived from Scottish thought. As Zoltán Haraszti discovered many years ago, the central thrust of Adams's analysis and argument in *Discourses on Davila* was little more than a paraphrase of one of the chapters in Adam Smith's *Theory of Moral Sentiments*.[31] Drawing on the motivational insights of Smith, Adams could develop better his own ideas on ambition, labor, emulation, and the passions for approbation, recognition, and distinction. He agreed fully with Smith that poverty is felt as a sign of disgrace and therefore man is motivated to work not merely for reasons of food and clothing but to acquire wealth as a badge of prestige. So great is the "desire for the attention, consideration, and congratulations of mankind," that human beings will even go against their self-interest to attain it: "To be wholly overlooked and to know it, are intolerable. Instances of this are not uncommon. When a wretch could no longer attract the notice of a man, woman, or child, he must be respectable in the eyes of his dog.—'Who will love me then?' was the pathetic reply of one, who starved himself to feed his mastiff, to a charitable passenger, who advised him to kill or sell the animal. In this *'who will love me then,'* there is a key to the human heart—to the history of human life and manners—and to the rise and fall of Empires."[32]

Adams's and Smith's perceptions of the sociological determinants of behavior presage the writings of Thorstein Veblen, as Arthur O. Lovejoy has noted.[33] Such perceptions also anticipate David Riesman's other-directed man and even Arthur Miller's *Death of a Salesman*, whose protagonist Willy Loman desperately identifies success with being "well liked." The market economy breeds a peculiar personality type; capitalism and competition register not so much the quest for profits as the self's need to be recognized by others. Yet while it is well known that Adams drew upon Smith for his insights

[31] Zoltán Haraszti, *John Adams and the Prophets of Progress* (New York, 1964), pp. 168–71.

[32] Adams, *Discourses*, pp. 35–36.

[33] Arthur O. Lovejoy, *Reflections on Human Nature* (Baltimore, 1961).

into the human condition, it is less noted that he drew the opposite conclusion.

Smith assumed that all behavior dissolved into the social relations of economic man, and as an intransigent individualist his pursuit of riches contributed to the general wealth of society. Adams, in contrast, distrusted economic man acting on his own natural impulses. Smith believed that individual actions had unintended social consequences, and hence selfish impulses translated into social benefits in a laissez-faire economy. Adams saw no irony between intention and outcome, at least not to the extent that he could feel confident that the new market economy would subdue the ravaging passions and rivalries that had destroyed the ancient and medieval republics. Nor did Adams ever entertain the notion—one that would become popularized by his admirer Hannah Arendt—that "public man" is somehow morally superior to private man. According to Arendt and other neoclassical scholars, the individual rises above his egoistic nature to the extent he leaves his private life behind and, as a citizen, expresses himself in politics and speech, participates rather than competes in the public realm, finds fulfillment in human relations and the life of action rather than mediation and the life of thought, and dedicates himself to the commonwealth, civic virtue, and "public happiness."[34]

Arendt was fond of quoting Adams's dictum that "it is action, not rest, that constitutes our pleasure."[35] Yet Adams, it will be recalled, made that observation in response to Machiavelli's naïveté when he wondered why the Roman nobility would not rest content with what it had. Adams saw men acting in the public realm not out of any sense of civic duty but rather because they had no morally autonomous private self, no identity or inner essence to give them the strength to resist society and endure a life of solitude apart from the reassuring gaze of others, a life in which the greatest fear was that no one will love them. Out of need to be recognized and loved, men desire power and wealth, and their desires are insatiable because they are prompted by "emulation," not by

[34] Hannah Arendt, *On Revolution* (New York, 1963).

[35] Ibid., p. 196.

what they need but what others have and value. "Action" signified for Adams not the medium in which political ideals are fulfilled but the alienated human condition that compels man to seek in motion what cannot be found in introspection. Thus all actions, whether those of Smith's economic man or of Arendt's political man, must be subjected to political controls.

But must they? The conclusion of this paper will attempt to answer that question by considering the observations of Alexis de Tocqueville.

Tocqueville's *Democracy in America* (1835–38) appears in some respects a reiteration of the French criticisms of the American Constitution that had been earlier registered at the time of its enactment. A man of democratic sympathies but aristocratic sensibilities, Tocqueville could hardly endorse the radical egalitarianism of Rousseau and writers like Mably and Turgot. Yet he agreed with them that almost all the balancing structural mechanisms of the American Constitution were unnecessary:

> I have always considered what is called a mixed government to be a chimera. There is in truth no such thing as a mixed government (in the sense usually given to the words), since in any society one finds in the end some principle of action that dominates all others.
>
> Eighteenth-century England, which has been especially cited as an example of this type of government, was an essentially aristocratic state, although it contained within itself great elements of democracy, for laws and mores were so designed that the aristocracy could always prevail in the long run and manage public affairs as it wished.
>
> The mistake is due to those who, constantly seeing the interests of the great in conflict with those of the people, have thought only about the struggle and have not paid attention to the result thereof, which was more important. When a society really does have a mixed government, that is to say, one equally shared between contrary principles, either a revolution breaks out or that society breaks up.[36]

[36] Alexis de Tocqueville, *Democracy in America*, ed. J. P. Mayer, trans. George Lawrence (Garden City, N.Y., 1969), p. 251.

Adams, who had indeed looked to England as the model for America, defended the American Constitution as a "mixed" and "balanced" government that promised both to represent and control discrete social divisions and thereby preserve liberty and protect property. Tocqueville, in contrast, argued that any society driven by contrary principles, by what Adams assumed to be an aristocratic elite in the Senate and the democratic mass in the House, would either break out in revolution or break up as a unit. Adams, in further contrast, expected violence and social disorder to be prevented by the soundness of America's governmental structure, and thus what remained fundamental over all other considerations—over economics, culture, and even religion—was the primacy of political institutions. Toward such an assumption Tocqueville could only be impatient, as indicated in a letter written to a friend in 1853:

> You say that institutions are only half my subject. I go farther than you, and I say that they are not even half. You know my ideas well enough to know that I accord institutions only a secondary influence on the destiny of men. Would to God I believed more in the omnipotence of institutions! I would have more hope for our future, because by chance we might, someday, stumble onto the precious piece of paper that would contain the recipe for all the wrongs, or on the man who knew the recipe. But, alas, there is no such thing, and I am quite convinced that political societies are not what their laws make them, but what sentiments, beliefs, ideas, habits of the heart, and the spirit of the men who form them, prepare them in advance to be, as well as what nature and education have made them.[37]

That the nature of society cannot be understood through its political institutions was also a premise of Scottish philosophy. But on this matter Adams remained closer to classical republicanism in viewing political institutions as absolutely indispensable in both understanding society and controlling it. The assumption was that the disorders of the social environment could be subdued to the extent that the mode of

[37] Alexis de Tocqueville, *Selected Letters on Politics and Society*, ed. Roger Boesche, trans. James Toupin and Roger Boesche (Berkeley, 1985), p. 294.

representation accurately reflected the polity's constituencies. Thus Adams, convinced America was reproducing Europe's social divisions, defended the Constitution on the grounds that a "mixed" government could best balance such divisions against one another. In short, he defended the Constitution on the basis of conflict when in reality it proved to be successful only because of the extent of consensus.[38]

One wonders what Tocqueville would say today about America's bicentennial celebration of the Constitution. One aim of *Democracy in America* was to suggest that the ideas set forth at the Philadelphia Convention in 1787 are not reliable guides to explaining the success of the new Republic. Tocqueville was the first "consensus" scholar, the first to see that, in contrast to the expectations of the Framers, Americans shared the same values and sentiments regarding property, labor, equality, liberty, and opportunity, the bourgeois values that became, along with religion and social mores, "habits of the heart." Where Adams and the Framers believed that political institutions must prevail over society and its citizens, Tocqueville saw all authority gravitating to society and its shifting and turbulent majorities. And where Adams saw all men driven by a "passion for distinction," Tocqueville saw all Americans driven by a desire to join, belong, submit, and conform.

There remains a further distinction between Adams and Tocqueville that returns us to the eighteenth-century debate over the Constitution. Unlike Tocqueville, Adams did not regard America as exceptional and instead saw its constitutional system as having transnational significance since it supposedly drew upon universal principles of political conduct. The French, however, believed that the new America was unique and that the "mixed" form of government Adams advocated, based on balancing its departments against one another, should be rejected both in Philadelphia and in Paris. In the first place, America had no antagonistic social strata requiring political control; in the second, France, which had inherited such strata like a historical curse, would only per-

---

[38] For an excellent analysis of the Framers' mistaken assumptions about conflict, see Louis Hartz, *The Liberal Tradition in America: An Interpretation of American Political Thought since the Revolution* (New York, 1955).

petuate the privileges of the old order by continuing with "mixed" government.[39] Adams insisted, with the *Federalist* authors, that the causes of faction could never be eliminated, hence their effects must be controlled. The French were just as certain that the abuses of class society could not be controlled without eliminating the political apparatus that had protected the few from the many, the idle aristocracy from the industrious bourgeoisie. But here Adams not only anticipates Marx in seeing class structures as inevitable regardless of the system of government, he goes further in insisting that power and exploitation will remain a permanent phenomenon even after property relations have been transformed unless institutional safeguards are established.

The ultimate irony of Adams's *Defence* is that it may have become less relevant to America than to France. If the Framers wrote the Constitution assuming America could not escape Europe's social divisions, the French forged their revolution assuming that they could escape them and dispense with the political mechanisms necessary to restrain them. Both proved wrong. Adams and the *Federalist* authors took it for granted that property and democracy were incompatible, and thus it followed that the few needed to be protected from the many, that bicameral legislatures were necessary because authority resides in the Senate and power in the people, and that a strong executive was essential in mediating social conflict. Such assumptions collapse under Tocqueville's observations of Jacksonian America, where the tyranny of the majority prevails yet poses no threat to property and where authority becomes little more than public opinion. What, then, remains of Adams's magisterial *Defence*? If Adams failed to grasp the exceptional nature of America, he did have a keen grasp of the nature of power as a phenomenon that cannot be abolished because it reflects the emotions and drives from which it sprung. Thus Adams may be credited for having predicted the course of the French Revolution as the tyranny of a single national assembly proclaiming sovereign authority without a mediating executive. Adams's pre-

---

[39] See the valuable study by Edward Handler, *America and Europe in the Political Thought of John Adams* (Cambridge, Mass., 1964).

dictions came several years before Edmund Burke's better-known reflections on the subject. But Adams shed no tears over the fate of the French aristocracy. Neither Calvinism nor Scottish commercialism had any place for the idle rich.

EDWARD J. ERLER

The Political Philosophy of the Constitution

As it was more than probable we were now digesting a plan
which in its operation would decide forever the fate of Republican Government we ought not only to provide every guard to
liberty that its preservation could require, but be equally careful
to supply the defects which our own experience had particularly pointed out.—JAMES MADISON

It has been frequently remarked that it seems to have been reserved to the people of this country, by their conduct and example, to decide the important question, whether societies of
men are really capable or not of establishing good government
from reflection and choice, or whether they are forever des-
tined to depend for their political constitutions on accident and
force.—ALEXANDER HAMILTON

ON THE OCCASION of the bicentennial of the Constitution, the
nation was confronted once again with a vigorous debate
about the origins of the regime. This time the debate concerned whether the origins—the intentions of the Framers—
should be the authoritative touchstone of constitutional interpretation. Controversies about the meaning and significance of the Constitution are hardly surprising, since they
form the most characteristic—and unique—feature of our
political life. In one way or another, all our important political
questions become constitutional questions, and these questions always—explicitly or implicitly—involve the character

NOTE: My epigraphs are from a speech of Madison's, June 26, 1787, at the
Convention, and from *Federalist* No. 1.

of the Founding. For it is the Founding that reveals the "standard maxim" of our political life, one that did not grow from a mythical or prehistoric past but was based on the universal principle that "all men are created equal." The origins of America thus exist in the full light of day and can be subjected to the most precise scrutiny. In great measure, the character of our national politics has depended upon the way in which we have viewed the work of the Founders.

The last few years have witnessed an extraordinary public debate between the attorney general of the United States and several members of the Supreme Court. This debate invites us once again to consider the meaning of the Constitution as an expression of first principles. Attorney General Edwin Meese advocated what he called a "jurisprudence of original intention" as an antidote to increased judicial activism.[1] He described the main outlines of this approach in the following terms: "Where the language of the Constitution is specific, it must be obeyed. Where there is a demonstrable consensus among the framers and ratifiers as to a principle stated or implied by the Constitution, it should be followed. Where there is ambiguity as to the precise meaning or reach of a constitutional provision, it should be interpreted and applied in a manner so as to at least not contradict the text of the Constitution itself."[2] This jurisprudential stance, Meese contended, is a necessary inference from the fact of a written constitution. The Constitution is organic law and thus superior in authority to any legislative enactment or interpretation by the Supreme Court.

Justice William Brennan responded to the attorney general's call for a return to the text of the Constitution by replying that it was both impossible and undesirable to attempt to interpret the Constitution in the light of the Framers' intentions: "Those who would restrict claims of right to the values of 1789 specifically articulated in the Constitution turn a blind eye to social progress and eschew adaptation of over-

[1] Edwin Meese, "Speech before the American Bar Association," July 9, 1985, reprinted in *The Great Debate: Interpreting Our Written Constitution* (Washington, D.C., 1986), p. 9.

[2] Edwin Meese, "Speech before the District of Columbia Chapter of the Federalist Society," Nov. 15, 1985, ibid., p. 36.

arching principles to changes of social circumstances."[3] The Constitution, according to Brennan, "is a sublime oration on the dignity of man, a bold commitment by a people to the idea of libertarian dignity protected through law."[4] But "the demands of human dignity will never cease to evolve."[5] Thus, the "sublime oration" on human dignity must be continually reinterpreted. And, of course, the principal role in the revision of the text belongs to the judiciary because, as Brennan notes, "judicial power resides in the authority to give meaning to the Constitution."[6]

There are some special demands of human dignity, however, that do not evolve. Being "fixed and immutable,"[7] these demands are somehow immune from social progress and evolution. The most dramatic of these, according to Brennan, relates to capital punishment. The Constitution explicitly excludes capital punishment from its proscription against "cruel and unusual punishment" by referring in the Fifth Amendment to "capital crimes" and by providing in the same amendment that "no person" can be deprived of "life, liberty, or property without due process of law." This latter provision, of course, clearly indicates that *with* due process of law, "persons" can be deprived of life. But the evolving standards of human dignity now dictate, according to Justice Brennan, that "capital punishment is under all circumstances cruel and unusual punishment prohibited by the Eighth and Fourteenth Amendments."[8] The Eighth Amendment was, of course, passed contemporaneously with the Fifth Amendment and therefore cannot possibly have been intended to proscribe capital punishment. An adherence to the literal language of the Constitution, in Brennan's view, would thus

[3] William Brennan, "The Constitution of the United States: Contemporary Ratification," Text and Teaching Symposium, Georgetown University, Oct. 12, 1985, ibid., p. 15.

[4] Ibid., p. 18.

[5] Ibid., p. 23.

[6] Ibid., p. 14.

[7] Ibid., p. 23.

[8] Ibid.

deny the Constitution's potential for serving as the vehicle of social progress. Brennan does not, however, attempt to explain how it is possible for some "fixed and immutable" demands to exist in a universe of constant change and progress. Perhaps these exceptions to progress are demanded by progress itself! Justice Brennan is strangely silent on this crucial point.

In any case, for Brennan, the original Constitution, before the advent of the Bill of Rights and the Reconstruction amendments, did not address the issue of human dignity, being almost exclusively concerned with the "abilities and disabilities of government." It was only the progressive evolution of the Constitution away from its defective origins that transformed it into "a sparkling vision of the supremacy of the human dignity of every individual."[9] Justice Thurgood Marshall joined the fray on the side of Justice Brennan, noting that during the bicentennial we should not be celebrating the work of the Framers, but the work of those who refused to acquiesce in the Framers' "outdated notions of 'liberty,' 'justice,' and 'equality.'"[10] The Constitution's compromise with slavery, according to Marshall, was a fatal defect that could not be remedied within the terms of the original document. "While the Union survived the civil war, the Constitution did not. In its place arose a new, more promising basis for justice and equality, the 14th Amendment, ensuring protection of the life, liberty, and property of *all* persons against deprivations without due process, and guaranteeing equal protection of the laws."[11] Thus, Marshall views the Fourteenth Amendment not as a completion of the principles embodied in the Constitution, but as a repudiation of the original document. For both Marshall and Brennan the origins (and the intentions of the Framers) can no longer be regarded as authoritative.

This contemporary debate necessarily impels us to a consideration of first principles. For it is only through a proper

[9] Ibid., p. 18.

[10] Thurgood Marshall, "Speech to the San Francisco Patent and Trademark Law Association," Maui, Hawaii, May 6, 1987.

[11] Ibid.

understanding of the origins of the regime that we can understand the character of this controversy about the principles of constitutional interpretation. If we find that somehow the origins are defective or outmoded, then the jurisprudence that looks upon the Constitution merely as a procedural instrument to facilitate social progress would certainly make more sense than the jurisprudence of original intent. If, on the other hand, the Founding has more theoretical and principled substance than Brennan and Marshall are willing to admit, then some version of an original intent jurisprudence is demanded by political prudence.

During the course of the debate in the Massachusetts ratifying convention in 1788, Fisher Ames, a leading Federalist, remarked in his defense of the new Constitution that "legislators have at length condescended to speak the language of philosophy; and if we adopt it, we shall demonstrate to the sneering world, who deride liberty because they have lost it, that the principles of our government are as free as the spirit of our people."[12] It seems rather curious to us today that Ames would refer to the Constitution as a philosophic document. One does not ordinarily speak of "the philosophy of the Constitution," because we know that constitutions are political, not philosophic, documents. We are more apt to view the Framers as pragmatists rather than philosophers. Indeed, we pride ourselves on being realists, able to see through what has been called "the lost language of the Enlightenment,"[13] a language replete with references to such concepts as natural rights and natural law. Our conceit is that we can understand the work of the Framers better than the Framers understood it themselves. After all, their reference to "the laws of nature and nature's God" as the ground of political right is symbolic not only of their own "romantic" self-delusions, but of the self-delusions of their age as well. Scientific realism has taught us that the eighteenth-century idea of

[12] Jonathan Elliot, ed., *The Debates in the Several State Conventions, on the Adoption of the Federal Constitution*, 2d ed., 5 vols. (Philadelphia, 1937), 2:155.

[13] Garry Wills, *Inventing America: Jefferson's Declaration of Independence* (New York, 1978), p. xiv.

"nature" cannot provide the standard of political justice be-cause—in the terms of one contemporary philosopher—na-ture is merely a "lottery," arbitrarily dispensing benefits and disadvantages. From this point of view, the ground of justice is not, as the Framers believed, "the laws of nature," but pos-itive laws which have as their explicit purpose the correction of the arbitrariness of nature.[14]

The most thorough and vigorous academic attempt to ex-pose the defects of the origins was undertaken by Charles A. Beard in his *Economic Interpretation of the Constitution of the United States* (1913). Beard's contribution was to portray the Framers as unprincipled men who created an undemocratic government designed to further their own class interests. Douglass Adair wrote that it was Beard's purpose "to expose the nature of [the] Constitution, to unmask its hidden fea-tures in order to show that it deserved no veneration, no respect, and should carry no authority to democratic Amer-icans of the twentieth century."[15] What Beard seemed to re-veal about the proceedings of the Constitutional Convention was that under the thin veneer of public-spiritedness affected by the delegates was a sinister and self-conscious aggrandize-ment of their own class interests. The Constitution, while masquerading as a democratic document, is really an eco-nomic document embodying the dominant class relations of the day. This interpretation, Beard remarked, is not to be gleaned from the language of the Constitution itself; rather, "the true inwardness of the Constitution" is revealed in the examination of the class interests of those who framed it.[16] The Constitution, therefore, is not to be viewed as a docu-ment with any theoretical or principled integrity. But as Adair cogently pointed out, this "economic interpretation" excludes the possibility of any theoretical interpretation *a*

[14] John Rawls, *A Theory of Justice* (Cambridge, Mass., 1971), p. 74.

[15] Douglass Adair, "The Tenth Federalist Revisited," in Trevor Col-bourn, ed., *Fame and the Founding Fathers: Essays by Douglass Adair* (New York, 1974), p. 85.

[16] Charles A. Beard, *An Economic Interpretation of the Constitution of the United States* (1913; reprint ed., New York, 1965), p. 152.

priori. After all, from the point of view of class analysis, theory or principle is only an epiphenomenon of the more basic (and more revealing) economic relationships.

> The Fathers, as pictured by Beard, were "practical" men who, knowing exactly what they wanted in the way of concrete economic privileges, were willing to stage a "coup d'état" to gain their ends. Collectively they were exhibited as being adepts in the use of force, fraud, and false propaganda. Beard gives no hint, however, that political theory played any consequential role in creating the Constitution; speculation there was in plenty in the Convention, but it was land and debt speculation, not speculative thought. Indeed, if it is possible to determine an individual's political motives by cataloguing his property, the irrelevance of theory should be apparent.[17]

While the details of Beard's economic interpretation were refuted long ago, the main thrust of his argument survives— the Framers were pragmatists who had little use for theory or principle except insofar as it was necessary to provide a gloss upon their interest-group brokering.

In 1961 John Roche published an essay entitled "The Founding Fathers: A Reform Caucus in Action."[18] In the intervening years this article has taken on the status of a minor classic.

[17] Adair, "Tenth Federalist Revisited," pp. 87–88. The same point of view is taken by Stanley Elkins and Eric McKitrick, "Youth and the Continental Vision," in Leonard W. Levy, ed., *Essays on the Making of the Constitution,* 2d ed. (New York, 1987), pp. 224–26 (originally published as "The Founding Fathers: Young Men of the Revolution," *Political Science Quarterly* 76 [1961]:181–216). In an early critique of Beard, Charles Warren, in his *The Making of the Constitution* (Boston, 1928), pp. 77–78, wrote that "an alignment of men as for or against a new Constitution, on the basis of property or non-property credits or debts, is an attempted simplification of the political situation in 1787, which facts and human nature do not support. It is impossible to draw a hard and fast economic line with reference to the attitude of classes of men towards the Constitution, and omit all consideration of their political faiths, ideals, inherited sentiments, personal antagonisms, past experience and patriotic desires. . . . It is faulty history to describe the subjects of division in 1787 in terms of class consciousness, for such a social phenomena did not then exist."

[18] John P. Roche, "The Founding Fathers: A Reform Caucus in Action," *American Political Science Review* 55 (1961):799–816.

Roche's thesis was straightforward and simple: "While the shades of Locke and Montesquieu *may* have been hovering in the background, and the delegates *may* have been unconscious instruments of a transcendent *telos,* the careful observer of the day-to-day work of the Convention finds no over-arching principles."[19] The concerns of the Framers, Roche continues, "were highly practical . . . they spent little time canvassing abstractions."[20] Their real business, instead, "was to hammer out a pragmatic compromise which would both bolster the 'National interest' and be acceptable to the people. What inspiration they got came from their collective experience as professional politicians in a democratic society."[21] The Constitution was therefore a "makeshift affair."[22] Roche's concern, unlike Beard's, is not that the Constitution was undemocratic, but that it established an unprincipled or pragmatic democracy. From this point of view—the view that has come to dominate scholarship—the Constitution is nothing more than a "bundle of compromises," a pragmatic accommodation of the various competing interests that were represented at the Convention. And, like all pragmatists, the Framers valued practice above principle—indeed, principle was no part of their practical calculations.

In Roche's view it was later generations—following the lead of the authors of *The Federalist*—who falsely imported into the Constitution "a high theoretical content."[23] Later interpreters sought to give the Convention proceedings some theoretical dignity in order to endow the Framers with the public-spirited motives they so conspicuously lacked. Perhaps those who seek a principled interpretation of the Founding are merely engaged in the necessary task of obscuring the origins of the regime by disguising the pragmatic machinations of the Framers. The Framers were hard-headed realists; it is the benefactors of their work who indulge in romantic theorizing.

[19] Ibid., p. 816.

[20] Ibid., p. 809.

[21] Ibid., p. 799.

[22] Ibid., p. 812.

[23] Ibid., p. 811.

According to Roche, the best example of the Framers' will-ingness to engage in pragmatic compromise is the "Rube Goldberg mechanism" of the electoral college: "It was merely a jerry-rigged improvisation which has subsequently been en-dowed with a high theoretical content."[24] During the course of the Convention, the mode of electing the president (as well as the other branches) was dominated by considerations drawn from the *principle* of the separation of powers. James Madison adumbrated that principle at the Convention to the general approbation of the members: "If it had been a fun-damental principle of free Govt. that the Legislative, Execu-tive & Judiciary powers should be *separately* exercised; it is equally so that they be *independently* exercised."[25] It was no simple task to provide for the independence of the various branches in a government that was intended to be "wholly popular." As Montesquieu had pointed out, it was easier to establish a constitutional separation of powers in a mixed regime because the different (and independent) interests of the classes in society would be reflected in the government itself.[26] There had been proposals in the Convention to have the president elected by Congress. But it was quickly recog-nized that this would compromise the independence of the executive and vitiate his role in the separation of powers. All proposals to have the president elected directly by the people were also rejected. Although direct election did not receive much support, it would also have tended to lessen the effec-tiveness of the separation of powers. To serve as a proper counterweight to the legislative branch, the president would have to have a *different* connection to the people, since it would be necessary on occasion for the president to serve the people "at the peril of their displeasure."[27] Thus, the mech-

[24] Ibid.

[25] Max Farrand, ed., *The Records of the Federal Convention of 1787*, rev. ed. 4 vols. (1937; reprint ed., New Haven, 1966), 2:56.

[26] See Edward J. Erler, "The Constitution and the Separation of Pow-ers," in Leonard W. Levy and Dennis J. Mahoney, eds., *The Framing and Ratification of the Constitution* (New York, 1987), pp. 151–66.

[27] *Federalist* No. 71, in Clinton Rossiter, ed., *The Federalist Papers* (New York, 1961), p. 432. See Gouveneur Morris's speech in Farrand, ed., *Rec-ords of the Convention*, 2:500; Harvey C. Mansfield, Jr., "Republicanizing

anism of the electoral college was designed specifically to produce not only an independent executive, but an energetic one as well. This mode of election—described by Alexander Hamilton as "if not perfect, at least excellent"—was dictated exclusively by considerations derived from the principle of the separation of powers. It appears jerry-built only from the perspective that presupposes that considerations of principle played no role in the Convention's deliberations.

Yet it is only too obvious that the Framers were not philosophers engaged in theoretical speculation—they were indeed practical politicians and only agitated questions of principle insofar as it was necessary to make prudential judgments. In other words, they were engaged in statesmanship—the accommodation of principle to particular circumstances. Even though the debates may have been tinged from time to time with the spirit of partisanship, the Framers did not regard the crucial compromises of the Convention as unprincipled accommodations. Instead, they saw themselves as statesmen adapting principle to meet the "exigencies of Government and the preservation of the Union." As Martin Diamond rightly noted, "The mere fact of compromise is not proof that principle, theory, and consistency were abandoned. Rather, the Framers successfully balanced the rival claims of theory and practical necessity. Despite the compromises which produced it, the Constitution is an essentially logical and consistent document resting upon a political philosophy. . . . Men of principle may properly make compromises when the compromises adequately preserve fundamental principle."[28] The crucial ingredient that is missing from

the Executive," in Charles Kessler, ed., *Saving the Revolution: The Federalist Papers and the American Founding* (New York, 1987), pp. 175–78; and Morton J. Frisch, "The Constitutional Convention and the Study of the American Founding," *Benchmark* 3 (1987):105.

[28] Martin Diamond, *The Founding of the Democratic Republic* (Itasca, Ill., 1981), p. 35. Winston Churchill, surely one of the greatest statesmen of the twentieth century, characterized the role of statesmanship in his essay "Consistency in Politics," published in 1932. "[A] Statesman in contact with the moving current of events and anxious to keep the ship on an even keel and steer a steady course may lean all his weight now on one side and now on the other. His arguments in each case when contrasted can be shown

Roche's account of the Convention is the element of political statesmanship. For Roche, there is no middle ground between a conclave of philosophers and an assemblage of democratic politicians who are unabashedly aggrandizing their own self-interest. In the political universe created by Roche, every compromise is ipso facto a departure from principle. But as Diamond seems to suggest, every compromise implies an agreement in principle—otherwise no compromise would be possible. It may be true that most of the delegates to the Convention "were impatient with speculations about government that were unconnected with a particular time and place."[29] But it is not true, as Roche insists, that the Framers were merely "practical politicians in a democratic society," inspired exclusively by "their own political futures."[30] Roche's view does not understand the statesmanship—the genuine politics—that was the real achievement of the delegates to the Convention. This is the reason he insists upon ludicrously characterizing it as "a reform caucus" when the delegates themselves knew (and stated) that they were recurring to "first principles."

Roche rightly notes that the Framers "*made* history and did it within the limits of consensus."[31] Consensus, of course, defines the necessary limits of statesmanship in a regime that rests upon the consent of the governed. But Roche has an extremely narrow view of the limits of consensus in 1787 and the capacity of the people to respond to democratic leadership. Roche's view, however, did find some expression in the

---

to be not only very different in character, but contradictory in spirit and opposite in direction: yet his object will throughout have remained the same. His resolves, his wishes, his outlook may have been unchanged; his methods may be verbally irreconcilable. We cannot call this inconsistency. In fact it may be claimed to be the truest consistency. The only way a man can remain consistent amid changing circumstances is to change with them while preserving the same dominating purpose" (*Amid These Storms: Thoughts and Adventures* [New York, 1932], p. 39).

[29] Herbert J. Storing, "The Constitutional Convention," in Morton J. Frisch and Richard Stevens, eds., *American Political Thought: The Philosophic Dimension of American Statesmanship*, 2d ed. (Itasca, Ill., 1983), p. 67.

[30] Roche, "Founding Fathers," p. 805.

[31] Ibid., p. 799.

Convention—*but it was far from the prevailing opinion.* Pierce Butler, for example, warned that "we must follow the example of Solon who gave the Athenians not the best Govt. he could devise; but the best they wd. receive."[32] William Paterson—the principal author of the New Jersey Plan—expressed a similar concern, but one which also stemmed from his skepticism about the legitimacy of the Convention's power to devise a constitution that was not strictly federal in character. "Our object," he said, "is not such a Governmt. as may be best in itself, but such a one as our Constituents have authorized us to prepare, and as they will approve."[33]

Madison's answer to these expressions of reticence was emphatic:

> If the opinions of the people were to be our guide, it wd. be difficult to say what course we ought to take. No member of the Convention could say what the opinions of his Constituents were at this time; much less could he say what they would think if possessed of the information & lights possessed by the members here; & still less what would be their way of thinking 6 or 12 months hence. We ought to consider what was right & necessary in itself for the attainment of a proper Governmt. A plan adjusted to this idea will recommend itself.[34]

Madison, of course, was not insensitive to the role of opinion in popular government.[35] Writing in *The Federalist,* he agreed

---

[32] Farrand, ed., *Records of the Convention,* 1:125; Gunning Bedford made nearly the same statement on June 30: "We must like Solon make such a Governt. as the people will approve" (ibid., p. 491).

[33] Ibid., 2:250.

[34] Ibid., 1:215.

[35] In an article for the *National Gazette* published Dec. 19, 1791, Madison wrote: "Public opinion sets bounds to every government, and is the real sovereign in every free one," in William T. Hutchinson et al., eds., *The Papers of James Madison,* 19 vols. to date (Chicago and Charlottesville, 1962-), 14:170. See also "Charters" (p. 192): "All power has been traced up to opinion. The stability of all governments and security of all rights may be traced to the same source. The most arbitrary government is controuled where the public opinion is fixed"; and "British Government" (p. 201): "The boasted equilibrium of this government, (so far as it is a reality) is maintained less by the distribution of its powers, than by the force of public opinion."

with Butler's assessment of Solon's role in formulating the Athenian constitution. Although "according to Plutarch" Solon had "the sole and absolute power of newmodeling the constitution" of Athens, he "confessed that he had not given to his countrymen the government best suited to their happiness, but most tolerable to their prejudices."[36] Madison demonstrated that he understood the problem perfectly when he noted that "the most rational government will not find it a superfluous advantage to have the prejudices of the community on its side."[37] But, as Madison also knew, in undertaking "the singular and solemn . . . experiment for correcting the errors of a system by which this crisis had been produced," "it is impossible for the people spontaneously and universally to move in concert towards their object; and it is therefore essential that such changes be instituted by some *informal and unauthorized propositions*, made by some patriotic and respectable citizen or number of citizens."[38] While the people are incapable of acting "spontaneously and universally," they are nonetheless "the only legitimate fountain of power."[39] Indeed, Madison wrote a few years later that "a republic involves the idea of popular rights. A representative republic *chuses* the wisdom, of which hereditary aristocracy has the *chance;* whilst it excludes the oppression of that form."[40] And the republican form of government, more than any other, presupposes the capacity of the people to make wise choices, although not necessarily in the sense of being able to formulate the choices in the first instance.

This is the precise sense in which Madison addressed the Convention on July 5:

> The Convention ought to pursue a plan which would bear the test of examination, which would be espoused & supported by

[36] *Federalist* No. 38, Rossiter, ed., *Federalist Papers*, pp. 232–33.

[37] *Federalist* No. 49, ibid., p. 315.

[38] *Federalist* No. 40, ibid., pp. 252–53.

[39] *Federalist* No. 49, ibid., p. 313; in *Federalist* No. 22 (p. 152), Alexander Hamilton had remarked that "the fabric of American empire ought to rest on the solid basis of THE CONSENT OF THE PEOPLE. The streams of national power ought to flow immediately from that pure, original fountain of all legitimate authority."

[40] Hutchinson et al., eds., *Papers of Madison*, 14:179.

the enlightened and impartial part of America, & which they could themselves vindicate & urge. It should be considered that altho' at first many may judge of the system recommended, by their opinion of the Convention, yet finally all will judge of the Convention by the system. The merits of the system alone can finally & effectually obtain the public suffrage. He was not apprehensive that the people of the small States would obstinately refuse to accede to a Govt. founded on just principles, and promising them substantial protection.[41]

This view was echoed many times during the course of the Convention. Gouverneur Morris, among others, spoke in support of Madison: "We must look forward to the effects of what we do. These alone ought to guide us. Much has been said of the sentiments of the people. They were unknown. They could not be known. All that we can infer is that if the plan we recommend be reasonable & right; all who have reasonable minds and sound intentions will embrace it, notwithstanding what had been said by some Gentlemen."[42] What made the Convention a valuable improvement "on the ancient mode of preparing and establishing regular plans of government" was the fact that the task of formulating the Constitution was given to a deliberative body serving as the representatives of the people and that the resulting plan was to be submitted to an *enlightened* citizenry for its approval. This was a situation totally unlike the one faced by Solon.[43] Ancient republicanism was not the model for the Convention's "select experiment" in republicanism.[44]

The argument in the Convention was not about the neces-

[41] Farrand, ed., *Records of the Convention*, 1:528.

[42] Ibid., pp. 529–30. See also p. 372: "Mr. Randolph feared we were going too far, in consulting popular prejudices. Whatever respect might be due to them, in lesser matters, or in cases where they formed the permanent character of the people, he thought it neither incumbent on nor honorable for the Convention, to sacrifice right & justice to that consideration"; and p. 474 (Hamilton): "We must therefore improve the opportunity, and render the present system as perfect as possible. Their good sense, and above all, the necessity of their affairs, will induce the people to adopt it."

[43] *Federalist* No. 38, Rossiter, ed., *Federalist Papers*, p. 233.

[44] Farrand, ed., *Records of the Convention*, 1:256 (Edmund Randolph).

sity of working within the bonds of consensus but what the consensus was. Roche argues that "a serious case can be made that the advocates of the New Jersey Plan, far from being ideological addicts of states'-rights, intended to substitute for the Virginia Plan a system which would both retain strong national power and have a chance of adoption in the states."[45] But there was much uncertainty expressed in the Convention about how much of a consensus existed in favor of the confederal form of government. James Wilson, for example, made the point that it was not the people so much as the state politicos who were opposed to a national government. His remark deserves to be quoted at length:

> With *regard to the sentiments of the people*, he conceived it difficult to know precisely what they are. Those of the particular circle in which one moved, were commonly mistaken for the general voice. He could not persuade himself that the State Govts. & sovereignties were so much the idols of the people, nor a natl. Govt. so obnoxious to them, as some supposed. . . . Where do the people look at present for relief from the evils of which they complain? Is it from an internal reform of their Govt.? No. Sir, It is from the Natl. Councils that relief is expected. For these reasons he did not fear, that the people would not follow us into a national Govt. and it will be a further recommendation of Mr. R.'s plan that it is to be submitted to *them* and not to the Legislatures, for ratification.[46]

This was a view that was frequently expressed in the Convention. It was not the people who were most likely to object to a plan that encroached upon the existing federal relationship, but those who held positions of power under that system.[47] Apart from considerations of legitimacy, the members

[45] Roche, "Founding Fathers," p. 806.

[46] Farrand, ed., *Records of the Convention*, 1:253.

[47] See, among others, ibid., p. 133 (James Wilson): "The opposition was to be expected . . . from the *Governments*, not from the Citizens of the States"; p. 49 (Wilson): "On examination it would be found that the opposition of States to federal measures had proceeded much more from the Officers of the States, than from the people at large"; p. 123 (Rufus King): "The Legislatures also being to lose power, will be most likely to raise objections. The people having already parted with the necessary powers it is

of the Convention were under no illusions that it was the people, not the state legislatures, who were most likely to look favorably upon the innovations contained in the new Constitution. And, as for the problem of legitimacy, this would be resolved by the acceptance of the people.[48] Ironically, a strong case could be made that the Convention was more representative of the sentiments of the people than the various state legislatures. Later events seem to support this assertion.

Roche cites John Dickinson's oft-quoted statement of August 13 as an expression of the general attitude of the delegates. During the course of a rather desultory argument about whether the lower house should have the exclusive power of originating money bills, Dickinson remarked that "experience must be our guide. Reason may mislead us."[49] This statement is conclusive evidence for Roche that the delegates were practical politicians, not men of theory or principle. But read in its proper context, Dickinson's statement does not support Roche's contention. In the debate over this question, *there was no principle at stake.*[50] "It was not Reason," Dickinson proclaimed, "that discovered the singular & ad-

---

immaterial to them, by which Government they are possessed, provided they be well employed"; p. 137 (George Read): "If we do not establish a good Govt. on new principles, we must either go to ruin, or have the work to do over again. The people at large are wrongly suspected of being averse to a Genl. Govt. The aversion lies among interested men who possess their confidence"; 2:476 (Madison): "Mr. Madison considered it best to require Conventions; Among other reasons, for this, that the powers given to the Genl. Govt. being taken from the State Govts the Legislatures would be more disinclined than conventions composed in part at least of other men; and if disinclined, they could devise modes apparently promoting, but really thwarting the ratification."

[48] See below.

[49] Roche, "Founding Fathers," p. 799 (John Dickinson's remark is found in Farrand, ed., *Records of the Convention,* 2:278). Similar importance is placed on William Peterson's remark of June 9: "A little practicable Virtue [is] preferable to Theory" (Roche, "Founding Fathers," p. 806; Farrand, ed., *Records of the Convention,* 1:186); this remark is recorded in Paterson's notes, but not those of Madison, King, or Robert Yates.

[50] Madison had remarked on June 13 that "commentators on the Brit: Const: had not yet agreed on the reason of the restriction on the H. of L.

mirable mechanism of the English Constitution. It was not Reason that discovered or ever could have discovered the odd & in the eye of those who are governed by reason, the absurd mode of trial by Jury. Accidents probably produced these discoveries, and experience has given a sanction to them. This is then our guide."[51] Dickinson was replying to Wilson and Madison who had earlier argued that the experience of vesting the power to initiate money bills in the lower house of the state legislatures had been a source of faction and contention. Dickinson denied that the short experience of the state legislatures outweighed the long experience of Great Britain. "Shall we oppose to this long experience," he mused, "the short experience of 11 years which we had ourselves, on this subject."[52] In this argument *both* sides appealed to experience; but the question could not be resolved on the basis of experience alone. Which experience was authoritative?[53]

In *The Federalist*, Madison wrote that in considering the central problems of republican government, "theoretic reasoning, in this as in all other cases, must be qualified by the lessons of practice."[54] Experience must always be tested in the

---

in money bills. Certain it was there could be no similar reason in the case before us" (Farrand, ed., *Records of the Convention*, 1:233).

[51] Ibid., 2:278.

[52] Ibid.

[53] John Rutledge outlined the dilemma nicely when he remarked in reply to Dickinson that "the friends of this motion are not consistent in their reasoning. They tell us that we ought to be guided by the long experience of G.B. & not our own experience of 11 years: and yet they themselves propose to depart from it. The H. of Commons not only have the exclusive right of originating, but the Lords are not allowed to alter or amend a money bill." Dickinson, of course, had supported the proposal restricting the origination of money bills to the House but allowing the Senate to amend. It is not surprising, therefore, that Rutledge would inquire as to what experience Dickinson was using for his guide, as it was obviously not that of Britain or the American states (ibid., p. 279).

[54] *Federalist* No. 43, Rossiter, ed., *Federalist Papers*, p. 276; in *Federalist* No. 20, ibid., p. 138, Madison had written that "experience is the oracle of truth; and where its responses are unequivocal they ought to be conclusive

light of some standard that is itself not a part of the historical experience. Experience, not theoretic reasoning, is the qualifier—theoretic reasoning is thus the principal ingredient in this amalgam of theory and practice that Madison understood to be statesmanship. Madison succinctly expressed the statesman's view of the matter in the notes compiled for his speech to the Convention on August 7: "We must not shut our eyes to the nature of man, nor to the light of experience."[55] Experience is the guide only when seen or interpreted in the light of human nature—that is, in the light of political philosophy.

To concede that the Convention delegates conceived of their task in eminently practical terms is not to concede that there was no principled integrity in their deliberations. Even Roche notes that "what is striking to one who analyzes the Convention as a case-study in democratic politics is the lack of clear-cut ideological divisions in the Convention. Indeed," Roche proclaims, "I submit that the evidence—Madison's *Notes*, the correspondence of the delegates, and debates on ratification—indicates that this was a remarkably homogeneous body on the ideological level."[56] It is unlikely that Roche's use of the term *ideological* is meant to convey the idea of theoretical principle, but it is close enough for our present purposes. What divided the delegates at the Convention was not so much issues of ideology or principle but the practical details of implementing those principles. The famous compromises of the Convention should be understood not as a sign of a lack of principle, but in fact as attempts to accommodate constitutional principle. The Constitution may indeed be described as a "bundle of compromises," but the compromises hammered out at the Convention—every one

---

and sacred." It is doubtful from the context, however, that Madison ever considered experience to be "unequivocal." For a penetrating discussion of this issue, see Douglass Adair, "'Experience Must Be Our Only Guide': History, Democratic Theory, and the United States Constitution," in Colbourn, ed., *Fame and the Founding Fathers*, p. 107.

[55] Farrand, ed., *Records of the Convention*, 3:451.

[56] Roche, "Founding Fathers," p. 803.

of them seeking accommodation of a particular point of view—took place within a common theoretical horizon. And this was the theoretical horizon that had been created by the Declaration of Independence, a document that, as Thomas Jefferson explained, "was intended to be an expression of the American mind."[57]

John Hancock, president of the Continental Congress, in his official letter transmitting the Declaration of Independence to the States remarked that "the important Consequences resulting to the American States from this Declaration of Independence, considered as the Ground and Foundation of a future Government, will naturally suggest the Propriety of proclaiming it in such a Mode, as that the People may be universally informed of it."[58] It is significant to note that from the beginning the Declaration was considered to be the "Ground and Foundation" of any future government or governments in America. On June 19, 1787, in the course of the Convention, Luther Martin, who later left without signing the Constitution, rose to remark that "the separation from G[reat] B[ritain] placed the 13 States in a state of nature towards each other; that they would have remained in that state till this time, but for the confederation."[59] Martin, of course, was an advocate of a strictly confederal form of government. But the question of whether the states had ever been in the state of nature with one another was not simply a metaphysical dispute. If the thirteen colonies achieved their independence of each other at the same time they gained their independence from Great Britain, then the arguments for a strong national government that entrenched upon state sovereignty could hardly be credited.

James Wilson of Pennsylvania rose to answer Martin, re-

[57] Thomas Jefferson to Henry Lee, May 8, 1825, Thomas Jefferson, *Writings,* ed. Merrill D. Peterson (New York, 1984), p. 1500.

[58] Paul H. Smith, ed., *Letters of Delegates to Congress, 1774–1789,* 16 vols. to date (Washington, D.C., 1979-), 4:396; see Dennis J. Mahoney, "Declaration of Independence," in Leonard W. Levy, Kenneth L. Karst, and Dennis J. Mahoney, eds., *The Encyclopedia of the American Constitution,* 4 vols. (New York, 1986), 2:545–46.

[59] Farrand, ed., *Records of the Convention,* 1:324.

marking that he "could not admit the doctrine that when the Colonies became independent of G. Britain, they became independent also of each other." As Madison recorded in his notes, Wilson "read the declaration of independence, observing thereon that the *United Colonies* were declared to be free & independent, not *Individually* but *Unitedly* and that they were confederated as they were independent, States." This speech of Wilson's was quickly seconded by Hamilton, who "denied the doctrine that the States were thrown into a State of nature."[60] The interesting point about this colloquy is that both arguments rested "on a deeper stratum of agreement— as any disagreement which can be compromised must. The basic understanding of government and individual rights expressed in the Declaration of Independence was taken for granted. . . . But different conclusions were drawn."[61]

Indeed, both the small and the large republic arguments were drawn from the Declaration. Both were about how best to secure the republican regime of natural rights specified in that document. Roger Sherman succinctly expressed this sentiment when he stated that "the question is not what rights naturally belong to men; but how they may be most equally & effectually guarded in Society."[62] As Herman Belz has recently written, "Republicanism was the political philosophy of the American Revolution."[63] The radical core of this political philosophy was the substitution of natural rights for historical rights—the natural rights of man for the historical rights of Englishmen. Harry Jaffa writes:

> The preamble to the Declaration of Independence may be a succinct restatement of the theory that underlay the English Revolution of 1688, but it had little in common with the public rhetoric of that revolution. The latter explicitly accused James II only of violating a traditional constitution, not of violating natural rights. The teachings of John Locke may have served to justify revolution to Englishmen after the event; they served to

[60] Ibid., see also p. 552 (Elbridge Gerry).

[61] Storing, "Constitutional Convention," p. 61.

[62] Farrand, ed., *Records of the Convention*, 1:450.

[63] Herman Belz, "Constitutionalism and the American Founding," in Levy, Karst, and Mahoney, eds., *Encyclopedia of the Constitution*, 2:483.

justify Americans *in* the event. It is doubtful that many Englishmen ever would have been swayed by an appeal to universal
human equality; it is undeniable that this appeal was most powerful in the American Revolution.[64]

In short, the radical core of the American Revolution was the
change from history to nature as the ground of political
right. And it was this change that supplied the ground of the
new Constitution.

Generally, this translated into the notion of a constitutional
government that not only derived its legitimate powers from
the consent of the governed but operated by means of consent. The central tenet of the Declaration of Independence—
the principle that "all men are created equal"—provided the
natural right foundation of American constitutionalism. For
in equality the Framers found a nonarbitrary point of departure for the establishment of political right; equality, after all,
is the abiding characteristic of human nature. And, because
equality is grounded in human nature, it necessarily points
to nature or natural right. The human species is unique in
that it is the only species that has no natural rulers; human
beings are free to choose—or at least have the potential to
choose—their form of government, a privilege that was accorded by nature's God to no other species. The human species is therefore unique, and the regime founded on the
recognition of this uniqueness will also be unique.[65]

I think there can be little doubt that the Framers were
attempting to put into practice the principles of the Declaration of Independence. It is long past the time when we
could take seriously Beard's implication that the Constitution
represented a Thermidorian reaction *against* the principles
of the Declaration. Yet the Constitution was not totally successful. Insofar as it allowed the continued existence of slavery, it could never be a complete expression of the principles
of the Declaration. It was only after the passage of the Re-

[64] Harry Jaffa, *Equality and Liberty* (New York, 1965), p. 126.

[65] I have discussed this question *in extenso* in "Natural Right in the American Founding," in J. Jackson Barlow, Leonard W. Levy, and Ken Masugi,
eds., *The American Founding: Essays on the Formation of the Constitution* (Westport, Conn., 1988), pp. 195–223.

construction amendments that it could be said that the Constitution came into formal harmony with the Declaration.

But however much slavery was tolerated as an act of political expedience, its tolerance was considered by the Framers as an *exception* to the principles of the Declaration. This point was neatly expressed by Representative William A. Newell arguing for the passage of the Fourteenth Amendment before the House of Representatives in February 1866:

> The combined wisdom of . . . patriotic men produced our present Constitution. It is a noble monument to their ability; but, unfortunately, like all human instruments, it was imperfectly constructed, not because the theory was wrong, but because of the existence in the country of an institution so contrary to the genius of free government, and to the very principles upon which the Constitution was founded, that it was impossible to incorporate it into the organic law so that the latter could be preserved free from its contaminating influence. . . . The framers of the Constitution did what they considered best under the circumstances. They made freedom the rule and slavery the exception in the organization of the Government. They declared in favor of the former in language the most emphatic and sublime in history, while they placed the latter, as they fondly hoped, in a position favorable for ultimate extinction.[66]

The Framers treated slavery as a *necessary* evil to be expunged from the polity as soon as circumstances would allow.

The greatest force working toward the abolition of slavery would be the regime's dedication to the principle that "all men are created equal." This dedication would ensure that slavery would be considered as an exception to the principle and therefore never a legitimate part of the regime. Only a denial of the principle—a denial that would destroy the regime itself—could therefore justify slavery. But this would not be a principled justification; its only basis would be force without right. As Abraham Lincoln—surely America's profoundest explicator of the Founding—explained in 1857, the authors of the Declaration

> did not mean to assert the obvious untruth, that all were then actually enjoying that equality, nor yet, that they were about to

[66] *Congressional Globe*, 39th Cong., 1st sess., p. 866.

confer it immediately upon them. In fact they had no power to confer such a boon. They mean simply to declare the *right*, so that the *enforcement* of it might follow as fast as circumstances should permit. They meant to set up a standard maxim for free society, which should be familiar to all, and revered by all; constantly looked to, constantly labored for, and even though never perfectly attained, constantly approximated, and thereby constantly spreading and deepening its influence. . . . The assertion that "all men are created equal" was of no practical use in effecting our separation from Great Britain; and it was placed in the Declaration, not for that, but for future use.[67]

The Declaration thus, in Lincoln's view, set up "a standard maxim" of political right, a maxim derived from natural human equality and therefore grounded in natural right. Stephen A. Douglas's "squatter sovereignty," which would have left the decision of whether "to vote slavery up or down" to local majorities, was simply grounded upon positivism—that is, the right of the stronger (and in democracies the stronger is the majority). And it was Douglas who insisted that the Declaration of Independence had meant only to include those of British descent. This doctrine, of course, became a leading tenet of the infamous *Dred Scott* decision. Had there been a move at the Convention to abolish slavery, the Convention would have collapsed and the Constitution would have been stillborn. As Madison and the more thoughtful Federalists realized, without a strong national government the prospects of ever abolishing slavery would be remote.

Madison pointed out in the Convention that the principal division was not between the large and small states but between the slaveholding and nonslaveholding states.[68] The reason for this remark by Madison is evident: the division between large and small states—however much it may have agitated the Convention—did not trench directly upon the question of republican principles; the division between slaveholding and nonslaveholding states did. As Madison noted

[67] Abraham Lincoln, "Speech at Springfield, Ill.," June 26, 1857, in Roy P. Basler, ed., *The Collected Works of Abraham Lincoln*, 9 vols. (New Brunswick, N.J., 1953–55), 2:406.

[68] Farrand, ed., *Records of the Convention*, 1:486.

during the Convention, "Where slavery exists, the Republican Theory becomes still more fallacious."[69] The question of federalism could reach a workable compromise without directly threatening the purity of the republican principles that informed the work of the Convention. The arguments about federalism, after all, were about what form of government, national or federal, would best *secure* republican principles. Madison and the other leading Federalists were adamant that republican liberty demanded an energetic national government, while those favoring a more confederal form of government were just as adamant that the best advantages for republican liberty were found in the state governments. But the question of slavery—while it too found its compromise in the Convention—was a compromise with republican principles. This was the tragic flaw of the Founding, a flaw that almost proved fatal to the republic in the Civil War. That it did not was due to the fact that it was still possible to rededicate the nation to those founding principles that had, by necessity, received only an incomplete expression in the Constitution. Contrary to what Justice Marshall has said, the Constitution did survive the Civil War; it was not replaced but completed by the Reconstruction amendments.

Frederick Douglass, a former slave and an abolitionist leader, understood the matter in precisely this light. In a speech delivered in February 1863, Douglass remarked that "the birth of our freedom is fixed on the day of the going forth of the Declaration of Independence." "The slaveholders," he continued, "are fighting for Slavery, and the slave system being against nature—they are fighting against the eternal laws of nature. . . . A great man once said it was useless to re-enact the laws of God, meaning thereby the laws of Nature. But a greater man than he will yet teach the world that it is useless to re-enact any other laws with any hope of their permanence."[70] A few months later, Douglass explained the importance of the Declaration as the ground of the Con-

[69] Ibid., p. 319.

[70] Frederick Douglass, "The Proclamation and a Negro Army: An Address Delivered in New York, on 6 February 1863," in John Blassingame, ed., *The Frederick Douglass Papers*, 3 vols. to date (New Haven, 1979-), 3:564, 554.

stitution: "I hold that the Federal Government was never, *in its essence,* anything but an anti-slavery Government. . . . If in its origin slavery had any relation to the Government, it was only as the scaffolding to the magnificent structure, to be removed as soon as the building was completed."[71] The essence of the Constitution, of course, found its expression in the arguments of the Declaration of Independence—those arguments derived from human nature and couched in the language of "the eternal laws of nature."

It is certain that the members of the Reconstruction Congress saw themselves as explicitly addressing the task of completing the regime of the Founding. This was the thrust of the remarks of Representative Thaddeus Stevens before the House of Representatives in May 1866:

> I beg gentlemen to consider the magnitude of the task which was imposed upon the [Joint Committee on Reconstruction]. They were expected to suggest a plan for rebuilding a shattered nation—a nation which though not dissevered was yet shaken and riven . . . through four years of bloody war. It cannot be denied that this terrible struggle sprang from the vicious principles incorporated into the institutions of our country. Our fathers had been compelled to postpone the principles of their great Declaration, and wait for their full establishment till a more propitious time. That time ought to be present now.[72]

References to the Declaration of Independence as "organic law" were so frequent throughout the debates in the thirty-ninth Congress that it can hardly be doubted that the Reconstruction Congress was, in some sense, self-consciously attempting to restore the Declaration as the authoritative source of the Constitution's principles.[73]

[71] Frederick Douglass, "Negroes and the National War Effort: An Address Delivered in Philadelphia, Pennsylvania, on 6 July 1863," ibid., p. 596 (emphasis added).

[72] *Congressional Globe,* 39th Cong., 1st sess., p. 2459.

[73] See Daniel A. Farber and John E. Muench, "The Ideological Origins of the Fourteenth Amendment," *Constitutional Commentary* 1 (1984):259, 272.

A delicate question arose at the Convention with respect to its authority to propose a new Constitution. The Continental Congress had called the Convention "for the sole purpose of revising the Articles of Confederation, and reporting to Congress and the several Legislatures, such alterations and provisions therein, as shall . . . render the Federal Constitution adequate to the exigencies of Government, and the preservation of the Union."[74] The leading Federalists in the Convention did not try to disguise the fact that they wished to scrap the Articles of Confederation and erect a "real and regular Government, as contradistinguished from the old Federal system."[75] Madison's study of ancient and modern confederacies had convinced him that a confederacy could not be the foundation of genuine government. He told his fellow delegates that the Articles of Confederation rested on "improper principles," and that no amount of reform could transform it into a viable form of government.[76] As Hamilton later wrote in *The Federalist,* "The great and radical vice in the construction of the existing Confederation is in the principle of LEGISLATION for STATES or GOVERNMENTS, in their CORPORATE or COLLECTIVE CAPACITIES, and as contradistinguished from the INDIVIDUALS of whom they consist."[77] Hamilton's critique of those who still argued for the confederal principle was devastating: "They seem still to aim at things repugnant and irreconcilable; at an augmentation of federal authority without a diminution of State authority; at sovereignty in the Union and complete independence in the members. They still, in fine, seem to cherish with blind devotion the political monster of an *imperium in imperio.*"[78] Thus, as Madison explained, the "exigencies of Government" required that the principle of Confederation must give way to the national

[74] Quoted in *Federalist* No. 40, Rossiter, ed., *Federalist Papers,* pp. 247–48.

[75] Madison to Jared Sparks, Nov. 25, 1831, quoted in Warren, *Making of the Constitution,* p. 116.

[76] Farrand, ed., *Records of the Convention,* 2:8.

[77] *Federalist* No. 15, Rossiter, ed., *Federalist Papers,* p. 108.

[78] Ibid.

principle, and if some believed that it was politically impossible to recommend a national government, then it was possible to recommend one that was "partly national and partly federal" in form, but national in principle.

The Convention, Madison argued, was charged with accomplishing two principal objects: revising the Articles of Confederation and rendering the federal Constitution "adequate to the exigencies of government." In Madison's view, the two charges, at bottom, were contradictory. The Convention was therefore forced to choose the more important of the two—providing for the "exigencies of government." Ultimately, however, Madison had resort to the Declaration to justify the work of the Convention. Its members, he wrote, "must have reflected that in all great changes of established governments forms ought to give way to substance; that a rigid adherence in such cases to the former would render nominal and nugatory the transcendent and precious right of the people to 'abolish or alter their governments as to them shall seem most likely to effect their safety and happiness.'"[79] Thus Madison justified the Convention's work by an appeal to natural right, reasoning that the members of the Convention "must have borne in mind that as the plan to be framed and proposed was to be submitted to *the people themselves,* the disapprobation of this supreme authority would destroy it forever; its approbation blot out antecedent errors and irregularities."[80]

Another question touched upon the legitimacy of the Convention's work, that is, its decision not to follow the forms prescribed for ratification by the Articles of Confederation, which required submission to the state legislatures. Instead, the Convention chose to submit the new Constitution directly to the people. This became a matter of some controversy at the Convention, and some delegates were troubled by what they regarded as the highhandedness of the proposal. On June 5 Roger Sherman argued that popular ratification was unnecessary since the Articles already provided for the assent by the state legislatures. Madison was quick to respond, re-

[79] *Federalist* No. 40, ibid., p. 253.

[80] Ibid.

vealing the importance of the mode of ratification: if the state legislatures were allowed to approve the new instrument of government, the implication would be that the states were creating the new federal government and the whole would "be considered as a Treaty only of a particular sort, among the Governments of Independent States. . . . For these reasons as well as others he thought it indispensable that the new Constitution should be ratified in the most unexceptionable form, and by the supreme authority of the people themselves."[81]

The idea that the people were the ultimate authorities in republican government was a theme that was frequently voiced within the secret confines of the Convention proceedings. The decisive exchange on the manner of ratification occurred on August 31, near the end of the Convention's deliberations. Many delegates had come to realize that following the procedures of allowing state legislatures to pass on the new Constitution would likely spell its doom. Gouverneur Morris on this day "said he meant to facilitate the adoption of the plan, by leaving the modes approved by the several State Constitutions to be followed." Madison at this point was forced into making a very revealing speech supporting ratification by conventions chosen by the people. He noted that submitting the Constitution to the state legislatures would not succeed because "the powers given to the Genl. Govt. being taken from the State Govts the Legislatures would be more disinclined than conventions composed in part at least of other men; and if disinclined, they could devise modes apparently promoting, but really thwarting the ratification. . . . The people were in fact, the fountain of all power, and by resorting to them, all difficulties were got over." In this instance, Madison concluded, "first principles might be resorted to."[82]

As expected, Luther Martin rose to oppose Madison, pointing out "the danger of commotions from a resort to the

[81] Farrand, ed., *Records of the Convention*, 1:122–23.

[82] Ibid., 2:476. In a remark earlier in the proceedings that went largely unnoticed, Randolph spoke to this point with the utmost boldness: "There are certainly reasons of a peculiar nature where the ordinary cautions must be dispensed with; and this is certainly one of them. He wd. not as

people & first principles in which the Governments might be on one side & the people on the other." Rufus King replied that the states "must have contemplated a recurrence to first principles before they sent deputies to this Convention." With this, the Convention consented to the "resort to first principles" by approving the proposal to submit the Constitution to conventions chosen by the people.[83]

In his explanation of the Convention's decision in *The Federalist*, Madison was quite explicit. He called it a question "of a very delicate nature" to determine "on what principle the Confederation, which stands in the solemn form of a compact among the States, can be superseded without the unanimous consent of the parties to it." This question, he said, "is answered at once by recurring to the absolute necessity of the case; to the great principle of self-preservation; to the transcendent law of nature and of nature's God, which declares that the safety and happiness of society are the objects at which all political institutions aim and to which all such institutions must be sacrificed."[84] Here, then, at almost the literary center of *The Federalist* is Madison's reference to "the transcendent law of nature and of nature's God" as being the object of the resort to first principles. Everyone, of course, recognized this quotation as being from the Declaration of Independence. No one could have mistaken Madison's intention in relying on the Declaration to answer this question of such "a very delicate nature." The ultimate foundation of the Constitution is the Declaration and its requirement that all legitimate government be derived from the consent of the governed. And, as Madison noted later in *The Federalist,* the central tenet of "republican theory" holds that "the people are the only legitimate fountain of power, and it is from them that the constitutional charter under which the several branches of government hold their power, is derived."[85] This,

---

far as depended on him leave any thing that seemed necessary, undone. The present moment is favorable, and is probably the last that will offer" (1:255).

[83] Ibid.

[84] *Federalist* No. 43, Rossiter, ed., *Federalist Papers,* p. 279.

[85] *Federalist* No. 49, ibid., pp. 313–14.

Madison notes, is the greatest expression of the"manly spirit" of the Revolution.[86]

I think that there can be little doubt that the Framers of the Constitution were self-consciously attempting to give practical effect to those natural rights principles that had been enunciated in the Declaration of Independence. The spirit that pervaded the Convention was one of engaging in a great republican experiment. And if there were some whose sentiments disposed them in the direction of a mixed regime— and there were some—even they recognized that the lack of a preexisting class structure and the republican"genius" of the people would make anything but a republic impossible. As Madison wrote in *The Federalist,* "The first question that offers itself is whether the general form and aspect of the government be strictly republican. It is evident that no other form would be reconcilable with the genius of the people of America; with the fundamental principles of the Revolution; or with that honorable determination which animates every votary of freedom to rest all our political experiments on the capacity of mankind for self-government. If the plan of the convention, therefore, be found to depart from the republican character, its advocates must abandon it as no longer defensible."[87] Thus, what informs the Constitution is the "spirit of the revolution," that is, the Declaration.

Any genuine interpretation of the Constitution must therefore read the text of that document in the light of the principles of the Declaration. Neither Attorney General Meese nor Justice Brennan adopted this as a viable view of constitutional jurisprudence. Each took an extreme, Meese attempting to interpret the text without resort to principle, and Brennan resorting to principle—informed only by the vaguest notions of the "evolving demands of human dignity"—without reference to the Constitutional text. But it is only in the light of the principles of the Declaration that the text can be understood. The Fifth Amendment provides that "no person" shall "be deprived of life, liberty, or property, without due process of law." Does this clause include slaves?

---

[86] *Federalist* No. 14, ibid., p. 104.

[87] *Federalist* No. 39, ibid., p. 240.

Are slaves to be considered as "persons" or as "property"? We know how this question was answered in *Dred Scott*. But Chief Justice Roger Brooke Taney in the *Dred Scott* opinion was forced to conclude that blacks were not included in the Declarations's phrase "all men are created equal." Here, Taney was wrong, as Lincoln many times pointed out. But what is decisive is that the question can only be settled by reference to the principles of the Declaration, not by the literal language of the Constitution. A similar analysis could be made of Brennan's view of "cruel and unusual punishment." Here Brennan ignores the *explicit* language of the Constitution in the name of evolving concepts of human dignity. This view, if it were to prevail, would simply make the idea of a written constitution absurd, to paraphrase John Marshall in *Marbury v. Madison* (1803).

In the last years of his life, James Madison worked on a preface to his notes on the Constitutional Convention that he wanted to be published posthumously. The preface, although never finished, was finally published in 1840, four years after his death. In the peroration, Madison, almost fifty years after the event, reflected on the spirit and the motives of the delegates.

> Whatever may be the judgment pronounced on the competency of the architects of the Constitution, or whatever may be the destiny of the edifice prepared by them, I feel it a duty to express my profound & solemn conviction, derived from my intimate opportunity of observing & appreciating the views of the Convention, collectively & individually, that there never was an assembly of men, charged with a great & arduous trust, who were more pure in their motives, or more exclusively or anxiously devoted to the object committed to them, than were the members of the Federal Convention of 1787, to the object of devising and proposing a constitutional system which would best supply the defects of that which it was to replace, and best secure the permanent liberty and happiness of their country.[88]

Madison's words sound hopelessly naive to our jaded ears. That men could act for public-spirited motives for "the per-

[88] Adrienne Koch, ed., *Notes of Debates in the Federal Convention of 1787 Reported by James Madison* (New York, 1969), p. 19.

manent liberty and happiness of their country" seems incredibly superficial to an age that expects to find realistic motives in class consciousness or pragmatism. Yet I suspect we could be well served by a little naïveté in our attempt to recover the spirit of the Founding. Charles Warren characterized the attempt to interpret history in terms of economics or sociology as history that "leaves out of account the fact that a man may have an inner zeal for principles, beliefs, and ideals. . . . Those who contend, for instance, that economic causes brought about the War of the Revolution will always find it difficult to explain away the fact that the men who did the fighting thought, themselves, that they were fighting for a belief—a principle."[89] And if we find statesmen who were attached to principles and animated by ideas, I see no need to be embarrassed by that. This does not make us less sophisticated, but it may get us nearer the truth.

[89] Warren, *Making of the Constitution*, pp. 3–4.

ISAAC KRAMNICK

The Discourse of
Politics in 1787:
The Constitution and
Its Critics on
Individualism,
Community,
and the State

INTRODUCTION—MODES OF
DISCOURSE AND THE "GREAT
NATIONAL DISCUSSION"

ALEXANDER HAMILTON'S FIRST *Federalist* essay, published in
the New York *Independent Journal* on October 27, 1787,
pointed out that in deliberating on their new Constitution,
Americans were proving that men could create their own
governments "by reflection and choice" instead of forever
having to depend on "accident and force." Their debates on
their proposed frame of government would by no means be
decorous and genteel. Too much was at stake, and as Hamilton conceded, "a torrent of angry and malignant passions"
would be let loose in the "great national discussion." But his
"Federalist" essays, he promised, would provide a different
voice in the national debate; one that would rise above "the
loudness of their declamations and the bitterness of their
invectives."

How does one read the documentary record of that "great
national discussion" two centuries later? Most contemporary

scholars would follow the methodological guidelines offered by J. G. A. Pocock in this respect. The historian of political thought, he suggests, is engaged in a quest for the "languages," "idioms," and "modes of discourse" that characterize an age. Certain "languages" are accredited at various moments in time "to take part" in the public speech of a country. These "distinguishable idioms" are paradigms that selectively encompass all information about politics and delimit appropriate usage. Pocock writes of "continua of discourse," which persist over time in terms of paradigms that both constrain and provide opportunities for authors with a language available for their use. To understand texts and "great national discussions," then, is to penetrate the "modes of discourse" and the meanings available to authors and speakers at a particular moment in time. The scholar must know what the normal possibilities of language, the capacities for discourse, were. Paradigms change, to be sure, ever so slowly, and we recognize this subtle process through anomaly and innovations. But much more significant is the static and exclusive aspect of "modes of discourse." Pocock cautions us that one "cannot get out of a language that which was never in it." People only think "about what they have the means of verbalizing." Anyone studying political texts, then, must use "the language in which the inhabitants . . . did in fact present their society and cosmos to themselves and to each other."[1]

Problematic in this approach is the assumption that there is but one language, one exclusive or even hegemonic paradigm, that characterizes the political discourse of a particular moment in time or place. This was not the case in 1787. In the great debate of 1787–88 Federalists and Antifederalists tapped several idioms and languages of politics that were available to them, the terms of which they could easily verbalize. This paper examines four such "distinguishable idioms" that coexisted in the political discourse of Americans engaged in the debate over the Constitution. None dominated the field, and the use of one was compatible with the use of another by the very same writer or speaker. There was

[1] J. G. A. Pocock, *Virtue, Commerce, and History: Essays on Political Thought and History, Chiefly in the Eighteenth Century* (New York, 1985), pp. 13, 58, 290.

a profusion and confusion of political tongues among the Founders. They lived easily with that clatter; it is we, two hundred years later, who chafe at their inconsistency. Reading the Framers and the critics of the Constitution, one can discern the language of republicanism, of Lockean liberalism, of radical Protestantism, and of state-centered theories of power and sovereignty.[2]

CIVIC HUMANISM AND LIBERALISM IN THE CONSTITUTION AND ITS CRITICS

Contemporary scholarship seems obsessed with forever ridding the college curriculum of the baleful influence of Louis Hartz. In place of the "Liberal Tradition in America," it posits the omnipresence of neoclassical civic humanism. Dominating eighteenth-century political thought in Britain and America, it is insisted, was the language of republican virtue. Man was a political being who realized his *telos* only when living in a *vivere civile* with other propertied, arms-bearing citizens, in a republic where they ruled and were ruled in turn. Behind this republican discourse is a tradition of political philosophy with roots in Aristotle's *Politics*, Cicero's *De Re Publica*, Niccolò Machiavelli, James Harrington, Viscount Bolingbroke, and the nostalgic country's virtuous opposition to Sir Robert Walpole and the commercialization of English life. The pursuit of public good was held to be privileged over private interests, and freedom was defined as participation in civic life, not the protection of individual rights from interference. Central to the scholarly focus on republicanism has been the self-proclaimed "dethronement of the paradigm of liberalism and of the Lockean paradigm associated with it."[3]

---

[2] Even this list is not exhaustive. I leave to my colleagues the explication of several other less discernible idioms of politics in the debate of 1787, for example, the "language of jurisprudence," "scientific Whiggism," and the "moral sentiment" schools of the Scottish Enlightenment.

[3] J. G. A. Pocock, "An Appeal from the New to the Old Whigs? A Note on Joyce Appleby's Ideology and the History of Political Thought," Intellectual History Group *Newsletter* 3 (Spring 1981): 47. Republican revisionism, often read as a critique from the right of hegemonic liberal

In response to these claims for republicanism, a group of what Gordon S. Wood has labeled "neo-Lockeans" has insisted that John Locke and liberalism were alive and well in Anglo-American thought in the period of the Founding.[4] Individualism, the moral legitimacy of private interest, and market society are privileged in this reading over community, public good, and the virtuous pursuit of civic fulfillment. For these "neo-Lockeans" it was not Machiavelli and Montesquieu who set the textual codes that dominated the debate over the Constitution, but Thomas Hobbes and Locke and the assumptions of possessive individualism.

Can we have it both ways? We certainly can if we take Federalist and Antifederalist views as representing a single text of political discourse at the Founding. A persuasive case can be made that reads the Federalists as liberal modernists and the Antifederalists as nostalgic republican communitarians, seeking desperately to hold on to a virtuous moral order threatened by commerce and market society. The Federalist tendency was to depict America in amoral terms as a nation transcending local community and moral conviction as the focus of politics. The Federalists seemed to glory in an individualistic and competitive America, preoccupied with private rights and personal autonomy. This reading of America is associated with James Madison more than with anyone else, and with his writings in the *Federalist*.

The basis for Madison's famous adulation of heterogeneous factions and interests in an extended republic, which he introduced into so many of his contributions to the *Federalist*, was a famous speech he gave to the Constitutional Con-

---

scholarship, has been taken up by an unlikely ally, Critical Legal Studies, which from the left has embraced its communitarian focus and potential as an alternative to liberal possessive individualism. See, for example, Andrew Fraser, "Legal Amnesia: Modernism vs. the Republican Tradition in American Legal Theory," *Telos*, no. 60 (1984).

[4] Gordon S. Wood, "Hell Fire Politics," *New York Review of Books*, Feb. 28, 1985, p. 30. Wood's magisterial *The Creation of the American Republic, 1776–1787* (Chapel Hill, 1969), remains much the most brilliant guide to the American Founding. It should be apparent in the pages that follow the debt I and all who write on this era owe him.

vention on June 6, 1787. The only way the rights of minorities could be protected, he told the delegates, was to enlarge the sphere, and thereby divide the community into so great a number of interests and parties that "in the first place a majority will not be likely at the same moments to have a common interest separate from that of the whole or of the minority; and in the second place, that in case they shd. have such an interest, they may not be apt to unite in the pursuit of it. It was incumbent on us then to try this remedy, and with that view to frame a republican system on such a scale and in such a form as will controul all the evils which have been experienced."[5]

In *Federalist* No. 10 Madison described the multiplication of regional, religious, and economic interests, factions, and parties as the guarantor of American freedom and justice. He put his case somewhat differently in a letter to Thomas Jefferson: "*Divide et impera,* the reprobated axiom of tyranny, is, under certain conditions, the only policy by which a republic can be administered on just principles."[6] Pride of place among "these clashing interests," so essential for a just order, went to the economic interests inevitable in a complex market society. They were described in the often quoted passage from *Federalist* No. 10: "The most common and durable source of factions has been the various and unequal distribution of property. Those who hold and those who are without property have ever formed distinct interests in society. . . . creditors . . . debtors. . . . A landed interest, a mercantile interest, a moneyed interest. . . . The regulation of these various and interfering interests forms the principal task of modern legislation."

Government was, for Madison, much like it was for Locke, a neutral arbiter over competing interests. Indeed, in *Federalist* No. 43 Madison described the legislative task as providing "umpires," and in a letter to George Washington he described government's role as a "disinterested and dispas-

[5] Max Farrand, ed., *The Records of the Federal Convention of 1787*, rev. ed., 4 vols. (New Haven, 1937) 1:136.

[6] James Madison to Thomas Jefferson, Oct. 24, 1787, Gaillard Hunt, ed., *The Writings of James Madison*, 9 vols. (New York, 1900–1910), 5:31.

sionate umpire in disputes."[7] Sounding much like Locke in chapter 5—"On Property"—of the *Second Treatise,* Madison in No. 10 attributed the differential possession of property to the "diversity in the faculties of man," to their "different and unequal faculties of acquiring property." It was "the protection of these faculties" that constituted "the first object of government." As it was for Locke—who wrote that "justice gives every man a title to the product of his honest industry"—so, too, for Madison and the Federalists, justice effectively meant respecting private rights, especially property rights.[8]

Justice for the Federalists was less a matter of civic virtue, of public participation in politics, as emphasized by recent American historical scholarship, or of a Neoplatonic ideal of a transcendent moral order, as argued by scholars like Walter Berns, than it was a reflection of the Lockean liberal world of personal rights, and most dramatically of property rights. It was a substantive not a procedural or civic ideal of justice that preoccupied the Framers in 1787. It was much more often the content of laws, not the violation of due process, that condemned legislation as wicked. With striking frequency the condemnation of local states that interfered with private contracts or established paper money schemes was cast in the language of "unjust laws." In South Carolina such laws were labeled "open and outrageous . . . violations of every principle of Justice." In New Jersey debtor relief legislation was criticized because it was "founded not upon the principles of Justice, but upon the Rights of the Sword." The Boston *Independent Chronicle* complained in May 1787 that the Massachusetts legislature lacked "a decided tone . . . in favor of the general principles of justice." A "virtuous legislature," wrote a critic in 1786, "cannot listen to any proposition, however popular, that came within the description of being unjust, impolitic or unnecessary." In Massachusetts the legislation sought by the Shaysites was seen to be the establishment of "iniquity by Law," to be acts of "injustice," violating "the most

[7] Madison to George Washington, Apr. 16, 1787, ibid., p. 8.

[8] John Locke, *First Treatise,* in *Two Treatises of Government,* ed. Peter Laslett, 2d ed. (Cambridge, 1970), chap. 4, sec. 22.

simple ties of common honesty." The link between the procedural and substantive objections to state legislatures was
made clearly by Noah Webster. They were, he wrote, guilty
of "so many legal infractions of sacred right, so many public
invasions of private property, so many wanton abuses of legislative powers."[9]

Madison, too, read justice as the substantive protection of
rights. In his argument before the Convention on behalf of
a council of revision, he pleaded for the president and judges
to have the right to veto "unwise and unjust measures" of the
state legislatures "which constituted so great a portion of our
calamities."[10] This is equally evident in the pages of *The Federalist*. In No. 10 state actions reflecting "a rage for paper
money, for an abolition of debts, for an equal division of
property" were "schemes of injustice" and "improper or
wicked project(s)." The fruits of unjust and wicked laws were
"the alarm for private rights which are echoed from one end
of the continent to the other." Madison equated in No. 44 the
"love of justice" with hatred of paper money. Such "pestilen-
tial laws" required, in turn, sacrifices on "the altar of justice."
The end of government and of civil society was justice, Madison wrote in No. 51, and in No. 54 he refined this point
further by noting that "government is instituted no less for
protection of the property than of the persons of individuals." It was the same for Hamilton, who wrote in *Federalist* No.
70 that "the protection of property" constituted "the ordinary course of justice." In No. 78 Hamilton described the
"private rights of particular classes of citizens" injured "by
unjust and partial laws."

The commitment in the Preamble of the Constitution to
"establish justice" meant for the Framers that it would protect
private rights, which would help it achieve the next objective—to "insure domestic tranquility." Should there be

[9]*Gazette of South Carolina* (Charleston), Mar. 5, 1787; New Jersey peti-
tion, quoted in Wood, *Creation of the Republic*, p. 406; *Independent Chronicle*
(Boston), May 31, 1787; *Political Intelligencer* (Elizabethtown, N.J.), Jan. 4,
1786; Massachusetts reactions to Shays, quoted in Wood, *Creation of the
Republic*, p. 465; Noah Webster, "Government," *American Magazine* 1
(1787–88):75.

[10]Farrand, ed., *Records of the Convention*, 2:73–74.

doubts about this, we have Madison as our guide to what "establish justice" meant. On June 6 he had risen at the Convention to answer Roger Sherman's suggestion that the only objects of union were better relations with foreign powers and the prevention of conflicts and disputes among the states. What about justice? was the thrust of Madison's intervention. To Sherman's list of the Constitution's objectives Madison insisted there be added "the necessity, of providing more effectually for the security of private rights, and the steady dispensation of Justice. Interferences with these were evils which had more perhaps than anything else, produced this convention."[11]

The acceptance of modern liberal society in the Federalist camp goes beyond a legitimization of the politics of interest and a conviction that government's purpose was protecting the fruits of honest industry. There is also an unabashed appreciation of modern commercial society. William Bennett was quite right in his reminder to Americans that "commerce had a central place in the ideas of the Founders." Hamilton, for example, in *Federalist* No. 12, insisted that "the prosperity of commerce is now perceived and acknowledged, by all enlightened statesmen, to be the most useful as well as the most productive source of national wealth; and has accordingly become a primary object of their political cares. By multiplying the means of gratification, by promoting the introduction and circulation of the precious metals, those darling objects of human avarice and enterprise, it serves to vivify all the channels of industry, and to make them flow with greater activity and copiousness."

Hamilton was perfectly aware that his praise of private gratification, avarice, and private gain flew in the face of older ideals of civic virtue and public duty that emphasized the subordination of private interest to the public good. He turned this very rejection of the republican moral ideal into an argument for the need of a federal standing army. This was a further blow to the ideals of civic virtue, which had always seen professional armies as evil incarnate, undermining the citizen's self-sacrificial participation in the defense of

[11] Ibid., 1:134.

the public realm that had been the premise of the militia. America as a market society could not rely on the militia, according to Hamilton. "The militia," he wrote in *Federalist* No. 24, "would not long, if at all, submit to be dragged from their occupations and families." He was writing of manning garrisons involved in protecting the frontiers: "And if they could be prevailed upon or compelled to do it, the increased expense of a frequent rotation of service, and the loss of labor and disconcertation of the industrious pursuit of individuals, would form conclusive objections to the scheme. It would be as burdensome and injurious to the public as ruinous to private citizens."

In *Federalist* No. 28, another defense of standing armies, Hamilton acknowledged the eclipse of older civic ideals of self-sacrifice and participatory citizenship in commercial America: "The industrious habits of the people of the present day, absorbed in the pursuit of gain and devoted to the improvements of agriculture and commerce, are incompatible with the condition of a nation of soldiers, which was the true condition of the people of those [that is, the ancient Greek] republics."

Many of the Antifederalists, on the other hand, were still wedded to a republican civic ideal, to the making of America into what Samuel Adams called "a Christian Sparta." The very feature of pluralist diversity in the new constitutional order that Madison saw as its great virtue the Antifederalists saw as its major defect. For the Antifederalist Brutus, it was absurd that the legislature "would be composed of such heterogeneous and discordant principles, as would constantly be contending with each other." A chorus of Antifederalists insisted that virtuous republican government required a small area and a homogeneous population. Patrick Henry noted that a republican form of government extending continent-wide "contradicts all the experience of the world." Richard Henry Lee argued that "a free elective government cannot be extended over large territories." Robert Yates of New York saw liberty "swallowed up" because the new republic was too large.[12]

[12] Samuel Adams to John Scollay, Dec. 30, 1780, Harry A. Cushing, ed., *The Writings of Samuel Adams*, 4 vols. (New York, 1904–8), 4:239; Brutus, cited in Herbert J. Storing, "What the Anti-Federalists Were *For*," in Stor-

Montesquieu and others had taught Antifederalists "that so extensive a territory as that of the United States, including such a variety of climates, productions, interests, and so great differences of manners, habits, and customs" could never constitute a moral republic. This was the crucial issue for the minority members of the Pennsylvania ratifying convention: "We dissent, first, because it is the opinion of the most celebrated writers on government, and confirmed by uniform experience, that a very extensive territory cannot be governed on the principles of freedom, otherwise than by a confederation of republics."[13]

As important as the issue of size for the Antifederalists was their fear over the absence of homogeneity in the enlarged republic. In the course of arguing that a national government could not be trusted if it were to allow open immigration, Agrippa, the popular Antifederalist pamphleteer assumed to be James Winthrop, contrasted the much more desirable situation in "the eastern states" with the sad plight of Pennsylvania, which for years had allowed open immigration, and in which religious toleration and diversity flourished: "Pennsylvania has chosen to receive all that would come there. Let any indifferent person judge whether that state in point of morals, education, energy is equal to any of the eastern states which, by keeping separate from the foreign mixtures, have acquired their present greatness in the course of a century and a half, and have preserved their religion and their morals . . . reasons of equal weight may induce other states . . . to keep their blood pure."[14]

For most Antifederalists a republican system required similarity of religion, manners, sentiments, and interests. They were convinced that no such sense of community existed in an enlarged republic. No one set of laws could work within such diversity. "We see plainly that men who come from New

---

ing, ed., *The Complete Anti-Federalist*, 7 vols (Chicago, 1981), 1:47; Patrick Henry, Richard Henry Lee, and Robert Yates cited in Leonard W. Levy, ed., *Essays on the Making of the Constitution* (New York, 1969), p. ix.

[13] Cited in Wood, *Creation of the Republic*, p. 499; Pennsylvania citation in Levy, ed., *Essays on the Constitution*, p. x.

[14] Cited in Storing, ed., *The Complete Anti-Federalist*, 1:20.

England are different from us," wrote a southern Antifederalist. And a northern Antifederalist declared that "the inhabitants of warmer climates are more dissolute in their
manners, and less industrious, than in colder countries. A
degree of severity is, therefore, necessary with one which
would cramp the spirit of the other. . . . It is impossible for
one code of laws to suit Georgia and Massachusetts."[15]

A just society, for many Antifederalists, involved more than
simply protecting property rights. Government had more responsibilities than merely to regulate "various and interfering interests." It was expected to promote morality, virtue,
and religion. Many Antifederalists, for example, were
shocked at the Constitution's totally secular tone and its general disregard for religion and morality. They were equally
critical of the fact that Federalist arguments made in support
of it lacked any religious content.

Some Antifederalists were angered that the Constitution,
in Article VI, Section 3, prohibited the religious tests for officeholders while giving no public support to religious institutions. Amos Singletary of Massachusetts was annoyed that
it did not require men in power to be religious "and though
he hoped to see Christians, yet by the Constitution, a papist,
or an infidel, was as eligible as they." An Antifederalist in
North Carolina wrote that "the exclusion of religious tests
is by many thought dangerous and impolitic. . . . They suppose . . . pagans, deists, and Mahometans might obtain offices
among us." For David Caldwell this prohibition of religious
tests "constituted an invitation for Jews and pagans of every
kind to come among us." Since Christianity was the best religion for producing "good members of society . . . those
gentlemen who formed this Constitution should not have
given this invitation to Jews and Heathens."[16]

Antifederalists were convinced that religion was a crucial

[15] Jonathan Elliot, ed., *The Debates in the Several State Conventions, on the Adoption of the Federal Constitution*, 2d ed., 5 vols. (Philadelphia, 1866), 4:24; northern Antifederalist, cited in Gordon S. Wood, ed., *The Confederation and the Constitution* (Washington, 1979), p. 59.

[16] Amos Singletary in Elliot, ed., *Debates*, 2:44; North Carolina Antifederalist, ibid., 4:192; David Caldwell, ibid., 4: 199.

support of government. For Richard Henry Lee, "refiners may weave a web of reason as they please, but the experience of times shews a religion to be the guardian of morals." The state, according to some Antifederalists, had to be concerned with civic and religious education. Several made specific proposals for state sponsored "seminaries of useful learning" for instruction in "the principles of free government" and "the science of morality." The state, they urged, should encourage "the people in favour of virtue by affording public protection to religion."[17]

Some Antifederalists even suggested that the Constitution's indifference toward religion, and the Federalists' departure from the age-old belief in religion as the foundation of civil institutions and their new vision of government as simply an arbiter of interests or protector of rights, would ultimately lead America to ruin. The Antifederalist A. F. Charles Turner was one of these: "Without the prevalence of Christian piety and morals the best republican Constitution can never save us from slavery and ruin." He urged that the government "institute some means of education, as shall be adequate to the divine, patriotic purpose of training up the children and youth at large in that solid learning and in those pious and moral principles, which are the support, the life and the soul of republican government and liberty, of which a free constitution is the body."[18]

The Antifederalists were quite perceptive. By and large the Federalists shared a secular view of government. Government's function for them was to be a mere servant to its citizens, protecting their interests and their property. The state and political obligation was demystified, its conventional and ageless link to arcane religious sources, inscrutable and beyond human understanding, was being severed. Deference to political power was removed from the timeless realm of hereditary religious mystery. The state was rendered a simple and useful artifact created by ordinary self-seeking men

[17] Richard Henry Lee to Madison, Nov. 26, 1784, James C. Ballagh, ed., *The Letters of Richard Henry Lee*, 2 vols. (New York, 1911–14), 2:304, cited in Storing, ed., *The Complete Anti-Federalist*, 1:21.

[18] Cited in Storing, ed., *The Complete Anti-Federalist*, 1:23.

whose rational common sense prompted them to consent voluntarily to be governed.

In this secular vision of politics, religious and credal matters lay outside the realm of the magistrate. Here, too, Locke was the source of wisdom. *A Letter concerning Toleration* was as profound an influence on shaping liberal discourse as was his *Second Treatise*. In it Locke pushed aside the Christian conception of law as a worldly injunction requiring virtuous and moral living ultimately traceable to God's own standards of right and wrong. For Locke and for secular liberalism "laws provide simply that the goods and health of subjects be not injured by the fraud and violence of others." Locke added that "the business of law is not to provide for the truth of opinion, but for the safety and security of the Commonwealth and of every particular man's goods and person. The truth is not taught by law, nor has she any need of force to procure her entrance into the minds of men."[19]

In liberal discourse, involving as it did the privatization of so much that hitherto had been seen as the public role of politics, religion was one of the main victims. The commonwealth was rendered a secular entity uninterested in men's souls or men's virtue, for, as Locke noted, the state was not concerned with matters of belief because "no injury is thereby done to anyone, no prejudice to another man's goods."[20]

The great debate that occurred in England in the 1770s and 1780s between the Anglican establishment and the Dissenters over the repeal of the Test and Corporation Acts is an essential factor in explaining the hold of the liberal paradigm—with its vision of a secular state and a wall of separation between the minimal public realm that kept the peace and a vast private realm of moral, religious, and economic diversity and voluntarism—on writers like Madison, Jefferson, and Benjamin Franklin. It is necessary to delineate their view of this English episode if we are to understand the atti-

[19] John Locke, *Treatise of Civil Government and A Letter concerning Toleration*, ed. Charles L. Sherman (New York, 1937), p. 205.

[20] Ibid., p. 198.

178

tudes of the Federalist Framers of the Constitution toward religion and the state.

The Test and Corporation Acts dated from the Stuart Restoration and were originally directed against Catholics. They required that all officeholders under the British Crown receive the sacraments according to the rites of the Anglican Church. The acts went on to exclude nonsubscribers to the Anglican creed from holding any offices in an incorporated municipality and they forbade non-Anglicans from matriculating at Oxford or Cambridge. The main victims of these discriminatory laws in the eighteenth century were the Dissenters—the non-Anglican Protestant sects that included Baptists, Presbyterians, Unitarians, and Quakers. While a small minority of the total population, Dissenters were a talented and successful group at the forefront of achievement. They were the leading entrepreneurs, inventors, and scientists in the early Industrial Revolution, conventionally dated after 1760, and were leaders in political and cultural radicalism as well. No wonder, then, that in the 1770s and 1780s they sought to repeal the Test and Corporation Acts, which denied them, because of their religion, access to one of the most important means a society has to reward its successful people—public office.[21]

Franklin and Jefferson were close to this dissenting circle. Their English connections, as for many in the founding generation, were with the radical Dissenters that gathered behind the banners of the Rev. Richard Price and Joseph Priestley. The Rev. James Burgh, cited in *Federalist* No. 56, helped popularize this vision in the 1770s. The intellectual leader of these English radicals was Priestley, discoverer of oxygen, founder of unitarianism, and political radical, whose books and pamphlets on politics, religion, and education Jefferson read "over and over again." Priestley's writings on the disestablishment of the Anglican Church and on the separation of church and state were used in 1786 by Madison and

---

[21] The best source on this conflict is still Anthony Lincoln, *Some Political & Social Ideas of English Dissent, 1763–1800* (Cambridge, 1938). See also Isaac Kramnick "Religion and Radicalism: English Political Theory in the Age of Revolution," *Political Theory* 5 (1977).

Jefferson in planning the statute for establishing religious freedom in Virginia. In one of his many letters to Priestley, Jefferson wrote unabashedly that Priestley's was "one of the few lives precious to mankind."[22]

In his critique of the Test and Corporation Acts, Priestley assumed Locke's view of the state. The state, he argued, had no positive role to educate, nurture, or provide moral standards. It was not concerned with illuminating the good life or providing an arena for moral fulfillment through participatory citizenship. Instead, according to Priestley, it had only the specific, limited, and negative functions that were implicit in its contractual origins. Its sole purpose was the protection of individuals and their rights. It was simply an agent performing the useful but limited service of keeping order and protecting individuals from harm. The state dealt only with "things that relate to this life," while the church dealt with "those that relate to the life to come." The state, then, was restricted to a specific purpose—neither more nor less than to provide a "secure and comfortable enjoyment of this life, by preventing one man from injuring another in his person or property." The magistrate had no concern with opinion or beliefs. His sole duty, according to Priestley, "was to preserve the peace of society." The state punished only "if I break the peace of society, if I injure my neighbor, in his person, property or good name," not if I believe in different creeds. "How," Priestley asked, "is any person injured by my holding religious opinions which he disapproves of?"[23] It is this very liberal paradigm of the state and of religion which is reproduced in the Constitution and which so infuriated

[22] See Paul Leicester Ford, ed., *The Works of Thomas Jefferson*, 12 vols. (New York, 1904–5), 9:95, 102, 216, 380, 404, 10:69. See also Andrew A. Lipscomb and Albert Ellery Bergh, eds., *The Writings of Thomas Jefferson*, 20 vols. (Washington, D.C., 1903–4), 10:228, 13:352, 14:200, 15:232. See also Adrienne Koch, *The Philosophy of Thomas Jefferson* (Chicago, 1964), pp. 24, 27, 34; Daniel J. Boorstin, *The Lost World of Thomas Jefferson* (Boston, 1960), pp. 17–19, 113–19, 159–62; Colin Bonwick, *English Radicals and the American Revolution* (Chapel Hill, 1977), p. 285; Nicholas Han, "Franklin, Jefferson, and the English Radicals at the End of the Eighteenth Century," American Philosophical Society *Proceedings* 98 (1954):406–26.

[23] Joseph Priestley, *Conduct to Be Observed by Dissenters in Order to Procure the Repeal of the Corporation and Test Acts* (Birmingham, 1789), p. 6.

many Antifederalists. The lineal descent is clear, from Locke to Priestley to Madison and Jefferson. The very words of Locke and Priestley are repeated in Jefferson's *Notes on Virginia:* "The legitimate powers of government extend to such acts only as are injurious to others. But it does me no injury for my neighbor to say there are twenty Gods or no God. It neither breaks my leg, nor picks my pocket."[24]

There was, not surprisingly, also a tendency in some Antifederalist circles to see the exchange principles of commercial society, so praised by the Federalists, as threats to civic and moral virtue. Would not, one of them wrote, the self-seeking activities "of a commercial society beget luxury, the parent of inequality, the foe to virtue, and the enemy to restraint?" The spread of commerce would undermine republican simplicity: "As people become more luxurious, they become more incapacitated of governing themselves." As one Antifederalist put it, speaking critically of the silence of the Constitution on questions of morality, "Whatever the refinement of modern politics may inculcate, it is still certain that some degree of virtue must exist, or freedom cannot live." Honest folk like himself, he went on, objected to "Mandeville's position . . . that private vices are public benefits." This was not an unfamiliar theme to the men who would oppose the Constitution. Earlier Richard Henry Lee had singled out the same source of evil, "Mandevilles . . . who laugh at virtue, and with vain ostentatious display of words will deduce from vice, public good."[25]

For many Antifederalists, the problem with the Federalist position was the inadequacy of its vision of community based on mere interests and their protection. The Antifederalists suspected that such a community could not persist through what Madison had called in *Federalist* No. 51 "the policy of supplying, by opposite and rival interests, the defect of better motives." A proper republican community for these Antifederalists required a moral consensus, which, in turn, required similarity, familiarity, and fraternity. How, they asked, could

[24] Thomas Jefferson, "Notes on Virginia, Query No. 17," in Saul K. Padover, ed., *Jefferson on Democracy* (New York, 1946), p. 109.

[25] Cited in Storing, ed., *The Complete Anti-Federalist,* 1:7,23, 73; Ballagh, ed., *Letters of Lee,* 2:62–63.

one govern oneself and prefer the common good over private interests, outside a shared community small enough and homogeneous enough to allow one to know and sympathize with one's neighbors? The republican spirit of Jean-Jacques Rousseau hovered over these Antifederalists as they identified with small, simple, face-to-face, uniform societies.

Madison and Hamilton understood full well that this communitarian sentiment lay at the core of much of the Antifederalist critique of the new constitutional order and they dismissed it out of hand. In *Federalist* No. 35 Hamilton ridiculed the face-to-face politics of those "whose observation does not travel beyond the circle of his neighbors and his acquaintances." Madison in No. 10 described two alternative ways of eliminating the causes of factions and thus the politics of interest: one by "destroying the liberty which is essential to its existence; the other by giving to every citizen the same opinions, the same passions, and the same interests." They were both unacceptable alternatives to him. To do either would cut the very heart out of the liberal polity he championed. One might well want to agree with the recent and most perceptive assessment by Walter Berns:

> In voting to ratify the Constitution, Americans voted against the loose confederation of small, simple, virtuous and democratic republics in favor of a strong, complex, and commercial republic whose first object, Publius said, is "the protection of different and unequal faculties of acquiring property." Whether they knew it or not, and there can be no doubt that at least Publius knew it, they had voted to test the validity of the proposition advanced by the philosophers of natural rights, primarily John Locke and Montesquieu, that, when combined with certain institutional arrangements in the modern liberal state, commerce could serve as a substitute for morality."[26]

But one can go too far in making the case for the Antifederalists as antiliberal communitarians, or Rousseauean republicans. Some were, without doubt, but others, paradoxically enough, responded to the enlarged federal govern-

[26] Walter Berns, "Does the Constitution Secure These Rights?" in Robert A. Goldwin and William Schambra, eds., *How Democratic Is the Constitution?* (Washington, D.C., 1980), p. 73.

ment and the enhancement of executive power with a call for the protection of private and individual rights through a Bill of Rights. Even this, however, may be explained by their communitarian bias. If, after all, government was to be run from some distant city hundreds of miles away, by people superior, more learned, and more deliberative than they, by people with whom they shared no common characteristics, then one's individual rights needed specific protection. The basis for trust present in the small moral community where men shared "the same opinions, the same passions, and the same interests" was extinguished.

An equally strong case can be made for the Federalists as republican theorists, and here we see full blown the confusion of idioms, the overlapping of political languages in 1787. There is, of course, Madison's redefinition of and identification with a republicanism that involves "the delegation of the government . . . to a small number of citizens elected by the rest" as opposed to a democracy "consisting of a small number of citizens who assemble and administer the government in person." But what puts Madison firmly within the republican paradigm in No. 10 is his assumption that the representative function in an enlarged republic would produce officeholders who would sacrifice personal, private, and parochial interest to the public good and the public interest. What made the layers of filtration prescribed by the new constitutional order so welcome was their ultimate purpose, producing enlightened, public spirited men who found fulfillment in the quest for public good. It is this feature of Madison's No. 10 to which Garry Wills has drawn attention and which he and others see as the crowning inspiration of Madison's moral republicanism. Republican government over a large country would, according to Madison, "refine and enlarge the public views by passing them through the medium of a chosen body of citizens whose wisdom may best discern the true interest of their country, and whose patriotism and love of justice will be least likely to sacrifice it to temporary or partial considerations. Under such a regulation it may well happen that the public voice pronounced by the representatives of the people will be more consonant to the public good than if pronounced by the people themselves, convened for the purpose." The greater number of citizens choosing representatives in a larger republic would reject "unworthy candidates" and choose "men who possess the most attractive merit." A large republic and a national government would lead to "the substitution of representatives whose enlightened views and virtuous sentiments render them superior to local prejudices and to schemes of injustice." We know, given Madison's candor, what this meant.[27]

Working out the mechanisms by which this filtration process would "refine and enlarge" both public views and the quality of the men chosen to express them preoccupied the delegates at Philadelphia. This explains their lengthy deliberations as to whether governing officials like the president and senators should be appointed by state legislatures or by state senates (which in many cases had themselves been appointed) or, as in the case of the president, by "electors" who were themselves already once removed from the people. Such indirect processes of selection would, as Madison wrote in his notes, "extract from the mass of the society the purest and noblest characters which it contains." The very people involved in choosing the president or senators would be, according to John Jay in *Federalist* No. 64, "the most enlightened and most respectable." The Senate, Madison wrote in *Federalist* No. 63, would then be made up of "temperate and respectable" men standing for "reason, justice and truth" in the face of the people's "errors and delusions."

Madison privileged public over private elsewhere in the *Federalist* as well. In No. 49 he envisaged public "reason" and "the true merits of questions" controlling and regulating government, not particular and private "passions." Similarly, in No. 55 he saw "the public interests" at risk in large legislative assemblies where "passion" always triumphs over "reason." The smaller House of Representatives, constructed by the Federalists, would thus better insure the victory of public good over self-interest.

The class focus of the Federalists' republicanism is self-evident. Their vision was of an elite corps of men in whom civic spirit and love of the general good overcame particular and narrow interests. Such men were men of substance, in-

[27] See Garry Wills, *Explaining America: The Federalist* (New York, 1981).

dependence, and fame who had the leisure to devote their time to public life and the wisdom to seek the true interests of the country as opposed to the wicked projects of local and particular interests. This republicanism of Madison and the Federalists is, of course, quite consistent with the general aristocratic orientation of classical republicanism, which was, after all, the ideal of independent, propertied, and, therefore, leisured citizens with time and reason to find fulfillment as *homo civicus.*

Antifederalists, on the other hand, calling for the representation of each and every particular interest, come off in this reading much closer to interest-centered liberals. It is they, not Madison, it could be claimed, who articulate the politics of interest, to be sure in a language much more democratic and participatory. The classic expression of this Antifederalist interest theory of representation came from Melancton Smith, the great antagonist of Hamilton at the New York ratification convention. He told the delegates that "the idea that naturally suggests itself to our minds, when we speak of representatives, is that they resemble those they represent. They should be a true picture of the people, possess a knowledge of their circumstances and their wants, sympathise in all their distress, and be disposed to seek their true interests." Directly refuting the filtration model, Smith insisted that a representative system ought not to seek "brilliant talents," but "a sameness, as to residence and interests, between the representative and his constituents."[28]

Hamilton repudiated the Antifederalist interest theory in his *Federalist* No. 35. "The idea of an actual representation of all classes of the people, by persons of each class," so that the feelings and interests of all would be expressed, "is altogether visionary," he wrote. The national legislature, Hamilton recommended, should be composed only of "landholders, merchants, and men of the learned professions." Ordinary people, however much confidence "they may justly feel in their own good sense," should realize that "their interest can be more effectually promoted" by men from these three stations in life.

The confusion of paradigms is further evident when one

28 Elliot, ed., *Debates,* 2:246.

analyzes in more detail these Federalist and Antifederalist theories of representation. The interest- and locality-oriented Antifederalists tended to espouse the traditional republican conviction dominant in most states under the Articles, that if there had to be representation then representatives should at least be directly responsible to their constituents and easily removable should they prove not to be so. This, of course, taps a rich eighteenth-century republican tradition of demanding frequent elections. Implicit in the Federalist notion of filtration, however, is a denial of the representative as mere delegate or servant of his constituents. In Madison's republicanism the representative was chosen for his superior ability to discern the public good, not as a mere spokesman for his town or region, or for the farmers or mechanics who elected him. It followed, then, that Federalists rejected the traditional republican ideal of annual or frequent elections, which was so bound to the more democratic ideal of the legislator as delegate. It is no surprise to find Madison in *Federalist* Nos. 37, 52, and 53 critical of frequent elections and offering several arguments against them. The proposed federal government, he insisted, was less powerful than the British government had been; its servants, therefore, were less to be feared. State affairs, he contended, could be mastered in less than a year, but the complexity of national politics was such that more time was needed to master its details. More important than these arguments, however, was the basic ideological gulf that here separated Madison's republicanism from the Antifederalist republican proponents of annual elections. Madison's legislators of "refined and enlarged public views" seeking "the true interest of their country" ought not to be subject to yearly review by local farmers and small-town tradesmen.

THE LANGUAGE OF VIRTUOUS REPUBLICANISM

The meaning of virtue in the language of civic humanism is clear. It is the privileging of the public over the private. Sam Adams persistently evoked the idioms of Aristotle and Cicero. "A citizen," he wrote, "owes everything to the Commonwealth." He worried that Americans would "forget their own generous Feelings for the Publick and for each other as to set private interests in competition with that of the great Community." Benjamin Rush went so far in 1786 as to reject the very core belief of what in a later day would come to be called possessive individualism. Every young man in a true republic, he noted, must "be taught that he does not belong to himself, but that he is public property." All his time and effort throughout "his youth—his manhood—his old age—nay more, life, all belong to his country." For John Adams, "public Virtue is the only Foundation of Republics." Republican government required "a positive passion for the public good, the public interest. . . . Superiour to all private passions."[29]

This is not all that virtue meant, however. Subtle changes were taking place during the Founding of the American republic in the notion of virtue, and at their core was a transvaluation of public and private. Dramatic witness is given to these changes by Madison's *Federalist* No. 44, where he depicted paper money as a threat to the republican character and spirit of the American people. That spirit, however, was neither civic nor public in nature. The values at risk were apolitical and personal. Madison feared for the sobriety, the prudence, and the industry of Americans. His concern was "the industry and morals of the people." Americans, like Gov. William Livingston, seemed convinced in 1787 that their countrymen "do not exhibit the virtue that is necessary to support a republican government." John Jay agreed. "Too much," he wrote, "has been expected from the virtue and good sense of the People." But like Madison, when Americans became specific about exactly what the decline of virtue meant, the language was often self-referential and noncivic. Writing to Jefferson in 1787, his friends told of "symptoms . . . truly alarming, which have tainted the faith of the most orthodox republicans." Americans lacked "industry, economy, temperance, and the republican virtues." Their fall from virtue was marked not by turning from public life (was there not, indeed, too much of that very republican value in the overheated state legislatures) but by their becoming "a luxurious voluptuous people without Economy or Industry."

[29] Cushing, ed., *Writings of Adams*, 4:255, 3:365; Dagobert D. Runes, ed., *The Selected Writings of Benjamin Rush* (New York, 1947), pp. 99, 31; *Warren-Adams Letters*, 2 vols. (Boston, 1917–25), 1:201–2, 222.

Virtuous republican people could, in fact, be described in noncivic, personal terms by the very same men who used the language of civic humanism. John Adams could also see the foundation of virtuous government in men who are "sober, industrious and frugal."[30]

One of the most striking aspects of political discourse in this era is the formulaic frequency with which this different sense of virtue is heard. For Joel Barlow in a 1787 Fourth of July oration at Hartford the "noble republican virtues which constitute the chief excellence" of government were "industry, frugality, and economy." Richard Henry Lee described the virtuous as a "wise, attentive, sober, diligent and frugal people" who had "established the independence of America." A Virginian wondering whether America could sustain republican government asked, "Have we that Industry, Frugality, Economy, that virtue which is necessary to constitute it?"[31] The constitutions of Pennsylvania and Vermont actually enlisted the Machiavellian republican notion of the return to original principles for their noncivic definition of a virtuous people. They specified that "a frequent recurrence to fundamental principles, and a firm adherence to justice, moderation, temperance, industry, and frugality are absolutely necessary to preserve the blessings of liberty and keep a government free."[32]

The Antifederalists, ostensible communitarian and public-oriented foils to Madisonian interest-based liberalism, could also use this more personal idiomatic notion of virtue. The Articles were not at fault, wrote one; it was the decline of virtue in the middle 1780s, "banishing all that economy, frugality and industry, which had been exhibited during the war." For the Antifederalist pamphleteer Candidus, it was not

[30] Theodore Sedgwick, *A Memoir of the Life of William Livingston* (New York, 1833), p. 403; John Jay to Jefferson, Feb. 9, 1787, Julian P. Boyd et al., eds., *The Papers of Thomas Jefferson*, 24 vols. to date (Princeton, 1950-), 11:129, 219, 318–19, 328–29; *Warren-Adams Letters*, 1:202.

[31] Joel Barlow, cited in Wood, *Creation of the Republic*, p. 418; Ballagh, ed., *Letters of Lee*, 2:33; Virginian, cited in Wood, *Creation of the Republic*, p. 75.

[32] Cited in Orrin G. Hatch, "Civic Virtue: Wellspring of Liberty," *National Forum* 64 (Fall 1984):35.

a new constitution that America needed but a return to the virtues of "industry and frugality."[33]

The republican tradition had, to be sure, always favored economy over luxury. From Aristotle and Cicero through Harrington and the eighteenth-century opposition to Walpole, republican rhetoric always linked a virtuous republican order to the frugal abstention from extravagance and luxury. But there is more than the all-pervasive paradigm of republicanism at work here. The inclusion of industry in the litany of virtues directs us to another inheritance, to another language in which Americans in the late eighteenth century conceptualized their personal and political universe. Americans also spoke the language of radical Protestantism that was derived less from Oliver Cromwell and the Levellers than from Richard Baxter, John Bunyan, and the literature of work, of the calling, and of "industry." Central in radical Protestant writings was the vision of a cosmic struggle between the forces of industry and idleness. Their texts vibrated less with the dialectic of civic virtue and self-centered commerce than with the dialectic of productive, hardworking energy, on the one hand, and idle, unproductive sloth, on the other. Their idiom was more personal and individualistic than public and communal. Work was a test of self-sufficiency and self-reliance, a battleground for personal salvation. All men were "called" to serve God by busying themselves in useful productive work that served both society and the individual. Daily labor was sanctified and thus was both a specific obligation and a positive moral value. The doctrine of the calling gave each man a sense of his unique self; different work appropriate to each particular individual was imposed by God. After being called to a particular occupation, it was man's duty to labor diligently and to avoid idleness and sloth.

The fruits of his labor were justly man's. There was for Baxter an "honest increase and provision which is the end of our labour." It was, therefore, "no sin but a duty to choose a gainful calling rather than another, that we may be able to do good." Not only was working hard and seeking to prosper the mark of a just and virtuous man, and idleness a sign of spir-

[33] Elliot, ed., *Debates*, 2:240; "Essays by Candidus," in Storing, ed., *The Complete Anti-Federalist*, 4:129–30 (4.9.18).

itual corruption, but work was also the anodyne for physical corruption. Hard work disciplined the wayward and sinful impulses that lay like Satan's traces within all men. Baxter wrote that "for want of bodily labour a multitude of the idle gentry, and rich people, and young people that are slothful, do heap up in the secret receptacles of the body a dunghill of unconcocted excrementitious filth . . . and die by thousands of untimely deaths . . . it is their own doing, and by their sloth they kill themselves."[34]

The Protestant language of work and the calling is, of course, complementary to the liberal language of Locke with its similar voluntaristic and individualistic emphasis. Locke's *Second Treatise* and its chapter "On Property"—with its very Protestant God enjoining industrious man to subdue the earth through work and thus to realize himself—is, as Quentin Skinner insists, "the classical text of radical Calvinistic politics."[35] The radical Protestant discourse's kinship to Locke has less to do with the juristic discourse of rights than with the Protestant theme of work. In the Protestant vocabulary there is much mention of virtue and corruption, but these have primarily nonclassical referents. Virtuous man is solitary and private man on his own, realizing himself and his talents through labor and achievement; corrupt man is unproductive, indolent, and in the devil's camp. He fails the test of individual responsibility. Few have captured the compatibility of the liberal and radical Protestant paradigms as well as Alexis de Tocqueville, albeit unintentionally. In his *Democracy in America* he writes of the American character in noncivic, individualistic terms that are at bottom central to both liberal and Protestant discourse. Americans, Tocqueville wrote, "owe nothing to any man, they expect nothing from any man; they acquire the habit of always considering themselves as standing alone, and they are apt to imagine that their whole destiny is in their own hands."[36]

[34] Richard Baxter, *A Christian Directory: Or a Sermon of Practical Theology, and Cases of Conscience* (London, 1673), pp. 116, 225, 449.

[35] Quentin Skinner, *The Foundations of Modern Political Thought*, 2 vols. (Cambridge, 1978), 2:239.

[36] Alexis de Tocqueville, *Democracy in America*, ed. and abr. Richard D. Heffner (New York, 1956), p. 194.

A small group of contemporary scholars that includes Edmund S. Morgan, J. E. Crowley, Joyce Appleby, and John P. Diggins have described this alternative paradigm of Protestantism and the Protestant ethic in eighteenth-century America and with it a language quite congenial to individualistic liberalism and the capitalist spirit.[37] Next to the Bible, the texts of Protestant moralists like Baxter were the books most likely to be found in the libraries of eighteenth-century Americans.[38] From them Americans came to know the virtuous man as productive, thrifty, and diligent. Morgan and Crowley, especially, have documented how the American response to England's policy of taxation centered on a dual policy of self-denial and commitment to industry. Richard Henry Lee, as early as 1764, when hearing of the Sugar Act, assumed it would "introduce virtuous industry." The subsequent nonconsumption and nonimportation policy of colonial protestors led many a moralist, in fact, to applaud parliamentary taxation as a blessing in disguise, recalling America to simplicity and frugality. As Morgan notes, many perceived the boycott movements as not simply negative and reactive but as "a positive end in themselves, a way of reaffirming and rehabilitating the virtues of the Puritan ethic."[39]

Industry, simplicity, and frugality were not only the signs of a virtuous people but also of a free people. As one Rhode Island writer put it, "The industrious and the frugal only will be free."[40] In Boston, the *Evening Post* of November 16, 1767, noted that "by consuming less of what we are not really in want of, and by industriously cultivating and improving the natural advantages of our own country, we might save our

[37] Edmund S. Morgan, "The Puritan Ethic and the American Revolution," *William and Mary Quarterly*, 3d ser. 24 (1967); J. E. Crowley, *This Sheba, Self: The Conceptualization of Economic Life in Eighteenth-Century America* (Baltimore, 1974); Joyce Appleby, "Liberalism and the American Revolution," *New England Quarterly* 49 (1976); idem, *Capitalism and a New Social Order: The Republican Vision of the 1790s* (New York, 1984); John P. Diggins, *The Lost Soul of American Politics: Virtue, Self-Interest, and the Foundations of Liberalism* (New York, 1984).

[38] Crowley, *This Sheba, Self*, p. 50.

[39] Ballagh, ed., *Letters of Lee*, 1:7; Morgan, "Puritan Ethic and Revolution," p. 8.

[40] *Newport Mercury*, Feb. 28, 1774.

substance, even our lands, from becoming the property of others, and we might effectually preserve our virtue and our liberty to the latest posterity." Three weeks later the *Pennsylvania Journal* proclaimed: "SAVE YOUR MONEY AND YOU WILL SAVE YOUR COUNTRY." In one of her famous letters to her husband John, away at the Continental Congress, Abigail Adams reveals how salient the Protestant virtues were in the political context of her day. Americans, she writes, must "return a little more to their primitive simplicity of manners and not sink into inglorious ease" and they must "retrench their expenses . . . indeed there is occasion for all our industry and economy."[41]

From pulpit and pamphlet, Americans had long heard praises of industry and denunciations of idleness. For Benjamin Coleman, the minister of the Brattle Street Church, "all nature is industrious and every creature about us diligent in their proper work." Constant activity was the human *telos* for Ebenezer Pemberton, an end even after death. He complained of those who thought "the happiness of heaven consisted only in enjoyment and a stupid indolence." This Protestant paradigm of restless and disciplined human activity also spoke in the idiomatic terms of life as a race. The life of the virtuous Christian was "compared to a RACE, a warfare, watching, running, fighting; all which imply Activity, Earnestness, Speed, etc." The race, according to Nathaniel Henchman, called "for the utmost striving of the whole man, unfainting Resolute Perseverance."[42]

Idleness, on the other hand, was a denial of the human essence. To be idle was to neglect "duty and lawful employment . . . for man is by nature such an active creature, that he cannot be wholly idle." Idleness for Americans had specific class referents. It was the sinful mark of the poor or the great, those below and those above the virtuous man of the middle.

[41] *Pennsylvania Journal* (Philadelphia), Dec. 10, 1767; Abigail Adams to John Adams, Oct. 16, 1774, in Lyman H. Butterfield, ed., *Adams Family Correspondence*, 4 vols. (Cambridge, Mass., 1963–73), 1:173.

[42] Benjamin Coleman, *A Sermon at the Lecture in Boston after the Funerals . . .* (Boston, 1717), p. 14; Ebenezer Pemberton, *A Christian Fix'd at His Post* (Boston, 1704), pp. 6–7; Nathaniel Henchman, *A Holy and Useful Life, Ending in Happy and Joyful Death* (Boston, 1721), p. 8.

Cotton Mather made it clear that the idle poor had no claims on society. "We should let them starve," he wrote. As for the idle rich, Nathaniel Clapp expelled them from the very folds of Christendom. "If persons live upon the labours of others," he wrote, "and spend their time in idleness, without any employment, for the benefit of others, they cannot be numbered among Christians. Yes, if persons labour to get great estates with this design, chiefly that they and theirs live in Idleness, they cannot be acknowledged for Christians."[43]

America in the 1780s, Drew McCoy tells us, may well have had one of the fastest rates of population growth in her history.[44] For many this conjured up fears of vast increases in the numbers of the poor and idle. Only a cultivation of domestic manufacturers would keep these idle hordes from the devil's hands. Once again the marriage of necessity and virtue led Americans to turn from foreign imports to local manufacture and domestic hard work. As Morgan noted of the prewar boycott of the British, so McCoy characterizes similar promotion of native production in the 1780s "as the necessary means of making Americans into an active, industrious, republican people." Indeed, in February 1787 one observer notes how absurd it was for Americans to support manufactures "at several thousand miles distance, while a great part of our own people are idle." American manufactures would "deliver them from the curse of idleness. We shall hold out . . . a new stimulus and encouragement to industry and every useful art."[45]

In the generation of the Framers there is one intellectual influence who played, I suggest, a particularly important role in the Protestant discourse's preoccupation with idleness and industry. He seems at first an unlikely choice, but James Burgh, we are told by Caroline Robbins, Oscar and Mary Handlin, Bernard Bailyn, Forrest McDonald, Lance G. Banning, J. G. A. Pocock, and Carla Hayes, had a profound in-

---

[43] Cotton Mather, *Durable Riches: Two Brief Discourses* (Boston, 1695), p. 20; Nathaniel Clapp, *The Duty of All Christians* (Boston, 1720), p. 8.

[44] Drew R. McCoy, *The Elusive Republic: Political Economy in Jeffersonian America* (Chapel Hill, 1980), p. 116.

[45] *American Museum* 1 (1787):116, 119.

fluence on the founding generation.[46] Reprinted in Philadelphia in 1775, his three-volume *Political Disquisitions* "had a widespread influence . . . not only upon the leaders, but even upon the common folk. . . . Its phrases were familiar in the town meetings of Western Massachusetts," according to the Handlins. For Bailyn it was "the key book of this generation." There is also the evidence of contemporaries. John Adams was so impressed with *Political Disquisitions* that he announced in 1775 his intention "to make it more known and attended to in the several parts of America." It was, he claimed, "a book which ought to be in the hands of every American who has learned to read." In its Philadelphia printing, the work had listed as its "Encouragers" a veritable Who's Who of American politics: Samuel Chase, Silas Deane, John Dickinson, John Hancock, Thomas Jefferson, Roger Sherman, George Washington, and James Wilson. Indeed, in 1790 Jefferson, writing to a young friend on what he should read to prepare for a public career, recommended Adam Smith, Montesquieu, "Locke's little book on government," and James Burgh's *Political Disquisitions*.[47] No wonder, then, that Burgh is cited in *Federalist* No. 56.

Burgh's apparent influence has been used by recent American scholarship to further the arguments of republican revisionism. He stands as the crucial figure in the transmission

[46] Caroline Robbins, *The Eighteenth-Century Commonwealthman: Studies in the Transmission, Development, and Circumstance of English Liberal Thought from the Restoration of Charles II until the War with the Thirteen Colonies* (Cambridge, Mass., 1959), p. 365; Oscar and Mary Handlin, "James Burgh and American Revolutionary Theory," *Massachusetts Historical Society Proceedings* 73 (1961); Bernard Bailyn, *The Ideological Origins of the American Revolution* (Cambridge, Mass., 1967), p. 35; Forrest McDonald, "A Founding Father's Library," *Literature of Liberty* 1 (1978):13; Lance G. Banning, *The Jeffersonian Persuasion: Evolution of a Party Ideology* (Ithaca, N.Y., 1978), pp. 61–62; J. G. A. Pocock, "Virtue and Commerce in the Eighteenth Century," *Journal of Interdisciplinary History* 3 (1972): 122, 133; idem, *Virtue, Commerce, and History*, pp. 257, 260–61; Carla Hays, *James Burgh, Spokesman for Reform in Hanoverian England* (Philadelphia, 1980).

[47] Handlin and Handlin, "Burgh and Revolutionary Theory," p. 31; Bailyn, *Ideological Origins*, p. 41; Charles Francis Adams, ed., *The Works of John Adams*, 10 vols. (Boston, 1850–56), 9:351; James Burgh, *Political Disquisitions*, 3 vols. (Philadelphia, 1775), 3:iii-vi; Lipscomb and Bergh, eds., *Writings of Jefferson*, 8:31.

from Britain to the Revolutionary generation of traditional opposition, or country, concerns informed by a nostalgic worldview, neoclassical, civic humanist, or republican at its foundation. The three volumes of *Political Disquisitions* are, indeed, full of jeremiads on the decline of virtue and the omnipresence of corruption in Britain. Well might Bailyn see Burgh as the messenger bearing tales of the conspiracy against liberty. Literally hundreds of pages of *Political Disquisitions* are devoted to themes closely associated with the country-based, or commonwealthman, opposition of the early eighteenth century. Balanced parliamentary government is depicted as threatened by pervasive ministerial corruption and the lack of annual parliaments. Bribes and jobs have undermined the independence of the Commons. A standing army, luxury, the national debt, and placemen have brought Britain to the brink of ruin. Pages upon pages on each of these topics are devoted to reprinting Bolingbroke and *Cato's Letters* of John Trenchard and Thomas Gordon. Large amounts of space are also given to Harrington, Trenchard and Gordon's other writings, and Charles Davenant, even to Machiavelli, Livy, and Cicero. Long excerpts from parliamentary assaults on Walpole are included, as are numerous parliamentary speeches on place bills, annual parliament proposals, suffrage reform, and bills to fund the national debt.

But Burgh and his widespread influence in America is, in fact, striking evidence of the multiplicity of political discourses there in the 1770s and 1780s. In this very text that illustrates the pervasiveness of the republican paradigm, one also hears a powerful rendering of the language of radical Protestantism. The dissenting minister and schoolmaster from Newington Green in North London here, too, spoke the political language of Americans. Burgh had participated in the efforts of his fellow Dissenters to repeal the Test and Corporation Acts, a political crusade that had a crucial social aspect, as well. To read the demands for the end of civic disabilities based on religion is to discover that even more prominent than reference to Locke's arguments for toleration is the boastful insistence that the Dissenters were hardworking, talented achievers responsible through their industry for much of England's wealth. They, the Dissenters, deserved public rewards more than those who had done no more than be born Anglican and privileged.

Burgh's *Political Disquisitions* and its attack on placemen and British corruption must have evoked sensitive memories in America for, as Morgan has argued, a good deal of the earlier anger at British taxation had been fueled by colonial fears that new and expensive legions of useless officeholders would be introduced. The new customs officials were seen as idle placemen fattening themselves on the industry of the colonists. They were villified as "parasitical minions," as "idle, lazy, and to say no worse, altogether useless customs house locusts, caterpillars, flies and lice." These placemen were, according to the *Newport Mercury* in 1773, "a parcel of dependent tools of arbitrary power," sent across the sea to enrich themselves "on the spoils of the honest and industrious of these colonies." In 1774 the town meeting of Bristol, Rhode Island, complained in a formal resolve (in terms virtually identical to those, noted below, in Burgh's *Disquisitions* of the same year) "that so many unnecessary officers are supported by the earnings of honest industry, in a life of dissipation and ease; who, by being properly employed, might be useful members of society."[48]

Americans saw "in their midst," Morgan writes, "a growing enclave of men whose lives and values denied the Puritan ethic." Burgh did, indeed, fuel colonial fears of conspiracy, but the plot was seen as one against Protestant notions of virtue and justice as well. For Sam Adams this was the intent of taxation without representation, which was "against the plain and obvious rule of equity, whereby the industrious man is entitled to the fruits of his industry." Such taxes not only attacked property, but also the industry and frugality "for which liberty and property must be the expected reward." For Jefferson, the purpose of England's oppressive taxes was "to provide sinecures for the idle or the wicked." Burgh could be read with utmost interest by colonial Americans convinced that "the conspirators against our Liberties

---

[48] *Boston Evening Post*, Nov. 30, 1767; Cushing, ed., *Writings of Adams*, 1:216; *Newport Mercury*, June 2, 1773; Bristol, R.I., cited in Morgan, "Puritan Ethic and Revolution," p. 16.

are employing all their influence to divide the people . . . introducing Levity, Luxury and Indolence."[49]

His attack on corruption and placemen in *Political Disquisitions* was utterly different from the constitutional arguments of Bolingbroke because Burgh used the Protestant idiom of work and talent. Over it hovered the same vision of the cosmic struggle between industry and idleness that Morgan discerned in Revolutionary America. The flavor of Burgh's attack on placemen is epitomized in the very title he gave to the fourth chapter of his second volume, "Places and Pensions Are Not Given According to Merit." For Bolingbroke, Walpole's placemen represented the triumph of new, upstart, monied men in politics, replacing men of breeding and privilege whose natural responsibility it was to govern. For Burgh, placemen were symbols of a corrupt society in which public office and public rewards went to the rich and privileged instead of the industrious and talented. Burgh used the image of a virtuous middle between two corrupt extremes. Why do we deny the right of voting to alms receivers, he asked? Is it not because we assume that they, "being needy, will of course be dependent, and under undue influence." Then why do we let men who "receive alms," that is, pensions and places, sit in Commons, he asked. They too, "are upon the parish, that is the nation." "Half our nobility" is "upon the parish, I mean the nation," and they cost hundreds of thousands, "while we are sinking in a bottomless sea of debt." He calculated elsewhere in the volume that "the over drenched court sponges" cost the nation two million pounds a year. All the while, he argued, the real business of the nation was being done by lesser clerks in the offices of the placemen "who have but 50 pounds a year."[50]

Burgh's major concern was the violation of the principles of equal opportunity and careers open to the talented. "If the nation is to be plundered," he wrote, "it would be some comfort to think that the spoil was divided among the deserving," but, alas, "modest merit gets no reward." The present system

---

[49] Cushing, ed., *Writings of Adams*, 1:271; Morgan, "Puritan Ethic and Revolution," pp. 13–14; Boyd et al., eds., *Papers of Jefferson*, 1:232.

[50] Burgh, *Political Disquisitions*, 3 vols. (London, 1774), 2:60, 97, 99.

inhibited ambition, as the talented, he noted, knew full well
that they would be excluded. Public service should be a public
return for talent, merit, and hard work, he insisted. Like
Figaro's charge that Almaviva had received all he had merely
by having taken the trouble to be born, so Burgh complained
in *Disquisitions* that public offices in Britain went to the
"worthless blockheads" who just "take care to be the son of a
Duke." Burgh quoted his friend Benjamin Franklin on how
irrelevant merit was in Britain. Pensions and places went to
"men of family and fortune" who, instead of offering their
services to the public, acted as "greedy sordid hirelings." The
"nobility and gentry . . . scramble for the profitable places."
They served their country only for hire. Burgh offered an
alternative to placemen and pensioners, and it was a far cry
from Bolingbroke's. "If the nobility and gentry declined serving their country in the great offices of the state, without
sordid hire, let the honest bourgeoisie be employed. They
will think themselves sufficiently rewarded by the honour
done them."[51]

Burgh proposed, in fact, that public jobs, like public contracts, be filled by "sealed proposals." The talented individual
most capable of serving his country would then be selected.
If men of the meritorious middle class took over public service and Parliament, then public expenditures, he predicted,
would decline dramatically. These new men would not demand great salaries; indeed, they would work without pay,
and they would not dance "at Mrs. Conneley's masquerades."
They would "rise up early and sit up late and fill up the whole
day with severe labour." Such men would replace the over-
paid "lord who has no necessary business to fatigue him but
drinking, whoreing, masquerading and New Marketing."
Why should not "the honest bourgeoisie" be employed in the
offices of state? Burgh could not resist the Dissenter's urge to
demystify the state. "Public business being all a mere routine," all its offices, even the secretary of state, the lord cham-
berlain, or the lord steward, are "places which any man of
common sense and common honesty can fill."[52]

[51] Ibid., pp. 80, 85, 87, 90, 96, 97.

[52] Ibid., pp. 97–98.

Burgh argued that government should "reward industry." He would revive the law of Queen Anne's reign that gave magistrates the right "to take up idle people for the army." He envisaged a press gang to seize "all idle and disorderly persons" who had been complained of three times. Such persons would be "set to work during a certain time for the benefit of great trading or manufacturing companies." In such hard work and labor, the idle would be made virtuous. In *Political Disquisitions* Burgh articulated a theme he shared with virtually all the middle-class Dissenter reformers in the 1770s and 1780s—virtuous government would repeal the poor laws.

> A benevolent disposition revolts against every discouragement to the exercise of the Godlike virtue of charity. But truth is truth, and it must be acknowledged that the profusion of our charities is hurtful to the manners of our people. . . . All that policy is sound which tends to improve and increase industry and frugality among the working people, and all that economy is hurtful, which tends to produce in the poor people a contrary spirit and which occasions their becoming more burdensome to their richer fellow subjects than is absolutely necessary, because this lays an additional burden upon all our exports, and hurts our trade at foreign markets upon which all depends. Let our innumerable and exorbitant public charities be considered in this light. If the poor are led by them to look upon industry and frugality as unnecessary, they will neither be industrious nor frugal; and the consequence will be that they and their children will come upon the parish, instead of being maintained by labour and industry.[53]

In the course of the long journey through corrupt Britain that was the third volume of his *Disquisitions*, Burgh did single out several virtuous models for emulation. They make a fascinating list, all of a piece. What unites them is not a republican preoccupation with participation in public life but a Protestant zeal for industry and thrift. He emphasized the Americans and Dissenters in general as people of virtue with "their sobriety . . . their thrift and regular manner of living." They have "bounded . . . their riotous appetites" and their

[53] Ibid., 3:215, 220, 225.

"lust." Other models of virtue for Burgh were the Quakers, who "hold frugality and industry for religious duties," the Dutch, "disciplined and frugal," and the Swiss, with their "character of simplicity, honesty, frugality, modesty and bravery." The models of virtue were not the ancient public-spirited citizens of Athens, Sparta, Rome, or even Elizabethan England; they were modern Protestants all.[54]

Burgh warned Britain that time was running out for the Dissenters, who represented so great a potential for the regeneration of Britain, but who might well be forced to leave if the Test and Corporation Acts were not repealed. He linked this to Sparta's fall, since one of its causes was that "those among them, who were distinguished by their merit and their morals, were on this very account proscribed by the tyrants, and hated by their creatures, so that they were forced to forsake their country."[55]

It is, then, a very Protestant vision of a reformed Britain that Burgh offered in the *Disquisitions*. He would have the virtuous magistrate stand in place of the omniscient God who forever watches over the lonely individual on his or her solitary pilgrimage and notes in his eternal book the pilgrim's successes and failures. "Did magistrates keep an attentive eye upon the behavior of individuals, and were they to keep a register of the complaints made against the idle and debauched, the register to be inspected upon every individual's applying for the benefit of public charity . . . it might appear whether he lived a life of labour and frugality, or brought himself to want by his own fault."[56]

Burgh, then, is himself a contradiction to those who insist on paradigm purity. His republican and civic humanist lamentations on the need for the regeneration of lost political virtues, so stressed by contemporary republican scholarship, coexist quite easily with a Protestant reading of virtue that is infinitely more compatible with the discourse of industry, individualism, and market society. Could it be that Burgh's phenomenal appeal to Americans lay in his very confusion of

[54] Ibid., pp. 30, 219, 172, 89, 410.

[55] Ibid., p. 88.

[56] Ibid., p. 226.

idioms? His importance in the political discourse of the 1780s may well have been the reflection of his ability to speak its varied tongues.

What better indication can there be of this than that Burgh was, in fact, soundly criticized by the very same man who had earlier been his champion. Unlike the contemporary scholars who currently write about Burgh, John Adams must have detected more than one discourse of politics in the *Political Disquisitions*. By 1789 Adams was no longer a Burgh booster. In that year he lumped *Political Disquisitions* with *Common Sense* and Mrs. Macauley's *History* as "extremely mistaken" and dangerously "ill-informed favorites." This may not have involved Adams's total revaluation of Burgh, but might have been merely the rejection of part of a varied whole. So Adams suggested, for he conceded that, despite Burgh's "erroneous opinions," his writings were still "excellent in some respects."[57] More than that Adams did not tell us. We can only conjecture which Burgh idiom he shared and which frightened him.

The paradoxes multiply. Communitarian critics of an individualistic interest-based politics could also speak the Protestant language of sobriety and industry and also locate these virtues in the particularly virtuous middle ranks of life. The Antifederalists were in good company, then, when they enlisted the Protestant language of sobriety, frugality, and industry to condemn what they saw as the aristocratic character of the new constitutional order. Melancton Smith, the bearer of a proud Calvinist name, best made the Protestant case for the virtuous middle against Hamilton's aristocratic Constitution at the New York ratifying convention. It was an evil Constitution, Smith claimed, because it restricted representation to the idle few and excluded those who were morally superior. What is crucial to note is that virtue here is apolitical and noncivic. "Those in middling circumstances, have less temptation—they are inclined by habit and the company with whom they associate, to set bounds to their passions and appetites—if this is not sufficient, the want of means to gratify them will be a restraint—they are obliged to employ their time in their respective callings—hence the substantial yeo-

[57] Adams, ed., *Works of Adams*, 9:558–59.

manry of the country are more temperate. Of better morals, and less ambitious than the great."[58]

In a recent collection of essays, J. G. A. Pocock has suggested that in the eighteenth century "virtue was redefined," but he is wide of the mark in suggesting that "there are signs of an inclination to abandon the word" or in claiming that it was simply redefined "as the practice and refinement of manners." Virtue had for some time been part of the Protestant discourse with its nonrepublican image of virtuous man as productive, thrifty, and frugal. By the second half of the century this noncivic personal reading of virtue would be secularized, as in Adam Smith's negative assessment of the aristocrat who "shudders with horror at the thought of any situation which demands the continual and long exertion of patience, industry, fortitude, and application of thought. These virtues are hardly ever to be met with in men who are born to those high stations."[59]

Virtue was for many becoming privatized in the latter part of the eighteenth century. It was being moved from the realm of public activity to a quality of personal character. The virtuous man partook less and less of that republican ideal that held sway from Aristotle to Harrington, the man whose landed property gave him the leisure necessary for civic commitment in the public arena, be its manifestations political or martial. Property was still important in the Protestant paradigm—not, however, as grantor of leisure, but as the rightful fruit of industrious work.

Gordon Wood has noted that Carter Braxton more than any other in the founding generation of Americans sensed the tension between a republicanism based on public virtue, the "disinterested attachment to the public good, exclusive of all private and selfish interest," and an American polity where in reality most practiced a private virtue in which man "acts for himself, and with a view of promoting his own particular welfare." The republican favoring of public over private had

[58] "Speeches by Melancton Smith," in Storing, ed., *The Complete Anti-Federalist*, 6:158–59 (6.12.17–18).

[59] Pocock, *Virtue, Commerce, and History*, p. 48; Adam Smith, *The Theory of Moral Sentiments*, ed. D. D. Raphael and A. L. Macfie (Oxford, 1976), pp. iii, 24.

never been, according to Braxton, the politics of "the mass of the people in any state." In this observation lay Braxton's real insight. Republican virtue was historically the ideal of a circumscribed, privileged citizenry with an independent, propertied base that provided the leisure and time for ful- fillment in public life through the moral pursuit of public things, *res publica*. But Americans, Braxton wrote, "who in- habit a country to which Providence has been more bounti- ful," live private lives of hard work and virtue, and their industry, frugality, and economy produce the fruits of honest labor.[60] From our perspective, we can credit Braxton with perceiving the decline of republican hegemony in the face of the alternative worlds of Lockean liberalism and the Protes- tant ethic. What we now know is that one hears more and more in the course of the late eighteenth century a different language of virtue, one that ejects the assumptions of civic humanism. Citizenship and the public quest for the common good were for some replaced by economic productivity and industrious work as the criteria of virtue. It is a mistake, how- ever, to see this simply as a withdrawal from public activity to a private, self-centered realm. The transformation also in- volved a changed emphasis on the nature of public behavior. The moral and virtuous man was no longer defined by his civic activity but by his economic activity. One's duty was still to contribute to the public good, but this was best done through economic activity, which actually aimed at private gain. Self-centered economic productivity, not public citizen- ship, would become a badge of the virtuous man. At the heart of this shift from republican to Protestant notions of virtue was the transvaluation of work and leisure. Many Americans in 1787 would dissent vigorously from the centuries-old re- publican paradigm set forth in Aristotle's *Politics:* "In the state with the finest constitution, which possesses just men who are just absolutely and not relatively to the assumed situation, the citizens must not live a mechanical or commercial life. Such a life is not noble, and it militates against virtue. Nor must those who are to be citizens be agricultural workers, for they must

[60] Carter Braxton, *An Address to the Convention of . . . Virginia, on the Sub- ject of Government . . .* (Williamsburg, 1776). For Wood's discussion of this text, see his *Creation of the Republic,* pp. 96–97.

have leisure to develop their virtue, and for the activities of a citizen."[61]

THE LANGUAGE OF POWER AND THE STATE

Lost today in the legitimate characterization of the Constitution as a document bent on setting limits to the power exercised by less than angelic men is the extent to which it is a grant of power to a centralized nation-state; this reflects a persistent bias toward Madison over Hamilton in reading the text. While posterity emphasizes the complex web of checks and balances and the many institutionalized separations of powers, the participants in the "great national discussion," on whichever side they stood, agreed with Hamilton that the Constitution was a victory for power, for the "principle of strength and stability in the organization of our government, and vigour in its operations."[62]

A pro-Constitution newspaper, the *Pennsylvania Packet*, wrote quite similarly in September 1787. "The year 1776 is celebrated for a revolution in favor of liberty. The year 1787 it is expected will be celebrated with equal joy, for a revolution in favor of government." The theme was repeated by Benjamin Rush, also a defender of the Constitution. Rush wrote in June 1787 to his English friend Richard Price that "the same enthusiasm now pervades all classes in favor of government that actuated us in favor of liberty in the years 1774 and 1775."[63]

Critics of the Constitution saw the same forces at work. For Patrick Henry "the tyranny of Philadelphia" was little different from "the tyranny of George III." The Antifederalist told the Virginia ratification convention that "had the Constitution been presented to our view ten years ago . . . it would have been considered as containing principles incompatible

[61] Aristotle, *The Politics*, trans. Thomas A. Sinclair (Harmondsworth, 1983), p. 415.

[62] Elliot, ed., *Debates*, 2:301.

[63] Benjamin Rush to Richard Price, June 2, 1787, Lyman H. Butterfield, ed., *Letters of Benjamin Rush*, 2 vols. (Princeton, 1951), 1:418–19.

with republican liberty, and, therefore, doomed to infamy." But the real foil to Hamilton, using the very same whig language, was Richard Henry Lee, who wrote in 1788, "It will be considered, I believe, as a most extraordinary epoch in the history of mankind, that in a few years there should be so essential a change in the minds of men. Tis really astonishing that the same people who have just emerged from a long and cruel war in defense of liberty, should now agree to fix an elective despotism among themselves and their posterity."[64]

But always there were other and louder voices using this same language in defense of the Constitution. Benjamin Franklin wrote that "we have been guarding against an evil that old states are most liable to, excess of power in the rulers, but our present danger seems to be defects of obedience in the subjects." For the *Connecticut Courant* it was all quite simple. The principles of 1776 had produced a glaring problem, "a want of energy in the administration of government."[65]

In the political discourse of 1787 there is a fourth paradigm at work, the state-centered language of power. It, too, reaches back into the classical world, to the great lawgivers and founders Solon and Lycurgus, and to the imperial ideal of Alexander and Caesar. Not republican city-states but empire, and much later the nation-state, are its institutional units. Its doctrines and commitments are captured less by *zoon politicon, vivere civilere, res publica,* and *virtu* than by *imperium, potestas, gubernaculum,* prerogative, and sovereignty. Its prophets are Dante, Marsilius of Padua, Jean Bodin, Cardinal Richelieu, Hobbes, Machiavelli of *The Prince* (not the *Discourses*), and James I. This language of politics is focused on the moral, heroic, and self-realizing dimensions of the exercise and use of power.

For Charles H. McIlwain the recurring answer to this power-centered language of politics was the discourse of *jur-*

---

[64] Henry in Elliot, ed., *Debates,* 3:436, 607; Lee, cited in Wood, *Creation of the Republic,* p. 469.

[65] Benjamin Franklin to Charles Carroll of Carrollton, May 25, 1789, Albert H. Smyth, ed., *Writings of Benjamin Franklin,* 10 vols. (New York, 1905–7), 10:7; *Connecticut Courant,* cited in Wood, *Creation of the Republic,* p. 432.

isdictio; for contemporary scholars it would be "the law-centered paradigm" or the "language of jurisprudence and rights."[66] For our purposes, it is important to recognize how the discourse of power and sovereignty renders problematic the reading of the "great national discussion" as simply a dialogue between republicanism and liberalism. To be sure, as the language of Protestantism complemented and supported liberalism, so the state-centered language of power is closer to and more easily compatible with the discourse of republicanism. Hamilton was fascinated by the nation-state builders in early modern Europe, but his power-centered politics was still connected with much of the older republican ideal. It shared the reading of man as a political animal, as a community-building creature. It, too, favored public life and public pursuits over a reading of politics that stressed the private context of self-regarding lives of individuals. It did not, however, share the participatory ideals of moral citizenship, basic to much of the republican tradition, and this most dramatically sets it off as a separate discourse.

In *Federalist* No. 1 Hamilton proclaimed "his enlightened zeal" for "the energy" and "vigor of government." His achievement, and that of the other young men at Philadelphia, was the creation of the American state. Some decades later Hegel could find nothing in America that he recognized as the "state."[67] But that was in comparison with established European states, and in that sense he was quite right. What little there was of an American state, however, was crafted by Hamilton, Madison, and the other Framers of the American Constitution who began their work de novo, from nothing. There was no royal household whose offices would become state bureaus, no royal army from a feudal past to be transformed into an expression of the state's reality.

It was the experience of war that shaped the vision of America's state-builders. The war against Britain provided them with a continental and national experience that re-

[66] Charles H. McIlwain, *Constitutionalism: Ancient and Modern,* rev. ed. (Ithaca, N.Y., 1947).

[67] Georg Wilhelm Friedrich Hegel, *The Philosophy of History,* trans. J. Sibree (New York, 1956), pp. 84–87.

placed the states-centered focus of the pre-1776 generation. A remarkable number of Framers of the Constitution either served in the Continental army or were diplomats or administrative officials for the Confederation or members of the Continental Congress. Indeed, thirty-nine out of the fifty-five delegates to the Constitutional Convention had sat in the Continental Congress. This is where the generational issue, so brilliantly described by Stanley Elkins and Eric McKitrick, is so crucial.[68] Most of the key figures in the Federalist camp had forged their identity in war service in the national cause and in dealing with the reluctance of individual states to assist that Continental effort. Washington, Henry Knox, and Hamilton were key figures in military affairs. Robert Morris was superintendent of finance, whose unhappy task it was to try to finance the war. John Jay had been president of the Confederation for a short while and a central actor in trying to implement a common foreign policy for the thirteen states. While most of the Antifederalists were states-centered politicians whose heroics took place before 1776, most of the Federalists were shaped by the need to realize the national interest in an international war. Their common bond was an experience that transcended and dissolved state boundaries.

Madison and Hamilton had sat on the same committee of the Continental Congress in 1782–83, working on the funding of the war and the maintenance of the French alliance. From experiences like this they and their state-building colleagues came to view the thirteen states as a "country," a country among countries. If it was going to live in a world of nation-states, it needed sovereign powers similar to theirs— to tax, to regulate trade, to coin money, to fund a debt, to conduct a foreign policy, and to organize a standing army.

The lack of such an American state was profoundly dispiriting to Hamilton. In *Federalist* No. 85 he lamented that "a nation without a national government is, in my view, a sad spectacle." In No. 15 he was even more distraught: "We have neither troops, nor treasury, nor government for the Union . . . our ambassadors abroad are the mere pageants of mimic sovereignty." One can, in fact, construct a theory of the origin

[68] Stanley Elkins and Eric McKitrick, "The Founding Fathers: Young Men of the Revolution," *Political Science Quarterly* 76 (1961):181–216.

and development of the state in *The Federalist,* all from Hamilton's contributions. The state is defined in No. 15 as a coercive agent having the power to make laws. To perform this function, according to Hamilton, required a stable and predictable system of taxation (Nos. 30 and 36) and agencies of force, that is, armies and police (Nos. 6 and 34). Especially important for Hamilton's theory of state development are *Federalist* Nos. 16 and 17. In the former he insists that "the majesty of national authority" cannot work if impeded by intermediate bodies: "It must carry its agency to the persons of the citizens." Independent and sovereign nations do not govern or coerce states; they rule over individuals.

Hamilton's preoccupation with money and arms as essential for state-building and his zeal to push aside any intermediate bodies between the state and individuals, while directly relevant to the case he is making on behalf of the Constitution, is also heavily influenced by his perceptive reading of the pattern of state-building in Europe. This is revealed in the all important *Federalist* No. 17, where he compares America under the Articles of Confederation to the "feudal anarchy" of medieval Europe. Clearly, for Hamilton, the separate American states were intermediate "political bodies" like "principal vassals" and "feudal baronies," each "a kind of sovereign within . . . particular demesnes." Equally self-evident is his sense that the pattern of European development with the triumph of coercive, centralized nation-states should be reproduced in America under the Constitution. On both sides of the Atlantic, then, the state will have "subdued" the "fierce and ungovernable spirit and reduced it within those rules of subordination" that characterize "a more rational and more energetic system of civic polity." Nor is this state-building scenario unrelated to liberal, ideological concerns. Hamilton, in *Federalist* No. 26, reads very much like the liberal theorists of the state Hobbes and Locke when he writes of the role that the "energy of government" plays in ensuring "the security of private rights." However, he is interested less in the limited liberal state than in the heroic state, and heroic state-builders cannot fear power, for power is the essence of the state. That power is so often abused does not rule out its creative and useful role, was the message of a Hamilton speech to the New York legislature in early 1787:

> We are told it is dangerous to trust power anywhere, that power is liable to abuse, with a variety of trite maxims of the same kind. General propositions of this nature are easily framed, the truth of which cannot be denied, but they rarely convey any precise idea. To these we might oppose other propositions equally true and equally indefinite. It might be said that too little power is as dangerous as too much, that it leads to anarchy, and from anarchy to despotism. . . . Power must be granted or civil society cannot exist; the possibility of abuse is no argument against the thing.[69]

All of the power-centered paradigm's euphemisms for power—"strength," "vigor," and "energy"—come together in Hamilton's conception of the presidential office. The presidency was the heart of the new American state for Hamilton, just as the monarch and chief magistrate was for older European nation-states. In Hamilton's president could be heard the echoes of *potestas* and *gubernaculum*. Had he not argued at Philadelphia for a life term for presidents? Short of that, in *Federalist* No. 72 Hamilton defended the president's eligibility for indefinite reelection. How else, he asked, would a president be able to "plan and undertake extensive and arduous enterprises for the public benefit?" The president was the energetic and creative builder of an energetic state. In *Federalist* No. 70 Hamilton argued: "Energy in the executive is a leading character in the definition of good government. . . . A feeble executive implies a feeble execution of the government. A feeble execution is but another phrase for a bad execution; and a government ill executed, whatever it may be in theory, must be in practice, a bad government."

Hamilton saw a close relationship between a state with energy and power at home and a powerful state in the world of states. At the Constitutional Convention he angrily replied to Charles Pinckney's suggestion that republican governments should be uninterested in being respected abroad and con-

---

[69] Harold C. Syrett et al., eds., *The Papers of Alexander Hamilton*, 27 vols. (New York, 1961–87), 4:11.

cerned only with achieving "domestic happiness": "It has been said that respectability in the eyes of foreign nations was not the object at which we aimed, that the proper object of republican government was domestic tranquility and happiness. This was an ideal distinction. No government could give us tranquility at home, which did not possess stability and strength to make us respectable abroad."[70]

Hamilton was preoccupied with the interrelationship between commerce, state power, and international politics. A powerful state in his vision was a commercial state. In the competitive international system, nation-states sought to improve or protect their commercial strength, which led inevitably to wars. Powerful states thus needed standing armies and strong navies. In *Federalist* No. 24 Hamilton insisted that "if we mean to be a commercial people, it must form a part of our policy, to be able to defend that commerce." In contrast to Thomas Paine and many isolationist Antifederalists, Hamilton rejected the notion that wars were fought only "by ambitious princes" or that republican government led inexorably to peace. Hamilton, the realist, ridiculed in *Federalist* No. 6 "visionary or designing men," who thought republics or trading nations immune from the natural conflicts of nation-states, who talked "of perpetual peace between the states" or who claimed that "the genius of republics is pacific": "Have republics in practice been less addicted to war than monarchies? Are not the former administered by men as well as the latter? Are there not aversions, predilections, rivalships and desires of unjust acquisitions that affect nations as well as kings? Are not popular assemblies frequently subject to the impulses of rage, resentment, jealousy, avarice and of other irregular and violent propensities?"

But Hamilton did not want to build an American state with all that that required—a financial and commercial infrastructure, energetic leadership, and powerful military forces— merely to allow America to hold its own in a world system where conflict, competition, and clashing power were an inevitable part of the human and international condition. He had a grander vision for the American state, a call to great-

---

[70] Farrand, ed., *Records of the Convention*, 1:466–67.

ness. In *Federalist* No. 11 he wrote of "what this country can become," of a future glory for America of "a striking and animating kind." Under a properly "vigorous national government, the natural strength and resources of the country, directed to a common interest, would baffle all the combinations of European jealousy to restrain our growth." If Americans would only "concur in creating one great American system," the American state would be "superior to the control of all transatlantic force or influence, and able to dictate the terms of the connection between the old and the new world." In the face of a vigorous and energetic American state Europe would cease to be "mistress of the world." America would become ascendant in the Western Hemisphere.

Hamilton's horizons were dazzling. His internationalism transcended the cosmopolitan vision of his fellow Federalists as it had transcended the localism of the Antifederalists. The victory of the state center over the American periphery would, in his fertile imagination, catapult America from the periphery of nations to the center of the world system.

It would be a heroic achievement for Hamilton and his colleagues in Philadelphia to create such a powerful American state. It would bring them everlasting fame, and, as Douglass Adair has told us, that may well have been the ultimate motive that prompted their state-building. In his *Federalist* No. 72 Hamilton suggested that political leaders who undertook "extensive and arduous enterprises for the public benefit" were prompted by "the love of fame, the ruling passion of the noblest minds." He was at one and the same time describing his ideal of an energetic president, the subject of the paper, and the heroic enterprise of constitutional state-building that he and his fellow Federalists had embarked upon. It would bring them the fame and immortality of a Lycurgus as described by Madison in *Federalist* No. 38. The classical and Renaissance discourse of power was replete with praise for creative wielders of *potestas*. Literate men in the eighteenth century, like Hamilton and Madison, knew that Plutarch in his *Lives of the Noble Greeks and Romans* reserved the greatest historical glory for the "lawgiver" and the "founder of commonwealth." In a text equally well known in this period, Francis Bacon's *Essays,* the top of a fivefold scale of "fame and honour" was occupied by "Conditores Imperium, Founders of States and Commonwealths." David Hume, an English eighteenth-century philosopher widely read by both Hamilton and Madison, echoed this theme. He wrote that "of all men that distinguish themselves by memorable achievements, the first place of honour seems due to legislators and founders of states who transmit a system of laws and institutions to secure the peace, happiness and liberty of future generations." Hamilton must have seen himself and his fellow state-builders as achieving such everlasting fame. Ten years earlier, in a pamphlet attacking congressmen for not better realizing the potential of their positions, he had written of true greatness and fame. He signed the pamphlet with the pseudonym Publius, a fabled figure in Plutarch's *Lives* and the name later used by the authors of the *Federalist*. Hamilton's vision transcended the walls of Congress in the infant nation and spoke to the historic discourse of power. "The station of a member of Congress is the most illustrious and important of any I am able to conceive. He is to be regarded not only as a Legislator, but as the founder of an empire. A man of virtue and ability, dignified with so precious a trust, would rejoice that fortune had given him birth at a time and placed him in circumstances so favourable for promoting human happiness. He would esteem it not more the duty, than the privilege and ornament of his office, to do good to mankind."[71]

We must not lose sight of the other side of the "great national discussion," however. Hamilton's discourse of power, with its vision of an imperial American state, attracted the fire of Antifederalists like one of Franklin's lightning rods. It was Patrick Henry who most angrily and most movingly repudiated the Federalist state in his speech to the Virginia ratifying convention. Henry's American spirit was Tom Paine's. With the Federalist state America had lost its innocence, and "splendid government" was its badge, its dress. On the ruins of paradise were built, if not the palaces of

---

[71] Francis Bacon, "Of Honors and Reputation," in *Essays*, ed. Richard Whatley, new ed. (London, 1886); David Hume, "Of Parties in General," *The Philosophical Works of David Hume*, 4 vols. (Edinburgh, 1826), 3:57; Syrett et al., eds., *Papers of Hamilton*, 1:580–81.

kings, then armies and navies and mighty empires. Henry evoked a different language of politics.

> The American spirit has fled from hence; it has gone to regions where it has never been expected; it has gone to the people of France, in search of a splendid government, a strong, energetic government. Shall we imitate the example of those nations who have gone from a simple to a splendid government? Are those nations more worthy of our imitation? What can make an adequate satisfaction to them for the loss they have suffered in attaining such a government, for the loss of their liberty? If we admit this consolidated government, it will be because we like a great, splendid one. Some way or other we must be a great and mighty empire; we must have an army, and a navy, and a number of things. When the American spirit was in its youth, the language of America was different; liberty, sir, was then the primary object."[72]

What was Madison's relationship to the discourse of power and the Hamiltonian state? Madison was a state-builder, too, but his state was quite different from Hamilton's, and upon these differences would turn a good deal of American politics, not only during the next two decades, but down to this day as well. Madison and Hamilton were in agreement on many things—the need to establish an effective, unified, national government, the serious threats to personal property rights posed by the state legislatures and the role that establishing a central government would play in their protection, the need to have the central government run by worthy, enlightened, and deliberative men, and the necessity of the Constitution to provide the essential framework for commercial development through the creation of a national market, public credit, a uniform currency, and the protection of contract. To be sure, Madison's vision was tilted toward agrarian capitalism and Hamilton's toward manufactures and commerce, but where they markedly disagreed, however, was in giving positive, assertive power, "energy," and "vigor" to the state.

Hamilton saw the new American state as an assertive power, valuable in and for its own sake. He saw the nation-

---

[72] Elliot, ed., *Debates*, 3:53.

state with its own historic and heroic goals, seeking power in a competitive international system of other power-hungry states. Madison saw the nation-state necessary only to protect private rights and thus ensure justice. Like Locke, he saw the need for a grant of power to the state, but a grant of limited power. Madison saw the central government providing an arena for competitive power, where the private bargaining of free men, groups, and interests would take place, and the state would define no goals of its own other than ensuring the framework for orderly economic life. All the state would do was regulate "the various and interfering interests," or as Madison put it in his letter to Washington in straightforward Lockean terms, be an impartial umpire in disputes. Energy in politics for Madison would come from individuals and groups seeking their own immediate goals, not from an energetic state seeking its own heroic ends.

What about Madison's governing elite of "enlightened views and virtuous sentiments," "whose wisdom may best discern the true interest of their country," of which he wrote in *Federalist* No. 10? Madison's "true interest" was not the "national interest" of Hamilton's realism. Nor was it some ideal, transcending purpose or goal to which wise leadership would lead the state and those still in the shadows. Madison's enlightened leaders would demonstrate their wisdom and virtue more by what they did not do than by what they did. Being men of cool and deliberate judgment, they would not pass unjust laws that interfered with private rights. They would respect liberty, justice, and property and run a limited government that did little else than preside over and adjudicate conflicts in a basically self-regulating social order. Did not Madison's *Federalist* No. 62 criticize the "excess of law making" and the voluminousness of laws as the twin "diseases to which our governments are most liable?"

If the men in the state legislatures under the Articles had acted with such self-restraint, there would have been no need for the institutions of the central state, but among generally fallen men they were an even more inferior lot, fired by local prejudices and warm passions. Should the unexpected happen and cooler men of enlightened views seek to do too much, that is, undertake "improper or wicked projects," then

Madison's new constitutional government would rapidly cut them down as its multiplicity of built-in checks and balances preserved the Lockean limited state.

Madison's limited Federalist state might well appear meek and tame set next to Hamilton's energetic and vigorous one, but it was a matter of perspective. To the Antifederalists even Madison's state, limited as it was by checks and balances and its cool men resisting the temptations of lawmaking, seemed a monstrous betrayal of the Revolution and its spirit. The Constitution could be seen, then, as the last act of the American Revolution. Like most revolutions, the American began as a repudiation of the state, of power, and of authority in the name of liberty. Like most revolutions it ended with a stronger state, the revival of authority, and the taming of liberty's excesses.

The American state would never be quite as bad, however, as the Antifederalists' worst fears. They had assumed, for example, that "Congress will be vested with more extensive powers than ever Great Britain exercised over us." They worried that "after we have given them all our money, established them in a federal town, given them the power of coining money and raising a standing army . . . what resources have the people left?" The reason it would not be quite that bad is because the new American state created by that "triple headed monster" of a Constitution was much closer to Madison's state than to Hamilton's—at least, that is, for the rest of the eighteenth century and through most of the nineteenth. The twentieth century would be another matter and another story.

CONCLUSION

The Federalists triumphed in the "great national discussion" that was the debate over the ratification of the Constitution. But posterity has not remembered simply the victorious advocates of the Constitution in 1787 and 1788. The Antifederalists have lived on in the American imagination, as well. Their worst fears were never realized, which proves the exceptionalism of the American Revolution when compared with others. The Antifederalists, while losers in 1788, were neither liquidated nor forced to flee. Nor, more significantly, were their ideas extinguished. Their values lived on in America, as they themselves did, and have been absorbed into the larger pattern of American political culture. The states have endured as vital parts of the American political scene and, in the unique configuration that is American federalism, have retained tremendous power in numerous areas of public policy. In celebrating the Bicentennial of its Constitution, America celebrates both the Federalists and the Antifederalists, for the living American Constitution is by now a blend of the positions both sides took during the "great national discussion," however untidy that may seem to constitutional purists.

Just as there was ultimately no decisive victor in the political and pamphlet battle, so, too, there was none in the paradigm battle. No one paradigm cleared the field in 1788 and obtained exclusive dominance in the American political discourse. There was no watershed victory of liberalism over republicanism. These languages were heard on both sides. So, too, were the two other paradigms available to the Framer's generation, the Protestant ethic and the ideals of sovereignty and power. So it has remained. American political discourse to this day tends to be articulated in one or another of these "distinguishable idioms," however untidy that may seem to professors of history or political philosophy.

The generations of Americans who lived through the founding and the framing have left us clear evidence of the variety of their paradigms. They imprinted on the landscape of their experience place-names by which future generations would know them and their frames of reference. They took the physical world as their text and wrote on it with the conceptual structures of their political language. My corner of the American text, upstate New York, was settled by Revolutionary war veterans in the last decades of the eighteenth century. When they named their parcels of land, they knew in what tongues to speak. There is a Rome here, as well as Ithacas and Syracuses. There is a Locke, a mere ten miles from Ithaca. There is a Geneva, at the foot of Seneca Lake. And for the statebuilders fascinated with founders of states, there is even a Romulus, New York. Such is the archaeology of paradigms far above Cayuga's waters.

JEAN YARBROUGH

The Constitution and Character: The Missing Critical Principle?

If there be . . . [no virtue among us], we are in a wretched situation. No theoretical checks, no form of government, can render us secure. To suppose that any form of government will secure liberty or happiness without any virtue in the people, is a chimerical idea.—JAMES MADISON

[Although] the American war is over, . . . this is far from being the case with the American Revolution. On the contrary, nothing but the great drama is closed. It remains yet to establish and perfect our new forms of government and to prepare the principles, morals, and manners of our citizens for these forms of government after they are established and brought to perfection.—BENJAMIN RUSH

IN RECENT YEARS, a new republican paradigm has revolutionized our understanding of the Founding period. In place of the older, liberal tradition, which viewed the Declaration and the Constitution as essentially Lockean documents, this new generation of scholars has focused on republican virtue or civic humanism in their study of the Founding.[1] Yet what is

NOTE: My epigraphs are from a speech of Madison's at the Virginia ratifying convention, June 1788, and an address by Rush, January 1787.

[1]Gordon S. Wood, *The Creation of the American Republic, 1776-1787* (Chapel Hill, 1969); John T. Agresto, "Liberty, Virtue, and Republicanism: 1776–1787," *Review of Politics* 39 (1977):473–504; Thomas L. Pangle, "The *Federalist Papers*' Vision of Civic Health and the Tradition out of Which That Vision Emerges," *Western Political Quarterly* 39 (1986):577–

remarkable about many of these studies, Gordon S. Wood's *Creation of the American Republic* in particular, is their tendency to view the Constitution as the end of classical republicanism. In short, Wood tends to agree with the earlier, liberal tradition (and with contemporary critics of republican revisionism, notably John P. Diggins and Joyce Appleby) that the Framers, while adopting the rhetoric of republicanism, were Lockean liberals. On the crucial question of character, this means that the Framers abandoned the traditional republican concern with virtue and substituted in its place institutional arrangements that would pit interest against interest and power against power.

Although the aim of this essay is to correct what I regard as a simplification of the Framers' intentions on the question of character, I acknowledge that, on the face of it, such a conclusion is not altogether implausible. After all, the Preamble to the Constitution, which sets forth the *ends* for which this "more perfect Union" is established, says nothing about the formation of character or the pursuit of human excellence.[2] Nor does the body of the text. Critics rightly note that the Constitution itself neglects the *institutions* that traditionally shaped republican character. Its failure to provide for

---

602. And compare with the liberal interpretation articulated by Martin Diamond in *"The Federalist,"* in Morton J. Frisch and Richard Stevens, eds., *American Political Thought: The Philosophic Dimension of American Statesmanship* (New York, 1971), and reaffirmed more recently by John P. Diggins, *The Lost Soul of American Politics: Virtue, Self-Interest, and the Foundations of Liberalism* (New York, 1984); Joyce Appleby, "What Is Still American in the Political Philosophy of Thomas Jefferson?" *William and Mary Quarterly,* 3d ser. 39 (1982):287–309. Not all historians see the Constitution as marking the end of republican "ideology." Some notable exceptions include J. G. A. Pocock, *The Machiavellian Moment: Florentine Political Thought and the Atlantic Republican Tradition* (Princeton, 1975); Lance G. Banning, *The Jeffersonian Persuasion: Evolution of a Party Ideology* (Ithaca, N.Y., 1978); Drew R. McCoy, *The Elusive Republic: Political Economy in Jeffersonian America* (Chapel Hill, 1980).

[2]The only exception is James Wilson's speech of July 13, 1787, before the federal Convention in which Wilson observed that "the cultivation and improvement of the human mind was the most noble object of government" (Max Farrand, ed., *The Records of the Federal Convention of 1787,* rev. ed., 4 vols. [New Haven, 1949], 1:605).

the education of statesmen and citizens alike ranks as the most glaring but by no means the only such omission.[3] Similarly, critics point out (though here their objections are more muted) that the decision not to acknowledge a dependence upon God, or to require a religious test for officeholders, flies in the face of the traditional alliance between religion and republicanism. Finally, they note that the Constitution makes no provision, beyond voting in biennial elections, for citizens to participate in public affairs. Indeed, the Framers seem to regard collective exclusion of the people from political life as a singular improvement, a point explicitly made in that most authoritative explication of the Constitution, the *Federalist.*

These omissions, important in their own right, gain from a comparison with the enormous attention lavished by the Convention upon commercial matters. Indeed, the centrality of commerce in the constitutional order has led some critics to conclude that it is this principle, more than any other, that shapes the American character. But far from shaping republican citizens, animated by a love of freedom, they see the commercial principle, and its grounding in self-interest, as undermining the virtues necessary to public life.[4]

Although these omissions are indisputable, the way they are interpreted distorts the Framers' intentions. Indeed, it is because the Framers were statesmen of the highest order that they took the question of character seriously. But they were compelled both by their *liberal* republican principles and various political necessities to approach this important issue indirectly.

This essay will begin by considering the effect of commerce on the American character. Seeking to understand the commercial principle as the Framers did, it returns to the

---

[3] Ibid., 2:322, 325. For a discussion, see Wilson Carey McWilliams, "The Constitution and the Education of Citizens" (Paper presented at the Seventy-ninth Annual Meeting of the American Political Science Association, Chicago, September 1983). Also, Paul Eidelberg, *The Philosophy of the American Constitution* (New York, 1968), esp. pp. 247–60.

[4] See especially, McWilliams, "Constitution and Education." Also Benjamin Barber "The Compromised Republic: Public Purposelessness," in Robert H. Horwitz, ed., *The Moral Foundations of the American Republic* (Charlottesville, 1977).

eighteenth-century philosophers—especially Montesquieu, David Hume, and Adam Smith—who most directly influenced the Framers' thinking about commerce and commercial republicanism. Although these philosophers fully understood that commerce would undermine the more austere virtues of classical republicanism, they expected it to call forth virtues of its own, virtues that were more appropriate to a world where citizens defined themselves chiefly in terms of work, rather than participation in public affairs.[5] Thus the Framers' embrace of the commercial republic is best understood not as the triumph of self-interest over virtue but as the replacement of the self-denying aristocratic virtues with those virtues more compatible with a liberal democratic republic. To stress only the appeal to self-interest without considering the virtues they expected commerce to engender is to lose sight of the moral argument that informs their position.

After elaborating the philosophical arguments in favor of commerce, the paper shifts to a discussion of the practical alternatives this principle involved. The debate between Thomas Jefferson and Alexander Hamilton about whether to remain a predominantly agrarian republic or to encourage a more diverse manufacturing society reveals most clearly the extent to which America's early statesmen understood commerce—and the choices it presented—as a moral as well as an economic principle. Nevertheless, not even the most enthusiastic supporter of this principle relied upon it exclusively to form the character of the people. In varying degrees, they all recognized that commerce might corrupt the habits and manners necessary for self-government and sought by other means to strengthen the virtues that would act as a brake on excessive materialism.

The next section of the paper examines what effect the federal distribution of power might have on the question of character. While the Framers made no more than passing references to character at the Federal Convention, and failed to provide for it in the Constitution or to discuss it in the *Federalist*, they passed over the subject not because they were indifferent to these concerns or because they took its contin-

[5] See the discussion in McCoy, *Elusive Republic.*

uation for granted[6] but because these matters were the preserve of the states, and the states were unlikely to ratify any charter that asked them to surrender these powers to the central government. Moreover, to recommend that the newly created federal government become actively involved in education, religion, and civic participation flew in the face of even the most radical nationalists' understanding of the scope of federal powers.[7]

Consequently, if we are to understand the significance of character in the American constitutional system, we must redirect our attention toward the state constitutions. In contrast to the federal Constitution, the Revolutionary state constitutions actively sought to promote the moral and civic virtues that would restrain the excesses of the commercial principle. And although the leading statesmen-educators divided on the question of which system would best form republican character—religion and a stern moral education or a more secular and enlightened emphasis on history and literature coupled with the right economic and social environment—there is no doubt that they considered some combination of these institutions to be vital to the preservation of free government.

THE MORAL ARGUMENT
FOR COMMERCE

Given the centrality of commerce to the modern liberal republic, we need to consider at the outset precisely what was meant by this term. At the most general level, commerce meant simply trade or exchange. But in the writings of Hume and Smith, which traced the various stages of economic development through which societies passed, from simple hunt-

[6] Martin Diamond, in his earlier writings, along with Diggins and McWilliams, argues that virtue is no longer necessary. In his later work "Ethics and Politics: The American Way," Diamond suggests that the Framers took its continuation for granted (Horwitz, ed., *Moral Foundations*, pp. 39–72). For this second interpretation, see also Marc Plattner, "American Democracy and the Acquisitive Spirit," in Robert A. Goldwin and William Schambra, eds., *How Capitalistic Is the Constitution?* (Washington, D.C., 1982), pp. 1–22.

[7] Consider especially *Federalist* Nos. 17 and 45.

ing and grazing, through agriculture, and finally to commerce and manufacturing, commerce referred specifically to the processes in advanced societies that encouraged the production and exchange of surplus goods for the sake of profit. A commercial society was one where every man was free "to pursue his own interest in his own way"[8] and where his interest extended beyond the minimal concern with self-preservation. In keeping with this broad understanding, these eighteenth-century philosophers generally had in mind a market economy in which government policy allowed, or even encouraged, individuals to acquire, enjoy, and most important, *increase* their property and wealth.

We are so accustomed to a society where the pursuit of wealth is considered appropriate and desirable that it is difficult to appreciate the moral revolution necessary to bring this idea to fruition. Yet Montesquieu had taught that commerce was incompatible with republicanism, at least in its classical form. The spring, or ruling principle, of the ancient Greek and Roman republics was virtue, understood as unswerving dedication to the common good. When republics permit, to say nothing of encourage, citizens to pursue their material well-being, the people lose interest in public affairs. Wealth and luxury corrupt virtue, and republican institutions degenerate.

Yet Montesquieu's assessment of commerce was ultimately more complicated. After observing that commerce makes "a traffic of all the humane, all the moral virtues,"[9] and even more important, undermines the patriotism and military valor on which republics depend, he went on to suggest that commerce promotes certain virtues of its own. "The spirit of commerce is naturally attended with that of frugality, economy, moderation, labour, prudence, tranquility, order, and rule."[10]

---

[8] Adam Smith, *The Wealth of Nations* (New York, 1909), p. 447. See also the discussion in McCoy, *Elusive Republic*, pp. 13–47; and Forrest McDonald, "The Constitution and Hamiltonian Capitalism," in Goldwin and Schambra, eds., *How Capitalistic Is the Constitution?* pp. 49–74.

[9] Charles de Secondat, baron de Montesquieu, *The Spirit of the Laws*, trans. Thomas Nugent (Chicago, 1952), book 20, chap. 2, p. 146.

[10] Montesquieu, *Spirit of the Laws*, book 5, chap. 6, p. 21.

The Scottish philosophers Hume and Smith expanded on this insight. Although Smith readily acknowledged that these were not "the greater and more splended virtues," he judged them "respectable," even "amiable,"[11] for they were rooted in the deepest desires of ordinary individuals. It was precisely such a democratic morality that the eighteenth-century political philosophers sought to fashion.[12]

Nor was it simply the bourgeois virtues that commerce tended to promote. Montesquieu, Hume, and Smith all noted the connection between commerce and justice, the first of the social virtues. To be sure, they did not mean the classical notion of distributive justice—that each should receive what by nature is most suitable for him. Rather, they had in mind the "exact justice" of contractual agreements and the rules of fair play, where each receives what is owed him or what he can fairly obtain, without regard to his intrinsic moral worth.[13] In such a society, justice was chiefly understood as the protection of property rights, though property rights broadly conceived. These liberal philosophers saw no tension between the protection of property rights and other more individual rights. Hence commerce, by protecting the acquisition of property, would provide greater security to all men's fundamental rights.

Nor did their praise of commerce stop here. Turning his attention to the full range of human excellences, Hume insisted that the luxury "which nourishes commerce," and which in turn is nourished by it, gives rise to the highest intellectual and moral virtues. In contrast to the classical republican tradition, which blamed luxury for the corruption of republican virtue, he argued that commerce promotes "knowledge and humanity," "mildness and moderation."[14]

[11] Adam Smith, *Theory of Moral Sentiments* (Indianapolis, 1969), part 6, sec. 1, pp. 353–54.

[12] Ralph Lerner, "Commerce and Character: The Anglo-American as New Model Man," *William and Mary Quarterly*, 3d ser. 36 (1979):3–26.

[13] Montesquieu, *Spirit of the Laws*, book 20, chap. 2, pp. 146–47; Smith, *Theory of Moral Sentiments*, part 2, sec. 2, p. 162.

[14] David Hume, "Of Refinement in the Arts," in *Essays: Moral, Political, and Literary*, ed. Eugene F. Miller (Indianapolis, 1985), p. 270. Ironically, Hume's pupil Adam Smith, whose work is popularly associated with a full-

Although the argument that progress in the technical arts lays the foundation for the advance of scientific and intellectual knowledge is not new, the claim that luxury promotes the social virtues is striking. The whole point of Jean-Jacques Rousseau's *First Discourse* had been to show that we achieve civilization only at the expense of virtue. Part of this disagreement turns, of course, on the meaning of virtue. What Rousseau had in mind were the austere, self-denying civic virtues of antiquity, while Montesquieu and the Scottish philosophers regarded humanity and benevolence as the highest moral virtues. What in their view distinguished civilized nations from earlier, barbaric times was that "among civilized nations, the virtues which are founded upon humanity are more cultivated than those which are founded upon self-denial and the command of the passions."[15] And since it was commerce that "softened" the manners of men, disposing them to humanity and universal benevolence, Montesquieu and the Scottish philosophers found much to recommend in this principle.

Still, even Hume recognized that this principle could be pushed too far, as evidenced by his distinction between "innocent" and "vicious luxury." And other Scots, notably Lord Kames, who exercised a profound influence upon Jefferson, remained even more cautious about the amount of luxury and wealth compatible with republican manners and morals. But these were minor quarrels, disputes at the margin, so to speak. No one except perhaps Rousseau considered the classical republics superior, and his influence on the Founders was minimal. Those who had the most to teach the Americans insisted that the defects of the commercial principle were caused by its excesses, and not by the principle itself. The only serious debate in America was what constituted the extreme.

---

blown defense of capitalism, was more cautious. While acknowledging that the pursuit of wealth was necessary for the well-being of society as a whole, he nevertheless expressed grave reservations about its effect upon the individual. For a discussion of these tensions see Joseph Cropsey, *Polity and Economy: An Interpretation of the Principles of Adam Smith* (The Hague, 1957).

[15] Smith, *Theory of Moral Sentiments*, part 5, chap. 2, pp. 334–35.

The argument thus far has attempted to show that the great eighteenth-century political philosophers believed commerce improved character by promoting not only the bourgeois virtues but the higher moral and intellectual excellences. We shall now consider their corresponding revaluation of the passions as the seat of those virtues and the connection between this revolution and the elevation of commerce to a moral and political good.

Unlike classical political philosophy, which taught that virtue depends on the restraint of the passions, modern political philosophy, beginning with Thomas Hobbes, erected a moral system based on the emancipation of men's desires. In both Hobbes and John Locke, this emancipation was linked to the demotion of more dangerous aristocratic passions like pride and the elevation of the more democratic desires for self-preservation and a comfortable life. It was precisely because most men's desires were so limited in their reach that the passions could be given free reign.[16]

Continuing in this general direction, both Hume and Smith agreed that morality must accord with the passions of ordinary men. But, breaking with Hobbes and Locke, the Scottish philosophers denied that a hierarchy of the passions could be definitively established. Although most men were motivated by selfish desires, there were other more generous passions, like benevolence, that also prompted men to action. And even among the selfish passions, the fear of violent death was not always paramount. In some individuals, "ambition, avarice, self-love, vanity" might also predominate. Of particular interest to us is avarice.

The rehabilitation of avarice by eighteenth-century political philosophy has been widely noted.[17] Whereas Christian moral teaching, following the lead of Aristotle, denounced avarice as one of the deadliest sins, both Hume and Smith praised the desire for wealth for its social utility. Not only did

[16] Leo Strauss, *The Political Philosophy of Thomas Hobbes: Its Basis and Genesis,* trans. Elsa M. Sinclair (Chicago, 1966).

[17] Lerner, "Commerce and Character"; Albert O. Hirschman, *The Passions and the Interests: Political Arguments for Capitalism before Its Triumph* (Princeton, 1977); Gerald Stourzh, *Alexander Hamilton and the Idea of Republican Government* (Stanford, 1970), pp. 73–75.

avarice tend to promote desirable bourgeois virtues, but in contrast to pride, lust, ambition, love of power, and the like, avarice was less violent and more reasonable. Compared to political and religious quarrels, property disputes in a commercial society were less likely to end in violent discord. Accordingly, Hume sought to encourage avarice and to use this passion to check other more dangerous desires.[18] Unlike Niccolò Machiavelli, Hume did not suggest that avarice could now be considered a virtue, and he dissociated himself from Bernard Mandeville's formula "private vice, public virtue." But in the final analysis, the distance is narrowed since Hume "excuses" the desire for wealth on the ground that it promotes the public good. And the passions that are useful not only to ourselves, but also to others, cannot truly be called vicious.[19]

It was, then, a new understanding of the virtues, accompanied by the rehabilitation of avarice or, to speak more precisely, acquisitiveness,[20] that made possible the Constitution of the commercial republic. But if Americans generally agreed on the moral and political desirability of the commercial principle, there still remained the narrower questions about what kind of commerce America should pursue and how much wealth was compatible with a society striving to retain some link with the republican tradition. It is these issues that the debates between Jefferson and Hamilton over agriculture and manufacturing sought to resolve. For both sides, but especially for the Jeffersonians, what was at stake in this quarrel was not merely the economic policy of the republic, but its very soul.

[18] David Hume, "Of Parties in General" and "Of Commerce," in *Essays*.

[19] In his early essay "Of Avarice," Hume condemns this passion as a vice. But what he has in mind here is the miserly hoarding of wealth. Significantly, he dropped this essay from later collections. In a later essay, "Of Refinement in the Arts," Hume distinguishes between the hoarding of wealth and the desire for it. He has no quarrel with acquisitiveness, so long as it is rightly used. In this connection, see Diamond, "Ethics and Politics," pp. 63–65.

[20] For a good discussion of this distinction, see Diamond, "Ethics and Politics," esp. p. 64.

COMMERCE AND AGRARIAN VIRTUE

One of the distinctive features of Jefferson's thought was his belief that the essence of republicanism was to be found not in the formal structures of government but in the manners and spirit of the people.[21] In thinking about how to preserve this spirit, Jefferson discovered a powerful connection between republican virtue and agrarianism. He first set forth this argument in the *Notes on Virginia,* written in 1782, long before the Constitution of the commercial republic was even a remote possibility. There he wrote:

> Those who labour in the earth are the chosen people of God, if ever he had a chosen people, whose breasts he has made his peculiar deposit for *substantial and genuine virtue.* It is the focus in which he keeps alive that sacred fire, which otherwise might escape from the face of the earth. Corruption of morals in the mass of cultivators is a phenomenon of which no age nor nation has furnished an example. It is the mark set on those, who not looking up to heaven, to their own *soil and industry,* as does the husbandman, for their subsistence, depend for it on the casualties and caprice of customers. Dependance begets subservience and venality, suffocates the germ of virtue, and prepares fit tools for the designs of ambition. . . . generally speaking, the proportion which the aggregate of the other classes of citizens bears in any state to that of its husbandmen, is the proportion of its unsound to its healthy parts, and is a good-enough barometer whereby to measure its degree of corruption.[22]

But even after the Constitution was drafted, and indeed throughout his long political career, Jefferson continued to insist on the moral superiority of the agrarian way of life. Writing to James Madison from Paris about the proposed Constitution, he saw nothing in the document that might

[21] Thomas Jefferson to Samuel Kercheval, July 12, 1816; to John Taylor, May 28, 1816, Andrew A. Lipscomb and Albert Ellery Bergh, eds., *The Writings of Thomas Jefferson,* 20 vols. (Washington, D.C., 1903–4), 15:33–44, 17–23.

[22] Thomas Jefferson, *Notes on the State of Virginia,* ed. William Peden (Chapel Hill, 1954), pp. 164–65. Emphasis added.

threaten the agrarian character of the country. After listing his objections, Jefferson concluded, "I think we shall [remain virtuous] as long as agriculture is our principal object, which will be the case while there remains vacant lands in any part of America. When we get piled upon one another in large cities, as in Europe, we shall become as corrupt as in Europe."[23] What were the virtues that Jefferson considered agriculture uniquely qualified to promote? His comments here and elsewhere suggest industry, independence, self-development, tranquility, order, and moderation. Because the farmer works for himself, he labors assiduously; because he must please neither customers nor bosses, he keeps his self-respect and independence. Then too, although the farmer works hard, he is not compelled to labor incessantly, as European workers are, merely to survive. Cultivating one's own plot of land requires a number of diverse skills; unlike the factory worker who performs the simple monotonous tasks dictated by the division of labor, the farmer is not degraded by his job. Accordingly, he has both the leisure and the incentive to participate in public affairs. For Jefferson, the material independence generated by a nation of freeholders lays the foundation for moral and political autonomy in a way that no other occupation can. Finally, the natural discipline imposed by the growth cycle affords the farmer a comfortable subsistence, while avoiding the extremes of luxury and poverty. "The moderate and sure income of husbandry begets permanent improvement, quiet life, and orderly conduct both in public and in private."[24]

Although these virtues have sometimes been dismissed as merely bourgeois, that is, involving only the qualities that promote success in private economic undertakings, Jefferson saw the matter quite differently. A nation of property-

[23] Jefferson to James Madison, Dec. 20, 1787, Lipscomb and Bergh, eds., *Writings of Jefferson*, 6:385–93.

[24] Jefferson to George Washington, Aug. 14, 1787, Julian P. Boyd et al., eds., *The Papers of Thomas Jefferson*, 24 vols. to date (Princeton, 1950-), 12:38. See also Smith, *Wealth of Nations*, book 3, chap. 1. For a discussion of these points, see Edward J. Lynch, "Commerce and the American Character: Constitutional Stability amid Technological Changes," *Newsletter*, University of Virginia (Apr. 1985).

holding farmers, enjoying the modest fruits of their labors, would produce a vigilant citizen body, alert to any and all encroachments on their political rights. We shall have occasion later to consider whether Jefferson was correct, but for the present it is important to note that, in his opinion, agrarian virtue had both a moral and a civic component.

The opposite side of Jefferson's faith in agriculture to promote these "substantial and genuine" virtues was his blanket condemnation of manufacturing. Having lived abroad in France, where the government's mercantile policies had artificially supported the manufacture of luxuries at the expense of agriculture, needlessly impoverishing the peasants, he sought to discourage all but the most essential manufactures in America. Although he recognized that agricultural abundance would eventually force Americans off the farms, he rejected out of hand any turn to manufacturing. "I consider the class of artificers as the panders of vice and the instruments by which the liberties of a country are generally overturned."[25] Here Jefferson sounds a variation on the traditional republican argument that commerce undermines civic virtue, substituting for commerce, broadly understood, the more narrow focus on manufacturing as the source of republican corruption. For Jefferson feared that manufacturing would multiply men's desires, thereby undermining the moderation and self-restraint necessary for self-government. In the debate whether luxury was compatible with republican mores, he took the more austere position, warning that the pursuit of extravagant pleasures would fatally weaken the habits of self-government.

It was not, however, simply the "taste for superfluities" to which Jefferson objected; he also opposed the *kind* of wealth a manufacturing society tends to create. Unlike the moderate and steady wealth produced by farming, the entire manufacturing enterprise is based on speculation. Sudden and unlimited wealth can be made by betting correctly upon the public's desire for novelty. For Jefferson, such successes tend to erode republican morals: "The wealth acquired by speculation and plunder is fugacious in its nature, and fills society with the

[25] Jefferson to John Jay, Aug. 23, 1785, Boyd et al., eds., *Papers of Jefferson,* 8:426.

spirit of gambling."[26] Because speculation holds out the promise of growing rich without toil, it undermines the habits of industry and breeds resentment among those who cannot afford to bet and who must work for a living.[27]

Finally, Jefferson feared that manufacturing would lead to the concentration of propertyless workers in cities, as well as the centralization of economic and political power. Because he regarded both these developments as fatal to the republican experiment, he wished to preserve the agrarian way of life as long as possible.

Jefferson's passionate defense of agrarianism has sometimes been perceived as a romantic return to the pastoral ideal of the self-sufficient farmer, living in virtuous isolation from the rest of the world.[28] But as recent historians have shown, his actual economic policies were anything but romantic. First as secretary of state and later as president, he sought to encourage farmers to produce surplus crops for export to European markets, the profits from which would be used to purchase manufactured "necessaries" and "comforts" for American farmers back home.[29] For Jefferson, agriculture was not so much an alternative to commerce as an elaboration of the commercial principle. Ironically, it was *commercial* agriculture, employing the latest scientific techniques, that he relied on to foster the agrarian virtue necessary for republican government. To be sure, his reliance on commercial and scientific agriculture set him apart from the

[26] Jefferson to Washington, Aug. 14, 1787, ibid., 12:38.

[27] McCoy, *Elusive Republic*, p. 173. For the persistence of this theme into the Jacksonian era, see Marvin Meyers, *The Jacksonian Persuasion: Politics and Belief* (Stanford, 1957).

[28] Richard K. Matthews, *The Radical Politics of Thomas Jefferson: A Revisionist View* (Lawrence, Kans., 1984), pp. 43–48. Richard Hofstadter, *The Age of Reform: From Bryan to F.D.R.* (New York, 1955); Pocock, *The Machiavellian Moment*, chap. 9.

[29] McCoy, *Elusive Republic;* Joyce Appleby, "Commercial Farming and the 'Agrarian Myth' in the Early Republic," *Journal of American History* 68 (1982):833–49. For a thoughtful critique of Appleby's excesses, see Lance G. Banning, "Jeffersonian Ideology Revisited: Liberal and Classical Ideas in the New American Republic," *William and Mary Quarterly*, 3d ser. 43 (1986):3–19.

classical republican tradition, with its emphasis upon the self-sufficient farmer, but as Drew McCoy and Lance G. Banning have rightly argued, Jefferson was seeking some way to bring the republican tradition into the modern world. Commercial farming was the perfect compromise between the poverty-stricken farmers of antiquity and the decadent manufacturing society still to come.

That Jefferson viewed the agricultural South and West as the "last asylum" of freedom and virtue against the vice-filled manufacturing North is another irony that has been widely noted.[30] It is one thing to argue, as Noah Webster did, that republican government requires a broad distribution of land so that all citizens have a tangible stake in the laws;[31] it is quite another to hold that only farming can produce a virtuous citizenry. Putting aside for the moment the question of whether any occupation can, by itself, produce "substantial and genuine virtue," farming in America proved particularly unsuited to this end. Whatever Jefferson's preference for free labor, agriculture in the South was essentially a slave economy. And it was the existence of slavery, standing in open contradiction to the principles of the Declaration of Independence, that posed the greatest danger to republican manners and morals. Instead of promoting the virtues that Jefferson associated exclusively with agrarianism, the plantation system tended to encourage the aristocratic vices of indolence, arrogance, and prodigality.[32] But even in the western free states, farming had no special claim on the virtues: it was just another means of growing rich, and land speculation was rife.

Despite these fatal weaknesses, the important point is that

[30] Harry Jaffa, "The Virtue of a Nation of Cities," in Robert A. Goldwin, ed., *A Nation of Cities* (Chicago, 1966); McCoy, *Elusive Republic*, pp. 251–52; Alexis de Tocqueville, *Democracy in America*, ed. J. P. Mayer and Max Lerner (New York, 1966), p. 526.

[31] Noah Webster, "On the Education of Youth in America," in Frederick Rudolph, ed., *Essays on Education in the Early Republic* (Cambridge, Mass., 1965), pp. 43–77.

[32] In his *Notes on Virginia*, Jefferson indicted the corrupting effect of slavery on both master and slave. See also Forrest McDonald, *Novus Ordo Seclorum: The Intellectual Origins of the Constitution* (Lawrence, Kans., 1985).

Jefferson's defense of agrarianism was essentially moral. His agrarian republic was not a modern Sparta, and the virtues he expected farming to encourage—moderation, independence, tranquility, order, and industry—were in his view compatible with trade and profit, technology and scientific progress. That agriculture, especially in the South, failed to promote these virtues should not obscure Jefferson's argument for its primacy.

COMMERCE AND CHARACTER IN THE EXTENDED REPUBLIC

While Jefferson believed that the preservation of republican institutions required a predominantly agrarian society, the authors of *The Federalist* praised the Constitution for the multiplicity of interests it would promote. It was the sheer diversity of interests generated by an extended commercial society, and not the moral superiority of one, that promised a cure for the "diseases" of republican government. Accordingly, Publius looked with scorn on states that were composed of "little more than a society of husbandmen." One of the advantages of the new Constitution was that "progress" could be expected in other "branches of industry," particularly in manufacturing.[33] Publius looked forward to the day when American reliance on foreign imports would decrease, and "domestic manufactures . . . begun" by the surplus population that could no longer earn a living through farming.[34]

But if, according to *The Federalist,* no single occupation could claim moral superiority, Publius regarded the commercial principle, which generated this "variety and complexity," as a moral good. Following the great eighteenth-century political philosophers, Publius regarded the commercial principle itself—rather than any particular occupation that springs from it—as the source of society's vigor and enterprise. "The assiduous merchant, the laborious husbandman, the active mechanic, the industrious manufacturer—all or-

[33] *Federalist* No. 56.

[34] *Federalist* No. 41. Both this paper and No. 56 were written by Madison.

ders of men look forward with eager expectation and growing alacrity to the pleasing reward of their toils."[35] Thus, Publius supported the commercial principle for the same reason that Jefferson defended agrarianism: it tended to produce a certain kind of character. Indeed, the virtues of a diversified commercial society bore a remarkable resemblance to those of Jefferson's yeoman farmer, though perhaps this is not so surprising given Jefferson's fundamental acceptance of the commercial principle.

Yet maintaining a strict neutrality toward economic interests in public policy proved no simple matter. As is well known, within a few years Madison retreated from the position staked out in *The Federalist* and allied himself with Jefferson's agrarian republic. What has been less remarked upon is the subtle shift in Hamilton's position. In the "Report on Manufactures" Hamilton veered away from *The Federalist*'s argument and suggested that manufacturing had not only an economic, but also a moral, edge.[36] In a rebuke to Jefferson, who had praised the discipline imposed on the farmer by the natural growth cycles, Hamilton observed that the strictly seasonal nature of farming allowed the farmer more easily to "be remiss." By comparison, the work involved in manufacturing was "constant and regular," and thus a spur to the enterprising and ambitious. The implication was clear: if industry, order, and regularity were desirable, and neither Jefferson nor Hamilton doubted they were, then manufacturing was at least as good as, if not actually superior to, agriculture.

Not only does manufacturing encourage a more industrious work force, it extends this enterprising spirit to those who, in a strictly agricultural society, would have little scope for their desires. Hamilton praises manufacturing for stimulating industry among farmers' wives and children. The rise of "neighboring manufactories" would not only afford "occasional and extra employment to industrious individuals and families," thereby "multiplying their acquisitions and enjoyments," but it would, in the words of one scholar, "liberate

[35] *Federalist* No. 12.

[36] One important exception is Forrest McDonald, *Alexander Hamilton: A Biography* (New York, 1982), p. 235.

children from the oppressive drudgery that was routine on the farm."[37]

What is interesting here is that both Jefferson and Hamilton expected some variation of the commercial principle to promote many of the same virtues. In particular, their emphasis upon industry, assiduity, regularity, order, and self-development suggests that, despite their disagreement over the particular occupation that would best promote these virtues, they had more in common with each other than either had with the classical republican tradition. Both were attempting to fine-tune the commercial principle to foster the kind of character that was appropriate to a liberal democratic republic where most citizens spent their days at work, striving to improve their material condition, rather than in full-time political participation and military exploits.

Still, there was at least one important difference. Unlike Jefferson, who tended to focus on the needs and interests of ordinary citizens and who worried that excessive materialism would sap republican virtue, Hamilton feared that republican government might provide too little scope to satisfy the ambitions and desires of the best. Consequently, he sought to develop manufactures because he believed that only a diversified economy could provide sufficient opportunities "for minds of the strongest and most active powers." This did not mean that such men necessarily would seek their fulfillment in commercial endeavors, only that their ruling passions were more likely to be satisfied in complex societies that aimed at commercial and political greatness. For this reason as well, he regarded the transition to a manufacturing society not principally as an economic but as a political and moral good because it promised to improve the material condition of the many, while at the same time gratifying the ambitions of the few.

Because Hamilton's vision has largely triumphed, we have a particular interest in examining whether the commercial society he did so much to create has in fact exerted a salutary influence upon the American character. In general, commerce has tended to promote the bourgeois virtues and to

[37] Lynch, "Commerce and Character," p. 47.

open up opportunities for self-development for succeeding generations of Americans. It has created a greater sense of justice by abolishing all hereditary distinctions and making individual talent, effort, and fortune the sole determinants of worldly success. But these goods have not been achieved without a certain cost, and it is to the debit side of the ledger that I would like briefly to turn.

First, although Hamilton was well aware that commerce generated its peculiar defects—"insolence, an inordinate ambition, a vicious luxury, licentiousness of morals"[38]—he was apparently confident that these "darling" vices could be controlled by prudent statesmen so that their evils did not get out of hand. He seems not to have forseen that commerce might also erode the very virtues it was expected to generate. Yet as the commercial principle developed into capitalism, the necessity of stimulating new desires and devising new means of affording them—such as installment buying, credit cards, and other ingenious financial instruments—has undermined the frugality, honesty, industry, diligence, and self-denial for the sake of future gratification.[39] Not only do all classes of Americans fail to exercise these virtues as regularly as Hamilton hoped, there seems to be serious doubt whether they are necessary at all in today's corporate and financial world.

Second, Hamilton was apparently unconcerned about the effect of a highly specialized division of labor on the moral and civic character of the people. Unlike his mentor Adam Smith, who warned that "the man whose whole life is spent in performing a few simple operations . . . generally becomes as stupid and ignorant as it is possible for a human creature to become,"[40] Hamilton seems to have taken for granted that

[38] Cited in Ralph Rossum, "Statesmanship and the Future of the American Commercial Republic," in Ralph Rossum and Gary McDowell, eds., *The American Founding: Politics, Statesmanship, and the Constitution* (Port Washington, N.Y., 1981), 157–70, esp. p. 170.

[39] Irving Kristol, "'When Virtue Loses All Her Loveliness,'" in his *Two Cheers for Capitalism* (New York, 1979), pp. 239–53; Daniel Bell, *The Cultural Contradictions of Capitalism* (New York, 1976).

[40] Smith, *Wealth of Nations*, book 5, part 1; also Tocqueville, *Democracy in America*, p. 528.

these untutored laborers would recognize the wisdom of deferring to their betters.[41] But why should someone who has no experience in public affairs, and whose work so constricts his political imagination, recognize the qualities that are necessary for the successful conduct of politics?[42]

Last, Hamilton did not foresee that a triumphant commercial spirit would succeed all too well in dampening civic virtue. Nor is it clear that if he had, he would have regarded this as a problem. From his perspective the great difficulty facing a democratic republic was how to defuse the political passions of the people, not to arouse them. Moreover, Hamilton was far more interested in questions of statesmanship. Thus, to the extent that he reflected on the virtues that citizens should possess, he apparently regarded the bourgeois virtues as an adequate substitute for civic virtue, though not necessarily for all the virtues.[43] And for the promotion of these other virtues, as well as the discouragement of the vices that attend commercial society, he relied, perhaps extravagantly, on a level of statesmanship that has been sorely lacking in American political life.

But even if commerce were to succeed in fostering the bourgeois virtues more reliably than it had, we would still be justified in asking whether these virtues, and the commercial principle that inspires them, are sufficient to preserve republican government. I think they are not, and, more important, I think the Framers thought they were not. Although both Jefferson and Hamilton expected their particular economic arrangements to have a salutary effect on the American character, there is no evidence that they or any of the Framers regarded commerce as a *sufficient* moral foundation for republican government. On the contrary, they fully expected that the family, churches, schools, and local political associations would continue to inculcate the civic and moral virtues necessary for self-government. But under the federal parti-

[41] *Federalist* No. 35.

[42] See the discussion in Hannah Arendt, *On Revolution* (New York, 1963), especially the concluding chapter.

[43] For Hamilton's belated recognition of the importance of civic virtue, see Stourzh, *Alexander Hamilton*, pp. 120–25.

tion of power, these institutions were the responsibility of the states, and it is to the state constitutions that we must now turn.

FEDERALISM AND THE MORAL FOUNDATIONS OF THE CONSTITUTION

If, as America developed into a full-scale manufacturing society, the spirit of commerce tended to influence character in ways unforeseen by its defenders, while its detractors, who had anticipated these difficulties, offered no real alternatives, it is also the case that on questions of character the Constitution of 1787 was fundamentally "incomplete."[44] The Framers did not talk more about the institutions that most directly form the character of the people because there was no question that control over the family, education, religion, and political participation would continue to be the exclusive preserve of the states. Thus, to understand fully the importance of character in the constitutional order, it is necessary to consider how this issue is treated in the state constitutions of the Founding period.

A survey of these Revolutionary charters suggests that the states took the question of character seriously indeed, providing in different ways for religion, education, and political participation. And just as, at the federal level, there was general agreement on the salutary effects of commerce, so at the state level there was a consensus that the states must inculcate the more traditional virtues still deemed necessary for the preservation of republican institutions. But, again like the commerce dispute, there were differences of opinion among the states and their leaders about how best to promote moral and civic virtue. One group, which might be called the heirs to the Puritan tradition, continued to stress the connection between religion and morality, and their role in sustaining

[44]On this point, see especially the work of Donald Lutz, *Popular Consent and Popular Control: Whig Political Theory in the Early State Constitutions* (Baton Rouge, 1980), and idem, "The Founding of Popular Government in America: The United States Constitution as an Incomplete Text" (Paper presented at the Seventy-sixth Annual Meeting of the American Political Science Association, Washington, D.C., September 1980).

republican institutions. Another, followers of the Enlightenment, dismissed religion as "monkish superstition" and sought to form republican citizens through a secular public education, emphasizing history and science. But in practice the line between these two was often blurred. Thus, the state constitutions of New England, while maintaining the link between republican virtue and religion, also acknowledged that freedom required an educated citizen body. In addition, the New England constitutions were unique in protecting the township, or local unit of government, as a means of promoting the spirited participation necessary to republican government. And this insight, in turn, followed its own curious trajectory. Thus, it was Thomas Jefferson, the great apostle of the American Enlightenment, and foe of Puritanism, who most fully grasped the political significance of the New England township. Accordingly, he urged all the states to amend their constitutions to include this vital "peg" of republican government.

RELIGION AND REPUBLICAN VIRTUE

According to the republican tradition, religion was one of the principal institutions in forming the character of the people. But what Machiavelli and Montesquieu had in mind were the pagan religions of Greece and Rome, which performed an essentially political purpose, instilling in the people a love of country and unswerving dedication to the common good. Love of country, or civic virtue, was the radiating principle of ancient republics; as such, it was, in the view of Montesquieu, "the source of all private virtues."

Clearly, the Christian religion could not serve modern republics in the same way, for civic virtue must always remain subordinate to moral virtue and the pursuit of eternal salvation. Yet despite what Machiavelli considered to be the complete incompatibility of Christianity and republican virtue, the churches played a key role in the struggle for Independence. Especially in Puritan New England, the war against Great Britain was seen as punishment for past sins; victory, as proof of redemption.[45]

[45] Edmund S. Morgan, "The Puritan Ethic and the American Revolution," *William and Mary Quarterly*, 3d ser. 24 (1967):3–18.

But there was a second and more theoretical reason why Christianity was important to the Founders of the American republics. In a clear departure from the republicanism of Machiavelli, which separated civic virtue from moral excellence and stressed only the virtues of the citizen, the Americans united the two and made moral virtue the source of civic virtue.[46] As John Adams observed, although "public virtue is the only foundation of republics," it "cannot exist without private [virtue]." And since Americans widely believed that religion was one of the most powerful means of instilling morality, they relied upon the churches to play an active role in forming the people for self-government. As Mark de Wolfe Howe has noted, in contrast to the silence of the federal Constitution, at the state level and especially in New England, "a view of government prevailed which not merely permitted but required a state's public power to be exercised for the advancement of religion."[47]

Thus the New Hampshire constitution of 1784, reaffirmed in 1792 after the ratification of the federal Constitution, expressly declared that "morality and piety, rightly grounded on evangelical principles, will give the best and greatest security to government."[48] Similarly, the Massachusetts constitution of 1780, written largely by John Adams, asserted that "the happiness of a people, and the good order and preservation of civil government, essentially depend upon piety, religion, and morality." Finally, both Rhode Island and Connecticut, which retained their colonial charters until 1842 and 1819 respectively, expressed similar views. "True piety,

[46] On this general point, see Pocock, *The Machiavellian Moment*.

[47] Mark de Wolfe Howe, *The Garden and the Wilderness: Religion and Government in American Constitutional History* (Chicago, 1965), p. 25. After this paper was essentially completed, I read Stephen Botein's excellent "Religious Dimensions of the Early American State," in Richard Beeman, Stephen Botein, and Edward C. Carter II, eds., *Beyond Confederation: Origins of the Constitution and American National Identity* (Chapel Hill, 1987), pp. 315–32. Botein makes essentially the same point, if anything, in stronger terms.

[48] Francis Newton Thorpe, ed., *The Federal and State Constitutions, Colonial Charters, and Other Organic Laws of the United States*, 7 vols. (Washington, D.C., 1909). Unless otherwise noted, all citations in this section are from Thorpe.

rightly grounded on evangelical principles" in Rhode Island and "Humanity, Civility, and Christianity" in Connecticut were said to be the foundation and "Stability of Churches and Commonwealths" alike.

To achieve these ends, the constitutions of Massachusetts and New Hampshire required the public worship of God, as well as public instruction by "protestant teachers of piety, religion, and morality." This instruction was to be provided by the various denominations at their own expense and, in Massachusetts, by the legislature when no provisions were made voluntarily.

In contrast to Massachusetts and New Hampshire, where the Congregational churches held a favored position, Rhode Island was founded as a "lively experiment" in religious freedom. It is significant, therefore, that even Rhode Island provided for the public support of the Christian religion.[49] So essential was "true piety" to the morals and happiness of the community that New Englanders across the political spectrum saw no contradiction between liberty of conscience and public support of religion. As long as people were not compelled to confess to particular sectarian beliefs or conform to prescribed rituals and forms, liberty of conscience was held to be secure. Religious freedom did not extend to purely financial questions.[50]

As these provisions make clear, the concern of the New England constitution-makers was primarily political. These Puritan Fathers were less concerned with saving men's souls than with warding off corruption in the body politic. They provided for religious instruction and support because they believed that religion was the chief source of morality, and that morality was essential to the preservation of free institutions.

Outside New England, no other state *required* public worship or support of religion. But most of the mid-Atlantic and southern states continued to see religion as an indispensable prop for republican government. In keeping with this view, the Maryland constitution of 1776, in force until 1851, *per-*

[49] Eidelberg, *Philosophy of Constitution*, p. 270.

[50] Howe, *Garden and Wilderness*, p. 26.

mitted the legislature, "in its discretion," to "lay a general and equal tax for the support of the Christian religion." In addition, the constitutions of Delaware, Maryland, and Virginia explicitly declared the worship of God to be not only a right, but also a duty. Continuing this emphasis on the duties citizens owe their country, the Virginia constitution of 1776 reiterated the familiar New England opinion that "no free government, or the blessings of liberty, can be preserved to any people" without virtue, and then proceeded to list those virtues necessary to the maintenance of republican institutions: "a firm adherence to justice, moderation, temperance, frugality, and virtue, and by frequent recurrence to fundamental principles." This was not a constitution indifferent to the character of its citizens, though it was characteristic of Virginia to decline to make the connection between virtue and religion explicit.

Not so the constitution of Delaware. Here the link between religion and morality was as clear and definite as in any of the Puritan charters. Article I, section 1 of the constitution of 1792 began with the recognition that "it is the duty of all men frequently to assemble together for public worship of the Author of the Universe, and piety and morality, on which the prosperity of communities depend [*sic*], are thereby promoted." But in a significant reversal of Puritan priorities, the Delaware constitution subordinated this principle to freedom of conscience. Although religion is said to promote the piety and morality on which republican governments depend, "yet no man ought to be compelled to religious worship." Nevertheless, despite this considerable shift in the direction of a more liberal republic, the important point is that nearly all the states acknowledged in their fundamental charters the role of religion in promoting a virtuous citizenry and sought, in different ways, to encourage this vital institution. As Alexis de Tocqueville noted approvingly when he visited this country in 1832, Americans still felt "the urgent necessity to instill morality into democracy by means of religion."

This survey of the role of religion in the Revolutionary state constitutions sheds a different light on the question of character in the American constitutional order. The Constitution is silent on religion and its effect on republican character, but not because the Framers thought that the "new science of politics" had rendered virtue superfluous, although some, notably James Madison, did doubt the connection between established religion and morality. The principal reason it is silent is that, under the federal partition of powers, positive support for religion remained the responsibility of the states. And fearing the tyranny of a national religion, most of the Framers were content to leave this power *as it existed* with the states.[51]

Indeed, in the one area where the Constitution specifically empowered the federal government to legislate on such matters, namely territorial possessions, Congress reaffirmed the need for a virtuous citizenry and recognized the importance of religion in promoting this end. The Northwest Ordinance, adopted in July 1787 while the Framers were assembled in Philadelphia and reenacted under the first Congress in 1789, reiterated the views of the state constitutions that "religion, morality, and knowledge" were "necessary to the good government and happiness of mankind." To achieve these ends, Congress assisted religious schools in diffusing morality and knowledge throughout the territories. In areas where it was constitutionally appropriate to act, Congress was no less concerned than the states with encouraging religion as a reinforcement to morality.

EDUCATION AND REPUBLICAN VIRTUE

While the churches traditionally shaped republican character, the men of the Revolution, reflecting the faith of the Enlightenment, looked forward to the day when universal public education would assist[52] religion in teaching the people their rights and duties. Thus, immediately after the Constitution was ratified, America's statesmen-educators turned their attention to the task of establishing a system of

[51] Here again, Madison is the great exception. His proposed draft of the Bill of Rights would have extended the freedom of conscience provision of the First Amendment to the states.

[52] A few, notably Madison and Jefferson, hoped education would replace religion, but it needs to be emphasized that, although their vision has triumphed, in their own day they were quite outside the mainstream.

education appropriate for republican government. But again, because the republic was federal and not consolidated, these proposals were statewide rather than national in scope.

Nearly all the republican writers on education agreed that the purpose of primary education was to make the people good citizens, though they differed on how to achieve this end.[53] Some viewed education as an adjunct of religion and hoped to accomplish through the schools what the New England constitutions had thus far achieved through religious worship and instruction.[54]

Outside New England, the foremost proponent of this view was Dr. Benjamin Rush. Testifying before the Pennsylvania legislature, Rush observed that "the only foundation for a useful education in a republic is to be laid in RELIGION. Without this, there can be no virtue, and without virtue there can be no liberty, and liberty is the object and life of all republics."[55] Although Rush asserted that any religion which "reveals the attributes of the Deity or a future state of rewards and punishments" was preferable to no religion at all, he believed, in contrast to Machiavelli, that republicanism and Christianity had a special affinity. Because Christianity teaches the virtues of "humility, self-denial, and brotherly kindness" that are opposed to monarchical pride, "a Christian cannot fail of being a republican." For Rush, as for his friend John Adams, republican virtue was firmly rooted in the Christian moral virtues, liberally construed. To be a good republican, one must first be a good man.

Second only to the duty men owed their Creator was the

[53] I am not here concerned with the Founders' views of higher education. For a discussion of this issue, see Eugene F. Miller, "On the American Founders' Defense of Liberal Education in a Republic," *Review of Politics* 46 (1984):65–90, and Eva Brann, *Paradoxes of Education in a Republic* (Chicago, 1979).

[54] See, in particular, the speech of Charles Turner before the Massachusetts ratifying convention in Jonathan Elliot, ed., *The Debates in the Several State Conventions, on the Adoption of the Federal Constitution*, 2d ed., 5 vols. (Philadelphia, 1901), 2:172.

[55] Benjamin Rush, ". . . Thoughts upon the Mode of Education Proper in a Republic," in Rudolph, ed., *Essays on Education*, p. 10. See also, Miller, "Founders' Defense of Education."

"supreme regard" they owe to their country. Although the Declaration of Independence spoke the language of rights, Rush insisted that republican government created "a new class of duties" as well. Nor were these duties inconsiderable, mere derivatives from rights. Schools must teach each child to place country above self and to be willing to lay down his or her life for its defense. When the nation was at peace, citizens must serve the country when called to administer its laws impartially. The goal of Rush's education was to "convert men into republican machines."[56]

To teach these lessons, Rush did not rule out poetry and history, but for him the central text was the New Testament. Rush recognized, however, that its use in the classroom would lead to denominational disputes, and rather than dilute the Bible's message with "fashionable" but pallid nonsectarian principles, he recommended what in effect was a system of state-supported parochial schools.

With its strong emphasis upon religious and civic education, Rush's proposal appears to run contrary to the scientific and commercial spirit of the age. But Rush's faith in the progressive character of science, as well as his belief that "next to religion," commerce played the vital role in "humanizing mankind" and preserving republican government against aristocratic encroachment, suggests that he saw an accommodation between these principles. The aim of Rush's republican education was not, as it might first appear, to turn back the clock on commercial and scientific progress, but to restrain and guide these principles through the formation of a certain kind of character. It was, to be sure, an uneasy alliance, but far preferable to the delusion that the Constitution created a "machine that would go by itself."[57]

[56] Rush was also an early supporter of female education. Although this education would not neglect the traditional female arts, Rush considered civic and moral education essential. Because the desire for women's approval influences the actions and opinions of men, and because women form the earliest habits and impressions of children, it was necessary that in a republic, women "should think justly upon the great subjects of liberty and government."

[57] The expression dates back to James Russell Lowell, but has recently reappeared as the title of Michael Kammen's work.

Other early American writers on education, like Noah Webster, agreed with Rush that education "forms the moral character of men, and morals are the basis of government."[58] Indeed, for Webster, "the virtues of men are of more consequence to society than their abilities." But the same tension that runs through Rush's thought is also at work in Webster. Despite his concern with character, it was Webster who wished to correct Montesquieu's emphasis on virtue by substituting land as the "soul of the republic."

In keeping with this Harringtonian materialism, the virtues Webster sought to inculcate were eminently practical; "what is now called a *liberal education* disqualifies a man for business."[59] But again like Rush, a practical education emphatically did not mean a value-free education. For "the yeomanry of a republican state" Webster recommended "an acquaintance with ethics and with the general principles of law, commerce, money, and government." Unlike Rush, however, Webster opposed teaching sectarian principles in the classroom. Although he did not oppose a selective reading of the Bible, the Bible was not for Webster the centerpiece of republican moral education. Instead, he prepared the *American Spelling Book,* which included a nondenominational moral catechism, stressing humility, mercy, justice, truth, charity, and frugality, as well as a "federal" catechism, outlining the principles of the Constitution.

The Maryland clergyman Samuel Knox, whose essay shared the American Philosophical Society's prize in 1797 for the best plan of education suitable for republican America, agreed with Webster that a "liberal plan" of instruction should steer clear of sectarian disputes.[60] But Knox saw no infringement of religious liberty for students to begin and end the school day with a nondenominational prayer. He also endorsed reading essays selected to "impress on the tender minded a reverence for the Deity, a sense of His government

[58] Webster, "Education of Youth," p. 64.

[59] Ibid., p. 56.

[60] Samuel Knox, "An Essay on the Best System of Liberal Education Adapted to the Genius of the Government of the United States," in Rudolph, ed., *Essays on Education,* pp. 298–372.

of the world, and a regard for morals."[61] As the central text, Knox recommended "a well-digested, concise moral catechism" consisting loosely of natural theology, ethics, political philosophy, jurisprudence, and civil history.

Despite their differences, what all these proposals have in common is the belief that republican character depends on a moral education, which is rooted, however loosely, in religion. To be sure, it was a religion that had made its accommodation with the secular world, but it was religion nonetheless.[62] By contrast, Thomas Jefferson and his followers[63] insisted that good citizenship depended primarily on the diffusion of political and scientific knowledge. Unlike the Puritan Founders, who constantly stressed man's sinful and fallen nature, Jefferson believed in the innate capacity of the people for virtue. As long as they lived in a healthy, that is, agrarian, environment, the people could be trusted to follow their own moral instincts. As the natural repositories of virtue, they had little need of moral instruction or improvement.

To the extent that some instruction in the virtues was still desirable, Jefferson rejected any attempt to supply it through religion. In his proposals for universal male education in Virginia,[64] he opposed teaching the Bible on the ground that it would corrupt the young. In its place, he proposed substituting history. "History, by apprising them of the past, will enable them to judge of the future; it will avail them of the experience of other times and other nations; it will qualify them as judges of the actions and designs of men; it will enable them to know ambition under every disguise it may assume; and knowing it defeat its views."[65] Jefferson could replace the Bible with history because he did not believe that the causes of corruption and degeneration lay in the people.

---

[61] Ibid., p. 333.

[62] Tocqueville, *Democracy in America,* pp. 500–502.

[63] See, for example, Samuel Harrison Smith, "Remarks on Education," in Rudolph, ed., *Essays on Education,* pp. 167–224.

[64] Unlike Rush, Jefferson took no interest in female education.

[65] Jefferson, *Notes on Virginia,* p. 148.

To preserve their liberties, the people must be taught to recognize the vices of their rulers.

Despite the considerable differences in the means by which these statesmen-educators sought to teach moral and civic virtue, all of them agreed that the chief purpose of education, at least at the primary level, was to make the people good citizens. As befit a commercial republic, all these proposals stressed the practical subjects that would enable the people to protect their property and increase their wealth, but no one assumed that mere vocational training was sufficient. Only a republican education, which prepared citizens to exercise their freedom intelligently and with the necessary restraint, could preserve the Constitution and the way of life it ordained. But was this education to be obtained only in the classroom?

POLITICAL PARTICIPATION AND REPUBLICAN VIRTUE

For Jefferson it was not enough merely to be taught the virtues; the people must also have the opportunity to exercise them. And while he was confident that in the right environment the moral sense would direct people to their social duties, he was less certain that it would promote a vigorous civic spirit. As he never tired of warning, the central preoccupation of Americans with money and wealth (and this in a predominantly agrarian republic) would lead to a dangerous erosion of civic virtue. For Jefferson, it was not faction but political lethargy, induced by the insatiable desire for material gratification, that was the chief danger to republican institutions.

To encourage citizens to act on their newly acquired knowledge of republican virtue and corruption, Jefferson sought to create and constitutionally preserve local political associations where the citizens could assemble in person. Long an admirer of the civic spirit he saw flourishing in the New England townships, which were recognized and protected by state constitutions, he proposed that other states amend their constitutions to preserve such local units and, where no townships existed, as in Virginia, that they be created. He championed local self-government because, like Tocqueville, he believed that the occasional exercise of the vote was not sufficient to make people responsible citizens. To foster civic virtue, the citizens must have regular opportunities to act on all matters within their reach and competence. Because the wards gave people the opportunity to act as self-reliant, independent citizens, Jefferson considered them, along with education (and in place of the religious instruction favored by many of the early republican thinkers), as one of the two "pegs" of republican government. And although Jefferson's amendment failed to win approval in Virginia, it is further proof that after the Constitution was established, the Founders looked to the states in various ways to form the manners and morals of the people.

CONCLUSION

Although the Framers of the Constitution rejected the argument that republican government could be sustained by virtue alone, they were by no means indifferent to questions of character. Indeed, they supported the establishment of some form of commercial republic largely because they believed it would improve republican manners and morals, without infringing on the natural rights they sought to protect.

But the Framers did not rely on commerce alone to form republican manners and morals. Out of deference to the federal principle embodied in the Constitution, they looked to the states to strengthen the institutions that might, through the encouragement of religion, morality, and civic virtue, further perfect the American character. To a large extent, these institutions succeeded in promoting the moral and political virtues that are beyond the scope of commerce. But in the long run, commerce would prove the more powerful principle since it was built into the educational system and managed to insinuate itself into both the family and the churches—that is, into the very institutions the Framers relied on to restrain it. This was not, of course, their intention, though it resulted partly from their attempt to synthesize the republican and liberal traditions, or to encourage the moral and political virtues that were compatible with men's equality and natural rights.

Finally, what commerce did not overpower, the nationalizing tendencies of the Constitution, spurred by the Fourteenth Amendment, further eroded. That the states were eventually compelled by the federal courts to surrender many of their responsibilities for moral and civic virtue may be the great irony of the Framers' political science. For the Constitution's silence on questions of morality, religion, and virtue is no longer understood as the Framers' deference to the states, but as a *standard* toward which to hold them. And it is why, now more than ever, the recovery of their political thought is vital to the preservation of our republican institutions.

RALPH LERNER

Facing Up to the Founding

THE PROMISE OF REVOLUTIONARY CONSTITUTIONALISM

IN 1776 IT TOOK as many weeks to send a letter from New York to London as it now takes seconds to telephone. Even so, London was in this respect closer to New York than Savannah. Then, too, some Founders reached back to a still more remote age. Among the older members of the Constitutional Convention of 1787, there were those who could even remember political agitation over the Stuart Pretender to the British throne. It is a long way from that world to ours of intercontinental ballistic missiles.

There is no concealing the fact that, as polities go and time flies, the American political regime is old. Where some find this antiquity a cause for pride, others are embarrassed by it. Yet neither the praise nor the disdain takes due account of the renovating intention and program of the Founders. Because they lived and worked so long ago, are so "old" in that sense, we forget how actually youthful were their intentions, how radical and novel their proposed new order was meant to be.

They were, after all, revolutionaries, intent not only on overturning the inanities and inequities of an old order but on replacing it with something more rational, just, and suited to their conditions. But they were also thinking revolutionaries, given to discriminating judgments and actions. Far from starting afresh by wiping clean their map, calendar, and institutional landscape (as their counterparts in France were to do soon after), those American Founders were keen on retaining whatever of their old modes and orders still made sense or had proved serviceable. Their singularity consists not least in this: that long-held customs moderated their zeal while new enthusiasms gave redirected energy to old forms. They were and remain a rare case.

Rarity, however, is no proof against sharp criticism. The more thoughtful criticisms of their Revolutionary constitutionalism have stemmed from a concern with justice, on the one hand, and with honor or nobility, on the other. The egalitarian criticism raises the charge of injustice against the Founders' tender regard for property—to say nothing of their willingness to countenance holding human beings as property. This has been the more usual complaint, from our old and new novelists, from Progressive era historians such as Charles A. Beard and Vernon L. Parrington on down to today's critical legal studies professors. The antiegalitarian criticism, by contrast, raises the charge of pettiness against the Founders' preoccupation with domestic tranquillity, comfort, and prosaic self-improvement. This has been a common ground for critics as different as Alexis de Tocqueville and Aleksandr Solzhenitsyn. The sum of these two critiques is that the Founders bequeathed us neither justice nor honor. I suggest that thinking about these criticisms may disclose something of the Founders' deeper purposes.

It is not hard to find evidence of the Founders' solicitude for private property and its basis. Granted, the word *property* does not even appear in the original Constitution of 1787. Yet one dare not make much of that, considering how many provisions of the Constitution refer to particular forms of property or presuppose them. Taxes, duties, imposts, excises, lands, commerce, bankruptcies, bills of credit, the exclusive rights of authors and inventors, contracts, debts, engagements, slaves: all these are matters of explicit (if sometimes circumlocutional) Constitutional provision.

The Founders' Constitution is intensely concerned with the conditions under which individuals acquire and hold property. Far from viewing property as theft, they took it to be a right and a bulwark for the safe enjoyment of individuals' other rights. Although they feared the prospect of a deeply divided society in which a privileged few would array themselves against an impoverished multitude, they did not relish a society that suppressed human diversity. They expected, indeed hoped, that the free play of human faculties, in all their various and unequal forms, would give rise to various and unequal property holdings. This, they thought, should not be regretted, for the great end in view was none other than to promote and protect those potentialities that make human beings more than faces in a crowd.

For those who see property-centeredness as a basis for the exploitation of man by man, the Founders and their Constitution are suspect—or worse. An American heritage grounded in acquisitiveness, private holdings, and a (never quite exclusive) reliance on market forces, we are told, is a heritage to overcome. According to these critics, such a heritage cannot serve as the basis of a genuine community, for its primary impulse is rather to set people apart and at odds with one another. From this perspective, then, the main features of American constitutionalism—representation, separation of powers, the rule of law, the language of rights—are sufficiently understood as means by which those who already have property secure their enjoyment of it. If that is the case, then those features ought to be viewed as cynical charades by which those who have little are led to believe that they have much and by which those who have much may continue to get more.

Our age, the modern age, is deeply suspicious of, even resentful toward, unequal results (outside the sports arena). Accordingly, it views a heritage that encourages inequality as a bad inheritance. Insofar as that heritage permits the inculcation of habits of endless consumption and the passive acceptance of manufactured wants in a world of howling misery, it will be thought to deserve not only contempt but also opposition.

Yet this account of the Founders' intent is shallow and therefore unjust to men capable of a deep intention. If we look more patiently, closely, and deeply, we may discover in the Founders' tender regard for property an indication that they had larger political aims, aims not likely to be recognized as such by facile debunkers of private property. To be sure, they were interested in the economic growth that might result from such a policy. But they were also led by a firm belief that there is an intimate connection between property and other "loftier" rights. Far from holding the now common view that contrasts or even opposes property rights and human rights, the Founders thought, in the words of James Madison, that "as a man is said to have a right to his property, he may be equally said to have a property in his rights."[1] To ride roughshod over the one made it easier to ride roughshod over the other; caring for the one led to caring for the other.

Moreover, the Founders thought that property—and the opportunity to acquire it—pointed to an open society in which large numbers of citizens would have a stake and a voice. This very openness would work powerfully against both permanent privilege and permanent penury. Accordingly, any generation legislating for itself and its children—children of whose prosperity or poverty it could have no certain foreknowledge—would have a strong incentive to keep channels of upward mobility open to all. Economic inequality is the price to be paid for economic equality of opportunity; and that promise of opportunity, in turn, secures the allegiance of all segments of republican society.

The second criticism of the Founders' Revolutionary constitutionalism derives from an aristocratic, not an egalitarian, premise. This is a premise adhered to by individuals whose education was shaped by the authors of classical antiquity or by the beliefs of one or another old order. But it is not exclusively that of the Tocquevilles and de Gaulles of some ancien régime. It is clearly in the air when we hear a Henry David Thoreau intone that "there is but little virtue in the action of masses of men."[2]

Individuals with this elitist perspective on human affairs are likely to call attention to the modest political goals of the Founding. Typically, the charge is not that those goals are bad or exploitative or grossly unjust. Rather, those aims are taken to be mundane, banal, and small-minded. By these

---

[1] James Madison, "Property," *National Gazette*, Mar. 29, 1792, in Marvin Meyers, ed., *The Mind of the Founder: Sources of the Political Thought of James Madison*, rev. ed. (Hanover, N.H., 1981), p. 186.

[2] Henry David Thoreau, "Civil Disobedience" (1849), in Milton Meltzer, ed., *Thoreau: People, Principles, and Politics* (New York, 1963), p. 42.

lights, the vision of the Founders was productive of mediocrity; indeed, it has been argued, they expected mediocrity in the masses who would try to realize their vision. So by deliberately eschewing a more noble aim, the American regime falls victim to its own success.

But, someone might retort, what of that pioneer people who bridged rivers, cut through mountains, drained swamps, uprooted untold millions of tree stumps, endured unspeakable hardships of topography and climate—all in order to carve out a place for themselves? Do their colonization and securing of a vast empire, albeit on contiguous territory, suggest a people incapable of extraordinary and heroic efforts?

Critics will view these incontrovertible achievements as large but not great, massive but not noble. After all, those who undertook those tasks were inspired less by a desire for public acclaim than by a private and homely vision of how best to improve their individual situations and stations—the next rung up on a particular ladder. Their unceasing efforts to grasp the next increment of real or imagined advantage could hardly be mistaken for those astonishing struggles for perfection that fired the fabled aristoi of the past. From that perspective the Founders' regime presupposes a people accustomed to calculating odds, making deals, and figuring out cost-effective ways of satisfying their small though insatiable wants. Here, then, is a heritage of small stakes, small risks, and small gains—smallness, so to speak, writ large.

To some political aesthetes the mass of citizens thus appear tone-deaf and color-blind in the realms of beauty, glory, and finesse of person and form. Lacking good models and great expectations, the populace appears to suffer from atrophied imaginations: their visions of what human beings might be and what a civic public might become are alike diminished and trivialized.

If the freeing of these countinghouse appetites were all they had in mind, the Founders might truly stand guilty as charged. But, in fact, we can again say the Founders looked further. Their program of Revolutionary constitutionalism was indeed intended precisely to overthrow (or at the very least cut loose from) many of the institutions, laws, habits, and ways of thinking they associated with the old country, older times, and the old regime of honor. Their New Republic would constitute a great "nay" to the Old Regime and, in the process, make possible an allegiance to a new regime of honor.

To begin with, the Founders rejected the whole structure of settled privilege on which all of European tradition had been based. "We [British] are resolved," Edmund Burke told the French in 1790, "to keep an established church, an established monarchy, an established aristocracy, and an established democracy, each in the degree it exists and in no greater."[3] That set world Burke was celebrating was precisely the world the Founders rejected as unfit for America.

In rejecting that hierarchical world of existing establishments, the Founders were not moved by hostility to wealth, by hatred of religion, by resentment of inequality, or by suspicion of any fixity in political and social life. But looking from afar at that European world, they thought they saw a world of injustice and pretension, of wasted lives and wasted opportunities. On the whole, they thought, the past had more to be ashamed of than to take pride in.

America, properly founded and newly constituted, would present a different picture. Not a crabbed, grudging acknowledgment of a condition owing to all, but a forthright proclamation of everyone's inalienable rights. Not an idolatrous genuflection toward established power, but an insistence that the original and continuing source of all political authority lay in the body of the people themselves. Not a silent multitude of consenting adults (Burke's image was of "thousands of great cattle, reposed beneath the shadow of the British oak," quietly chewing their cud),[4] but an active, querulous citizenry, quick to be jealous, mistrustful of officialdom, and quick to act on their misgivings.

America, properly founded and newly constituted, would provide an arena for such a people to expand, develop, and mature. Rid at last of the encumbrances that kings, clerics, and nobles had contrived to suit their own ends, the ordinary

[3] Edmund Burke, *Reflections on the Revolution in France* (1790), ed. Thomas H. D. Mahoney (Indianapolis, 1955), p. 104.

[4] Ibid., p. 97.

people of America would demonstrate to an astonished world the capacity of mankind for self-government. Thus individuals would be at once free to arrange their own lives and forced to respect the rights of others. The Founders saw this exercise of rational freedom as both a precondition and result of self-government. With proper supports and necessary checks, ordinary people would gain the experience and understanding needed to make them their own best guardians. This was a revolutionary idea—and remains so.

Even though we are far removed from the eighteenth-century Enlightenment, the stamp of the Founders' principles and expectations may be detected at every turn in all levels of government and in the workings of private associations. Consider the recurrent demand—and hence claim—that a program of some sort should meet and solve a problem however complex, be it drug addiction, teenage pregnancy, or moribund industries. Consider the almost automatic expectation that power be checked, held accountable, and opened to public scrutiny. Consider, best perhaps, the place of religion—not only where it is but where it is not in American life.

The Founders thought that this experiment, if successful, would have worldwide significance. They did not blush to regard that outcome as a matter not only of prideful patriotism but of the most far-reaching philanthropy. They believed that if Americans could rise to the challenge, their example would contribute to the emancipation of men and women wherever they are bound by ignorance, superstition, and gross injustice. Thinking that, the Founders proceeded to school the American people in the language of equal rights and in the habits of self-governance. Indeed, the Revolutionary struggle itself was a great teacher: the speeches of James Otis and Patrick Henry, the writings of Thomas Jefferson and John Adams, the declarations of the Continental Congress, George Mason's Virginia Declaration of Rights. The Founders also proceeded to embody their principles in institutions that might mold the people into the kind of moderns they thought the experiment demanded. Outstanding in this respect were John Adams's contributions to the Massachusetts Constitution of 1780, the imperfectly realized efforts of Jefferson, Edmund Pendleton, and George Wythe to revise Virginia's legacy of British and colonial laws, the Confederation Congress's enactment of a framework for the governance of the vast public domain in the Northwest Territory, and (not least) the Constitution itself.

Far, then, from thinking small or being indifferent to glory, the Founders hoped to win lasting fame on the strength of their contributions to America's future significance and grandeur. Reviewing the charge that the Founders were small-minded, we find instead that their designs were vaultingly ambitious: they were, after all, raised under the regime they overthrew.

It is striking that the Founders sought to contain traditional religion within civil bounds by separating it from civil authority—and all this precisely so as to avoid the tyranny and idolatry of European state religious establishments. When ardor and righteousness can call upon the power of the state, they believed, no one's conscience is safe. Nor, for that matter, can the triumphing religion itself have the confidence that its adherents are indeed adherents rather than conscripts. By fostering the multiplication of sects and by shielding religion from the state and the state from religion, the Founders hoped to keep enthusiasm at a pitch that all might tolerate.

From their vantage point, a church militant was unlikely to be mistaken for a strong church, or religious fervor for religious conviction. Their readings in history and their direct experiences made them fearful and wary of the enthusiasm that could persecute and even murder. This may be an expression of the deism, anticlericalism, or secularism of some of the Founders. But the fact remains that they took care to cast their arguments in terms that Baptists or Quakers or Jews, that Congregationalists in Virginia or Anglicans in Connecticut, could understand and approve. Such parishioners—as well as those whose worship was even more private—could have the consolation that whoever or whatever it was to whom they believed they owed an account of their spiritual lives and intentions, it was not a being armed with the authority of the new United States government. In freeing the individual's spirit from clerical and political authority, the

Founders would not and could not believe that they were diminishing that spirit.

The Founders' heritage usually is made out to be simple and prosaic. A generation without poetry in their souls, their likenesses are said rightly to adorn the currency of this country. But this one-dimensional view is itself impoverished. The Founders' realism, worldliness, unsentimental view of human nature, and reliance on workaday motives, though commonplaces to us, are nevertheless no small thing. And there is more. The reverse of the one-dollar bill bears the picture of the Great Seal of the United States, that homespun exotic creation with its proud proclamation, *novus ordo seclorum,* the new beginning of the ages. To ignore that intention and that promise is to undervalue both the Founders and ourselves.

A DIALOGUE OF FATHERS AND SONS

Just as the Founders of the American republics looked back to a past that they both cherished and rejected, so too did they look forward to a future that might cherish and yet also in some sense reject them. Although the Founders were believers in self-evident truths, in inalienable rights, in the lasting correctness of the principles of republican government, they were far from insisting on the fixity of each and every feature of their thought and work. Pleased though they were with much of what they had wrought, they still wished for and expected better. They began with the American people as they found them. They flattered themselves in thinking that, thanks to their constitutional regime, the American people would in time grow stronger, wealthier, and wiser— and to that extent freer. The Founders neither expected nor desired the mindless adulation of their successors or the routine thoughtless application of their principles. Yes, they counted on the people growing habituated to certain forms of thinking and acting, and even on their affectionate attachment to those familiar ways. Beyond those particular attachments, however, was to be a growing calm, general understanding of what it takes to rule oneself. In looking forward to that, each succeeding generation would have something to labor for and to look up to.

Never far from the thoughts of a Washington, Franklin, Madison, Rush, Adams, or Jefferson was the concern for developing this kind of intelligent self-awareness in the people at large. Ultimately the success of the experiment would turn on that. Unless the people knew enough to be aware of their rights, unless they cared enough to act in concert with others to secure those rights, unless they were mindful of the demands and risks and opportunities of self-governance, their brave experiment would likely end up either tragedy or farce. The Founders could neither give guarantees about the outcome nor refrain from pointing toward and working for a favored outcome. With high self-consciousness they bequeathed what they considered a goodly heritage, one that permitted their heirs to show what they could rise to. If the Founders thought they could do no more, it is equally clear that they thought they could do no less.

The sons of the Founders likewise had a double vision. The generations of John Quincy Adams and of Abraham Lincoln saw their fathers' legacy as entailing upon them great burdens and great hopes. Although the American War of Independence might be over, the task of Founding was not yet complete. For both fathers and sons the establishment of Revolutionary constitutionalism in America marked not only a culmination of an age-old struggle but a promising and demanding new beginning. Beyond the peaceful enjoyment of rights, beyond the anticipated domestic prosperity and tranquillity, lay the challenge of using those goods to achieve something even finer. It was to that promise that some of the leading figures of the early generations turned their thoughts, propelled by a fervent belief in the power of education broadly conceived. Retracing those thoughts may help us to see more clearly the kind of regime they had in prospect.

Speaking in general terms of the Founders' stance toward their past tempts us into simplifications, even oversimplifications. In fact, the Founders' attitudes were neither simple nor undiscriminating. Along with their great "nay" to leading features of the old established order went a deep regard for their English inheritance of constitutional rights, traditional liberties, and the rule of law. If they were confident that earlier theory or political science might now be surpassed, they believed no less that the lessons of the past, historical experience, remained the best if not the only guide.

Yet in the new world aborning, it was the America of their design and not some mythic past that would be the model. America's proclaimed and freely chosen goals would be a cautionary reminder to itself and might serve as an inspiration to others. Thus one might say with Alexander Hamilton that "it remains for us to justify the revolution by its fruits."[5] Although this recurring theme was invoked in efforts to move a reluctant public opinion, it was more than a rhetorical trope. The Founders thought that their own good name was at stake in the success or failure of the American experiment; or rather, they staked their fame on the larger meaning of that experiment—the still unresolved question of a people's capacity to govern itself well. While the goal no longer was cast as the Puritans' holy city upon a hill, the new Zion, it remained in the Founders' eyes an eminence intensely interesting to mankind at large.[6] Indeed, it is arguable that the Founders' high pretensions were, in their eyes, a necessary corrective for the kind of public political life the American people were likely to lead. Such pretensions could recall to mind the larger meaning and value of the experiment, a prod especially needful in times of great heat over small issues. Where so much of ordinary life narrowed the citizenry's thoughts and tugged them earthward, reminders of high principle, grand example, and broad significance would be indispensable. In this sense the American heritage might save the American people from themselves.

Securing that high ground and erecting upon it something truly worth looking up to would require a peculiar education—one fitted for this people, in this place, and in these circumstances. The most pressing task was to persuade that

[5] Alexander Hamilton, "Second Letter from Phocion," April 1784, in Morton J. Frisch, ed., *Selected Writings and Speeches of Alexander Hamilton* (Washington, D.C., 1985), p. 89.

[6] See James Madison, "Address to the States, by the United States in Congress Assembled" (Apr. 26, 1783), in Meyers, ed., *Mind of the Founder*, p. 25; Alexander Hamilton, *Federalist* No. 1 (Oct. 27, 1787), in Frisch, ed., *Writings and Speeches of Hamilton*, p. 128.

people of their need for such an education. It was likely that men and women so preoccupied with the urgencies of making a living or of improving their economic situation would be little inclined to adorn or refine whatever they already judged serviceable enough. Indeed, at this distance it is hard for us to say how much of the perceived popular resistance to grander projects stemmed from external necessities or ignorant self-satisfaction.

Thus Benjamin Rush, for example, in thinking about the kind of education suitable for America, had no difficulty accepting the usual priorities of life in an undeveloped country: "Our principal business should be to explore and apply its resources, all of which press us to enterprize and haste. Under these circumstances, to spend four or five years in learning two dead languages [Greek and Latin], is to turn our backs upon a gold mine, in order to amuse ourselves in catching butterflies."[7] But Rush did not view himself as the founding father of George F. Babbitt's Zenith. From the outset of the struggle for Independence, he was intent on getting Americans to distinguish the short-range measures that proclaimed a revolution from the long-range measures that secured a revolution. Quite apart from his private distaste for those who "have little relish for the 'feast of reason and the flow of soul,'" Rush had sufficient political incentives to work for an America that was more than all-business. Nothing short of the reconstitution of the manners of the people would secure them against monarchical temptations and aristocratic subversion. "Republican seminaries" would go far in inculcating the technical skills and moral lessons that might render the people safe and knowing guardians of their own liberty.[8]

[7] Benjamin Rush, "Observations upon the Study of the Latin and Greek Languages," in *Essays, Literary, Moral and Philosophical*, 2d ed. (Philadelphia, 1806), p. 39.

[8] Benjamin Rush, "Address to the People of the United States" (1787), in Hezekiah Niles, comp., *Principles and Acts of the Revolution* (New York, 1876), p. 234; Rush to Arthur Lee, May 4, 1774, in Lyman H. Butterfield, ed., *Letters of Benjamin Rush*, 2 vols. (Princeton, 1951), 1:85; Rush, "Of the Mode of Education Proper in a Republic" (1786), in Dagobert D. Runes, ed., *The Selected Writings of Benjamin Rush* (New York, 1947), p. 94.

That same great objective lies at the core of the far-reaching reforms Jefferson proposed for Virginia in the early years of the Revolution. While some of those reforms were manifestly changes in institutions—in the way property was passed on from one generation to the next, in the way religious organizations were supported, in the way local civil government conceived of its functions—such changes were only part of the story. Viewed as a whole, Jefferson's revision of Virginia's laws may be thought of as an elaborate exercise in popular political education.[9] It is quite obvious that he wished to see that all the free boys and girls of the commonwealth learned the three R's and the useful lessons of history and, likewise, that those students of "the best learning and most hopeful genius and disposition" should be able to attend (at the public's expense) a college properly reconstituted to reflect and help secure "the late change in the form of our government."[10] He did not, however, leave it at that. Taking great pains and descending to the smallest particulars, Jefferson also constructed an elaborate network of responsibilities and accountabilities that involved not only overseers and aldermen but teachers, electors, and even students. Here would be more than a lesson in book-learning for the young, for Jefferson was intent on explaining by example precisely what he understood by self-governance. Here were lessons in living republicanism to be learned and applied at all levels by the citizenry. To this end he contrived institutions that would bring individuals together linked in common cause. Their mutual involvements would make it necessary for them to develop skills of listening and speaking, of thinking and judging, in short of behaving like a people who deserved a free society and would be capable of sustaining it. Nothing short of that could secure the Revolution's promise.

Although the contents and emphases of their several educational projects differed, both Benjamin Rush and Thomas

---

[9] This theme is developed in Ralph Lerner, *The Thinking Revolutionary: Principle and Practice in the New Republic* (Ithaca, N.Y., 1987), pp. 60–90.

[10] Thomas Jefferson, Revisal of the Laws, Bill nos. 79–80, in Julian P. Boyd et al., eds., *The Papers of Thomas Jefferson*, 24 vols. to date (Princeton, 1950-), 2:533, 538.

Jefferson agreed with Noah Webster in this: a proper system of education would fit every citizen to choose others and be chosen in turn himself for places of public trust.[11] With Rush, the moral teachings of the Bible and the pacific calculations of commerce would point young republicans in the right direction. With Jefferson, the stirring yet unhappy histories of earlier republics would yield useful lessons for moderns eager to avoid the past's fatal political errors. With Webster, a distinctive speller, reader, and dictionary would be the vehicles for shaping a new American nationality. None of these Founders was willing to leave the desired outcomes to the workings of chance; there was simply too much at stake.

Looking beyond schooling, James Wilson voiced the expectation that political participation itself might become a most valuable means of education, drawing individuals out of their workaday concerns and accustoming them to the ways of dignified citizenship.

> The man who enjoys the right of suffrage, on the extensive scale which is marked by our constitutions, will naturally turn his thoughts to the contemplation of publick men and publick measures. The inquiries he will make, the information he will receive, and his own reflections on both, will afford a beneficial and amusing employment to his mind. I am far from insinuating, that every citizen should be an enthusiast in politicks, or that the interests of himself, his family, and those who depend on him for their comfortable situation in life, should be absorbed in Quixote speculations about the management or the reformation of the state. But there is surely a golden mean in things; and there can be no real incompatibility between the discharge of one's publick, and that of his private duty. Let private industry receive the warmest encouragement; for it is the basis of publick happiness. But must the bow of honest industry be always bent? At no moment shall a little relaxation be allowed? . . .
>
> Under our constitutions, a number of important appointments must be made at every election. To make them is, indeed, the business only of a day. But it ought to be the business

[11] Thomas Jefferson, *Notes on the State of Virginia* (1784), ed. William Peden (Chapel Hill, 1954), pp. 146–49; Noah Webster, "On the Education of Youth in America" (1788), in *A Collection of Essays and Fugitiv Writings on Moral, Historical, Political and Literary Subjects* (Boston, 1790), pp. 23–26.

of much more than a day, to be prepared for making them well. When a citizen elects to office—let me repeat it—he performs an act of the first political consequence. He should be employed, on every convenient occasion, in making researches after proper persons for filling the different departments of power; in discussing, with his neighbours and fellow citizens, the qualities, which ought to be possessed by those, who enjoy places of publick trust; and in acquiring information, with the spirit of manly candour, concerning the manners and characters of those, who are likely to be candidates for the publick choice.

A habit of conversing and reflecting on these subjects, and of governing his actions by the result of his deliberations, would produce, in the mind of the citizen, a uniform, a strong, and a lively sensibility to the interests of his country.[12]

For all their preoccupations with the urgencies of the hour, the most notable Founders never lost sight of the needs of the morrow. Thus an anxious John Adams, even while spurning the seductive pleasures of French royal gardens and palaces in the name of his pressing public duties, still could sharply distinguish what was expected of him from what he expected of his descendants. "I must study politics and war, that my sons may have liberty to study mathematics and philosophy. My sons ought to study mathematics and philosophy, geography, natural history and naval architecture, navigation, commerce, and agriculture, in order to give their children a right to study painting, poetry, music, architecture, statuary, tapestry, and porcelain."[13] Establishing America's separate and equal station—politically, militarily, and commercially—among the powers of the earth was the first order of business, not the last.

A paterfamilias plans for his offspring, a Founding Father plans for his country: whatever the resemblances, the difficulties are incommensurable. Post-Revolutionary youth had so much to learn, an old Jefferson complained to his older

[12] James Wilson, *Lectures on Law* (1791), in Robert Green McCloskey, ed., *The Works of James Wilson*, 2 vols. (Cambridge, Mass., 1967), 1:404–5.

[13] John Adams to Abigail Adams, 1780, in Adrienne Koch and William Peden, eds., *The Selected Writings of John and John Quincy Adams* (New York, 1946), p. 66. This development took one generation longer than John Adams had calculated: John, John Quincy, Charles Francis, Henry.

comrade Adams; yet the young were not of a mind to learn from anyone. One would hope that experience might dent their mistaken self-sufficiency and that in time they might come to value education on a broad scale. Meanwhile, however, Jefferson's thoughts ran toward supplying the lack that young America could not yet detect: a university whose structure, curriculum, and faculty would be designed for this kind of new society.[14]

His partner in founding the new University of Virginia thought likewise. James Madison sought to anticipate and answer all the shortsighted arguments that neighboring Kentuckians might adduce against a proposed general system of state-funded education. He had a ready answer to objections prompted by democratic indifference, fear of elitism, and parsimony. But most revealing, perhaps, were Madison's political appeals to a free people, appeals that sought to transcend real or alleged social divisions: "It is certain that every Class is interested in establishments which give to the human mind its highest improvements, and to every Country its truest and most durable celebrity." It could be assumed that the quality of public lawmaking and of public life would all be enhanced by the diffused effects of "Learned Institutions." Beyond that, however, lay this even larger inducement:

> Throughout the Civilized World, nations are courting the praise of fostering Science and the useful Arts, and are opening their eyes to the principles and the blessings of Representative Government. The American people owe it to themselves, and to the cause of free Government, to prove by their establishments for the advancement and diffusion of Knowledge, that their political Institutions, which are attracting observation from every quarter, and are respected as Models, by the new-born States in our own Hemisphere, are as favorable to the intellectual and moral improvement of Man as they are conformable to his individual & social Rights. What spectacle can be more edifying or more seasonable, than that of Liberty & Learning, each leaning on the other for their mutual and surest support?[15]

[14] Thomas Jefferson to John Adams, July 5, 1814, in Lester J. Cappon, ed., *The Adams-Jefferson Letters: The Complete Correspondence between Thomas Jefferson and Abigail and John Adams*, 2 vols. (Chapel Hill, 1959), 2:434.

[15] James Madison to William T. Barry, Aug. 4, 1822, in Meyers, ed., *Mind of the Founder*, pp. 343–46.

The promise of Revolutionary constitutionalism had still to be fulfilled.

That promise remained a challenge to the succeeding generation. To see that clearly, one ought first to address the same questions to the sons: What was their stance toward *their* past? What did they see as their most pressing needs? What did they take to be the longer-range needs of American society? In choosing John Quincy Adams and Abraham Lincoln as examples, one can hardly claim to have invoked representative types of the middle period of American history. But by the same token, neither could one find individuals who had delved more profoundly into the questions at hand.

It is commonplace to regard John Quincy Adams as a kind of resident alien in the nineteenth century. By temperament, training, and taste he belonged to his father's era. Yet it is also fair to say that John Quincy did not let his admiration for the Revolution, and for those who made it, dull his critical faculties. The nineteenth century was barely six weeks old when, looking back, he heaped his scorn upon "the flood of philosophy which poured upon that self-conceited dupe, the eighteenth century." [16] A defensible belief in progress had overreached itself, with terrifying results. Believer though he was, John Quincy was not about to be carried away.

Lincoln was equally capable of distancing himself from "those old-time men" of '76 whose sentiments he confessed to loving so much; his stance was at least as complex as Adams's. On the one hand, he steadfastly presented himself as a conservative defender of the old policy of the fathers, especially when fending off attacks by adherents of Stephen A. Douglas who were portraying Lincoln as a revolutionary and a disrupter of union. [17] On the other hand, he presented himself as a modern, a believer in progress, one who took special delight in "the discovery of anything which is at once

[16] John Quincy Adams to Thomas Boylston Adams, Feb. 14, 1801, in Koch and Peden, eds., *Selected Writings*, p. 258.

[17] Abraham Lincoln, Peoria Speech on the Kansas-Nebraska Act, Oct. 16, 1854, in Richard N. Current, ed., *The Political Thought of Abraham Lincoln* (Indianapolis, 1967), p. 74; Cooper Union Address, Feb. 27, 1860, ibid., pp. 150–53.

new and *valuable.*"[18] He understood—and showed—the ease with which the Founders' high ambitions could be dissected and demystified. But with equal ease Lincoln lampooned the snippy self-satisfaction and self-delusion of Douglas's "Young America."[19]

The proper bearing of sons toward fathers had to be at once modest and discriminating. If one approached the problem by first considering America's role in the world, the matter would appear in a clearer light. Lincoln's audience was all too ready to presume American superiority in inventiveness and to extrapolate from that to American superiority across the board. In comparison, the rest of the world was immured in custom and ignorance (and increasingly so, it seemed, as one moved eastward). "In anciently inhabited countries, the dust of ages—a real downright old-fogyism—seems to settle upon, and smother the intellects and energies of man." It was in this context that Lincoln spoke of a new country as "most favorable—almost necessary—to the immancipation of thought, and the consequent advancement of civilization and the arts."

But this presumption in favor of the New World and of Young America (nothing of course is newer than "the most *current* youth of the age") grievously underestimated the debt of the young to the old. We moderns "owe everything which distinguishes us from savages" to the legacy of Old Fogy—the habit of observation and reflection, the sundry discoveries and inventions that resulted from that habit, and finally, the gradual awareness that ordinary folk, too, are capable of rising to equality. "It is difficult for us, *now* and *here*, to conceive how strong this slavery of the mind was; and how long it did, of necessity, take, to break it's shackles, and to get a habit of freedom of thought, established." Analogously, Young America owed almost everything to the Old Fogy Founders who had invented the country on a new principle,

[18] Lincoln, Cooper Union Address, ibid., p. 149; Wisconsin State Fair Address, Sept. 30, 1859, ibid., pp. 136, 138.

[19] Lincoln, Springfield Young Men's Lyceum Address, Jan. 27, 1838, ibid., pp. 18–19; Springfield Temperance Society Address, Feb. 22, 1842, ibid., p. 32; Lecture on Discoveries and Inventions, Feb. 11, 1859, ibid., pp. 112–15.

a principle that now appears to us as old. Just as the one emancipation—that of the mind from a "false and under estimate of itself"—was less the work of a day than of a century, so too might be the other sort of emancipation. Here was a lesson that the followers of both Stephen A. Douglas and William Lloyd Garrison might take to heart.[20] There was a past to remember and cherish even as there was a past to overcome.

Indeed, it was the denigration of that older principle (Jefferson's "abstract truth, applicable to all men and all times") and the consequent perversion of liberty to imperialistic purposes that so exercised both Lincoln and John Quincy Adams. The open or covert sapping of those founding principles called, however, not for their public repudiation and consignment to the rubbish heap of history but for a restoration or recovery of the "axioms of free society." No task was more urgent. Hence Lincoln (echoing the Founders) could view popular education in the principles of the regime as "the most important subject which we as a people can be engaged in." Perhaps nothing less would suffice: an entire people had to become passionately attached to a system of rational liberty.[21] Precisely because Abraham Lincoln and John Quincy Adams—like Henry Clay—saw an intimate connection between "the light of reason, and the love of liberty," they tended to view whatever jeopardized the one as likely to jeopardize the other.[22]

Neither Lincoln nor Adams found it easy to think of America's longer-range needs and opportunities abstracted from

[20] Lincoln, Lecture on Discoveries and Inventions, ibid., pp. 114–21.

[21] Lincoln to Henry R. Pierce et al., Apr. 6, 1859, ibid., pp. 123–24; "Appeal to the Voters of Sangamon County," Mar. 9, 1832, ibid., p. 7; Springfield Young Men's Lyceum Address, ibid., pp. 16–17, 21.

[22] Lincoln, Eulogy on Henry Clay, July 6, 1852, ibid., pp. 61–62. See also John Quincy Adams to Richard C. Anderson, May 27, 1823, in Koch and Peden, eds., *Selected Writings*, pp. 345–52. None of this precluded the surprising turn of an impoverished European republicanism which showed "that the *arts* and *sciences* themselves, that genius, talents, and learning, are in the most enlightened periods of the human history liable to become objects of proscription to political fanaticism" (John Quincy Adams to John Adams, July 27, 1795, ibid., p. 247).

the festering wound of slavery. Perhaps this is only another way of saying that for both men "this is a world of compensations; and he who would *be* no slave, must consent to *have* no slave"; those whose private interest or ambition or passion made them indifferent or neutral toward the fundamental principle of human equality could not be trusted either to guard that principle or to respect it.[23] Just as the plainest print could not be read through a gold eagle, so too would an attitude of "don't care" obscure the foundations of the regime. The result would be a population coolly prepared to expand or contract human slavery depending on the comparative returns of alternative forms of investment, a population unilaterally disarmed of any principle by which it might combat the machinations of ruthless demagoguery. To contain or forfend those evils, John Quincy Adams and Lincoln sought to create a vast continental empire of liberty. Their commitments to internal improvements, free soil, free labor, indeed to an *educated* population of laborers, may be seen as so many ways of binding a diverse public in a diverse land to a singular and ennobling ideal.

For both men there was a deep and continuing connection between the principles of American Revolutionary constitutionalism and the moral and intellectual improvement of the human race. Accordingly, the project of reducing American principles to practice took on for them the hues of genuine nobility. For Lincoln this mighty effort was an emphatically human achievement—the triumph of a particular people in a particular land to be sure, but with universal consequences.[24] To John Quincy Adams, speaking in an age when "the spirit of improvement [was] abroad upon the earth," it

[23] Lincoln to Pierce et al., Apr. 6, 1859, in Current, ed., *Political Thought of Lincoln*, p. 124. See also Lincoln, Springfield Young Men's Lyceum Address, ibid., p. 19; Springfield Speech on the Dred Scott Decision, June 26, 1857, ibid., p. 93; and John Quincy Adams, Diary entry for Nov. 24, 1843, in Koch and Peden, eds., *Selected Writings*, p. 407.

[24] Lincoln, Wisconsin State Fair Address, in Current, ed., *Political Thought of Lincoln*, p. 138. See also the image of man as a miner who discovers and exploits the untapped treasures that constitute "the whole world, material, moral, and intellectual" (Lecture on Discoveries and Inventions, ibid., p. 115).

seemed inconceivable that a government charged with the powers enumerated in the Constitution should hold itself incapable of advancing the mechanical and elegant arts, literature, and "the sciences, ornamental and profound." Equally, it seemed to Adams churlish and "unworthy of a great and generous nation" not to join with other civilized nations in the exploration of the earth and the heavens. European contributions to those branches of science posed a direct challenge to the Americans—and to the grandest implications of their Revolutionary principles. "But what, in the meantime, have *we* been doing?"[25] A people posing such a question to themselves could not be charged with holding only petty aspirations.

Facing up to the Founding has entailed for Founders and successors alike a willingness to step back and take stock, to orient oneself toward the larger purposes that from the outset gave the Revolutionary cause its impulse and meaning. This brief review of some of those worthies has focused on their several hopes and expectations, especially as they perceived them to be bound up with the education of the new, rising generation. In illustrating through word and deed their ways of respecting and transcending *their* past, those early fathers and sons have shown us, their successors, how we in turn might face up to their achievements. Whatever we may owe the past in the way of gratitude and honor, it is something better than mindless idolatry or rote incantation. Rather, like thoughtful critics, like men and women of independent judgment, we are invited to face up to the legacy of the Founders by taking their nobler intentions and supporting reasons seriously. In so doing, we not only pay them a deserved compliment but come closer to being the kind of self-governing people they wished for.

One cannot review the thoughts of those early Revolutionary constitutionalists without being impressed by both their sobriety and hopefulness. If they cherished certain features

[25] John Quincy Adams, First Annual Message, Dec. 6, 1825, in Koch and Peden, eds., *Selected Writings*, pp. 360–64, 366–67; Oration delivered before the Cincinnati Astronomical Society, Nov. 10, 1843, ibid., pp. 400–401, 405–6.

of their colonial or imperial legacy, it was with a view to surpassing those older ways. If they expected this continent to serve as a testing ground for the conversion of their theoretical principles into homegrown practices, it was with more than half a thought to displaying models that others might be tempted to emulate and adapt. Treading a narrow path (and not always successfully) between pretension and parochialism, between bombast and pettiness, those fathers and sons acted on a common assumption. Here, they thought, was something that Americans of all kinds and conditions might most reasonably take pride in: a general willingness to face up to their own highest expectations. For Founders and successors alike, the promise of America would always lie just over the horizon.

PETER S. ONUF

Anarchy and the Crisis of the Union

REPORTING ON THE progress of the controversy over the ratification of the federal Constitution in Pennsylvania, William Shippen, Jr., wrote that "fear of anarchy" explained widespread support for the proposed system. Even though he was convinced "this fear is imaginary, nothing can remove it."[1] In view of remarkably stable political conditions in the new nation and its prospects for economic growth, many other Americans were equally puzzled by the talk of crisis and calamity. "If we are undone," quipped one South Carolinian, "we are the most splendidly ruined of any nation in the universe."[2] But proponents of constitutional reform were not describing the existing situation in the states; they were predicting the future, and their predictions centered on the behavior of states responding to external threats—including those presented by other states—in the event of disunion.

Federalist rhetoric was effective because it exploited chronic concerns about the preservation—and even the substantial reality of—American independence in the "savage" realm of international politics. At the same time, the growing independence of the separate states threatened to create the anarchic conditions in America that would open the door to European intervention. Only by the "terror" of their collected power, warned Harrington, could the American states

[1] William Shippen, Jr., to Thomas Lee Shippen, Nov. 29, 1787, Merrill Jensen et al., eds., *The Documentary History of the Ratification of the Constitution*, 10 vols. to date (Madison, 1976-), 2:424.

[2] *South Carolina Gazette and Public Advertiser* (Charleston), May 18–21, 1785, quoted in Gordon S. Wood, *The Creation of the American Republic, 1776–1787* (Chapel Hill, 1969), p. 395.

"preserve perpetual peace with the nations of Europe."[3] Both by mimicking the European state system and by inviting European interference, the politics of the "disunited states" would soon be Europeanized.

Students of the American Founding have long recognized the importance of the new nation's vulnerable international situation for proponents of a more "energetic" union. But scholars generally have failed to relate these concerns to contemporary thinking about the nature of an "extended republic" that included—and was designed to preserve—distinct, semisovereign states. This essay will explore Federalist responses to a "crisis" in the American state system that they thought jeopardized the survival of the states individually and collectively. An examination of crisis rhetoric, focused particularly on the protean notion of anarchy, demonstrates the importance of international and interstate relations—and their close connection—to proponents of national constitutional reform. Concern with such issues constituted a crucial dimension of the "cosmopolitan" perspective that distinguished Federalists from their adversaries in the ratification controversy.[4]

The Federalists' understanding of anarchy grew out of their increasingly pessimistic assessments of the new nation's international situation. They feared that a "state of nature" would emerge among the United States as the effectiveness of the union diminished, thus preparing the way for the thorough

[3] Harrington [Benjamin Rush], "To the Freemen of Pennsylvania," *Pennsylvania Gazette* (Philadelphia), May 30, 1787, Jensen et al., eds., *Documentary History of Ratification*, 13:116–20, esp. p. 119. The editors of this enormously useful series have determined that Rush's essay was reprinted at least thirty times in eleven different states.

[4] Frederick W. Marks III, *Independence on Trial: Foreign Affairs and the Making of the Constitution* (Baton Rouge, 1973). For an excellent treatment of the problem of national "respectability," see David F. Epstein, *The Political Theory of the Federalist* (Chicago, 1984), pp. 59–110. Wood, *Creation of the Republic*, and Forrest McDonald, *Novus Ordo Seclorum: The Intellectual Origins of the Constitution* (Lawrence, Kans., 1985), the leading studies of contemporary political thought, pay little attention to the problem of union.

Europeanization of American politics. In focusing on external threats, proponents of national constitutional reform implicitly acknowledged the durability of the states and their ability to contain domestic dissidence and lawlessness usually denoted by the term *anarchy*.

Although Shays's Rebellion seemed to justify conventional anxieties about the degeneration of democracy, commentators generally focused on Shays himself, as an exemplar of "tyranny" or "despotism." The more fevered accounts suggested that Daniel Shays, with the secret support of the British as well as the renegade state of Vermont, was simply the stalking horse for a counterrevolutionary conspiracy. Americanus warned his countrymen to guard against "every plot which is aimed at your INDEPENDENCE," or else Vermont, Canada, and the Iroquois—"savages" of every variety—"will join forces to the monster REBELLION."[5] Anarchy thus was not endemic in the American states, the inevitable tendency of popular government run amuck, but rather a condition created by conspirators (themselves perhaps the tools of a foreign power) to introduce despotism. For example, "Tar and Feathers" called the seceders from the Pennsylvania Assembly who sought to block the call for a ratification convention "disciples of SHAYS." These malcontents intended "to introduce *anarchy* into these states, that they might be an easy prey to *their lord* and *master,* DANIEL SHAYS."[6]

However much some Federalists distrusted the common people and feared popular licentiousness, the tendency of their rhetoric was to externalize the threat of anarchy. Of course, if republicans were naturally prone to anarchy the reform project was doomed from the start. Further, as Gordon S. Wood points out, Shays's Rebellion was anomalous. Reformers could exploit the disorders in Massachusetts for propaganda purposes, but they recognized that their real problems derived from the strength or "despotism" of state

[5] Americanus, *New York Journal,* Mar. 15, 1787, Jensen et al., eds., *Documentary History of Ratification,* 13:71–73; Peter S. Onuf, *Origins of the Federal Republic: Jurisdictional Controversies in the United States, 1775–1787* (Philadelphia, 1983), pp. 174–79.

[6] "Tar and Feathers," *Independent Gazetteer* (Philadelphia), Oct. 2, 1787, Jensen et al., eds., *Documentary History of Ratification,* 2:152–53.

governments, not from their weaknesses.[7] The states' self-sufficient strength encouraged them to pursue independent policies, thus subverting the union and creating a lawless state of nature—or condition of anarchy—among the states.

The danger of anarchy was all the more insidious to Federalists because it was *not* apparent in widespread social disorder, but instead described the inevitable tendency of sovereign states in disunion. Some Americans refused to acknowledge that Americans could ever be brought to "cut the throats of their brothers and sons," assuming that a sense of common identity would disarm the states; others, through partiality to their own states, failed to recognize the growing discrepancy between state interests and the common good.[8] Thus the challenge for proponents of constitutional reform was to overcome inertia and complacency by demonstrating the imminence of anarchy. The present "state of tranquillity" made it possible to provide "some rule" for the states that "will enforce a regard to the general interest." But if Americans failed to seize this providential moment, "we [will] have only exchanged tyranny for anarchy."[9]

AMERICA AND EUROPE

In 1783 Thomas Pownall, former royal governor of Massachusetts and a sympathetic observer of the American War for Independence, addressed the "Sovereigns of America." Pownall was convinced that the Americans had inaugurated an epoch of equal rights, "equal liberty, universal Peace, and an unobstructed intercommunication of happiness in Human Society." The United States would be nothing like Eu-

[7] See Wood, *Creation of the Republic,* pp. 409–13, on "democratic despotism."

[8] Thomas Jefferson to James Madison, Jan. 30, 1787, William T. Hutchinson et al., eds., *The Papers of James Madison,* 19 vols. to date (Chicago and Charlottesville, 1962-), 9:247–52. For similar sentiments see the report on dissension in the Wyoming Valley, *State Gazette of South Carolina* (Charleston), Apr. 13, 1786, and "A Dialogue," *Falmouth Gazette* (Portland, Mass.), Mar. 23, 1786.

[9] Item in *Pennsylvania Herald* (Philadelphia), May 9, 1787, Jensen et al., eds., *Documentary History of Ratification,* 13:96–97.

rope, whose sovereigns were always at each other's throats in a never-ending struggle for dominance. "As to political civilization," he wrote, Europeans "scarce [can] be said to have emerged out of their Savage State." In contrast, the new American system "is founded on a law of Nations that coincides with the law of Nature." Warfare was not the "natural" condition among republican states dedicated to the preservation of individual rights and the pursuit of "happiness." Indeed, Pownall suggested, these political communities existed to serve the interests of their citizens; they were simply means toward the progressive perfection of "human society." It did not follow, however, that the Americans could avoid the sordid realities of power politics. Here was the point of Pownall's "Address": the American "Sovereign must come forward amongst the Nations, as an active existing Agent."[10]

Pownall anticipated the arguments of American constitutional reformers. Balancing his enthusiasm for the American experiment with a realistic assessment of world politics, he told the Americans they would have to become like Europeans, "sovereigns" in a world of hostile sovereignties, in order to secure their independence. American reformers agreed, urging their countrymen to prevent the Europeanization of American politics by creating a "respectable" national government. This alone could guarantee the survival of the new American republics, leagued in peaceful harmony under a regime of law. Only when the European states had emerged from "savagery" could the Americans dispense with collective security arrangements.[11]

Pownall grasped the central paradox in America's relations with Europe: although the United States was no longer part of the Old World, it would have to master Old World politics to preserve its independence. Pownall explained the new nation's situation by juxtaposing European "savagery" and American "civilization," a reversal of the conventional equa-

[10]T[homas] Pownall, *A Memorial Addressed to the Sovereigns of America* (London, 1783), pp. 54, 53, 129.

[11]See Felix Gilbert, *To the Farewell Address: Ideas of Early American Foreign Policy* (Princeton, 1961); James H. Hutson, *John Adams and the Diplomacy of the American Revolution* (Lexington, Ky., 1980); Gerald Stourzh, *Benjamin Franklin and American Foreign Policy*, 2d ed. (Chicago, 1969).

tions flattering to—and characteristic of—the neocolonial mentality. Most importantly, he focused his comparison specifically on the behavior of states toward each other, not on the achievements in arts, manners, industry, or commerce that ordinarily denoted the progress of civilization. European sovereigns were "savage" because they did not recognize any higher, controlling law: thus they remained in a lawless, anarchic "state of nature." Monarchy, Pownall intimated and the Americans insisted, was a historical anachronism, sustained by force and violence.[12] By overawing their subjects—by making war on them as well as on each other—the sovereign savages of Europe had preserved their power even while human society became more civilized.[13]

American Revolutionaries and their European friends believed that the discrepancy between political science and the general progress of civilization could only be overcome by a

[12] Noah Webster was convinced that the "basis of every [European] constitution . . . was laid by barbarians, in whom the military spirit was predominant" (Noah Webster, Jr., *Sketches of American Policy* [Hartford, 1785], p. 21). On Webster's ideas see Richard M. Rollins, *The Long Journey of Noah Webster* (Philadelphia, 1980), pp. 39–55, esp. pp. 44–46. Robert H. Wiebe, *The Opening of American Society: From the Adoption of the Constitution to the Eve of Disunion* (New York, 1984), pp. 67–89, discusses the Americans' neocolonial mentality.

[13] Few European commentators indicted Old World politics so categorically. The French financier Jacques Necker believed that the "blind and unruly passions" of "nations, in their savage state" had been "softened in some measure by the effect of civilization" ("Extract from Neckar's Treatise on the Administration of the Finances of France," from *New York Independent Journal*, n.d., in *Virginia Gazette* [Richmond], Feb. 8, 1786). The balance of power had introduced a measure of rationality and predictability into international relations; international law treatises codified the emergence of civilized standards in state practice. Hutson emphasizes the centrality of the balance of power and interest of state in American thinking about international relations. He says this "realism" was not incompatible with liberal premises: "Americans genuinely believed that [the balance of power] was a progressive principle in international affairs" (*Adams and Diplomacy*, p. 10). See also Daniel George Lang, *Foreign Policy in the Early Republic: The Law of Nations and the Balance of Power* (Baton Rouge, 1985), and Peter S. and Nicholas G. Onuf, "American Constitutionalism and the Emergence of a Liberal World Order," in George Athan Billias, ed., *American Constitutionalism Abroad: Selected Essays in Comparative Constitutional History* (Westport, Conn., 1990), pp. 65–89.

thorough reconstitution of the states that constituted international society. "National felicity" and international peace would be secured, William Vans Murray predicted, when "nations can be brought to stand towards each other, under relations similar to such as connect moral agents."[14] But, beyond the counsels of prudence, irresponsible monarchical regimes had no reason to be "moral." Led astray by their savage passions, monarchs perpetuated a state of war at their own and each other's subjects' expense. As Thomas Paine told the Americans in *Common Sense,* monarchy was simply a survival of darker ages, an artificial, unnatural incubus on modern civilized society.[15]

Because their governments were founded on the great principles of natural law, Americans believed they would be immune to the savage enmities of the Old World. Freed from the shackles of British mercantilism, "we have it in our power to extend a beneficial commerce" to all nations.[16] The United States had no enemies: "We now view the whole human race as members of one great and extensive family."[17] Guided by enlightened self-interest, the American states would disdain war and conquest; they had already renounced the conventional prerogatives of sovereign, war-making states by joining in Confederation. For enthusiastic observers like Richard Price, the English radical, the American union represented a practical application of republican principles to international relations. Through Confederation, a regime of law would supplant the lawless "state of nature" among sovereign states: it was "not impossible that by such means universal peace may be produced and all war excluded from the world."[18]

[14] William Vans Murray, "Political Sketches" (written in 1784–85), *American Museum* 2 (1787):220–48, quotation on p. 241.

[15] Thomas Paine, *Common Sense,* 3d ed. (1776), in Merrill Jensen, ed., *Tracts of the American Revolution, 1763–1776* (Indianapolis, 1966), pp. 400–446, esp. pp. 409–18.

[16] Jonathan Loring Austin, *An Oration, Delivered July 4, 1786* (delivered in Boston; Boston, 1786), p. 16.

[17] James Campbell, "An Oration, in Commemoration of the Independence of the United States of North America . . . July 4, 1787" (delivered in Philadelphia), *American Museum* 3 (1788):21.

[18] Richard Price, *Observations on the Importance of the American Revolution, and the Means of Making It a Benefit to the World* (1785), in Bernard Peach,

Ezra Stiles, Benjamin Franklin, and other American commentators agreed that the American Revolution had begun a "new chapter in the law of nations." Although less impressed than Price with the prospects for extending the principles of Confederation, they shared his faith that warfare would become increasingly anachronistic. Stiles predicted that the recognition of states' true interests that the Revolution inspired eventually would confine hostilities so as not to interrupt the "civil, social and commercial intercourse of subjects." The war-making apparatus of the monarchical state would wither away: "Even navies will, within this century, be useless." Thus would be inaugurated "a generous, and truly liberal system of national connexions."[19]

Yet, as Pownall suggested, this new epoch in international history depended on the Americans' ability to preserve and perfect their own union. Notwithstanding the successful outcome of the war, the prospects seemed doubtful to many observers. Hostile British commentators gleefully reported that the American states were now poised for conflict—with each other. A writer in the *London Times* was convinced America was "on the point of falling into that anarchy which generally attends a country torn from an ancient state."[20] Before the war, the empire had guaranteed peace and harmony among the colonies; ironically, the British—as the common enemy—continued to provide the efficient cause of union during the war years. Critics of the ministry therefore urged an early peace: as Charles James Fox told Parliament, "The American provinces are not united by any other bonds of

---

ed., *Richard Price and the Ethical Foundations of the American Revolution* (Durham, N.C., 1979), pp. 177–224, esp. p. 187.

[19] Ezra Stiles, *The United States Elevated to Glory and Honor* (1783 Connecticut election sermon), 2d ed. (Worcester, 1785), p. 85. Benjamin Franklin's views are set forth in a letter to Benjamin Vaughan, July 10, 1782, excerpted and discussed in Stourzh, *Franklin and Foreign Policy*, pp. 229–30. On the connections between commerce and civilization in contemporary thought, see the stimulating discussion in Albert O. Hirschman, *The Passions and the Interests: Political Arguments for Capitalism before Its Triumph* (Princeton, 1977).

[20] Item in *Times* (London), Jan. 29, 1785. These reports are surveyed in Leon Fraser, *English Opinion of the American Constitution and Government (1783–1798)* (New York, 1915), pp. 31–43.

friendship than those which you yourselves, by your hostilities, impose. Their usual animosities and jealousies will return with an elastic force, when once the incumbent weight which now presses them down is removed." Reports of numerous separatist movements on the frontiers as well as of virulent factional splits in the old states seemed to bear out Fox's prediction: "Every day brings forth accounts of the anarchy that prevails throughout the American provinces."[21]

British writers were particularly impressed by the weakness of Congress and the union. In an influential tract that helped abort an Anglo-American commercial treaty, Lord Sheffield wrote that "the authority of Congress can never be maintained over those distant and boundless regions" supposedly secured to the United States at the Peace of Paris: "Her nominal subjects will speedily imitate and multiply the examples of independence."[22] Some Americans agreed that the vast size of the new nation was its leading liability. "There is but one path that can lead the United States to destruction," Benjamin Rush wrote, "and that is their extent of territory. It was probably to effect this, that Great Britain ceded to us so much waste land."[23]

Size was a source of weakness both because it encouraged settlers to pursue their own interests in defiance of state and national authority and because it made the country vulnerable to Indian attacks and European interference. Another English writer warned that "a general confederacy of the Indian nations" in the Northwest presented a "formidable" danger to the overextended union. Comparing the prematurely senescent United States to the declining Roman Empire, he suggested that "eruptions from the north-western hives of hardy intrepid savages, would resemble the inroads of the Goths and Vandals, that spread such terror and desolation over Europe." As the fragmentation of old states and

[21] "Sketches of the Present Times," including Charles James Fox quotation, *Times* (London), Feb. 2, 1786.

[22] Earl of Sheffield [John B. Holroyd], *Observations on the Commerce of the American States* (London, 1783), p. 105.

[23] Nestor [Benjamin Rush], "To the People of the United States," *Independent Gazetteer*, June 3, 1786.

the overextension of settlement weakened the union, America's enemies would gain in strength.[24] With "a great many over the whole continent" growing "quite tired of their independence," the states will "be shortly ripe for that punishment they so justly merit."[25] When the union collapsed, Europeans would rush to fill the vacuum of effective power. "Politicians" in London reportedly "offer considerable wage[r]s that the new States are divided among the different powers of Europe in the course of five years." The only obstacle to recolonization would be getting hostile European states to reach an agreement about how to divide the continent.[26]

Many Americans endorsed this gloomy assessment of their situation, agreeing with George Washington that the continent was "fast verging on anarchy." "Thirteen sovereignties pulling against each other, and all tugging at the foederal head, will soon bring ruin on the whole," the former American commander-in-chief predicted.[27] Only a more energetic union, a Philadelphian wrote in 1785, "can protect the United States from the insults and abuses of Barbarians, whether civilized or uncivilized."[28] In the following year— shortly before Shays's uprising—a Bostonian warned that the states should not "trifle any longer": to do so "is to sport with their existence, and to offer themselves a prey to any invader, or to a tyrant, or to anarchy."[29] These concerns shaped the

[24] Item datelined London, Dec. 1–12, 1785, *Maryland Gazette* (Annapolis), Mar. 10, 1786. For a similar warning see Turgot's letter, Mar. 22, 1778, Peach, ed., *Price and the Revolution*, pp. 215–24, esp. p. 222.

[25] Letter from Suffolk, Va., June 1, 1785, *London Chronicle*, Aug. 6, 1785, Samuel Cole Williams, *History of the Lost State of Franklin* (New York, 1933), pp. 87–88; letter dated Kingston, Jamaica, July 25, 1785, *Falmouth Gazette*, Sept. 10, 1785.

[26] Item datelined London, Aug. 6, 1785, *Virginia Gazette*, Oct. 15, 1785.

[27] George Washington to Madison, Nov. 5, 1786, *Documentary History of the Constitution of the United States*, 5 vols. (Washington, D.C., 1901–5), 5:33–35.

[28] Item datelined Philadelphia, May 30, 1785, *Virginia Journal* (Alexandria), June 9, 1785.

[29] Item datelined Boston, July 19, 1786, *State Gazette of South Carolina*, Aug. 24, 1786.

Federalists' definition of the American "crisis," prompting them to seek a more perfect, energetic union. The crucial question, as they framed it, was whether governments founded on equal rights and the sovereignty of the people could coexist peacefully. Would the New World be different from the Old?

Federalists argued that the fulfillment of America's promise—and the further progress of mankind—depended on vindicating the principles of natural right and law, by perfecting a continental union of free republics. The new Constitution alone could secure this paramount goal, Federalists insisted, and answer Pownall's challenge. The proposed system, Joel Barlow averred, thus was "calculated for the great benevolent purposes of extending peace, happiness, and progressive improvement" throughout the world.[30] "The principles of the American Revolution are those of eternal Peace," he later added: "Purge the earth of its tyrants, and it will no more be tormented by war."[31]

AMERICAN ANARCHY

Federalist proponents of the new Constitution agreed with British commentators that the tendency of American politics was toward disunion, and that the anarchy of disunion would soon lead to tyranny and counterrevolution. We are "on the eve of war," Edmund Randolph told the Philadelphia convention.[32] After belatedly endorsing the Constitution, Randolph returned to Virginia to expatiate on the dangers of disunion. Union alone could restrain the "dogs of war," he warned: "I see the dreadful tempest, to which the present calm is a prelude, if disunion takes place. I see the anarchy which must happen if no energetic government be established. . . . If an-

[30] Joel Barlow's Oration to the Cincinnati, Hartford, July 4, 1787, *American Museum* 2 (1787):135–42, esp. p. 138.

[31] Joel Barlow, *A Letter Addressed to the People of Piedmont* (New York, 1795), p. 27; see also idem, *Advice to the Privileged Orders, in the Several States of Europe* (1792; reprint ed., New York, 1795), pp. 4–5.

[32] Speech of Edmund Randolph, May 29, Max Farrand, ed., *The Records of the Federal Convention of 1787*, rev. ed., 4 vols. (New Haven, 1937), 1:26 (Madison's notes, except where otherwise indicated).

archy and confusion follow disunion, an enterprising man may enter into the American throne. . . . No greater curse can befall her than the dissolution of the political connection between the states."[33] The association between anarchy and war was close in Federalist rhetoric. Promoters of the Constitution identified the formal conditions for a "state of war" among the states—the absence of "political connection"— with the inevitable consequence, "tumults" and disorder. The idea of war embraced both the latent rivalry of sovereign states in a lawless "state of nature" and the actual outbreak of violent conflict always immanent in this condition.

The Federalists' Hobbesian assumptions about international relations were familiar to Americans. It was axiomatic, Cato told readers of the *New-Haven Gazette* in January 1787, that a state must be sufficiently strong to defend itself. Otherwise "it must expire under the sword of its foes, or sink into submission, both of which are equally the extinction of its felicity."[34] The imminent collapse of the union would multiply potential dangers by exposing each state to the "natural" rivalry of other American as well as European states.

Hugh Henry Brackenridge was persuaded that the United States were already in this liminal "natural" situation, so full both of danger and of promise. He contrasted the opportunity "of forming a constitution, which shall be the wonder of the universe," with the awful possibility of a war of all against all. Seeking to reassure delegates who thought the Framers had exceeded their charge to amend the Articles, Brackenridge told the Pennsylvania convention the American people were "on the wild and extended field of nature, unrestrained by any former compact." "We are not on federal ground," he concluded: "The former Articles of Confederation have received sentence of death."[35] Noah Webster agreed that "the present situation of our American states is very little better

[33] Speeches of Randolph, Virginia convention, June 24 and [17], Jonathan Elliot, ed., *The Debates in the Several State Conventions, on the Adoption of the Federal Constitution*, 2d ed., 5 vols. (Philadelphia, 1876), 3:603, 470–71.

[34] Cato, *New-Haven Gazette*, Jan. 25, 1787.

[35] Speech of Hugh Henry Brackenridge, Pennsylvania convention, Sept. 28, 1787, Jensen et al., eds., *Documentary History of Ratification*, 2:93.

than a state of nature." As a result, "our boasted state sovereignties are so far from securing our liberty and property,
that they, every moment, expose us to the loss of both."[36]

Federalists linked the apparently imminent dissolution of
the union with the onset of anarchy. "Are not the bands of
Union so absolutely relaxed as almost to amount to a dissolution?" asked James Madison.[37] A North Carolinian con-
curred: "These states are now tottering on the brink of
anarchy."[38] With the Articles under "sentence of death," the
proposed Constitution represented the only hope for preserving peace and harmony among the states. A Massachusetts writer compared the *"Disunited* States of America . . . to
Thirteen distinct, separate, independent, *unsupported* Columns," vulnerable to "rapid destruction from the ruthless
Attacks of *Anarchy,* on the one Hand, and of *Despotism,* on the
other."[39] Charles Cotesworth Pinckney developed a similar
argument in the South Carolina debates. "Anarchy" would
probably follow rejection of the Constitution, thus encour-
aging "some daring despot to seize upon the government,
and effectually deprive us of our liberties."[40]

Anarchy certainly conjured up conservative anxieties
about "liberty degenerating into licentiousness & ye turbulence of factions" and "the flames of internal insurrection"
bursting out "in every quarter."[41] Even now, Pennsylvanian

[36] [Noah Webster], *An Examination into the Leading Principles of the Federal
Constitution* (1787), in Paul Leicester Ford, ed., *Pamphlets on the Constitution
of the United States* (Brooklyn, 1888), pp. 25–65, esp. p. 55.

[37] Speech of James Madison, Virginia convention, June 14, 1788, Elliot,
ed., *Debates,* 3:399.

[38] James White to Gov. Richard Caswell, Nov. 13, 1787, Edmund Cody
Burnett, ed., *Letters of the Members of the Continental Congress,* 8 vols. (Washington, D.C., 1921–36), 8:681–82.

[39] Item from *Massachusetts Gazette,* n.d., in *Maryland Journal* (Baltimore),
Dec. 25, 1787.

[40] Speech of Charles Cotesworth Pinckney, South Carolina convention,
Jan. 17, 1788, Elliot, ed., *Debates,* 4:281–82.

[41] Edward C. Papenfuse, "An Undelivered Defense of a Winning Cause:
Charles Carroll of Carrollton's 'Remarks on the Proposed Federal Constitution,'" *Maryland Historical Magazine* 71 (1976):220–51, esp. p. 232;

Jasper Yeates asserted, "the government of laws has been almost superseded by a licentious anarchy."[42] Federalists were determined to resist this "licentiousness, which advances nigh to a contempt of all order and subordination," and they saw the preservation of the union as their most important line of defense.[43] The forces of lawlessness and disorder disguised their ultimate goals by claiming to uphold state "sovereignty." But by subverting the union and therefore setting the states at each other's throats, enemies of constitutional reform would in fact "annihilate all government."[44] In the event of disunion, Federalists warned, even the largest states would be "weak and contemptible" and thus "unable to protect themselves from external or domestic insult."[45]

Social anxieties merged with dire predictions about the behavior of the "disunited states" in Federalist rhetoric. As a result, it was the strength, or war-making capacity, of fully sovereign states that was most immediately frightening. Without some "confessedly paramount . . . legal authority," "the worst sort of unsubdueable anarc[h]y might be expected to result."[46] But while the states grew stronger and more dangerous to each other, they would collectively be more vulnerable to external threats. As a result, no stable balance of power among the states was likely to emerge and the condition of anarchy would prove short-lived. "If the great union

---

speech of James Wilson, Pennsylvania convention, Dec. 11, 1787, Jensen et al., eds., *Documentary History of Ratification*, 2:577. See also [Oliver Ellsworth], "Landholder," no. 5, *Connecticut Courant* (Hartford), Dec. 3, 1787, Jensen et al., eds., *Documentary History of Ratification*, 3:482.

[42] Speech of Jasper Yeates, Pennsylvania convention, Nov. 30, 1787, Jensen et al., eds., *Documentary History of Ratification*, 2:439.

[43] "Letter from New York," *Connecticut Journal*, Oct. 24, 1787, ibid., 3:386.

[44] "A Plain Citizen," *Independent Gazetteer*, Nov. 22, 1787, ibid., 2:291.

[45] Speech of Charles Pinckney, South Carolina convention, May 14, 1788, Elliot, ed., *Debates*, 4:331.

[46] John Brown Cutting to Jefferson, July 11, 1788, *Documentary History of the Constitution*, 5:770–79, esp. p. 771. The reference is to hostilities between North Carolina and the Franklin separatists.

be broken," Gen. William Heath told the Massachusetts convention, "our country, as a nation perishes; and if our country so perishes, it will be as impossible to save a particular state as to preserve one of the fingers of a mortified hand."[47]

Whether or not anarchy among the states gave way to utter "licentiousness" within them, the result would be the same. America, Civis concluded, "will either fall into the hands of an aspiring tyrant, or be divided among European powers."[48] The British already had "busy emissaries throughout the states," Charles Pinckney warned; and "how long," he asked, "can we flatter ourselves to be free from Indian cruelties and depredations."[49] Wars among the states, European intervention, and Indian attacks would all lead Americans to embrace order, even at the expense of their liberties. It hardly mattered if the "teeth of the lion" were "again made bare" and the British sought to reconquer their lost colonies,[50] or if some American "Caesar or Cromwell" should "avail himself of our divisions."[51] In any case, were the American states so foolish as to reject the Constitution, "the arm of tyranny" would "impose upon us a system of despotism" and the Revolution would be undone.[52]

STATES AT WAR

Federalists argued that the union would quickly degenerate into a "parcel of jarring contemptible states" if the new Constitution were not ratified.[53] This disunited condition would

[47] Speech of Gen. William Heath, Massachusetts convention, Jan. 30, 1788, Elliot, ed., *Debates*, 2:121.

[48] Civis, "To the Independent Electors of Maryland," Jan. 26, 1788, *Maryland Journal*, Feb. 1, 1788.

[49] Charles Pinckney's Letter, Jan. 2, 1788, *State Gazette of South Carolina*, May 5, 1788, Paul Leicester Ford, ed., *Essays on the Constitution of the United States* (Brooklyn, 1892), pp. 411–13, esp. pp. 411–12.

[50] [Ellsworth], "Landholder," no. 10, *Connecticut Courant*, Mar. 3, 1788, Ford, ed., *Essays on the Constitution*, pp. 189–92, esp. p. 192.

[51] [Webster], *Examination of the Constitution*, in Ford, ed., *Pamphlets on the Constitution*, pp. 25–65, esp. p. 63.

[52] Speech of Richard Law, Connecticut convention, Jan. 9, 1788, Jensen et al., eds., *Documentary History of Ratification*, 3:559.

[53] Civis, *Maryland Journal*, Feb. 1, 1788.

be inherently unstable and unpredictable. Connecticut's Oliver Ellsworth was afraid the states would "fly into a variety of shapes and directions, and most probably into several confederations and not without bloodshed."[54] The common assumption in all such speculations was that as states exercised the powers of independent sovereignties, they would lose their distinctive republican character and become progressively Europeanized. In the event, the subsequent "shapes and directions" of American politics hardly mattered: the constant threat of war would bring despotic governments to power and demolish liberty. Therefore, Federalists agreed, the unrestrained state "sovereignty" that would follow disunion was incompatible with the preservation of liberty as well as with the republican character—if not the very survival—of the states themselves.

Madison developed the Federalist critique of state sovereignty in his speech of June 29 at the Constitutional Convention. It was clear to him that "the same causes which have rendered the old world the Theatre of incessant wars, & have banished liberty from the face of it, wd soon produce the same effects here." Although the American states might begin their independent careers with the most enlightened republican constitutions, external threats would subvert the constitutional balance on which liberty depended. "In time of actual war," Madison told his fellow delegates, "great discretionary powers are constantly given to the Executive Magistrate. Constant apprehension of war, has the same tendency to render the head too large for the body."[55] Whether fighting or preparing to fight, every state would have to support a standing army, thus further jeopardizing liberty.

A strong union was the only guarantee of American independence. Taking the floor immediately after Madison, Alexander Hamilton warned that this unrestrained pursuit of state interest would inevitably lead to European entanglements: "Alliances will immediately be formed with different rival & hostile nations of Europe, who will foment disturbances among ourselves, and make us parties to all their own

[54] Speech of Oliver Ellsworth, Aug. 22, Farrand, ed., *Records of the Convention*, 2:375.

[55] Speech of James Madison, June 29, ibid., 1:464.

quarrels."[56] The British and Spanish were already tampering with western loyalties and, if the union collapsed, they would surely find many eager new clients. As if to substantiate Hamilton's prediction, Delaware's Gunning Bedford warned—in one of the most sensational speeches at Philadelphia—that the small states were prepared to seek foreign alliances. If large state delegates did not concede equal representation, he threatened, the small states would "find some foreign ally of more honor and good faith, who will take them by the hand and do them justice."[57] Although determined to hold out for proportional representation, the large states took such threats to heart. For his part, Virginian Edmund Randolph "was far from thinking the large States could subsist of themselves any more than the small; an avulsion would involve the whole in ruin."[58] "Something must be done," future Antifederalist Elbridge Gerry concluded, "or we shall disappoint not only America, but the whole world."[59]

Nationalists like Madison and Hamilton would have been happy to do away with the states altogether. Taking the anarchy argument to its logical conclusion, Gouverneur Morris thought "one government better calculated to prevent wars" and "render them less expensive or bloody than many."[60] But the impasse over representation served notice that the failure to secure a central role for the states in the new plan would certainly lead to its rejection by voters in the states—even if it could be rammed through the national convention. The certain result, Federalists had long since convinced themselves, would be "disunion and civil war," with all their attendant horrors.[61]

Federalists had to show that state sovereignty was an insub-

[56] Speech of Alexander Hamilton, June 29, ibid., p. 466.

[57] Speech of Gunning Bedford, June 30, ibid., p. 492.

[58] Speech of Randolph, July 2, ibid., p. 515.

[59] Speech of Elbridge Gerry, July 2, ibid., p. 515.

[60] Speech of Gouverneur Morris, May 30, ibid., p. 43 (McHenry version).

[61] Alexander Hamilton to Madison [June 8, 1788], Hutchinson et al., eds., *Papers of Madison*, 11:99–100.

stantial "phantom" while the states remained in union, but would lead to the destruction of republican liberty if the union collapsed.[62] "The States and the advocates for them were intoxicated with the idea of their *sovereignty*," Gerry noted. In fact, "we never were independent States, were not such now, & never could be even on the principles of the Confederation."[63] The exaggerated pretensions of state governments could not be allowed to jeopardize the real rights and interests of individual Americans or of the states themselves. Hamilton thus distinguished between the legitimate "rights of a state" and the factious "interests" of state governments.[64] Such invidious "state distinctions" must be sacrificed, William Pierce of Georgia concluded, "but without destroying the States."[65]

Political and constitutional developments in the states justified the Federalists' distinction between government and people. The tendency was toward more elaborate constitutional limitations on state legislatures matched by increasingly effective efforts of suspicious constituents to control their representatives. According to emerging American concepts of representation, government officials could no longer claim the absolute authority stipulated by the prevailing definition of sovereignty. As a result, Gordon Wood has shown, James Wilson and other Federalists theorists could ground a more powerful central government on the undelegated, undiminished sovereignty of the people.[66] They could also assert that a "more perfect union" would curb the states' illegitimate pretensions to "sovereignty" and thus secure the limits on governmental power that the people had attempted to set in the state constitutions. By radically expanding the scope of state power—and transforming state sovereignty

[62] Speech of Rufus King, June 30, Farrand, ed., *Records of the Convention*, 1:489.

[63] Speech of Gerry, June 29, ibid., p. 467.

[64] Speech of Hamilton, New York convention, June 25, 1788, Elliot, ed., *Debates*, 2:319–20.

[65] Speech of William Pierce, June 29, Farrand, ed., *Records of the Convention*, 1:467.

[66] Wood, *Creation of the Republic*, pp. 530–32, 544–47.

from a "phantom" into a "substantial" reality—disunion would reverse the direction of American constitutional development.

The challenge to the Federalists was to show that republican liberty would not survive if state governments exercised sovereign powers. They insisted that the American states, notwithstanding their republican character, could not coexist peacefully in the absence of effective union. "State sovereignty," "Plain Truth" wrote in the Philadelphia *Independent Gazetteer,* "is as incompatible with the federal Union, as the natural right of human vengeance is with the peace of society."[67] The Federalists' premise was that all states were reduced to the same hostile and violent level when confronting each other in their "natural" condition. It was a mistake to believe the "Genius of republics pacific," Hamilton warned: "Jealousy of commerce as well as jealousy of power begets war."[68] It was in their *internal* constitutions, where the rule of law superseded government by force and fear, that republics could properly be denominated "pacific"; Federalists might even concede that the authentic interests of republican citizens in promoting commercial intercourse throughout the world were also pacific. But, by definition, the interests of governments, not citizens, determined the course of international relations.

States spoke the language of domination, power, and relative advantage; their commitments were calculated and contingent, and the only sanction they recognized was force. "A nation stands alone, as an individual in the state of nature," explained Cato, "and every other [nation] is naturally its hostile rival; for societies have not even the sympathy of men to moderate their enmities."[69] In America, the present power of state governments was limited both by the constitutions under which they acted and by the constraints of the union, a civilized society of republics—albeit a dangerously imper-

[67] "Plain Truth," *Independent Gazetteer,* Nov. 10, 1787, Jensen et al., eds., *Documentary History of Ratification,* 2:216–23, esp. pp. 218–19.

[68] Hamilton's notes for a speech, June 18, Farrand, ed., *Records of the Convention,* 1:307.

[69] Cato, *New-Haven Gazette,* Jan. 25, 1787.

fect one—that preserved peace and harmony. In the event of disunion, however, the states would assume a new, mutually hostile character. John Jay catalogued the resulting horrors to New York voters: "Every State would be a little nation, jealous of its neighbors, and anxious to strengthen itself by foreign alliances, against its former friends. Then farewell to fraternal affection, unsuspecting intercourse; and mutual participation in commerce, navigation and citizenship. Then would arise mutual restrictions and fears, mutual garrisons,—and standing armies."[70] States as sovereignties would distort and disrupt the "natural," mutually beneficial "intercourse" of citizens and states. It was their very "artificiality" that made sovereign states so frightening and therefore so lethal to fundamental principles of republican government.

REAL AND APPARENT INTERESTS

In June 1787, when the Framers were beginning their deliberations in Philadelphia, Edward Carrington warned his fellow Virginian Madison that any "attempt to confederate upon terms materially opposed to the particular Interests" of the respective states, would lead to the "dismemberment" of the union; then "the prospects of America will be at an end as to any degree of National importance."[71] But it would be equally dangerous, Madison and his colleagues believed, to allow the existing union to collapse. Disunion would lead to interstate conflict, foreign intervention, and the return of despotism. The prosperity of the continent as well as the preservation of liberty depended on constitutional reform. In the words of a Maryland Federalist, a more perfect union alone could transform America "from being a parcel of jarring contemptible states" into "a great, free, happy, and flourishing empire."[72]

Sensitive to the new nation's precarious international posi-

[70] [John Jay], *An Address to the People of the State of New York* (1788), in Ford, ed., *Pamphlets on the Constitution*, pp. 67–86, esp. p. 84.

[71] Edward Carrington to Madison, June 13, 1787, Hutchinson et al., eds., *Papers of Madison*, 10:52–53.

[72] Civis, *Maryland Journal*, Jan. 26, 1788.

tion and convinced that conflicting state policies impeded recovery from the postwar economic slump, Federalists insisted on the necessity of immediate action. The new nation was doomed to betray its enormous promise if it failed to establish an energetic union. Antifederalists were less impressed with the magnitude of commercial and diplomatic problems, warning that the proposed solution—a powerful, "consolidated" national regime—jeopardized republican liberty and threatened to destroy the states.[73] But both sides agreed that Americans faced a critical choice, whether the "crisis" was the cause or—as Antifederalists charged—the effect of reform agitation. Federalists and Antifederalists used remarkably similar language to describe the inevitable consequences of disunion or consolidation. By emphasizing—and exaggerating—the dangers of either extreme, this polarized rhetoric created optimal conditions for a "miraculous" compromise.[74] Both parties agreed that the people of the states had to act decisively—either by endorsing a stronger union or by foiling the Federalists' consolidationist plot—in order to prevent counterrevolution and preserve American liberty and independence. At the same time, however, each party proclaimed that its own program best served the goals the other ostensibly sought to promote. Antifederalists therefore urged that more explicit guarantees of state rights and interests would strengthen the union, while Federalists insisted that a strong union would, as Carrington urged, secure "particular" inter-

[73] For a recent account that emphasizes the severity of the postwar depression and the intractability of diplomatic problems under the Articles, see Richard B. Morris, *The Forging of the Union, 1781–1789* (New York, 1987), esp. pp. 130–61, 194–219. Merrill Jensen minimized economic dislocations, attributing the notion of a "critical period" to Federalist propaganda (*The New Nation: A History of the United States during the Confederation, 1781–1789* [New York, 1950], pp. 422–28).

[74] Onuf, *Origins of the Republic*, pp. 186–209. On Antifederalist thought see Cecelia M. Kenyon's influential essay "Men of Little Faith: The Anti-Federalists on the Nature of Representative Government," *William and Mary Quarterly*, 3d ser. 12 (1955):3–43; Herbert J. Storing, "What the Anti-Federalists Were *For*," in Storing, ed., *The Complete Anti-Federalist*, 7 vols. (Chicago, 1981), 1:1–100, and James H. Hutson, "Country, Court, and Constitution: Antifederalism and the Historians," *William and Mary Quarterly*, 3d ser. 38 (1981):337–68.

ests and preserve the states. Combined with their common anxieties about the future, this convergence of goals enhanced the possibility of eventual accommodation.

The exigencies of the debate over the Constitution thus drove the Federalists to disavow a thoroughgoing nationalist intent, however much some of them might have preferred a truly consolidated continental republic.[75] Indeed, the obliteration of the states would have constituted an admission that the republican New World had not escaped Old World "savagery." The Federalists thus insisted that the Constitution alone could secure the states' political salvation: the Articles of Confederation were hopelessly inadequate. According to William Davie, "The encroachments of some states on the rights of the others, and of all on those of the Confederacy, are incontestible proofs of the weakness and imperfection of that system."[76] "Instead of supporting or assisting each other," said Hugh Williamson, the states "are uniformly taking advantage of one another."[77] Because the states were vulnerable in proportion to the weakness of the Confederation, only a more perfect union could guarantee their survival.

Antifederalists were justifiably suspicious of this solicitude for the states: after all, the Federalists also insisted that state sovereignty constituted the leading threat to the survival of republican government in America. But Antifederalist rhetoric worked toward compromise, both by forcing their opponents to acknowledge a central role for the states and by expressing "discordant notions" of state interest that revealed how "wretched" the disunited "situation" of the states would

[75] For a lucid discussion of how the authors of the *Federalist* were compelled to modify their original positions, see Albert Furtwangler, *The Authority of Publius* (Ithaca, N.Y., 1984). I emphasized the importance of the states in the Founders' thinking about the extended republic in "American Federalism and the Politics and Expansion," in Hermann Wellenreuther, ed., *German and American Constitutional Thought: Contexts, Interaction, and Historical Realities* (New York, 1990), pp. 50–69.

[76] Speech of William R. Davie, July 24, 1788, Elliot, ed., *Debates*, 4:17–23, esp. p. 20.

[77] Hugh Williamson, "Remarks on the New Plan of Government," *State Gazette of North Carolina* [1788], Ford, ed., *Essays on the Constitution*, pp. 393–406, esp. p. 403.

be "were the present plan rejected."[78] Antifederalists sought to expose the dangerous general tendencies of the proposed government by identifying specific threats to "particular interests." The practical result, however, was to invite their opponents to explain how much the new system would benefit individual states, thus deflecting attention away from its "tendency to annihilate all the state governments indiscriminately."[79]

The Federalists were prepared to occupy the moderate middle ground opened up by compromises at the Philadelphia Convention and the subsequent exchange of polemics. Their strategy was to suggest that constitutional reform was instigated by the states themselves in order to secure their own essential interests. They frequently invoked the analogy of individuals emerging from a natural state. For instance, North Carolinian James White said "States in Confederacy" were "like individuals in society" who "must part with some of their privileges for the preservation of the rest."[80] In a society of states, added "Plain Truth," each state had to sacrifice its "sovereignty," just as each man emerging from the "state of nature" could not reserve the "natural right of being the judge" in his own case.[81] The federal Constitution would protect the states by preventing them from exercising sovereign powers. "It gently subtracts from the liberties of each" state, "Social Compact" explained, while providing "for the security of all."[82] James Wilson used different language to express the same thought: "More liberty is gained by associating, than is lost by the natural rights which [the new government] absorbs."[83]

[78] "Federalism," Mar. 8, 1788, *Maryland Journal*, May 9, 1788.

[79] Letters of Luther Martin, no. 3, Mar. 25, 1788, *Maryland Journal*, Mar. 28, 1788, Ford, ed., *Essays on the Constitution*, pp. 372–77, esp. p. 375.

[80] White to Caswell, Nov. 13, 1787, Burnett, ed., *Letters of the Members*, 8:681–82.

[81] "Plain Truth," *Independent Gazetteer*, Nov. 10, 1787, Jensen et al., eds., *Documentary History of Ratification*, 2:218.

[82] "Social Compact," *New-Haven Gazette*, Oct. 4, 1787, ibid., 3:356–57.

[83] Speech of Wilson, Pennsylvania convention, Nov. 24, 1787, ibid., 2:335–36.

In the Federalist formulation, less turned out to be more. As "sovereignties" that acknowledged no superior authority, the states would remain "weak and contemptible."[84] But, the Federalists promised, the states would grow strong and prosperous once they disclaimed sovereign powers and submitted to the rule of law in a more perfect union. The key premise in their argument was that a chronic state of war would jeopardize the population and power of the separate states while subverting their republican character. Surrounded by hostile powers and threatened by domestic dissidents, the states stood precariously on the brink of violence. By eliminating the pervasive danger of incipient violence, the Constitution would enable the states to fulfill their republican destiny.

Reformers asserted that the weakness of the union and its inability to restrain the separate states was the Confederation's leading liability. In 1786 a Massachusetts writer predicted that any "efforts of a feeble union" to discipline "a powerful delinquent State" would necessarily "become *war*, instead of justice; and the punishing violations by right of war, is incompatible with every idea of government."[85] In the ratification debates, Oliver Ellsworth of Connecticut developed this crucial distinction between law and violence. Because the Confederation Congress could not exercise any legal authority over recalcitrant states, its only choices were to employ force against them or to capitulate. "A war of the states" would follow any attempt to impose the will of the union forcefully, while capitulating to the states would only hasten the union's collapse and lead to the same lamentable result. But the Federalists argued that the new system would substitute "coercion of law" for "coercion of arms." "This Constitution," concluded Ellsworth, "does not attempt to coerce sovereign bodies, states in their political capacity."[86]

Federalists countered Antifederalist warnings about con-

[84] Speech of Charles Pinckney, South Carolina convention, May 14, 1788, Elliot, ed., *Debates*, 4:331.

[85] Item datelined Charleston, Mass., *Maryland Gazette* (Baltimore), Apr. 14, 1786.

[86] Speech of Ellsworth, Connecticut convention, Jan. 7, 1788, Jensen et al., eds., *Documentary History of Ratification*, 3:548–54, esp. 553. See the discussion in Onuf, *Origins of the Republic*, pp. 190–91.

solidation by emphasizing the safety and security of the states under the Constitution. Roger Sherman thought the new system "well framed . . . for preserving the governments of the individual states." Any tendency toward consolidation would be checked by the state legislatures as they jealously defended their own internal "sovereignty." At the same time, however, it was in the legislatures' "interest" to support an effective central government that could protect the states "against foreign invasion" and preserve "peace and a beneficial intercourse" among them.[87] By minimizing the many sources of danger to the states under the existing Confederation, a stronger union would necessarily make the states stronger. Shielded by law, the states would no longer have to threaten each other with armed force to vindicate their rights.

The crucial question in the ratification debate was whether the states could preserve their integrity and independence under the new scheme. For Antifederalist William Grayson, the answer was simple enough: "Will not the diminution of state power and influence be an augmentation of those of the general government?"[88] The Federalist answer was paradoxical: by foregoing the conventional sovereign powers—notably to conduct foreign policy—the states were better secured in their essential rights and interests. "It appears very evident to me," wrote Pelatiah Webster, "that the Constitution gives an establishment, support, and protection to the internal and separate police of each State, under the superintendency of the federal powers, which it could not possibly enjoy in an independent state. Under the Confederation each State derives strength, firmness and permanency from its compact with the other states." The Federalist premise was that the legitimate rights of a republic could be distinguished from the powers of a lawless "sovereignty" in a state of nature. Under the Constitution, the states would be prohibited from pursuing policies that jeopardized their own republican character as well as the rights of neighboring republics. Para-

[87] [Roger Sherman], "A Citizen of New Haven," *Connecticut Courant*, Jan. 7, 1788, Jensen et al., eds., *Documentary History of Ratification*, 3:524–27, esp. pp. 527, 524.

[88] Speech of William Grayson, Virginia convention, June 12, 1788, Elliot, ed., *Debates*, 3:287–88.

doxically, it was only by monopolizing all the powers conventionally exercised by independent sovereignties that the new central government could assure the survival of republican governments in the states. But Federalists insisted that the states—as republics—gave up nothing under the new system; "the new Constitution," Webster concluded, "leaves all the Thirteen States, *complete republics,* as it found them."[89]

Federalists aimed their rhetorical attacks at actual and potential abuses of state power: the possibility of short-run gain in an unstable, highly competitive situation inevitably would corrupt and destroy republican governments. Therefore it was necessary, Hamilton said, "to attend to the distinction between the real and the apparent interests of the states."[90] Without an effective union, states pursuing their "apparent interests" would not be able to restrain themselves from "privateering upon each other" for commercial or territorial advantage;[91] nothing would "hinder" large, powerful states from "oppressing" their small, weak neighbors.[92] The economic dominance of states with large ports would lead to commercial discrimination against other states; states with large land reserves could anticipate lower taxes, while drawing wealth and population from their circumscribed neighbors. The disadvantages of some states—depopulation, depression, and social instability—thus would be translated into advantages for taxpayers and governments in other states.

The distinction between "real" and "apparent" interests

[89] Pelatiah Webster, *The Weakness of Brutus Exposed: Or, Some Remarks in Vindication of the Constitution* (1787), in Ford, ed., *Pamphlets on the Constitution,* pp. 117–31, esp. pp. 128, 121, my emphasis. See also speech of Wilson, Pennsylvania convention, Dec. 4, 1787, Jensen et al., eds., *Documentary History of Ratification,* 2:493–501, esp. p. 496, and Charles Carroll of Carrollton in Papenfuse, "An Undelivered Defense," p. 247.

[90] Speech of Hamilton, New York convention, June 25, 1788, Elliot, ed., *Debates,* 2:317–20, esp. p. 318.

[91] Item in *Middlesex Gazette* (Middletown, Conn.), Oct. 22, 1787, Jensen et al., eds., *Documentary History of Ratification,* 3:394–96, esp. p. 394.

[92] Speech of Ellsworth, Connecticut convention, Jan. 4, 1788, ibid., pp. 541–45, esp. p. 542.

was plausible to Americans on several grounds. Republican ideology and the Revolutionary commitment to a common cause taught Americans to distrust factious or partisan "self-interest" and posit a transcendent public interest. Thus, a Boston writer claimed that "the true interests of the several parts of the Confederation are the same."[93] Concepts of popular sovereignty also implied a common interest among the people-at-large and justified a distinction between them and potentially "factious" governments with their own distinct, "apparent" interests.[94] Federalists thus could argue that self-interested "state demagogues" and "great men" opposed the new system even though it served the real interests of the states themselves.[95]

Gordon Wood has shown that challenges to the legitimacy of state governments gained momentum with the development of new standards in the writing and interpretation of constitutions that seemed to subject governments as well as citizens to the rule of law.[96] Although the imperial crisis had driven Americans to embrace a Blackstonian notion of legislative sovereignty, representatives were unable and often unwilling to sustain claims to omnipotence over the course of the next decade. American republicanism came to be as closely identified with constitutional limitations on government as with government by popular consent. But the notion of responsible, limited government under law was jeopardized by the deterioration of the union: in relation to each other, the American states were irresponsible, acknowledging no lawful limits to their sovereignty. The new state constitutions had abolished sovereignty—the despotic power to command submission—from the states themselves, only to have the discredited doctrine gain new vitality and respectability in the realm of interstate relations. This was the discrepancy that Federalists exploited so brilliantly.

[93] Item in *American Herald* (Boston), Oct. 1, 1787, ibid., 13:285–86, esp. p. 286.

[94] Wood, *Creation of the Republic*, pp. 363–89.

[95] Henry Knox to [?], [September 1787], Jensen et al., eds., *Documentary History of Ratification*, 13:279–80; George Nicholas draft of address, Feb. 16, 1788, Durrett Collection, University of Chicago.

[96] Wood, *Creation of the Republic*, pp. 453–63.

The logic of constitutional development in the states worked against claims to unlimited power by their governments. But the collapse of the union threatened to reverse this tendency: nothing could then restrain the states from extending their power at each other's expense—and at the expense of their own citizens. Robert Livingston, for instance, was convinced that New York's very "existence, as a state, depends on a strong and efficient federal government."[97] Federalists insisted that only a strong union could save the states from themselves. Constitutionally limited republican government would not long survive under the lawless, anarchic conditions that disunion would entail.

The "great desideratum," wrote Madison, was to establish a national government "sufficiently neutral between different parts of the Society to controul one part from invading the rights of another, and at the same time sufficiently controuled itself."[98] This, Federalists proclaimed, was the Framers' great achievement. The federal Constitution would preserve the American republics by preventing them from behaving like disconnected, antagonistic "sovereignties"; at the same time, constitutional limitations on the new central government would protect the states from consolidation. Therefore, Pelatiah Webster concluded, the new system would not "melt down and destroy" the states, but would instead "support and confirm them all."[99]

PERPETUAL PEACE

When Federalists emphasized the advantages of the new union for the separate states they were obviously responding to political reality. Most Americans, Federalists included,

[97] Speech of Robert Livingston, New York convention, June 19, 1788, Elliot, ed., *Debates*, 2:211. See also "A Jerseyman," "To the Citizens of New Jersey," *Trenton Mercury*, Nov. 6, 1787, Jensen et al., eds., *Documentary History of Ratification*, 3:146–51, esp. p. 150, and speech of Archibald MacLaine, North Carolina convention, July 25, 1788, Elliot, ed., *Debates*, 4:68–69.

[98] Madison to Jefferson, Oct. 24, 1787, Hutchinson, et al., eds., *Papers of Madison*, 10:205–20, esp. p. 214.

[99] [Webster], *Weakness of Brutus*, in Ford, ed., *Pamphlets on the Constitution*, pp. 117–31, esp. p. 129.

were committed to republican self-government in the states, however much they distrusted those who actually exercised authority and even when they challenged existing constitutional arrangements. Nor could many Americans, in view of their own Revolution against British tyranny, lightly dismiss the dangers of a powerful, potentially despotic "consolidated" regime erected on the ruins of the states.

By definition, of course, there could be no union without states. Reformers were forced to acknowledge that the ultimate measure of the new union's "perfection" would be the vigor and vitality of the states—not their obliteration. In doing so, they advanced new claims for the global significance of America's republican revolution: not only had the individual states instituted the most rational and beneficent governments known to modern man, but the states were about to adopt a system that would save them from anarchy and disunion and preserve their character as peaceful republics. Thus the Federalists presented the Constitution as a kind of peace plan for the American states and as an inspirational example to the Old World.

James Wilson was the most ingenious exponent of the idea that the American union constituted a model world order. "Here is accomplished," exulted Wilson at the Pennsylvania ratification convention, "what the great mind of Henry IV of France had in contemplation" when he developed one of the most famous peace plans. States would now submit to law, not force: "A tribunal is here founded to decide, justly and quietly, any interfering claim." The central government was the "great arbiter," and "the whole force of the Union can be called forth to reduce an aggressor to reason." Wilson thought these new arrangements "an happy exchange for the disjointed contentious state sovereignties!"[100] Marylander Alexander Contee Hanson also claimed that Americans were making the dream of that "great soul . . . HENRY THE FOURTH" into a reality. Seeking to perfect an enduring balance of power, the French king had first "conceived the idea" of a "true and perfect confederate government" for Europe. Now the United States was about to become a "true federal

---

[100] Speech of Wilson, Pennsylvania convention, Dec. 11, 1787, Jensen et al., eds., *Documentary History of Ratification*, 2:572–84, esp. p. 583.

republic, . . . always capable of accession by the peaceable and friendly admission of new single states."[101]

Both Wilson and Hanson noted that Montesquieu—the Antifederalists' favorite philosopher—also endorsed the idea of a federal republic. Such a confederation, wrote Wilson, guaranteed "all the internal advantages of a republic, at the same time that it maintained the external dignity of a Monarchy."[102] This was precisely the combination of national respectability and local liberty called for by Thomas Pownall and other European friends of the American experiment. A strong continental government, capable of collecting and wielding the power of a mighty empire, alone could secure "perpetual peace" and preserve republican government in America.

The Americans would show Europe how interstate relations could be governed by law and reason. They would also be prepared to welcome new states into their union: extending the confederation was their rational, republican alternative to wars of conquest. If the new government would have "energy enough to maintain the Union of the Atlantic states," predicted Madison, it would prove equally capable of binding new western states to the existing union.[103] Thus, Francis

[101] Aristides [Alexander Contee Hanson], *Remarks on the Proposed Plan of a Federal Government, Addressed to the Citizens of the United States of America, and Particularly to the People of Maryland* (1788), in Ford, ed., *Pamphlets on the Constitution*, pp. 217–57, esp. p. 248. For an Antifederalist response see John Francis Mercer's ingenious argument that Europe already constituted a *"great federal republic"* without—and because of the absence of—a central government ("Farmer," no. 7, *Maryland Gazette* [Baltimore], Apr. 15, 1788, Storing, ed., *The Complete Anti-Federalist*, 5:64–66 [5.1.108–11], esp. p. 65). Stiles referred to Henry IV's peace plan in *United States Elevated*, p. 31. The plan itself is reprinted in Edward Everett Hale, ed., *The Great Design of Henry IV, from the Memoirs of the Duke of Sully*, intro. by Edwin D. Mead (Boston, 1909), and its authorship and intent are discussed in F. H. Hinsley, *Power and the Pursuit of Peace: Theory and Practice in the History of Relations between States* (Cambridge, 1963), pp. 24–27.

[102] *The Substance of a Speech Delivered by James Wilson* (delivered Nov. 24, 1787; publ. 1788), in Jensen et al., eds., *Documentary History of Ratification*, 2:340–50, esp. p. 342. See also Hanson, *Remarks on the Federal Government*, in Ford, ed., *Pamphlets on the Constitution*, pp. 217–57, esp. 223–24n.

[103] Madison to George Nicholas, May 17, 1788, Hutchinson et al., eds., *Papers of Madison*, 11:44–51, esp. p. 45.

Corbin exclaimed, the Americans would extend their union "to all the western world; nay, I may say, ad infinitum." No matter how large the union became, he added, its extent cannot render the new "government oppressive." The states would "retain such powers" as will give them "the advantages of small republics, without the danger commonly attendant on the weakness of such governments."[104]

The Federalists' advocacy of a strong, "respectable" union represented more than a realistic capitulation to the imperatives of power politics. Reformers also promoted a more powerful central government in order to preserve what they considered the essential differences between Old World and New World politics. Acknowledging no legal superior, European "sovereignties" always confronted one another with suspicion and hostility. In contrast, the American states—as long as they upheld their union—would live in peace. By eschewing the prerogatives of sovereignty and submitting to the rule of law, they would fulfill their republican destiny.

[104] Speech of Francis Corbin, Virginia convention, June 7, 1788, Elliot, ed., *Debates*, 3:108, 107.

CALVIN C. JILLSON

Ideas in Conflict: Political Strategy and Intellectual Advantage in the Federal Convention

No PERIOD IN American political history has attracted more sustained scholarly attention than that extending from the fateful shots at Lexington and Concord to the rise of the first Washington administration. No single event of this formative period more fundamentally shaped the new nation's future political development than did the Federal Convention of 1787 and its product—the American Constitution. As a result, each generation of Americans has sought to interpret and understand the Constitution in ways that buttress and support their fundamental vision of American politics and of the critical issues that their politics must confront. Interpretation of the constitution-making process, and therefore of the character and meaning of the document itself, has developed from stark simplicity to great complexity, while more recently the analytic focus has shifted from the role of narrow interests to that of broadly shared political principles.

Scholars still clash over the relative impact of John Locke and Montesquieu, or of liberal individualism and classical republicanism, on the hearts and minds of the Founding generation. Nonetheless, very little attention has been paid to the complex question of how principles and interests interacted with each other in the Convention.[1] This essay will identify

[1] Jack N. Rakove, "The Great Compromise: Ideas, Interests, and the Politics of Constitution Making," *William and Mary Quarterly*, 3d ser. 44 (1987):427–57, is an important exception.

principle and interest-based coalitions in the debates and roll-call voting record of the Convention; will specify the kinds of issues upon which each coalition structure was most active; and will describe how the coalitions organized to pursue various principles influenced the coalitions organized to pursue particular interests and vice versa. Coalitions arising from the interests of large states and small, northern states and southern, states claiming large swaths of western land and states without such claims, and commercial and agrarian states are well known. Divisions in the Convention based in conflicting sets of political principles are much less clear. Therefore, this essay will focus to a greater extent on the origins of coalitions based in principles than on those based in interests.

THE CONFLICT OVER PRINCIPLES AS A CLASH OF POLITICAL SUBCULTURES

The fundamental dispute over the role of principles in American political life has been between those who see Lockean individualism and those who see the communitarian strains of republicanism as central to the American experience.[2] More than thirty years ago, Louis Hartz summarized the collective wisdom of the first half of this century by providing a compelling description of the impact of a uniformly Lockean political culture on the origins and future course of American political development. Hartz argued that, as a result of Locke's influence, "the uniform values by which the colonial American was beginning to live" as the Revolution approached were organized around a single "master assumption." This "master assumption," which Hartz described as "instinctive to the American mind," affirmed "the reality of atomistic social freedom."[3] More recently Bernard Bailyn, Gordon S. Wood, J. G. A. Pocock, and others have described a republican political culture that came powerfully together during the decades surrounding 1776 to constitute a volatile

[2] John P. Diggins, *The Lost Soul of American Politics: Virtue, Self-Interest, and the Foundations of Liberalism* (New York, 1984).

[3] Louis Hartz, *The Liberal Tradition in America: An Interpretation of American Political Thought since the Revolution* (New York, 1955), pp. 59, 62.

Revolutionary ideology.[4] Nonetheless, scholars such as Joyce
Appleby, Isaac Kramnick, E. James Ferguson, Ralph L. Ketcham, and John P. Diggins have reasserted the importance of
Lockean liberalism and economic individualism to the political culture of the Founding period.[5] It is apparent at this
point that both liberal and republican political ideas were at
large in the American political culture of the Founding period. The question is, How did they interact with each other?[6]

While Hartz, Bailyn, Pocock, and others have sought to
describe one pervasive American political culture, other
scholars have attempted to explain widely acknowledged patterns of social, cultural, and political tension in postcolonial
America in terms of distinctive regional variations in the
American political culture.[7] In moving the analytic focus
from the general American character to its regional variations, these scholars have drawn attention to the interaction
of classical republican assumptions with those of Lockean liberalism.[8] Daniel J. Elazar contends that

[4] Bernard Bailyn, *The Ideological Origins of the American Revolution* (Cambridge, Mass., 1967), pp. 94–143; Gordon S. Wood, *The Creation of the
American Republic, 1776–1787* (Chapel Hill, 1969), pp. 43–44; J. G. A. Pocock, *The Machiavellian Moment: Florentine Political Thought and the Atlantic
Republican Tradition* (Princeton, 1975), p. 506.

[5] Joyce Appleby, "The Social Origins of American Revolutionary Ideology," *Journal of American History* 64 (1978):935–58; Isaac Kramnick, "Republican Revisionism Revisited," *American Historical Review* 87 (1982):629–
64; E. James Ferguson, "Political Economy, Public Liberty, and the Formation of the Constitution," *William and Mary Quarterly*, 3d ser. 40
(1983):389–412; Ralph Ketcham, *Presidents above Party: The First American
Presidency, 1789–1829* (Chapel Hill, 1984); Diggins, *American Politics*.

[6] Wood, *Creation of the Republic*, pp. 626–27; also see Diggins, *American
Politics*, p. 31; Forrest McDonald, *Novus Ordo Seclorum: The Intellectual Origins of the Constitution* (Lawrence, Kans., 1985), pp. viii, 285.

[7] Seymour Martin Lipset, *The First New Nation* (New York, 1963), pp. 2–
8, 18, 26–34; Clinton Rossiter, *1787: The Grand Convention* (New York,
1966), p. 23; Wood, *Creation of the Republic*, pp. 626–27; McDonald, *Novus
Ordo Seclorum*, pp. viii, 60–80.

[8] Daniel J. Elazar, *Cities of the Prairie: The Metropolitan Frontier and American Politics* (1970; reprint ed., Lanham, Md., 1984); idem, *American Federalism: A View from the States*, 2d ed. (New York, 1972); Robert Kelley, *The
Cultural Pattern in American Politics: The First Century* (New York, 1979).

the American political culture is rooted in two contrasting conceptions of the American political order, both of which can be
traced back to the earliest settlement of the country. In the first
(liberalism), the political order is conceived as a marketplace in
which the primary public relationships are products of bargaining among individuals and groups acting out of self-interest. In
the second (republicanism), the political order is conceived to be
a commonwealth . . . in which the citizens cooperate in an effort
to create and maintain the best government in order to implement certain shared moral principles.[9]

Clearly, although Elazar has not explored the Founding
period in anything like the depth of either Hartz or Bailyn,
he has subsumed their basic points by suggesting that regional subcultures represent characteristic syntheses of selected and distinctively weighted values drawn from a
common matrix of liberal and republican principles.

The moralistic political culture is a product of Puritan New England in its efforts to create the holy commonwealth. . . . Government is considered a positive instrument with a responsibility
to promote the general welfare. . . . The individualistic political
culture is a product of the Middle states['] . . . overriding commitment to commercialism and . . . pluralism. . . . Government
is instituted for strictly utilitarian reasons. . . . The traditional-
istic political culture is a product of the plantation agrarianism
of the South. . . . It reflects an older, precommercial attitude
that accepts a substantially hierarchical society . . . authorizing
. . . those at the top of the social structure to take a . . . dominant
role in government.[10]

The substantive meanings that Elazar, Robert Kelley, and
others have outlined for the political subcultures dominating
the several regions of the new American nation rest directly

[9] Elazar, *Cities of the Prairie*, pp. 258–59; also see Samuel Huntington,
"American Ideals and American Institutions," *Political Science Quarterly* 97
(1982):8; Ketcham, *Presidents above Party*, pp. 184–85; Joyce Appleby, *Capitalism and a New Social Order: The Republican Vision of the 1790s* (New York,
1984), p. 22; McDonald, *Novus Ordo Seclorum*, pp. 291–92.

[10] Elazar, *Cities of the Prairie*, pp. 261–65; also see idem, *American Federalism*, pp. 93–102; Robert Bellah et al., *Habits of the Heart: Individualism and
Commitment in American Life* (New York, 1985), pp. 27–28.

upon extensive bodies of descriptive historical writing. Descriptions of New England's distinctive variant of the American political culture invariably draw heavily on the work of Perry Miller, Edmund S. Morgan, Alan Simpson, and others in contending, in Kelley's words, that "the Congregational New Englanders['] . . . model for America was an idealized version of New England's orderly peasant democracy: communal, pious, hard working, austere, and soberly deferential."[11] New England's insular local culture of democratic deference had, however, come under considerable strain in the decades immediately before and after the outbreak of the Revolution.[12] Kelley argues that "a crucial transformation from *Puritan* to *Yankee* was in fact underway. . . . By the mid-1700s . . . a growing passion for liberty . . . and a far more unrestrained search for wealth and individual advancement were shifting the balance in New England's social order."[13] As a result, by the mid-1780s, New England's village democracies had become more raucously partisan and, from the perspective of the traditional elites, more dangerously unstable. Shays's Rebellion in the winter of 1786 confirmed the elite's growing sense that, although the democratic and participatory heritage of the region could not be denied, state politics could be stabilized through the creation of a strengthened national government.

No single comment better illuminates the attitude of the New England delegates as they made their way to Philadelphia than that offered by Henry Adams a full century ago,

[11] Kelley, *Cultural Pattern in American Politics*, p. 83; also see Elazar, *American Federalism*, p. 108; Edmund S. Morgan, "The Puritan Ethic and the American Revolution," *William and Mary Quarterly*, 3d ser. 24 (1967):7; David D. Hall, "Understanding the Puritans," in John M. Mulder and John W. Wilson, eds., *Religion in American History: Interpretive Essays* (Englewood Cliffs, N.J., 1978), p. 3; John Kincaid, *Political Culture, Public Policy, and the American States* (Philadelphia, 1982), pp. 9–10; Timothy H. Breen, "Persistent Localism: English Social Change and the Shaping of New England Institutions," *William and Mary Quarterly*, 3d ser. 32 (1975):3–28.

[12] Joyce Appleby, "Liberalism and the American Revolution," *New England Quarterly* 49 (1976):7.

[13] Kelley, *Cultural Pattern in American Politics*, p. 52; David P. Szatmary, *Shays's Rebellion: The Making of an Agrarian Insurrection* (Amherst, 1980), pp. 1–18.

when he wrote that "New England society was organized on a system—a clergy in alliance with a magistracy; universities supporting each, and supported in turn—a social hierarchy, in which respectability, education, property, and religion united to defeat and crush the unwise and vicious."[14] Delegates adhering to New England's *localist* political culture sought, throughout the Convention, to stabilize local democratic institutions by adding the leavening influence of a moderate elite at the national level. Since the people were uninformed, unpredictable, and, as recent events had shown, at least potentially perverse, New England's delegates would attempt to ground the national political establishment on the state legislatures rather than on the people themselves.

An equally distinctive variant on the American political culture was the southern *elitist* tradition. "Its representatives . . . were secular men, prickly about personal freedom. . . . Most were of the aristocracy. Their manners were baronial."[15] Charles S. Sydnor, Rhys Isaac, and others have made this point arguing, in Sydnor's words, that in the southern colonies, "in local affairs, the members of the gentry were the government."[16] Elazar contends that in the South, "those who do not have a definite role to play in politics are not expected to be even minimally active as citizens."[17]

Once again, the distinctive character of the southern political culture has long been well understood. In fact, Edmund Burke, in trying to interpret for his legislative colleagues the nature and source of colonial resistance to parliamentary policy, explained that "in Virginia and the Carolinas they have a vast multitude of slaves. . . . Freedom is to them . . . a kind of

[14] Henry Adams, *The United States in 1800* (Ithaca, N.Y., 1955), p. 77, reprinted from *History of the United States of America, during the First Administration of Thomas Jefferson*, 2 vols. (New York, 1889), vol. 1.

[15] Kelley, *Cultural Pattern in American Politics*, p. 84; also see W. J. Cash, *The Mind of the South* (New York, 1941), pp. 31–33; Robert E. Shalhope, "Republicanism and Early American Historiography," *William and Mary Quarterly*, 3d ser. 39 (1982):342.

[16] Charles S. Sydnor, *American Revolutionaries in the Making* (Chapel Hill, 1952), p. 85; Rhys Isaac, *The Transformation of Virginia, 1740–1790* (Chapel Hill, 1982), pp. 88–114.

[17] Elazar, *Cities of the Prairie*, pp. 264–65.

rank and privilege. . . . In such a people, the haughtiness of domination combines with the spirit of freedom . . . and renders it invincible."[18] The southern delegates, like their colleagues from New England, wanted their states to deal with the national government through state legislatures securely controlled by established elites. Southern purposes, however, were different from those of the New England delegates. Where the New England delegates sought to stabilize local democracies, the southern delegates sought to insulate local aristocracies. Throughout the Convention, southern elitists sought to minimize popular contact with the national government, just as they had limited popular control of state and county government. The national government would stand behind them when needed (slave rebellions, Indian attacks, foreign incursions), but it would not be allowed to challenge their control of local affairs.

Nearly seventy years ago Frederick Jackson Turner argued that "the Middle region . . . had a wide mixture of nationalities, . . . a varied economic life, many religious sects. In short, it was a region mediating between New England and the South, and the East and the West."[19] Historians following Turner's lead have concluded that while the middle states had no uniform social or economic character, they had, as a direct result of their diversity, a distinctive political style that anticipated the full development of American pluralism. Patricia U. Bonomi helped to reassert this line of argument in the 1970s by contending that "the principal contribution of the middle colonies was not—as with the South and New England—to our cultural heritage, but to the foundation of our political habits."[20] Milton M. Klein has also noted that "this middle region exhibited the traits which were to become

[18] Philip B. Kurland and Ralph Lerner, *The Founders' Constitution*, 5 vols. (Chicago, 1987), 1:4.

[19] Frederick Jackson Turner, "The Significance of the Frontier in American History" (1920), reprinted in George Rogers Taylor, ed., *The Turner Thesis, concerning the Role of the Frontier in American History*, 3d ed. (Lexington, Mass., 1972), p. 21.

[20] Patricia U. Bonomi, "The Middle Colonies: Embryo of the New Political Order," in Alden T. Vaughan and George Athan Billias, eds., *Perspectives on Early American History* (New York, 1973), p. 65.

characteristic of the nation as a whole: it was national in outlook, easy and tolerant in its social attitudes, composite in its
demographic makeup, individualistic and competitive in its
manners."[21]

It is not surprising that delegates from the middle states,
being generally more familiar and comfortable with the
rough and tumble of popular democratic politics, sought a
broad popular franchise as the base for a powerful and independent national government. This *national* orientation,
with its confidently democratic assumptions, would do battle
with both the localist political culture of New England and
the elitist political culture of the South throughout the Convention.

Thus, underpinning the general intellectual and political
dynamics of American political culture during the Founding
period were three regionally based subcultures, each drawing
heavily though distinctively on both liberal and republican
political images, traditions, and principles. Through quanti-
tative and textual analysis, this essay will explore the intellectual composition and the regional distribution of the ideas,
values, and attitudes that formed American political culture
at this time and will demonstrate that these provide a sound
basis for understanding important factional divisions that appeared in the work of the Federal Convention.

PRINCIPLES AND INTERESTS
AS INFLUENCES ON
CONSTITUTIONAL DESIGN

The clash of these regional political cultures echoed loudly
through the Convention, but not at all times and not on all
issues. As different types of issues and choices appeared, the
delegates reacted on different levels and on the basis of different influences and motives. Debate moved between two
levels of constitutional construction that represented significant shifts in the relative influence of general principles (the

[21] Milton M. Klein, "Shaping the American Tradition: The Microcosm
of Colonial New York," *New York History* 59 (1978):181; Douglas Green-
berg, "The Middle Colonies in Recent American Historiography," *William
and Mary Quarterly,* 3d ser. 36 (1979):400.

distinctive visions of regionally based political subcultures) and specific interests (state size or existing patterns of control over resources) on the results of the Convention's deliberations.[22]

At what I will refer to as the *higher* level of constitution making, the delegates confronted broad considerations of regime design; these questions concerned the character and form that the national government ought to take. Here the differences in regional political cultures, over such issues as what government should be about and who should be most directly involved in administering it, were critically important. The Founders had to decide whether the new government should continue as a confederation only modestly strengthened, whether it should be broken into three more internally homogeneous and manageable regional confederations, loosely affiliated at the national level, or whether a decisive move toward a truly national government should be attempted.[23] Once the path toward national government was chosen, the delegates had to decide whether that new government should be based directly on the people, with attendant risks of volatility and instability, or sheltered from direct popular influence in order to promote order and stability; whether the Congress should be unicameral or bicameral; whether its members should be selected by the state legislatures or by the people; how legislative power should be distributed across the more popular lower house and the at least potentially aristocratic upper house; and whether the executive should be composed of one man or several, serving for a fixed term or for life, and empowered to declare war and make treaties independently or not. These questions and others dealing with broad issues of regime design simply could not be determined by the specific economic status or social characteristics of the individual delegates. Rather, they

[22] See Calvin C. Jillson and Cecil Eubanks, "The Political Structure of Constitution Making: The Federal Convention of 1787," *American Journal of Political Science* 28 (1984):435–58; Calvin C. Jillson, *Constitution Making: Conflict and Consensus in the Federal Convention of 1787* (New York, 1987), for a full discussion.

[23] James H. Hutson, ed., *Supplement to Max Farrand's The Records of the Federal Convention of 1787* (New Haven, 1987), pp. 9–32.

were determined by the delegates' general assumptions about how human nature was likely to interact with alternative political structures to create a good social order.

A specific example may help to clarify this argument. No one except George Washington realistically could expect to be president in the immediate or even the foreseeable future, so for most of the delegates the question of executive organization and powers had to be resolved on the basis of which design seemed most likely to result in an executive establishment both strong enough to be efficient and constrained enough to be safe. This was not because the delegates were deliberately disregarding their personal interests in favor of broader-principled concerns while considering questions at the higher level of constitutional choice but because they simply could not see clearly what difference choices concerning such broad structural questions would make to them as individuals, to their states, or to their regions. Therefore, they had no alternative but to base their decisions on their own regionally distinctive beliefs—regarding the more diffuse and general interests of the community and the nature, role, and purpose of national political institutions.

However, as the new government's general institutional design and the relationships that would pertain among its component parts became clear, the individual delegates moved closer to the realm of practical politics and to the kinds of influences that operate there. The questions that dominated this *lower* level of constitutional design concerned the distribution of future political power and economic benefit through control over such decisions as those concerning commerce, slavery, western lands, and the allocation of seats in the legislature and in the electoral college. The key fact about each of these issues is that they had a straightforward, immediately evident, distributive character about them. Therefore, questions at this level were commonly decided with direct reference to the political, economic, and social characteristics of the individual delegates, their states, or their regions, rather than to more general political principles.

The issue of counting slaves for purposes of representation exemplifies the point and establishes the distinction being made between higher and lower levels of constitutional choice. Clearly, slavery and the trade in slaves had a principled dimension, and delegates in the Convention mentioned this occasionally, but no extended debate occurred on the morality of human slavery. Instead, discussion centered on how slavery and the continued importation of slaves would affect the distribution of power in the House and Senate. No delegate could possibly miss the fact that counting slaves for purposes of representation would enhance the power of individual plantation owners, of slaveholders as a class, of the individual states from Maryland south, and of the South as a region, and would disadvantage the opposite interests.

When the Convention concentrated on higher-level questions of regime design, coalitions formed along lines defined by the new nation's regional political subcultures. During these phases of the Convention's work, the delegates from the more nationally oriented Middle Atlantic states opposed the more locally oriented delegates representing New England and the deep South. When the focus shifted to lower-level choices concerning the distribution of authority within and over the institutions of government, the states split along lines defined by economic and geographic interest, state size, and region (large versus small or North versus South). In fact, one can be even more specific. On lower-level issues involving power within and control over institutions (seats in the legislature or electoral votes), the states split large against small. On issues touching specific policy interests (commerce, slavery, control of the West), the states split North against South.

Finally, the coalitions based on shared principles and those based on shared interests were not independent, but rather they clearly, consistently, and decisively influenced each other over the entire course of the Convention. Coalitions of principle were undercut and weakened by considerations of interest, and coalitions of interest were equally subject to being disrupted by considerations of principle. As a direct result, the Convention was forced to move slowly forward through the well-known series of compromises, bargains, and accommodations for which it is so justifiably renowned.

NATIONAL VERSUS CONFEDERAL GOVERNMENT: AN EARLY CLASH OF PRINCIPLES

The Convention's opening days of substantive debate, May 29 to June 9, saw a formidable clash of principles at the higher level of constitutional design.[24] James Madison's notes indicate that on the morning of May 29, "Mr. [Edmund] Randolph opened the main business" with a long speech analyzing the defects of the existing Confederation. He closed his remarks by offering fifteen resolutions "which he proposed to the convention for their adoption, and as leading *principles* whereon to form a new government."[25] The resolutions, known to history as the Virginia Plan, served as the Convention's agenda during its first nine weeks.

Before a debate on the Virginia Plan could begin, Alexander Hamilton sought more clearly to frame the fundamental issue confronting the Convention. Robert Yates records that "it was observed by Mr. Hamilton before adjourning that it struck him as a necessary and preliminary inquiry to the propositions from Virginia whether the united States were susceptible of one government, or required a separate existence connected only by leagues offensive and defensive and treaties of commerce."[26] Hamilton wanted the Convention immediately to confront the very basic choice of a national government versus one or more confederacies of sovereign states. A brief record provided by Madison's notes for May 30 shows how this fundamental issue was posed.

> The propositions of Mr. Randolph which had been referred to the Committee being taken up. He moved on the suggestion of Mr. G[ouverneur] Morris that the first of his propositions to wit "Resolved that the articles of Confederation ought to be so corrected & enlarged, as to accomplish the objects proposed by

[24] Merrill Jensen, *The Making of the Constitution* (New York, 1964), p. 43; David G. Smith, *The Convention and the Constitution* (New York, 1965), pp. 36–41.

[25] Max Farrand, ed., *The Records of the Federal Convention of 1787*, rev. ed., 4 vols. (New Haven, 1937), 1:24.

[26] Farrand, ed., *Records of the Convention*, 1:27.

their institution; namely, common defence, security of liberty & general welfare["] . . . should be postponed in order to consider the . . . following. . . . that a *national* Government ought to be established consisting of a *supreme* Legislative, Executive & Judiciary.[27]

The substitute motion, conceived by Hamilton and offered by Morris, abandoned the idea of marginally improving the old structure of the Articles and explicitly proposed a government "national" and "supreme." Only Connecticut opposed the motion, New York divided between Hamilton and Yates, while six delegations cast their votes in favor. With this affirmative vote behind them, the delegates moved directly, though cautiously, to the issue of representation. Madison's notes clearly display a determination to win general approval of some version of proportional representation while avoiding the explicit details that might bring on premature confrontations between North and South or between large states and small. Madison's records show:

> The following Resolution being the 2d. of those proposed by Mr. Randolph was taken up. viz—"that the rights of suffrage in the National Legislature ought to be proportioned to the quotas of contribution, or to the number of free inhabitants. . . ." Mr. Madison observing that the words *"or to the number of free inhabitants."* might occasion debates which would divert the Committee from the *general question* whether the principle of representation should be changed, moved that they might be struck out.[28]

Madison wanted to delay the ominous, though at some point unavoidable, clash between and among the several states over the distribution of seats (power) in the legislature. Therefore, he and Randolph offered a more abstractly phrased amendment to the second resolution that proposed " 'that the rights of suffrage in the national Legislature ought to be proportioned,' " to which it was moved to add, " 'and not according to the present system.' " The proposal was ap-

[27] Ibid., p. 33.

[28] Ibid., pp. 35–36.

proved by a vote of seven to zero, with Delaware refusing to vote because its instructions forbade it to relinquish the equal vote that each state enjoyed in the Confederation Congress.[29]

While many delegates were in general sympathy with the program for thoroughgoing reform being pursued by Madison, Hamilton, and Morris, many others remained wary, preferring the more cautious approach to the Convention's business being suggested by John Dickinson. Dickinson proposed that the Convention simply "resolve . . . in order to let us into the business. That the confederation is defective; and then proceed to the definition of such powers as may be thought adequate to the objects for which it was instituted."[30] Table 1 highlights the deep division engendered by these alternative approaches to the Convention's business. The nationalists (Factor 1) sought to undertake immediately the radical changes necessary to institute a truly national government, while the localists (Factor 2) favored incremental changes in the existing Confederation.

Because most delegates arrived at the Convention assuming that the national government would have to be strengthened, the nationalists held the initial advantage. They had a program for strengthening the national government that they could rally strongly behind. Localists, having no program of their own, could offer only ambivalent opposition. Hence, no state from the Middle Atlantic region participated even modestly on Factor 2, while Massachusetts and North Carolina, though loading most heavily on Factor 2, abandoned their localist colleagues with some frequency to reinforce the nationalists on Factor 1. As a result, the nationalists, as we shall see, were able to sweep all before them during the Convention's first ten days. Thereafter, effective opposition formed with startling rapidity.

The debates of May 31, concerning whether the people or the state legislatures should select the members of the House of Representatives, dramatically illuminate the conflicting assumptions upon which the nationalists from the Middle Atlantic states and the localists from New England and the South acted in the Convention. New England's confidence in

[29] Ibid., p. 36.

[30] Ibid., p. 42.

Table 1. Nationalists vs. localists: the clash of political principles. Two-factor solution to roll-call votes 1–36, May 29 to June 9 (Varimax Rotation)

	1 Nationalists	2 Localists	h^2
New Hampshire	absent	absent	absent
Massachusetts	(.60)	(.67)	.81
Connecticut	−.21	(.63)	.44
New York	(.76)	.29	.66
New Jersey	absent	absent	absent
Pennsylvania	(.82)	−.10	.68
Delaware	(.70)	.08	.49
Maryland	(.77)	−.12	.60
Virginia	(.66)	.32	.54
North Carolina	(.51)	(.68)	.73
South Carolina	−.04	(.86)	.74
Georgia	.27	(.81)	.73
Sum of squares	3.50	2.93	6.43
% variance explained	35.00	29.30	64.30

the people had been badly shaken by Shays's Rebellion, while the conservatism of the South rejected popular control of politics at any level in favor of elite management. Connecticut's Roger Sherman immediately objected to "election by the people, insisting that it ought to be by the State Legislatures." He contented that "The people . . . immediately should have as little to do as may be about the Government. They want information and are constantly liable to be misled."[31] Elbridge Gerry, from neighboring Massachusetts, supported Sherman, noting that "in Massts. it has been fully confirmed by experience [Shays's Rebellion] that they are daily misled into the most baneful measures."[32] Pierce Butler of South Carolina, the only delegate from the lower South to speak on this question, simply noted that he "thought an election by the people an impracticable mode."[33] Delegates from New England and the lower South would consistently support selection to national offices by the state legislatures as opposed to the people.

[31] Ibid., p. 48.

[32] Ibid.

[33] Ibid., p. 50.

The delegates from the Middle Atlantic states, represented on this issue by George Mason, James Wilson, and Madison, argued passionately for popular selection. "Mr. Mason argued strongly for an election of the larger branch by the people. It was to be the grand depository of the democratic principle of the Govt." Wilson "was for raising the federal pyramid to a considerable altitude, and for that reason wished to give it as broad a basis as possible."[34] Madison supported Mason and Wilson, explaining that he "considered the popular election of one branch of the national Legislature as essential to every plan of free Government. . . . He thought too that the great fabric to be raised would be more stable and durable if it should rest on the solid foundation of the people themselves, than if it should stand merely on the pillars of the Legislatures."[35] When the vote was taken popular selection was passed, six to two, with two states divided. Madison then records that "the remaining Clauses of Resolution 4th. relating to the qualifications of members of the National Legislature being postpd. nem. con. as *entering too much into detail* for general propositions."[36]

The Convention, now fully caught up in the nationalists' call for a thoroughgoing reform, moved quickly through the clauses of the sixth resolution of the Virginia Plan. The sixth resolution read:

> Resolved that each branch ought to possess the right of originating Acts; that the National Legislature ought to be empowered to enjoy the Legislative Rights vested in the Congress by the Confederation & moreover to legislate in all cases to which the separate States are incompetent, or in which the harmony of the United States may be interrupted by the exercise of individual Legislation; to negative all laws passed by the several States, contravening in the opinion of the National Legislature the articles of Union; and to call forth the force of the Union agst. any members of the Union failing to fulfill the duty under the articles thereof.[37]

[34] Ibid., p. 49.

[35] Ibid., pp. 49–50.

[36] Ibid., pp. 50–51; see also p. 60.

[37] Ibid., p. 21.

Debate over the clause empowering the Congress "to legislate in all cases to which the separate States are incompetent," again exposed southern reluctance to delegate broad
power to the national government. "Mr. [Charles] Pinckney,
& Mr. [John] Rutledge objected to the vagueness of the term
incompetent, and said they could not well decide how to vote
until they should see an exact enumeration of the powers
comprehended by this definition."[38] As yet, however, the
early momentum of the nationalists could not be checked.
Madison simply declared that "he should shrink from nothing which should be found essential to such a form of Govt.
as would provide for the safety, liberty and happiness of the
Community."[39] Though this declaration did nothing to satisfy the South Carolinians' request for a more specific description of the substantive areas in which the state
governments might be thought to be incompetent, the clause
was approved overwhelmingly. The remainder of the clause,
including the power "to negative all State laws contravening
in the opinion of the Nat[ional] Leg[islature] the articles of
Union," was, at the suggestion of Benjamin Franklin, approved without further debate.[40]

Madison's vision of a democratic republic of continental
dimensions, guided by a powerful national government that
would moderate and check the ill-formed and often precipi-
tous initiatives of the several states, was directly challenged
on June 6 by Connecticut's Roger Sherman. Sherman reasoned that extensive national powers could not be well used
because "the objects of the Union . . . were few."[41] Moreover,
great power should not be given to the national government
because most "matters civil & criminal would be much better
in the hands of the States."[42] Therefore, Sherman concluded,
"the Genl. Government [should] be a sort of collateral Government which shall secure the States in particular difficul-

[38] Ibid., p. 53.

[39] Ibid.

[40] Ibid., p. 54.

[41] Ibid., p. 133.

[42] Ibid.

ties . . . I am agt. a Genl. Govt. and in favor of the independence and confederation of the states."[43] This view of the national government as "collateral" to, or supplemental of, the state governments in times of peculiar exigency (as in Shaysite or slave rebellions, Indian uprisings, or foreign invasions) is at the core of the localist vision dominating the delegations from New England and the lower South.

The nationalists wanted a central government, not for the purpose of protecting state and local institutions and elites from outside pressures, but precisely for the purpose of exercising some outside control over these volatile and often shortsighted state and local institutions and elites. Therefore, Madison met Sherman's opposition to a "Genl. Govt." by challenging his assumption that the responsibilities of the national government would be few (defense, commerce, and disputes between the states). Madison "combined with them the necessity, of providing more effectually for the security of private rights, and the steady dispensation of Justice."[44] Most of the delegates, including Sherman, found it hard to disagree when Madison argued that interested local majorities had been "the source of those unjust laws complained of among ourselves."[45] Yet Madison's solution to the problem of majority tyranny struck many of the delegates as dangerously speculative. He argued that "the only remedy is to enlarge the sphere . . . as far as the nature of Government would admit. . . . This [is] the only defense against the inconveniences of democracy consistent with the democratic form of Government."[46]

The Virginia Plan, as it emerged from the Convention's first full week of debate, envisaged a powerful national government "consisting of a Supreme Legislative, Judiciary, and Executive." The legislature, clearly the dominant branch, would consist of two houses, the seats in each branch to be distributed in proportion to the populations or the quotas of contribution to the various states. The powers awarded to this

[43] Ibid., pp. 142–43.

[44] Ibid., p. 134.

[45] Ibid., p. 135.

[46] Ibid., p. 136.

national legislature were amazingly broad, particularly when compared to the strict limits imposed on the Congress under the Articles of Confederation. The national Congress would have exclusive power to legislate in all areas where *it* might judge the states to be "incompetent" or in which *it* conceived that uncoordinated activities might disrupt the "harmony" of the nation. Moreover, the Congress would have the authority "to negative all laws passed by the several States contravening, in the opinion of the national legislature, the articles of union; or any treaty subsisting under the authority of the Union." Both the executive and the judiciary would be appointed by the legislature. The executive would be a single person, chosen by the national legislature, for a nonrenewable term of seven years. A national judiciary, to consist of a Supreme Court, would be appointed by the Senate, with lower courts to be organized and appointed as needed by the national legislature. Finally, "the Legislative, Executive, and judiciary powers within the several States" were "to be bound by oath to support the articles of union."[47]

It took some time before the initiative and momentum captured by the nationalists early in the Convention could be reversed, and when that occurred it was not solely the work of the localists from New England and the lower South. As we shall see, the large-state nationalists overreached themselves to such a degree that they frightened their small state colleagues into assuming a defensive position that required equal voting rights for the states, large and small, in the Senate. The localists had feared for some time, if they had not precisely known, that the nationalists sought a consolidated national government. Yates recorded on June 6 that "Madison is of opinion, that when we agreed to the first resolve of having a national government, consisting of a supreme executive, judicial and legislative power, it was then intended to operate to the exclusion of a federal government."[48] As of June 6 many of the small-state nationalists had failed fully to consider the position of their states in a consolidated national government such as the one for which they had been working

[47] Ibid., pp. 225–28.

[48] Ibid., p. 141.

during the Convention's opening week. Their attention would soon be riveted on precisely this concern.

At the close of business on June 6, Charles Pinckney gave notice that he wished to reconsider the clause in the sixth resolution that gave the national Congress the power to negative "such laws of the States as might be contrary to the articles of Union, or Treaties with foreign nations." Pinckney moved on June 8 dramatically to expand the range of the national negative to include "all Laws which they [the Congress] shd. judge to be improper."[49] He defended his motion by arguing "that such a universality of power was indispensably necessary to render it effectual; that the States must be kept in due subordination to the nation."[50] Madison agreed, adding that "he could not but regard an indefinite power to negative legislative acts of the States as absolutely necessary to a perfect system."[51]

The thought of a national government in which proportional representation allowed the large states to control both houses of the Congress, and in which a negative over all state laws allowed them to control policy in the smaller states, was a shocking prospect for most of the delegates. The localists of New England and the lower South objected immediately. Hugh Williamson of North Carolina "was agst. giving a power that might restrain the States from regulating their internal police."[52] Gerry of Massachusetts could "not see the extent of such a power, and was agst. every power that was not necessary. . . . A Natl. Legislature with such a power may enslave the States."[53]

Delegates from New England and the lower South had defended local interests against nationalist assaults from the Convention's opening day, so such sentiments from these familiar sources are not surprising. More importantly, though, delegates representing the small states of the Middle Atlantic

[49] Ibid., p. 164.

[50] Ibid.

[51] Ibid.

[52] Ibid., p. 165.

[53] Ibid.

region were so alarmed by the proposal that it changed their very approach to the Convention. Gunning Bedford, representing tiny Delaware, drew his colleagues' attention to the fact that "Delaware would have about one-ninetieth for its share in the General Councils, whilst Pa. & Va. would possess one-third of the whole."[54] Bedford was convinced that this disparity of power between the large states and the small represented great danger for the small states. He asked, "Is there no difference of interests, no rivalship of commerce, of manufactures? Will not these large States crush the small ones whenever they stand in the way of their ambitions or interested views."[55] Bedford concluded with the observation that "it seems as if Pa. & Va. by the conduct of their deputies wished to provide a system in which they would have an enormous & monstrous influence."[56]

Madison, though sensing the power that differences in state size had for disrupting the coalition of large and small Middle Atlantic states, sought to hold his coalition of middle-state nationalists together with veiled threats. He "asked Mr. B[edford] what would be the consequence to the small States of a dissolution of the Union. . . . If the large States possessed the Avarice & ambition with which they were charged, would the small ones in their neighborhood, be more secure when all the controul of a Genl. Govt. was withdrawn."[57] To many delegates from the small states, whether to this point they had been committed nationalists or confirmed localists, Madison's comments seemed to offer the unpleasant choice of being dominated politically by the large states under a consolidated national government or militarily in the fractious chaos that might follow the collapse of the Articles.

The small states reacted immediately and firmly. When the vote was taken on the question of the expanded negative, only the three largest states—Massachusetts, Pennsylvania, and Virginia—voted in favor. The Delaware vote divided, while the seven remaining states (Connecticut, New York,

[54] Ibid., p. 167.

[55] Ibid.

[56] Ibid.

[57] Ibid., p. 168.

New Jersey, Maryland, the Carolinas, and Georgia) opposed, with the small states joining the localists.[58] Clearly, the attempt by Pinckney and Madison to expand the negative activated a cleavage based on state size that undercut and seriously disrupted the nationalist coalition of large and small Middle Atlantic states. Once activated, the division between the large states and the small dominated the Convention for the next three weeks.

POLITICAL POWER IN THE LEGISLATURE: LARGE STATES VERSUS SMALL

Table 2 shows how dramatically the voting alignments changed when the Convention's attention shifted from higher- to lower-level questions of constitutional choice. With a government "national and supreme" approved, but a "universal negative" over state legislation effectively rejected, the issue of what kind of government to create and where to place decisive power within it was abandoned in favor of the even more contentious issue of who would wield the power awarded to the new government. When the central question before the Convention became who would control the dominant institution—the legislature—in this new national government, the rapidly growing states of the lower South and Massachusetts, all formerly consistent opponents of great power at the national level, joined the equally consistent advocates of national power from Pennsylvania and Virginia to defend proportional representation in both the House and the Senate. These large states were opposed by five smaller states from the Middle Atlantic region, several of which formerly had been among the most consistent of the nationalist delegations, demanding equal representation in at least one branch of the proposed legislature. This alignment of large states against small on the issue of representation has been so thoroughly explored in the traditional historical literature that I will spend only enough time on it to establish both the distributive character of the dominant issues during this pe-

[58] Ibid.

Table 2.   Large states vs. small states: interests in conflict. Two-factor solution to roll-call votes 37–156, June 11 to July 16
(Varimax Rotation)

	1 Large states	2 Small states	h²
New Hampshire	absent	absent	absent
Massachusetts	(.80)	.13	.66
Connecticut	.13	(.59)	.37
New York	−.02	(.52)	.27
New Jersey	−.13	(.75)	.58
Pennsylvania	(.65)	.09	.43
Delaware	−.08	(.74)	.56
Maryland	.25	(.78)	.68
Virginia	(.73)	.08	.54
North Carolina	(.79)	.12	.64
South Carolina	(.55)	−.22	.36
Georgia	(.69)	−.10	.49
Sum of squares	3.13	2.45	5.58
% variance explained	28.45	22.25	50.70

riod and the continuing influence of principles on the interested behavior of the delegates.

The confrontation between the delegates from the large states and the small became the focus of the Convention's business on June 11 when Connecticut's Roger Sherman proposed that the House of Representatives be apportioned according to the number of a state's free inhabitants and that each state have one vote in the Senate. Delegates representing the large states continued to defend the decision of May 30 in favor of proportional representation in both houses. On May 30 the critical question of the basis of proportionality—free inhabitants, total population, wealth, or some other standard—had been postponed as too divisive. Now conflict was the order of the day and divisive details were unabashedly pushed to the fore. Madison records that "Mr. [Rufus] King and Mr. Wilson in order to bring the question to a point moved 'that the right of suffrage in the first branch of the national Legislature ought not to be according to the rule established in the articles of Confederation [equality], but according to some equitable ratio of representation,'" which after some discussion passed in the affirmative, seven to three with one state divided.[59] The large-state coalition unanimously voted "yes" and was joined by Connecticut in pursuit of Sherman's suggested compromise. New York, New Jersey, and Delaware opposed, while the Maryland delegates were divided on the issue.

Wilson then moved to fasten the allegiance of the slave states to the large-state coalition by confirming the traditional three-fifths counting of their slaves for purposes of representation. The Convention accepted this by a vote of nine to two. Only New Jersey and Delaware opposed.[60] Despite the fact that southern interests had been strengthened by the counting of three-fifths of their slaves, Sherman called for the second half of his proposed compromise, voting by states in the Senate. Equality for the small states in the Senate was denied by a vote of six to five with the six Factor 1 states standing against the five Factor 2 states of table 2. Having blocked the small states, Wilson and Hamilton pushed forward the large-state demand that "the right of suffrage in the 2d. branch ought to be according to the same rule as in the 1st. branch."[61] The large states were successful by the same six to five alignment. Thus, proportional representation in both houses, at least for a time, had been reconfirmed following a head-on clash in which the large states had defeated the small.

Nonetheless, the small-state demand for power in the new system was not the only influence at work in the Convention. Principles continued to have their influence as well. For many of the delegates, the idea of popular election to offices of the national government was still a worrisome prospect. Delegates from Massachusetts and the lower South were still plagued by deep reservations about the relative fitness of the people, when compared with the members of the state legislatures, to select men to high national office. Increasingly, their desire to balance popular election to the House with some direct role for the state legislatures in selecting members to the Senate eroded their commitment to proportional representation in both houses.

[59] Ibid., p. 196.

[60] Ibid., p. 201.

[61] Ibid., p. 202.

On June 25, when the Convention's focus shifted to selection of senators, the tension between nationalist and localist delegates within the coalition of large states became clearer. James Wilson opened debate on this issue with a very long and articulate speech based on the premise that the new nation was composed of a "great & equal body of citizens . . . among whom there are no distinctions of rank, and very few or none of fortune."[62] Wilson concluded from this that both branches of the national legislature, Senate as well as House, should be selected directly by the people.

Nathaniel Gorham of Massachusetts was not so sure. The Massachusetts delegation had supported the nationalists' call for proportional representation in both houses from the beginning. But they had been equally consistent in working to secure the localist objective of a prominent role for the state legislatures in the new system (recall Massachusetts' position of Factors 1 and 2 of table 1). North Carolina had pursued a similar agenda (again, see table 1). By now it was clear to all that the delegates most strongly in support of proportional representation in both the House and the Senate—Wilson, Hamilton, and Madison among them—also wished virtually to exclude the states from an active role in the new system. In response, several key delegates concluded that an appropriate role for the states could only be preserved by tying them firmly to the Senate. After considering Wilson's case for popular selection of both houses, Gorham declared that he was now "inclined to a compromise as to the rule of proportion. He thought there was some weight in the objections of the small States."[63] North Carolina's Williamson also "professed himself a friend to such a system as would secure the existence of the State Govts."[64] A vote was then taken on the clause, "that the members of the 2d. branch be chosen by the indivl. Legislatures."[65] Only Pennsylvania and Virginia opposed, while nine states voted to approve state legislative selection of members of the national Senate. All three states of the lower South and Massachusetts abandoned Pennsyl-

[62] Ibid., p. 403.

[63] Ibid., p. 404.

[64] Ibid., p. 407.

[65] Ibid., p. 408.

vania and Virginia to join the five states on Factor 2 of table 2. Madison appended an explanatory footnote to this vote which indicates that he understood quite clearly the nature of the opposition that Pennsylvania and Virginia faced on this issue. Madison wrote that "it must be kept in view that the largest States particularly Pennsylvania and Virginia always considered the choice of the 2d. Branch by the State Legislatures as opposed to a proportional Representation to which they were attached as a fundamental principle of just Government. The smaller States who had opposite views were reenforced by the members from the large States most anxious to secure the importance of the State Governments."[66]

Madison made at least two critical points here. First, he felt that acknowledging the legitimacy of a prominent role for the state governments in selecting members of the Senate mediated against a later decision in favor of a proportional distribution of Senate seats. Second, he pointed to the fundamental flaw in the large-state coalition as a vehicle for nationalist aspirations when he noted that some "members from the large States" were "anxious to secure the importance of the State Governments."

On June 29 Madison's position continued to erode as the Connecticut delegates again argued the merits of the compromise position that they had adhered to since first putting it forward on June 11. Presenting Connecticut's case, Oliver Ellsworth declared, "We were partly national; partly federal. The proportional representation in the first branch was conformable to the national principle & would secure the large States agst. the small. An equality of voices was conformable to the federal principle and was necessary to secure the Small States agst. the large. He trusted that on this middle ground a compromise would take place. He did not see that it could on any other."[67]

Ellsworth's motion was put to a vote on July 2. Even after weeks of intense debate, the result was, with one critical variation, the familiar six to five large-state versus small-state

[66] Ibid.

[67] Ibid., pp. 468–69.

split. The Georgia delegation split evenly, resulting in a five-five-one tie.[68] With the proceedings apparently at an impasse, Gen. Charles Cotesworth Pinckney of South Carolina "proposed that a Committee consisting of a member from each State should be appointed to devise & report some compromise."[69] Only Wilson and Madison, who understood quite clearly that "compromise" meant the loss of proportional representation at least in the Senate, opposed the formation of a compromise committee.[70] On July 5 the compromise committee, headed by Gerry of Massachusetts, reported to the Convention. The report was in two parts: "1st That in the first branch of the Legislature each of the States now in the Union be allowed one Member for every forty thousand inhabitants . . . and that no money shall be drawn from the public Treasury but in pursuance of appropriations to be originated by the first Branch. 2ndly That in the second Branch of the Legislature each State shall have an equal Vote."[71]

Following the July 5 committee report of equality in the Senate, which resolved, at least for a time, the balance between the large states and the small in the legislature, a related North-South sectional clash of interests came to the fore. For the next two weeks the jealous regions battled over the allocation of seats in the first House of Representatives.[72] Again, the distributive issue of the allocation of power within and over the legislature riveted the Convention's attention. The first committee assigned to adjust these clashing interests

[68] Ibid., p. 510.

[69] Ibid., p. 511.

[70] George Bancroft, *History of the United States*, vol. 6, *The Formation of the American Constitution* (New York, 1882), p. 245; Andrew C. McLaughlin, *The Confederation and the Constitution* (New York, 1905), p. 234; Max Farrand, *The Framing of the Constitution of the United States* (New Haven, 1913), p. 97; John P. Roche, "The Founding Fathers: A Reform Caucus in Action," *American Political Science Review* 55 (1961):809.

[71] Farrand, ed., *Records of the Convention*, 1:524.

[72] Charles Warren, *The Making of the Constitution* (1928; reprint ed., New York, 1967), pp. 293–94; Staughton Lynd, *Class Conflict, Slavery, and the United States Constitution* (New York, 1976), pp. 239, 243.

was made up of Morris, Gorham, Randolph, Rutledge, and King, with Gouverneur Morris in the chair. On July 9 the Morris committee reported back, the key section of its proposal reading: "As the present situation of the States may probably alter as well in point of *wealth* as in the number of their *inhabitants* that the Legislature be authorized from time to time to augment the number of representatives."[73] Madison recorded that the question was "taken without any debate" and passed easily.

Nonetheless, because many southerners worried that leaving reapportionment to the discretion of the legislature, with its initial northern majority, might work to the detriment of a growing South, a second committee, headed by King, was appointed. Their recommendation, delivered on July 10, sparked one of the clearest North-South confrontations in the Convention. Rutledge, following General Pinckney's second, moved "that N. Hampshire be reduced from 3 to 2. members."[74] King rose to defend the committee's work against this assault from the South by pointing out "that the four Eastern States having 800,000 souls, have ⅓ fewer representatives than the four Southern States, having not more than 700,000 souls rating the blacks, as 5 for 3. The Eastern people will advert to these circumstances, and be dissatisfied."[75] Williamson was still concerned that "the Southn. Interest must be extremely endangered by the present arrangement. The Northn. States are to have a majority in the first instance and the means of perpetuating it."[76]

On July 12 Virginia's Randolph offered a proposal built around the formula of a mandatory census to serve as the basis for requiring the reallocation of House seats with slaves being rated at three-fifths. The Pennsylvanians agreed to the proposal, if it could be attached to a suggestion made earlier by Massachusetts' King and by Gouverneur Morris, who cautioned that the measure could be made more acceptable to opinion in the North by including slaves indirectly, "saying

[73] Farrand, ed., *Records of the Convention*, 1:557–58.

[74] Ibid., p. 566.

[75] Ibid.

[76] Ibid., p. 567.

that they should enter into the rule of taxation."[77] The Massachusetts and Pennsylvania delegates were willing to see the South's representation increased only if these states were also prepared to shoulder an increased share of the tax burden that the new central government was certain to create. Randolph's motion, once suitably altered, passed easily.

On July 16 the final vote was taken "on the question for agreeing to the whole Report as amended & including the equality of votes in the 2d. branch."[78] It passed by the narrow margin of five to four, with one divided. Massachusetts and North Carolina, whose delegates had declared as early as June 25 that they shared the desire of the small-state men to secure the role of the state governments in the new system, provided the margin of victory, but not before they and the Convention as a whole were convinced that closely held regional interests had also been defended. The Massachusetts vote divided, while North Carolina joined the four smaller states of Connecticut, New Jersey, Delaware, and Maryland to carry the day against Pennsylvania, Virginia, South Carolina, and Georgia. With this vote the small states finally secured the equal suffrage in the Senate for which they had contended so long and risked so much, and the South secured a mandatory reallocation process that all assumed would give her a majority in the national councils within a few years. Therefore, both the small states and the states of the deep South had clear reasons for defending the compromise solution that had finally been achieved on representation and for opposing any attempt to reopen this divisive issue.

ACCESSIBILITY OF GOVERNMENT: NATIONALIST HOPES VERSUS LOCALIST FEARS

The nationalist and localist coalitions that had opposed one another during the Convention's opening days again became dominant immediately following the Connecticut Compro-

[77] Ibid., p. 595.

[78] Ibid., 2:15.

mise as the Convention's focus turned once again to questions at the higher level of constitutional design. These familiar coalitions, nationalists from the Middle Atlantic states opposing localists from New England and the lower South, still divided by differences concerning the nature of republican government, controlled the Convention's business for the next five weeks, well into late August.[79] The issues that they confronted concerned not only the nature and role of the executive in republican government but also the nature of and rationale for restrictions on citizenship, citizen participation, and officeholding in the new government. Questions that had long perplexed republican theorists, such as how powerful a republican executive safely could be and how homogeneous a republican citizenry must be, dominated this phase of the Convention's work.

On the one hand, the nationalists held a positive view of the ordinary citizen's ability to participate meaningfully in a properly balanced and structured government. The nationalists reasoned that one could give great authority to government if one could depend on its structure to forestall tyranny by maintaining separate centers of power. On the other hand, the localists continued to have serious doubts about the quality of citizen participation and about the likelihood that mere institutions could guarantee the consistently benign use of political power housed in a distant national government. Therefore, the localists thought history no less than common sense warned them to fight tyranny and corruption by anticipating its varied forms and by erecting constitutional barriers and prohibitions wherever experience suggested that danger might lurk.

New Hampshire and Massachusetts formed the northern wing of the localist coalition while the three states of the deep South still formed its southern wing. Connecticut, the only state unambiguously to change coalitions as a result of the compromise solution on representation, joined the coalition of large and small Middle Atlantic states backing a powerful national government. Though the nationalists would seem to have had at least a six to five advantage, their coalition was much less cohesive than was that of the localists. The reason

[79] McDonald, *Novus Ordo Seclorum*, p. 240.

Table 3.   Accessibility of government: nationalist hopes vs. localist fears. Two-factor solution to roll-call votes 157–399, July 17 to Aug. 29

(Varimax Rotation)

	1 Localists	2 Nationalists	h^2
New Hampshire	(.75)	.14	.58
Massachusetts	(.70)	.12	.51
Connecticut	.24	(.52)	.33
New York	absent	absent	absent
New Jersey	.08	(.58)	.35
Pennsylvania	.16	(.71)	.53
Delaware	.19	(.55)	.34
Maryland	− .04	(.66)	.43
Virginia	.19	(.63)	.43
North Carolina	(.71)	.21	.55
South Carolina	(.79)	.06	.63
Georgia	(.70)	.19	.52
Sum of squares	2.84	2.36	5.20
% variance explained	25.82	21.45	47.27

for this, I believe, is that the localists sought mainly to limit the power and flexibility of the national government and, as a result, they could cooperate without necessarily trusting each other. Power denied and restricted, it was thought, would protect the interests of the states by default. The nationalist coalition, on the other hand, sought broadly to empower the national government. Therefore, delegates working within the nationalist coalition had to worry not just about giving the government adequate power but about who would wield this power and for what purposes. On the latter question, with the clash between the large states and the small over representation still clearly in mind, the small-state nationalists found it very difficult to view their colleagues from the large states with anything other than profound suspicion. As a result, when the nationalist and localist coalitions resurfaced following the Connecticut compromise, the initiative swung quite decisively to the localists.

The central issue at the higher level of constitutional design to be confronted by the Convention, once the Connecticut Compromise had settled the distribution of power among the states in the legislature, was how the chief magistrate and his executive department should relate to the legislative branch.[80] Should he be subservient to the people's more direct representatives in the legislature, or should he have the power and independence to control and check a potentially volatile and erratic legislature. The stage had been set for this discussion of the role of the executive in republican government during the Convention's opening days.[81] As in early June, the localist delegations worked to create a dependent executive selected by the legislature, for the relatively long term of six years, with no possibility of a reappointment, while the nationalist delegations sought to create an independent executive chosen through a nonlegislative mechanism, either by the people or by a specially appointed electoral college, for a shorter term of four years, with the possibility that excellent service could be rewarded by a reappointment.

The broad question of the appropriate relationship between legislative and executive power in a republican government arose again on July 17 (the day immediately following the adoption of the Connecticut Compromise) when the clause "to be chosen by the National Legisl" came before the Convention. Pennsylvania's Gouverneur Morris warned that the executive "will be the mere creature of the Legisl: if appointed & impeachable by that body. He ought to be elected by the people at large, by the freeholders of the Country."[82] South Carolina's Charles Pinckney rejected Morris's argument, noting once again and in language almost identical to that which he had used to oppose popular election to the federal House, that "an Election by the people . . . [was] liable to the most obvious & striking objections. They will be led by a few active & designing men."[83] Williamson supported Pinckney by arguing that "there was the same difference be-

[80] M. J. C. Vile, *Constitutionalism and the Separation of Powers* (Oxford, 1967), pp. 132–42; Wood, *Creation of the Republic,* p. 138.

[81] Calvin C. Jillson, "The Executive in Republican Government: The Case of the American Founding," *Presidential Studies Quarterly* 9 (1979):386–402.

[82] Farrand, ed., *Records of the Convention,* 2:29.

[83] Ibid., p. 30.

tween an election in this case, by the people and by the legislature, as between an appt. by lot, and by choice."[84] The
Convention apparently agreed with Pinckney and Williamson as it defeated popular selection of the executive by a vote
of nine to one, only Pennsylvania voting in favor. Legislative
selection was then approved by a unanimous vote.

To counter the localists' achievement of selection by the
national legislature, the nationalists, again behind Morris,
successfully moved to strike out "to be ineligible a second
time," arguing quite plausibly that to do otherwise would be
to institutionalize inexperience at the helm of the national
government. Reeligibility virtually assured in the minds of
many that, in Madison's words, "the Executive could not be
independent of the Legisl[at]ure, if dependent on the pleasure of that branch for a re-appointment."[85] Further consideration would be necessary.

When these questions reappeared on July 19, Madison patiently reargued the nationalist view that, "if it be a fundamental principle of free Govt. that the Legislative, Executive
& Judiciary powers should be *separately* exercised; it is equally
so that they be *independently* exercised. . . . It is essential then
that the appointment of the Executive should either be
drawn from some source, or held by some tenure, that will
give him a free agency with regard to the Legislature."[86] The
delegates from New England and the lower South understood Madison's reasoning quite clearly; they simply rejected
it out of hand. Gerry again noted that "he was agst. a popular
election. The people are uninformed, and would be misled
by a few designing men."[87] Rutledge simply declared that he
"was opposed to all the modes except appointmt. by the Natl.
Legislature. He will be sufficiently independent, if he be not
re-eligible."[88]

These profound differences between nationalists and lo-

[84] Ibid., p. 32.

[85] Ibid., p. 34.

[86] Ibid., p. 56.

[87] Ibid., p. 57.

[88] Ibid.

calists again offered the Connecticut delegation the chance to play a mediating role. Connecticut's delegates had, virtually from the Convention's opening day, supported a stronger national government, based on the state legislatures as opposed to the people, in which the smaller states would be well positioned to defend their interests against their larger neighbors. When the Convention unanimously agreed to "reconsider generally the Constitution of the Executive," Ellsworth proposed an executive "to be chosen by electors appointed by the Legislatures of the States in the following towit—one for each State not exceeding 200,000 inhabts. two for each above yt. number & not exceeding 300,000. and, three for each State exceeding 300,000."[89] Delaware seconded the motion. This system would create the independent executive that the nationalists wanted and would give the smaller states a greater role in his selection than their populations alone would warrant.

Ellsworth's motion was immediately divided into its three parts and the questions were taken separately. First, the general question, "shall ye Natl. Executive be appointed by Electors," was addressed.[90] The six nationalist states on Factor 2 of table 3 were solidly in favor of electors, with the three localist states of the deep South opposed and Massachusetts divided (New Hampshire's delegates did not arrive until July 23). Selection of electors by state legislatures was then approved easily, but "the part relating to the ratio in which the States sd. chuse electors was postponed nem. con."[91] Again, just as in the earlier case of legislative representation, once the general principle governing executive selection was determined (by electors to promote independence), the resolve of each state to be well positioned in the new system quickly broke apart the nationalist coalition.[92] This problem in lower-level constitutional design, the allocation of presidential electors among the states, was directly confronted on July 20.

[89] Ibid.

[90] Ibid., p. 58.

[91] Ibid.

[92] Charles C. Thach, *The Creation of the Presidency* (1923; reprint ed., Baltimore, 1969), p. 102.

Madison, always the advocate and defender of proportional representation, worried "that this would make in time all or nearly all the States equal."[93] With this demand for proportional representation still dominating the large-state delegations, the decision confronting the smaller members of the nationalist coalition was quite simple. Their equality in the Senate gave them more leverage in a system of legislative selection than they would have under the system of electors envisaged by the larger members of their coalition. Therefore, when the larger members of the nationalist coalition (Pennsylvania and Virginia) sought to bend the small members' (Connecticut, New Jersey, Delaware, and Maryland) proposed allocation scheme to their own advantage, the small states responded by abandoning electoral selection altogether.[94]

As a result, the more cohesive localist coalition was able to reimpose preference for legislative selection, a long term, and ineligibility. With Massachusetts off the floor, the localists mustered the votes of New Hampshire, Connecticut, and New Jersey in the North, and North Carolina, South Carolina, and Georgia in the South, against the contiguous middle states of Pennsylvania, Delaware, and Maryland, with Virginia divided.[95] The broad design for a national government now clearly in view, the Convention adjourned for ten days to give the Committee of Detail "time to prepare and report the Constitution."

The fundamental choices facing the Convention when it reconvened on August 6 concerned the relationships that would pertain between the national government, citizens of the existing states, potential officeholders, new immigrant citizens, and the new territories then rising in the West. The debates on residency requirements for election to the House and Senate provide clear insight into the very different understandings being pursued by nationalists and localists of the dangers inherent in men wielding political power in the process of governance. Gouverneur Morris abandoned his

[93] Farrand, ed., *Records of the Convention*, 2:63.

[94] Ibid., pp. 64, 101, 121.

[95] Ibid., p. 121.

nationalist colleagues to propose a fourteen-year residency requirement for senators, "urging the danger of admitting strangers into our public Councils." Not surprisingly, Charles Pinckney agreed that "as the Senate is to have the power of . . . managing our foreign affairs, there is peculiar danger and impropriety in opening its door to those who have foreign attachments."[96] Butler of South Carolina supported Pinckney, observing that foreigners bring with them "ideas of Govt. so distinct from ours that in every point of view they are dangerous," thereby wholly justifying the requirement for "a long residence in the Country."[97]

Many nationalists thought this tremulous concern for the character and impact of new immigrants to be unnecessary, illiberal, and unbecoming to the nation. Madison indicated that although he was "not averse to some restrictions," certainly the fourteen-year prohibition suggested by Morris, to say nothing of the reasons for such restrictions offered by Pinckney and Butler, were wrong. Madison argued that the same object could be accomplished by ordinary legislative acts controlling naturalization and citizenship. But even more, Madison worried that this approach would "give the tincture of illiberality to the Constitution." Franklin also noted the "illiberality" of the proposal as well as the probable adverse impact on European opinion of ideas approaching the xenophobic imbedded in the very text of the Constitution. James Wilson, a Scotsman by birth but an American since before the Revolution, noted the impact that such a provision would have on him personally and then joined Madison and Franklin in remarking upon "the illiberal complexion which the motion would give to the system."[98]

Morris's motion for a fourteen-year residency requirement, as well as one for thirteen and another for ten years, were all defeated four to seven. On each vote, the localist states of New Hampshire, South Carolina, and Georgia, joined by New Jersey, were defeated by an otherwise solid bloc of Middle Atlantic states. Finally, nine years was pro-

[96] Ibid., p. 235.

[97] Ibid., p. 236.

[98] Ibid., pp. 235–37.

posed and approved, after Rutledge argued that a seven-year requirement existed for the House, and since the Senate was to be more powerful, a longer requirement was justified. Though defeated on residency requirements for the Senate, several of the delegates from the middle states were eager to try to liberalize and moderate related requirements.

When Wilson led a move to reduce the residency require-ment for service in the House from seven years to four, Gerry responded that he "wished that in future the eligibility might be confined to Natives." What is more, Gerry hastened to assure his colleagues that "he was not singular in these ideas. A great many of the most influential men in Massts. reasoned in the same manner."[99] Williamson spoke next to reassure Gerry that the southern localists also understood the dangers that foreign ideas and the men who carried them might rep-resent to the settled habits of New England and the South.

Hamilton and Wilson, from the more polyglot cultures of New York and Philadelphia, spoke to highlight the benefits and minimize the dangers of future immigration. Hamilton noted that he "was in general agst. embarrassing the Govt. with minute restrictions," and that "the advantage of encour-aging foreigners was obvious." Wilson "cited Pennsylva. as a proof of the advantage of encouraging emigrations," point-ing to the public service that state had enjoyed from its recent immigrants as well as "the population & prosperity" to which they had added.[100]

Gouverneur Morris attempted to respond to his colleagues most immediate concerns by proposing "that the limitation of seven years should not affect the rights of any person now a Citizen."[101] A familiar chorus of voices from the localist delegations sounded to the effect that even this presumption in favor of immigrants who had attained citizenship under current states laws would constitute a danger. South Caro-lina's Rutledge observed that "the policy of the precaution was as great with regard to foreigners now Citizens; as to those who are to be naturalized in future." Connecticut's

[99] Ibid., p. 268.

[100] Ibid., pp. 268–69.

[101] Ibid., 2:270.

Sherman offered the very remarkable observation that "the U. States have not invited foreigners nor pledged their faith that they should enjoy equal privileges with native Citizens."[102] Madison, Morris, and Wilson protested, but when the votes were recorded, a familiar pattern was evident. The localist coalition collected the votes of New Hampshire and Massachusetts in the North, the Carolinas and Georgia in the South, while a defector from the less cohesive nationalist coalition, in this case Delaware, delivered the victory to them. Once again, a united localist coalition had successfully exploited the divisions within the more diffuse nationalist coalition to transform its fears into constitutional prohibitions.

SLAVERY, COMMERCE, THE EXECUTIVE, AND THE WEST: STATE AND REGIONAL INTEREST

As the Convention entered its final three weeks, several important issues at the lower level of constitutional choice, including some provision for the critical economic issues surrounding slavery, commerce, and control of the western lands, as well as the contest for control of the executive selection process, stood unresolved. Initially, it seemed that the dominant localist coalition would resolve each of these issues in its own favor against the increasingly desultory opposition of the nationalists. As the nationalist coalition tottered toward collapse, the more cohesive localists appeared to gather new strength as its northern and southern wings quickly and smoothly reached an initial accommodation on the divisive regional issues of the slave trade and commercial regulation. In the end, neither the localists nor the nationalists would survive the shift in the Convention's attention from issues at the higher level of constitutional design to those at the lower level.

The apparent strength of the localist coalition as it turned to deal with the critical issues of commerce and the trade in slaves quickly proved to be illusory. When debate on the slave trade opened on the morning of August 22, Gen. Charles

---

[102] Ibid.

Cotesworth Pinckney went directly to the distributive interests that specific members of the localist coalition had in these matters. He cited the regional economics of the conflict between the states of the upper South (Maryland and Virginia of the nationalist coalition) and the states of the lower South (the Carolinas and Georgia of the localist coalition) on the continued trade in slaves. General Pinckney said, "S. Carolina & Georgia cannot do without slaves. As to Virginia she will gain by stopping the importations. Her slaves will rise in Value, & she has more than she wants." For the shipping interests so dear to the New England wing of the localist coalition Pinckney held out the prospect that "the more slaves, the more produce to employ the carrying trade; The more consumption also, and the more of this, the more of revenue for the common treasury."[103] Rufus King of Massachusetts responded to the distributive economic logic offered by Pinckney with some of his own. King simply "remarked on the exemption of slaves from duty whilst every other import was subjected to it, as an inequality that could not fail to strike the commercial sagacity of the Northn. & middle States."[104] General Pinckney agreed with his northern colleague that a moderate tax would not be improper. Therefore, Pinckney, thinking the matters of commerce and the trade in slaves essentially resolved between New England and the lower South "moved to commit the clause that slaves might be made liable to an equal tax with other imports."[105] Gouverneur Morris, noting Pinckney's willingness to compromise on this aspect of the matter, acted to broaden the ground for compromise to include the entire area of slavery, commerce, and export taxes, saying "these things may form a bargain among the Northern & Southern States."[106]

The commitment of these three questions to a compromise committee as a package left little doubt as to the expected outcome. When the committee report was produced on Au-

[103] Ibid., p. 371.

[104] Ibid., p. 373.

[105] Ibid.

[106] Ibid., p. 374.

gust 24, the localist coalition appeared to have carried the day easily with regard both to the lower South's interest in the continued importation of slaves (allowed until 1800 subject only to a modest import tax) and the northern interest in commercial regulation (no special congressional majorities to be required).

Further, when General Pinckney moved on August 25 "to strike out the words 'the year eighteen hundred' as the year limiting the importation of slaves and to insert the words 'the year eighteen hundred and eight,'" the northern members of the localist coalition were more than willing to allow this additional eight-year increment to their southern colleagues.[107] The vote on the clause as amended to read 1808 passed when three states from the Northeast—New Hampshire, Massachusetts, and Connecticut—joined Maryland and the three states of the deep South against the central states of New Jersey, Pennsylvania, Delaware, and Virginia.

The provisions of the compromise report dealing with the northern interest in controlling commercial policy proved to be much less tractable. When the commerce section was finally debated on August 29, Charles Pinckney immediately moved to strike out the section of the report allowing simple majority decision on commercial questions in favor of a special majority of at least two-thirds. Fearing that the whole compromise might come unhinged, the older Pinckney chastised his young cousin for mistrusting their northern colleagues. Though General Pinckney argued that the "liberal conduct towards the views of the South Carolina [allowing the trade in slaves to continue until 1808]" demonstrated by the northern states had convinced him that "no fetters should be imposed on the power of making commercial regulations," feelings in most of the southern delegations ran strongly to the view of the younger Pinckney that commercial regulation by simple majority was an open invitation to southern oppression.[108] Edmund Randolph, the very man who had introduced the Virginia Plan in the first week of the Convention, now declared "that there were features so odious in the

[107] Ibid., p. 415.

[108] Ibid., pp. 449–50.

Constitution . . . that he doubted whether he should be able to agree to it. A rejection of the motion [Pinckney's for two-thirds majorities] would compleat the deformity of the system." [109] Despite this warning, Pinckney's motion was defeated four votes to seven. A solid bloc of northern states from New Hampshire to Delaware, joined only by South Carolina, defeated the remaining four southern states of Maryland, Virginia, North Carolina, and Georgia. The payoff to General Pinckney and the slaveholders of South Carolina was immediately forthcoming when the Convention passed the following resolution without debate: " 'If any person bound to service or labor in any of the U-States shall escape into another State, he or she shall not be discharged from such service or labor, . . . but shall be delivered up to the person justly claiming their service or labor.' " [110]

Many in the South were convinced that the northern majority would oppress southern commerce if this opportunity were open to them. South Carolina's decision to trade away a southern ability to block potentially dangerous commercial legislation for marginally more favorable terms in regard to slavery broke the lower South as a solid voting bloc. With the southern wing of the localist coalition shattered, one might have expected the nationalists to reassert their control of the Convention. But when this opportunity arose, they were in no position to take advantage of it. The battle over legislative representation that had pitted large states against small during June and July had created such mistrust that the nationalist coalition never regained the cohesion that it had enjoyed during the Convention's opening days. In the face of regular defections by the small Middle Atlantic states to the localist coalition (on issues such as executive selection and residency requirements for service in the Congress), Pennsylvania and Virginia sought in late August to minimize their vulnerability by abandoning the small states on the still undecided question of executive selection.

The question that arose on the morning of August 24 was whether legislative selection of the executive would be con-

[109] Ibid., p. 452.

[110] Ibid., pp. 453–54.

ducted by separate ballots in the House and Senate or, as suggested by Rutledge in the hope of driving a wedge between Pennsylvania and Virginia and their small-state allies, by "joint ballot" of both houses voting together. Sherman immediately "objected to it as depriving the *States* represented in the *Senate* of the negative intended them in that house," while Wilson "urged the reasonableness of giving the larger States a larger share of the appointment."[111] Just as Rutledge had hoped that they would, Pennsylvania and Virginia jumped at the chance to support legislative selection, after opposing it for months, because it had now been shaped to maximize their influence at the expense of their small-state allies. The small states were depending heavily upon a separate ballot in the Senate to give them some meaningful control over the executive branch. Control of the executive selection process, together with their equal vote in the Senate, would supply the institutional means to defend themselves against the large states. The dangers represented by the Pennsylvania and Virginia votes in favor of a "joint ballot" selection were not lost on the small states. Once again the Convention was dealing with distributive issues at the lower level of constitutional choice, in this case the distribution among the states of control over the process of executive selection, and, once again, it was the large states against the small.

Considerations of state size returned to the fore immediately following conclusion of the very divisive debate over commercial regulation when debate moved to the provision in the Committee of Detail report that dealt with conditions for the admission of new states into the union. Debate centered around Gouverneur Morris's motion that "New States may be admitted by the Legislature into this Union: but no State shall be erected within the limits of any of the present States, without the consent of the Legislature of such State, as well as the Genl. Legislature."[112] Pennsylvania and Virginia claimed vast stretches of territory in the West while the small Middle Atlantic states held claim to almost none.

[111] Ibid., pp. 401–2.

[112] Ibid., p. 455.

National control of the western lands had been a demand of the small Middle Atlantic states since the Revolution. New Jersey, Delaware, and Maryland had been the last three states to ratify the Articles of Confederation, chiefly because the larger states were reluctant to relinquish their claims to exclusive control of the unsettled West. Now, in the view of the small central states, the large states were again trying to monopolize the benefits to be derived from this tremendous resource. Maryland's Daniel Carroll moved a commitment of this issue to a committee of a member from each state, assuring the House that this was "a point of a most serious nature," which if it "be disregarded, he believed that all risks would be run by a considerable minority, sooner than give their concurrance."[113] Carroll's colleagues were unimpressed by his warning. When the vote was taken, New Jersey, Delaware, and Maryland stood against the remaining eight states. Morris's substitute motion requiring the affected state to consent to any division of its territory was then approved by the same eight to three margin.

These decisions on executive selection and control of the western lands made it unmistakably clear to the delegates from the smaller states that those from the large states were again attempting to assert a dangerously exclusive control over the institutions and the resources of the new government. If the large states effectively dominated the executive selection process and the vast resources represented by the West, their influence in the new system would be decisive, while that of the smaller states would be negligible. The behavior of Virginia and Pennsylvania, on the issues of executive selection and control of the western lands, split the coalition of middle state nationalists as certainly as the behavior of South Carolina, on the issues of commerce and the slave trade, split the coalition of New England and southern localists. With both of the coalitions that had dominated the Convention's business since the mid-July compromise on representation now in disarray, the delegates on August 31 appointed a committee, chaired by New Jersey's David Brearley, to which "it was agreed to refer such parts of the Constitution

[113] Ibid., p. 462.

as have been postponed, and such parts of Reports as have not been acted on."[114]

BREARLEY COMMITTEE REPORT AND THE NEW NORTHERN MAJORITY

The Brearley committee delivered its major proposals on September 4 and 5. Attention was immediately drawn to provisions at the lower level of constitutional design dealing with control over the executive selection process, and with what many perceived to be a redistribution of power within the new government to the Senate as the stronghold of the small states. The committee report envisaged a return to electoral selection, but, perhaps more importantly, it proposed that the failure of any one candidate to achieve a majority of the electoral votes would result in the reference of the five leading candidates to the Senate (where the small states had an equal vote with the large states) for final selection. The committee was working with an idea that would dominate the remainder of the debate on the executive branch: the distribution among the states of control over the two phases of executive selection—nomination and final election. The small-state men on the Brearley committee believed that electoral votes would be scattered and would rarely result in majority support for anyone. But even if no one was expected to attract a majority, candidates from the large states could be expected to get more votes, giving those states an advantage on the nomination round of the process. This indicated the need for a second round, in the interest of majority election, and on this final election round the advantage of the large states needed to be balanced. How better to achieve this than to entrust final selection to the Senate where all states exercised an equal vote?

Further, the Brearley committee determined that treaties, as well as ambassadorial, Supreme Court, and other major administrative appointments, were to be made by the president "with the advice and consent of the Senate."[115] And fi-

[114] Ibid., p. 481.

[115] Ibid., pp. 498–99.

nally, although the House would charge the president in impeachable offenses, the final disposition of these charges would occur in the Senate. These provisions provoked consternation in many delegates because they seemed to give the smaller states what many of the delegates thought would be direct control over the appointment, conduct in office, and removal of the president. Yet, as the Convention entered its final days, neither the large states nor the southern states were in a position effectively to oppose the committee's report and the determined phalanx of small Middle Atlantic and northeastern states that stood behind it.

Not since the small states had resolutely demanded an equal vote in at least one house of the proposed Congress were they more adamant than they were on the question of control over the process of executive selection. On this and related issues, the small states of the Middle Atlantic region were consistently opposed by Pennsylvania and Virginia while the lower South was ambivalent. The remarkable extent to which the South as a regional bloc of votes was broken as a force in the Convention, not only on the matter of the executive, but more generally on all issues during the final two weeks, is highlighted by tables 4 and 5. Only Virginia, of the five states south of Delaware, maintained a consistent opposition to the small states of the new northern majority. In fact, Maryland and Georgia frequently joined the small states to the north in systematically enhancing the role and influence of the Senate.

Nonetheless, some opposition to the Brearley committee report did demand consideration. Charles Pinckney opposed the process for executive selection because "as the President's reappointment will thus depend on the Senate he will be the mere creature of that body."[116] Such a decisive Senate influence over the process of executive selection posed starkly the danger of an aristocracy, a possibility that many were coming to apprehend as more ominous than the potential for monarchy that lurked in the presidency. The problem for those in opposition was obviously one of convincing the northern majority, with its decisive voting advantage and its patent

[116] Ibid., p. 511.

Table 4. A new northern majority: the role of the small states. Two-factor solution for roll-call votes 441–569, Sept. 4–17 (Varimax Rotation)

	1 Northern majority	2 Large-state opposition	h²
New Hampshire	(.75)	.45	.76
Massachusetts	(.65)	.34	.54
Connecticut	(.79)	.14	.64
New York	absent	absent	absent
New Jersey	(.82)	.06	.67
Pennsylvania	.22	(.68)	.51
Delaware	(.75)	.07	.56
Maryland	.49	.47	.46
Virginia	−.00	(.85)	.72
North Carolina	.08	.46	.22
South Carolina	.42	.49	.42
Georgia	.49	.51	.50
Sum of squares	3.55	2.45	6.00
% total variance	32.27	22.27	54.54

Table 5. A new northern majority: the role of the small states. Three-factor solution for roll-call votes 441–569, Sept. 4–17 (Varimax Rotation)

	1 Northern majority	2 Large-state minority	3 Southern minority	h²
New Hampshire	(.72)	.44	.25	.77
Massachusetts	(.62)	(.55)	−.18	.73
Connecticut	(.78)	.22	.03	.63
New York	absent	absent	absent	absent
New Jersey	(.81)	.04	.18	.69
Pennsylvania	.16	(.80)	.03	.66
Delaware	(.74)	.04	.18	.59
Maryland	.45	.23	(.59)	.61
Virginia	−.07	(.76)	.38	.73
North Carolina	.04	.05	(.81)	.65
South Carolina	.38	(.55)	.11	.45
Georgia	.45	.37	.45	.53
Sum of squares	3.29	2.26	1.51	7.06
% total variance	29.90	20.50	13.90	64.30

stake in maintaining Senate authority, that there was real danger in failing to avoid an undue concentration of power in the Senate. Even in the face of an increasingly general reaction against an overly powerful Senate as an invitation to aristocracy, it was not possible to reach an agreement until a solution was found that preserved small-state control without involving the Senate.

Nonetheless, all major groups were relieved of their principal concerns when Williamson suggested that instead of the Senate, "this choice should be made by the Legislature, voting by *states* and not *per capita*." To simplify matters, the Senate was dropped, leaving the House of Representatives voting by states, which passed over the opposition of only Delaware.[117] With this final decision, the selection process for the executive was completed. The new northern majority had gained what it most wanted, final control of the executive selection process, while the opposition had been allowed to avoid what it most feared, supplementing the power of a potentially aristocratic Senate.

On September 6 James Wilson indicated that "he thought the new mode of appointing the President, with some amendments, a valuable improvement; but he could never agree to purchase it at the price of the ensuing parts of the Report."[118] The remaining battles of the Convention were fought over precisely these "ensuing parts of the Report." Opposition centered around attempts to remove powers from the Senate where possible, while the northern majority sought to defend and maintain the advantages that they had written into the Brearley committee's report. In a very real sense the tables had been completely turned on the original proponents of the Virginia Plan. Initially the small states had feared the House of Representatives as the "vortex" into which all power would inevitably slip. But events had taken such a turn that the large states, particularly Pennsylvania, Virginia, and the Carolinas, now feared that the Senate as constituted in the report before the Convention would soon incorporate all of the authority and functions of the new

[117] Ibid., p. 527.

[118] Ibid., p. 523.

government. Their goal was to weaken the Senate in favor of institutions, most obviously the House, in which they were more favorably situated.

The decisions taken on these "ensuing parts of the Report" are important because they show the northern majority to be active not just on the highly visible executive issue but on a whole series of secondary concerns as well. Each incremental contribution to senatorial authority increased the sense on the part of the smaller states that they were well placed to defend themselves in the new system. They would not only have an equal vote in the Senate as a result of the Connecticut Compromise, but that vote would now be exercised across a broad range of issues of content and consequence: appointment of the president in the event that the electoral process was not definitive; advice and consent responsibility on the appointment of all major officials, ambassadors, and judges; trial of all impeachments; and the amendment of money bills. In defense of these powers, the small northern states successfully resisted demands for change on the part of both the large state and southern minorities.

SUMMARY AND CONCLUSION

In sum, the Federal Convention of 1787, from its opening day to its final adjournment, confronted two distinct but intimately related aspects of constitutional design. The first was general: what kind of democratic republic should be constructed? As the delegates considered and discussed alternative visions of the relationship between human nature, the institutions of government, and the quality of the resulting social order, profound differences among them quickly became evident. I have sought to explain the tension at this higher level of constitutional choice as a function of stable patterns of conflict and cooperation among three related but distinct political subcultures within the new nation. The second was more specific: how would power over and benefit from the new government be distributed? When distributive questions came to the fore, such as those touching upon the allocation of representatives and presidential electors, the status of slavery, commerce, and western lands, questions directly affecting the political and economic interests of states and regions, divisions fell along the lines of state size and region. Indeed, it was only at this lower level of constitutional construction, where interests clashed so loudly and winners and losers were starkly clear, that the Convention was threatened with dissolution.

James Madison and the middle state nationalists clearly held the intellectual advantage when the Convention opened in late May 1787. Almost all the delegates arrived in Philadelphia with the understanding that political power at the national level had to be enhanced. As a result, by June 6, the nationalists had won approval of a government "national and supreme," with proportional representation in both houses of a legislature, empowered to "negative" state legislation that contravened the new Constitution. This powerful national government had the strong support of a majority of the delegates representing the states of the Middle Atlantic region, while many delegates representing the states of New England and the lower South found both its power and its independence from the more familiar state governments disconcerting.

The nationalists' desire to restrain the volatile state legislatures led them to attempt dramatically to expand the range of the national negative on state legislation. The localist delegates from New England and the lower South opposed this move on principle as another dangerous imposition on the states, while the delegates representing the large and small states of the nationalist coalition split on the basis of state size. The delegates representing the smaller nationalist states, following Bedford's impassioned denunciation of the expanded negative, focused firmly on the fact that this great national power would be wielded over the states, their states included, almost exclusively by others. These delegates, for a time, set aside their principled commitment to a powerful national government in order to secure the political power and influence of their states in the new system.

When the fundamental issue facing the Convention turned from principle (national vs. confederal government) to power (proportional vs. equal representation of the states in the House and Senate), the coalitions dominating the Convention's business quickly changed from nationalists vs. localists to large states vs. small states. By July 5, after three weeks of intense debate, the small states won equal voting rights in the Senate when key delegates from several of the large states with localist leanings (Massachusetts, the Carolinas, and Georgia) decided to forego the political power that proportional representation in both the House and the Senate promised them in favor of their principled concern to secure the role of the states in the new system by granting each of them an equal vote in the Senate. In this instance, principles undercut interests. Attention immediately turned to the initial distribution of seats in the House between the states of the North and the South. Between July 5 and 16, a series of compromise committees hammered out an agreement that included a mandatory census every ten years, followed by a mandatory reallocation of House seats. This convinced the southern delegates that rapid population growth in their region would soon lead to majority control of the House.

With the scope of and control over legislative power thus resolved, the Convention's focus turned on July 17 to the other great center of power in the new government, the executive. As the scope and character of executive power came under review, the dominant coalition pattern active in the Convention once again quickly became the localist periphery against the nationalist center. The balance of power between these coalitions was, however, much different from what it had been during the Convention's opening days when the nationalists held the initiative. From mid-July to late August a very solid localist coalition dominated a nationalist coalition weakened by the obvious possibility that its large and small members might again be turned against each other.

The localist delegates envisaged a weak executive selected by the legislature and subservient to it. The nationalist delegates envisaged an executive selected by independent electors and powerful enough to act as a check on the legislature. When the nationalist coalition succeeded on July 19 in narrowly winning electoral selection, the delegates, recalling the recent battles over legislative apportionment, immediately turned to the question of how these electors would be distributed among the states. The fundamental flaw in the nationalist coalition, the opposition of interests based on state size, quickly reemerged. When Pennsylvania and Virginia refused to budge from their demand for a distribution of electors based on population, the small Middle Atlantic states abandoned them to join the localists supporting legislative selection of the executive. Once again, as during the Convention's opening days, principled positions adopted by the nationalists had been lost when considerations of power came to the fore and divided large states from small.

Following a ten-day adjournment in favor of the Committee of Detail, the nationalists and the localists faced off again over a series of issues that included the nature of citizenship, possible restrictions on officeholding, the appropriate legislative origin of money bills, and the potential for corruption inherent in the movement of legislators into positions in the executive branch. To control the behavior of both citizens and government officials, the nationalists wanted to depend upon well-constructed institutions, while the localists sought the assurance of tightly crafted constitutional restrictions and prohibitions. With debilitating consistency the nationalist coalition was weakened on these and similar issues by the defection of one or more of its smaller members to the localist coalition.

The nationalist coalition, vulnerable but still competitive from mid-July to late August, was finally broken on August 24 and 25 when Pennsylvania and Virginia, frustrated throughout August by their inability consistently to control their small-state colleagues, sought to strengthen their political position in the new government by abandoning the small states on the critical issues of executive selection and control of the western lands. The small Middle Atlantic states became quite firmly convinced that the large states were still dedicated to the goal of carving out an undue and dangerous influence for themselves in the new system.

The localist coalition also proved in late August to be critically vulnerable to the rise of state and regional interests. The solid southern wing of the localist coalition, made up of the Carolinas and Georgia from the Convention's opening day, was destroyed by South Carolina's willingness to trade what her neighbors thought was unacceptably dangerous northern control over national commercial policy for the right to continue importing slaves until 1808 and for the added protection of a fugitive slave provision in the new Constitution. South Carolina's action, in the face of stern warnings from the other southern delegations, broke the South as an effective force in the Convention.

The Convention entered September with both the nationalist and the localist coalitions in disarray, but with several critical issues still unresolved. A committee headed by New Jersey's David Brearley, charged with resolving these issues, reported on September 1 and 4. The coalition that came together in the Brearley committee and that emerged to dominate the Convention's final ten days was northern and small state in character, excluding only the Carolinas (as southern states), and Pennsylvania and Virginia (as large states). The Senate was seen by all of the delegates as a small-state stronghold that might also soon become the last bastion of northern strength if the population of the South grew as rapidly as most expected. Therefore, the Brearley committee report saw the dominant northern majority, led by its small-state members, move strongly to secure what they and others thought would be substantial influence over the process of presidential selection and over such presidential responsibilities as nominations to high national office and the conduct of foreign policy.

No one doubts that what I have called principles and interests both exercise an independent influence on political behavior or that the products of that behavior will bear the distinctive marks of both influences. James Madison, with some fifty years of perspective on the Convention, made precisely this point in relation to the Federal Convention in a letter of February 12, 1831, to Theodore Sedgwick. Madison was convinced that "the two subjects, the structure of Govt and the question of power entrusted to it were more or less inseparable in the minds of all, as depending a good deal, the one on the other." Nonetheless, Madison thought that some partial discrimination of influences was possible because he noted that when the "question of power" was not directly involved, "the abstract leaning of opinions would better ap-

354

pear."[119] Modern analysts of the Convention still retain Madison's conviction that the interplay of principles and interests was critical to the debates and decisions of that body. Yet despite the presence of this widespread recognition, now nearly two centuries old, it is clear that we have no general understanding of the distinct roles played by principles and interests in molding political behavior. Nor do we understand the interaction between them as principles influence the view that men take of their interests and interests influence the principles that men hold and act upon.

Guiding principles, such as nationalism vs. localism, a pure separation of powers vs. an intricate system of checks and balances, define the structure and character of government only in general terms. Other considerations, primarily deriving from diverse political, economic, and geographic interests, suggest and often virtually determine the modifications, adjustments, and allowances that principled consistency must make to political expediency. Not surprisingly, philosophical consistency will be particularly at risk where "practical politicians in a democratic society . . . [must] take home an acceptable package and defend it—and their own political futures—against predictable attack" on the grounds that local interests have been ignored or sacrificed with dangerous consequences.[120] The problem that I have sought to confront in this essay is how the interaction of principles and interests operated in the specific case of the Federal Convention.

METHODOLOGICAL APPENDIX

For a complete treatment of factor analysis, see either Rudolph J. Rummel or Harry H. Harman.[121] In this study, I employ factor analysis principally in its role as a "confirmatory" or "hypothesis-testing" device. As Harman explains, "Confirmatory factor analysis may be used to check or test

[119] Ibid., 3:496.

[120] Roche, "Founding Fathers," p. 805.

[121] Rudolph J. Rummel, *Applied Factor Analysis* (Evanston, Ill., 1970); Harry H. Harman, *Modern Factor Analysis,* 3d ed. (Chicago, 1976).

. . . a given hypothesis about the structure of the data."[122] The introduction to this essay offers a hypothesis designed to explain the complex interactions that characterized the Federal Convention's business. Factor analysis will aid in showing whether the expected relationships comport with the empirical "structure of the data."

This study employs a principal component Q-factor analysis throughout.[123] I group states (variables in the matrix columns) on the basis of their responses to the 569 roll-call votes (cases in the matrix rows) taken during the Convention. The twelve states that sent delegations to the Convention comprise the variables in this study. They are New Hampshire, Massachusetts, Connecticut, New York, New Jersey, Pennsylvania, Delaware, Maryland, Virginia, North Carolina, South Carolina, and Georgia. The cases are the 569 roll-call votes taken during the Convention as recorded in Max Farrand's *Records of the Federal Convention of 1787*. Votes were coded for analysis as follows: 1—yes, 2—no, 3—absent, 4—divided. Each factor analysis in this study begins from a correlation matrix.[124] Since voting in the Convention was by state delegation, rather than by individual delegate, deletion of absences and divided votes allows each cell of each correlation matrix to define the degree of association between two states in yes-and-no voting.

[122] Harman, *Modern Factor Analysis*, p. 6.

[123] Rummel, *Applied Factor Analysis*, pp. 112–13.

[124] Norman Nie, *Statistical Program for the Social Sciences* (New York, 1970).

Contributors
Index

Contributors

JOHN P. DIGGINS is a Distinguished Professor of History at the Graduate School, CUNY. His recent books include *The Lost Soul of American Politics: Virtue, Self-Interest, and the Foundations of Liberalism* (1984), *The Proud Decades: America in War and in Peace, 1941–1960* (1988), and *The Rise and Fall of the American Left* (1991). He is currently working on "The Promise of Pragmatism."

EDWARD J. ERLER is professor of political science and chair of the department at California State University, San Bernadino. He is widely published in his principal fields of inquiry, political philosophy and constitutional law, having most recently authored *The American Polity: Essays on the Theory and Practice of Constitutional Government* (1991).

CALVIN C. JILLSON is the chair of the Department of Political Science at the University of Colorado, Boulder. He is the author of *Constitution-Making: Conflict and Consensus in the Federal Convention of 1787* (1988) and a series of articles on the Constitutional Convention and on the Congress under the Articles of Confederation. Professor Jillson and Professor Rick Wilson of Rice University are currently working on a book entitled *Congressional Dynamics: Structure, Coordination, and Choice in the First American Congress, 1774–1789*.

ISAAC KRAMNICK is the Richard J. Schwartz Professor of Government at Cornell University. He is the author of *Bolingbroke and His Circle: The Politics of Nostalgia in the Age of Walpole* (1968), *The Rage of Edmund Burke: Portrait of an Ambivalent Conservative* (1977), and most recently of *Republicanism and Bourgeois Radicalism: Political Ideology in Late Eighteenth-Century England and America* (1990). His current research takes him out of the eighteenth century. He is working on a biography of Harold Laski, the English socialist who died in 1950.

CONTRIBUTORS

RALPH LERNER is professor in the Committee on Social Thought and in the College of the University of Chicago. Apart from his work in medieval Jewish and Islamic political philosophy, he has specialized in American political thought of the period from the Revolution to the Civil War. He coedited (with Philip B. Kurland) *The Founders' Constitution* (5 vols., 1987) and is the author of *The Thinking Revolutionary: Principle and Practice in the New Republic* (1987).

JOHN M. MURRIN is professor of history at Princeton University. He is general editor of Garland Publishing's series *Outstanding Studies in Early American History,* coeditor of four books, including *Saints and Revolutionaries: Essays in Early American History* (1984), and the author of numerous articles on the legal profession and trial by jury in colonial America, the New York Charter of Liberties and Leisler's Rebellion of 1689, and American political culture and constitutionalism from the seventeenth century through the age of Jefferson. He is collecting his major essays for publication by Oxford University Press.

JENNIFER NEDELSKY is associate professor of law and political science at the University of Toronto. Her book *Private Property and the Limits of Constitutionalism* was published in 1990. Her work in the field of feminist theory has appeared in the *Yale Journal of Law and Feminism* and *Representations.*

PETER S. ONUF, professor of history at the University of Virginia, received his A.B. and Ph.D. from the Johns Hopkins University and has taught at Columbia University, Worcester Polytechnic Institute, Southern Methodist University, and University College, Dublin. His works on the Founding period include *The Origins of the Federal Republic: Jurisdictional Controversies in the United States, 1775–1787* (1983), *Statehood and Union: A History of the Northwest Ordinance* (1987), and, with Cathy D. Matson, *A Union of Interests: Political and Economic Thought in Revolutionary America* (1990).

J. R. POLE was, until his retirement in 1989, Rhodes Professor of American History and Institutions at Oxford University and a Fellow of St. Catherine's College, of which he is now an Emeritus

Fellow. He is a Fellow of the British Academy and of the Royal Historical Society, and a vice-president of the International Commission for the History of Representative and Parliamentary Institutions. His works include *Political Representation in England and the Origins of the American Republic* (1966), *The Pursuit of Equality in American History* (1978), of which a revised edition is under preparation, *Paths to the American Past* (1979), *The Gift of Government: Political Responsibility from the English Restoration to American Independence* (1983), and, as editor or coeditor, *Colonial British America: Essays in the New History of the Early Modern Era* (1984), *The American Constitution: For and Against* (1987), and *The Blackwell Companion to the American Revolution* (1991).

JEAN YARBROUGH is professor of government and legal studies, Bowdoin College, Brunswick, Maine. She has published numerous articles on the political thought of the Founders. These essays have appeared in *Polity, Publius: The Journal of Federalism, The Journal of Politics,* and *The Review of Politics.* She is currently at work on a study of the moral foundations of the American republic.

Index

Adair, Douglass, 139–40, 211
Adams, Abigail, 192
Adams, Henry, 307–8
Adams, John: and balance of political power, 121–26, 130–32; and class, inevitability of, 116–18; and commerce and acquisitiveness, benefits of, 120–22; death of, 34; and education, 264; and executive branch, 122–26; and faction, 119, 132; and French critique of American constitutions, 107–33; and human nature, 126–29; and inequality in society, 115–16; and legislative branch, 122–26; and liberty, 111–13; and political collectivism, 78, 80; and *Political Disquisitions*, 194, 201; and political individualism, 80; and political power, 118–19; property, defense of, 113–15; and reason, role of, 108–10; and religion, 25, 28; and virtue, role of, 110–11, 187–88, 239, 243
Adams, John Quincy, 266, 268–70
Adams, Samuel, 174, 186–87, 196
Affaires de l'Angleterre et de l'Amérique, 108
Agrippa, 85, 175
Allestree, Richard, 13
Allison, Francis, 17
American Spelling Book (Webster), 245
Americanus, 274
Ames, Fisher, 138
Anglican moralism, 11, 13, 15, 17, 23

Antifederalists, 61, 167, 169, 215–16; and American nation-state, vision of, 212–13; and Bill of Rights, 183; and commercial society, 181; and extended republic, 174–75, 182–83; and faction, 174–76, 181; and government, objects of, 176–77, 181; and religion, 176–77; and representation, 185–86; state-centered experience of, 207; and state sovereignty, 292–94, 296; and virtue, 188–89, 201–2
Appleby, Joyce, 191, 218, 305
Arendt, Hannah, 128–29
Aristotle, 168, 203–4
Articles of Confederation, 87–89, 108, 159–60, 162, 208, 283–84, 293, 314–15
Artisanal radicalism. *See* Radicalism, artisanal
Avarice, 225–26

Bacon, Francis, 211–12
Bailyn, Bernard, 111, 193–95, 304–5
Baker v. Carr, 73, 105
Bank of the United States, 9–10
Banning, Lance G., 193, 231
Barlow, Joel, 188, 282
Barron v. Baltimore, 100–102, 106
"Basic Doctrine of American Constitutional Law" (Corwin), 66
Baxter, Richard, 189–91
Beard, Charles A., 139–41, 154
Bedford, Gunning, 288, 323, 351
Belz, Herman, 153
Bennett, William, 173
Bentham, Jeremy, 35

INDEX